CAN BUFFALO.

THUNDER WITHOUT RAIN

BOOKS BY THOMAS McINTYRE

Days Afield

The Way of the Hunter

Dreaming the Lion

Seasons & Days

The Snow Leopard's Tale

Shooter's Bible Guide to Optics

Augusts in Africa

THUNDER WITHOUT RAIN

A MEMOIR WITH DANGEROUS GAME—GOD'S CATTLE, THE AFRICAN BUFFALO

THOMAS McINTYRE

ILLUSTRATIONS BY JOEL OSTLIND

FOREWORD BY DAVID MAMET

Skyhorse Publishing

Skyhorse Publishing books may be purchased in bulk at special discounts for sales promotion, corporate gifts, fund-raising, or educational purposes. Special editions can also be created to specifications. For details, contact the Special Sales Department, Skyhorse Publishing, 307 West 36th Street, 11th Floor, New York, NY 10018 or info@skyhorsepublishing.com.

Visit our website at www.skyhorsepublishing.com.
10 9 8 7 6 5 4 3 2

Library of Congress Cataloging-in-Publication Data is available on file.

Cover design by Kai Texel
Cover photo credit: Maggie Kinnard

Print ISBN: 978-1-5107-3834-8
Ebook ISBN: 978-1-5107-3836-2

Printed in the United States of America

CONTENTS

To *Pica hudsonia*.

…as for me, I am tormented with an everlasting itch for things remote.

–HERMAN MELVILLE, *MOBY-DICK*

A quatre ans, il faisait des romans, sur la vie
Du grand désert, où luit la Liberté ravie,
Forêts, soleils, rives, savanes!—

–WITH APOLOGIES TO ARTHUR RIMBAUD,
"LES POÈTES DE SEPT ANS"

As the epitaph of Marcel Duchamp's gravestone reads, "D'ailleurs, c'est toujours les autres qui meurent" (Besides it's always other people who die). This can also be interpreted in two ways, either specifically that it is always other people who die or–and the other interpretation is just as interesting–that the longer we live the more deaths we see, with one exception: our own. This is what no one has ever been able to see. We always see only the deaths of others. And that is something we can ponder, consider, even inveigh against. Is the function of the deaths of others to foster that which sustains life, and which appears to be inviolable, our integration into the enormous system of principles, into the dreadfully complicated web of cause and effect? There is only one thing capable of ripping it apart: our own death. This, however, we do not see–and that is why we do not perceive how the web of cause and effect of existence comes undone. All we can do is imagine it.

–LÁSZLÓ F. FÖLDÉNYI,
"KLEIST DIES AND DIES AND DIES"

I had no compunction at shooting a buffalo. Most other animals I always had a slight feeling of remorse.

–BUNNY ALLEN, *THE NEW YORK TIMES*, 1989

A thing of beauty is a joy for ever…

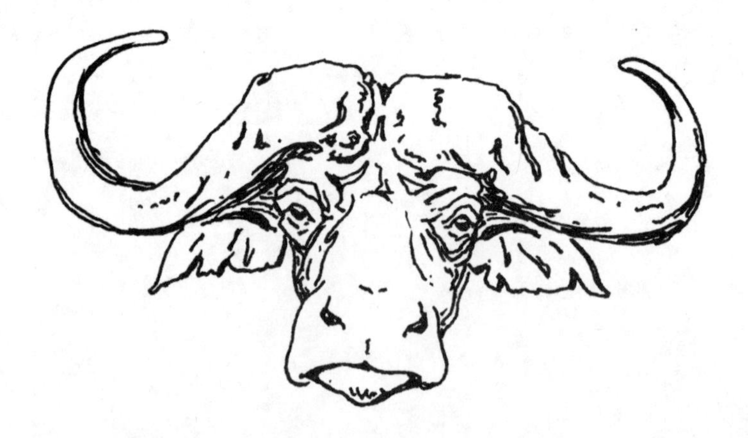

Foreword

Allan Bloom, in *The Closing of the American Mind* (1987), decried the absence, in his students, of *eros*, that is, of desire for the other—for a person, an object, or, indeed, for knowledge. Great enthusiast writing is, by his definition, profoundly erotic. It is written with gratitude, in the urge both to express, and to share. It is written for the similarly bitten (by boating, flying, photography, bicycling) and is eminently more readable than the mass of that drudgery going by the name of literature. For enthusiast writers have both something to share and sufficient respect for their subject to state their perceptions clearly.

One does not find purple prose in quilting and gardening magazines. But these contributions are short-form, and devoted not to the subject as a whole, but to one of its aspects, recently discovered or just recently understood.

Most long discourses on adventure (physical or mental) devolve into "writing." See: almost everything written about aviation, exploration, and, of course, travel.

Even Hemingway, in love with bull fighting, crossed the line, if not in *Death in the Afternoon*, most certainly in *The Dangerous Summer*. And Exupery's Vol de Nuit, and Markham's *West with the Night*, are unforgivably "writey."

To the contrary, see Ernie Gann's *Fate is the Hunter*, the best book ever written about aviation, and John Masters's *Bugles and Tigers*, about his experiences during the Raj, in the Indian Army.

Raymond Chandler or somebody wrote that a drinking problem is like a little Latin; if you've got it, sooner or later it will show up in your book. This is a tax on the reader: the inclusion of the author's credentials posing as information.

How to keep to the straight and narrow?

The answer, from the enthusiast rags, is gratitude, or, say, humility. For the love of the subject is, finally, a reverence for God, or, for the non-religious, for that world which He made.

Rebecca West wrote, "What I like I love." And in *Thunder Without Rain* we have a book written by one who likes life; which, to him, is understood as an adventure.

Bolitho saw life like that. He was, at once, *sui generis*, and the most shockingly readable of writers (try *Twelve Against the Gods*). Mencken said that Bolitho wrote like a man from Mars.

Tom McIntyre writes like a man from my beloved American century.

Here he tells us about his childhood:

"Downey had no especial culture of its own, not that of the Kizh or Mexicans or Irish, certainly not Black. The closest ethnic group was the Okies, who lived in neighboring South Gate. They came out of the dustbowl when South Gate was an industrial town. The Purex plant there along the Rio Hondo, when I was four, still showing the camouflage painting—green groves on corrugated steel siding—that had been applied during the war, to shelter national household cleanser production against enemy bombardment—no that is dishonest: the fear then among my father's generation in Southern California was not chimerical."

That self-correction should be precious to us all: I know it is to me.

Reading his book is not just a pleasure, it is a privilege.

Dave Mamet
Santa Monica
August, 2022

Preface

Thunder Without Rain is a creative work that strives to be as accurate and more important, as true as I am able to write it. In no way does it purport to be, or should be taken for, a reference, textbook, natural history, biography, scientific treatise, literary essay, thesis, political broadside, special pleading, or religious tract. What it may be is what the title and subtitle suggest.

PROLOGUE

Cape

AS THE EIGHTEENTH century unfurled at the terminus of Africa, a large Body of Cape Colonists, outfitted likely with the crotchety 80-caliber export haakbussen of the day–serpentines and embering slow matches–determined to give chase to the Wild buffalo. Garmented in linen falling collars, breeches, white stockings, and a smattering of indented cabassets, one of their number added, according to Artrium Magister Peter Kolben, the unreliable narrator of *The Present State of the Cape of Good Hope*, a notable item of apparel: a vest of deep crimson.

Kolben, or Kolbe, landing at the Cape, disembarked bearing letters of credence from the mayor of Amsterdam, with instructions to study the native peoples; describe the country; catalog the fauna; and being as well a student of astronomy, make observations of unnamed comets in what was for Europeans, the newfound southern sky. While for the first volume of his work he drew most of his intelligence about the indigenous Hottentot from the embroideries of Old Hollander settlers, rather than actual research, the second volume, devoted to natural history, is on relatively firmer footing.

In it, Kolben tells of the animal called Qu' ᔕ Arahô in the native language, the Cape's brown Red buffalo, or Buffle–Creatures, he writes, that in the Woods in every...*Hottentot* Country abound–being larger than the Black buffalo of Europe, which was presumably the domestic Water buffalo introduced to the Italian boot from India.

The African buffalo is, per Kolben in the translation Done into English from the Original High German by one Mr. Guido Medley, well proportioned, holds its head high, and is clad in Skins so hard and tough that 'tis difficult to kill 'em without very good Fire-Arms.

As Kolben assures us, a Cape-Buffalo is enrag'd at the Sight of red Cloth. Inflamed, it roars and stamps and tears up the Ground, and runs with such Fury at the offending party that it beats down all Opposition that is weaker than Walls, and will run through Fire and Water to come at him.

Thus was initiated the lore that trails the Buffalo to this day, like the lengthening penumbra of some municipality-destroying Japanese kaiju–a bovine Godzilla.

On the day of the recorded inaugural hunt for the Buffalo by Dutch Reformed colonists, one of the body donned that ruby Wastcoat, the word appearing in the typeface of the 1731 translation with a heavy capital W and an elongated s like the F-hole of a violin.

The company drove the Buffalo to the Water-Place, as 'tis call'd near the Cape-Harbour, before the Beast turn'd about and ran with all his Fury at the one of the Pursuers garbed in red. The Fellow gave the Buffalo a nimble Go-by, but it succeeded in wheeling and running him into the waves of Table Bay, plunging in after him. The Buffalo closed, and the swimmer dove beneath the surface to escape.

Losing sight of the scarlet-clad hunter, the Buffalo trod water for a time, then made for the opposite shore, some three miles off. And it would undoubtedly have achieved it, had a crew, at the taffrail of a ship in the harbor, not shot it as it swam. Hauling it on board, the men feasted jovially. The hide they presented to the governor who order'd it to be stuff'd with Hay and added to a collection he made out of such like Curiosities.

I have for some time considered the African buffalo more than a curio or even a hard-won trophy for big-game hunters–of whom I may be one, having begun the pursuit of them more than four-fifths of a lifetime ago, the Buffalo figuring in my imaginings far earlier than that, before I even gained the canonical age of reason. How it is that the African buffalo–to which few people, outside Africa, seem to have paused to take even the slightest note–has come to occupy for me in my thoughts a position of distinction as prominent as it has: key to the spirit of the chase and its traditions, to the history and culture of Africa, the lives and customs of native Africans ancient and modern, colonial encroachers, more than one work of literary fiction, my own curriculum vitae, and the existences and associated evolutions of animals and humans, bovine and hominin dispersing together throughout much of our continent of origin from the earliest times of both, the Buffalo always a little ahead?

This is an effort to find why this is a story worth the telling. If nothing else, in a case of my having taken more out of Buffalo than Buffalo have ever taken out of me, it is time, by attempting to tell such a story and thereby assay the value of this eminent animal, to give something, long belated, back.

CHAPTER ONE

Praenomen

I WAS TWENTY-TWO. I would not wait for Africa.

Three bull Buffalo, the first I ever saw, grazed at the edge of a Kenyan thicket at dawn. Spotting us in the ashen light, they went off, Broderick Crawford necked, noses lifted, black horn tips high. We trailed them through wet tall grass. Then less than a hundred yards ahead, a bull Black rhino drifted across. Steep withered and hook lipped, front horn an arm's length, its saddled back dusty red and belly wet-dark from bedding in the grass, it walked muzzle down, head heavy, scuffing the ground with its trifoliate front hooves as it lifted them, small poor-sighted eyes as impassible as art. The Pleistocene.

We froze, John Fletcher the professional hunter–P. H.–and I with thumbs on the safeties of our rifles. The Kifaru shouldered on, and we moved slowly forward until we came to a solid wall of bright green leaves into which the Buffalo vanished. We could hear them kneeing down in there, rumbling and grunting not discontentedly. Please, don't make me go. But before I said anything, Fletcher said, No, we'll come back in the afternoon.

In the last hour of light, the trackers picked up the spoor. We followed it into the thicket. Inside it was not as impenetrable as my imagination fancied it, ten to twenty feet visible around us. I grew stout hearted. Then came the crashing and snorting, trees splintering and limbs snapped off by horns and bosses, exasperated bellows of big animals on the scramble. We saw nothing except the shaking of the bush, and nobody knew in which direction tons of stampeding Buffalo were headed. The noise faded, becoming silence broken only by a soft, anonymously voiced, Fuck.

Lightning staggered across the Rift Valley below as we drove through the darkness on the escarpment. We met a band of red-togaed, ochre-haired morani. They rode with us a few miles before jumping off to walk into the night, talking and laughing, the last sign of them in the dark the flashing of the long polished blades of Lion-spears. Fletcher drove warily, dreading running over hares petrified in the headlights. I slumped in the left-hand seat, remembering the quaking of the ground from the hooves of Buffalo, feeling the aftershock in my spine still. I was twenty-two. As I said.

Etymologists relish indulging in theories of the origin of names. Africa was certainly not always Africa. One suspiciously modern proposal is that—for Moors, Nubians, Numidians, Carthaginians, né Khart-Haddans, and Aethiops—Alkebu-lan is the most-ancient indigenous name for the continent, meaning the place that is the mother of mankind or the garden of Eden. That claim, though, seems to be a baseless one in the service of a brand of neopaganism.

Herodotus, the Greek originator of written Western history, or for Plutarch, the father of lies, called Africa Libya, from a large group of Berber tribes, the Libu. To look for the Buffalo in Herodotus's Libya, begin with mythic Lake Tritonis. In what is today southern Tunisia, the saline twenty five hundred-square-mile endorheic-basin Chott el Djerid, resembling to some the head of a Wolf, is thought to contain the residue of the lake. Every summer nearly all of the chott evaporates, leaving behind fata morganas to sail over the searing flats; so if once real, what trace of Tritonis that may remain is at best conjectural.

Herodotus, though, imagined a Triton River feeding the earlier lake, west of it living the agrarian Maxyes occupying a hilly land densely forested, full of wild beasts–huge serpents were found there, and the Lion, Elephant, Bear, Asp, and Horned ass, which were believed to be Rhinoceros. Although Herodotus doesn't say, there were certainly Leopard as well–the species through Africa and Eurasia, a cosmopolite to this day–all together four of the animals identified now as the Big Five by safari hunters. Only the Buffalo was absent, though the Aurochs may have been there in its stead. Herodotus, not the first to reference Libya-Africa, nonetheless told the West most of what it knew about it for centuries to come, before Claudius Ptolemaeus–the polyhistor Ptolemy–and others added their pieces to the puzzle–a puzzle only to those not inhabiting the continent, Africans themselves always knowing where they lived.

An enticing hypothesis for the root of the name of Africa is credited to the A. D. fourth-century Latin writer Festus, who according to John Pory, the English translator in 1600 of Joannes Leo Africanus's 1550 Della descrittione dell'Africa, concluded that it derived from the Greeke worde φείκη, which signifieth horror or colde, and from ἄ the particle privative, as who shoulde say, Africa is a place free from all horror and extremitie of cold, because it lieth open to the heavens, and is sandie, drie, and desert. It is most likely, though, that the Romans who colonized the parts of North Africa conquered by Scipio Aemilianus, took the name from the Afri people believed to have lived around Carthage, limiting the word Africa, then, to the Punic colonies, though the designation later expanded to take in the continent as a whole.

With a little Latin and ingenuity, wrote Gustave Flaubert in his *Dictionary of Accepted Ideas*, etymology is the easiest thing in the world. Less Gallically, etymology, or the etymology of etymology, is the study of the inner meaning of a word. A professor of the classics has written that etymology claims an underlying semantic content in a word, placed there by ancient name-givers. So etymology, according to the professor, is about unwrapping the message the name-givers put inside a word.

Is etymology only in words?

The word Buffalo came after the word Africa, from Buffel in Middle French in 1510, before that from the Portuguese Bufalo for the Water buffalo of Asia, and earlier Medieval Latin Bufalus, a variant of Latin for the Wild ox, Bubalus. The Greeks knew of the Boubalos–which was more commonly the name for the Bubal hartebeest that roamed throughout Africa north of the ergs of the Sahara until its extinction in the twentieth century. The Greek was based on βοῦς, ox or cattle. Take it back to Proto-Indo-European and the word is *g^{w}ṓws, cattle.

Since being named *Bos caffer* in 1779 by Anders Erikson Sparrman–student of Linneaus, Captain Cook's one-time ship's surgeon, explorer of South and West Africa, member of the Royal Swedish Academy of Sciences–the African buffalo has been known by more than ninety separate species names. Today in binomial nomenclature, it has from the Cape through the western bulge of the continent to almost as far as Eritrea a single overall designation, *Syncerus caffer*. And what old message is there within the name, to be unwrapped?

This is a hunt for the etymology of the Buffalo of Africa in more than words. The enigma is that the effort to find the thing that is ineffable in the animal, is being waged with words. It's easier with Africa. You have only to look at the Buffalo and see in it the wild definition of a continent, and perhaps as well, of a genus we are pleased to refer to as *Homo*.

Looking for Africa, the French expat and I left from the farthest point of the west of the continent in Dakar, driving east on the N1 bitumen highway into the hazed cool January dawn, the sun rising from the vanishing point on the road. The light expanded and the country transitioned from coastal to urban to suburban to township to open low rolling savanna marked by the most African of éminence grises, massive palaver trees, baobabs whose bulk seemed a threat to crack the crust of the globe.

Only a short way along, the blacktop went to hell. We lurched in two hundred-yard spurts of acceleration, then braked to weave around potholes, up to speed again, braking again, slewing onto the sandy shoulder when no broken-down lorries obstructed it. For most of the long day, the road was like that, passing through villages and towns, each with its own row of stalls built from scrap-wood brushed with mismatched paint, groundnuts vended in plastic bags as big as down pillows. If we halted for more than a moment, mobs of rowdy little boys chanting cadeaux, cadeaux, surrounded us, thrust-out palms semaphoring.

Late in the afternoon we came to the major crossroads of Tambacounda, capital of eastern Senegal. Mungo Park passed through the walled town a number of times during his two expeditions–the second fatal–in search of the source of the River Niger. After Tambacounda we turned south toward the Guinea border; and the people we passed—pedaling black-tired bicycles, driving horse-drawn carts jumbled with firewood, elegantly slender women balancing bundles and baskets on their heads—seemed conspicuously more friendly and less excitable. Waves were returned with smiling bashful curiosity. No further demands for gifts were issued.

The road surface underwent significant improvement, perhaps because we were nearing Parc National du Niokolo Koba. A thirty five hundred-square-mile national treasure in the guidebooks, it offered unalloyed falsehoods about being home to hundreds of thousands of animals including Leopard, Elephant, Painted wolf, Hyena, rare Western Lord Derby eland, and Africa's largest Lion, perhaps relicts of the great and extinguished Barbary Coast subspecies. In fact, an extremely good day of touring might furnish brief sightings of coffee-brown Western roan, Sing-Sing waterbuck, Buffon's kob, Hartebeest, Oribi, Western bushbuck, Red duiker, grumbling Hippo, big sun-struck Croc, outsized Warthog, plus a solitary Leopard in a cage, along with Guinea fowl, Blue roller, and Rock hen, all glimpsed in single digits except for thronging troops of Baboon knuckling across the ground. As we passed the parc entrance off the highway, I wondered how many West African savanna buffalo, *Syncerus caffer brachyceros*, might be beyond the gate. On the better road, the driver up shifted the mini-truck past the tall forest; and we went into the oncoming eve.

At Mako, quarters of butchered beef hanging in the open air in the village's own rough roadside stalls, we crossed the Gambia bridge, the water fast and clear over smooth river stones, women gathered in the shallows with their long skirts tucked up, washing laundry; and just at nightfall we drove into Campement de Mako under the swaying strings of bare light bulbs and onto the gnashing raked gravel of the camp's vehicle area, finding small neat bungalows with the names of animals on the doors—Buffle, Hippo, Guib–gathered on bare earth around a tall anthill and under the large leaves of shade trees that grew into the outer darkness beyond sight. Tomorrow we'd hunt for the game birds of the area: Francolin à double éperon, Double-spurred francolin or spurfowl; Ganga quadribande, Four-banded sandgrouse; Tourterelle pleureuse, African mourning dove; Tourterelle rieuse, African collared dove; and Pigeon à épaulettes violettes, Bruce's green pigeon.

That night, encompassed by African stillness near the high bank of the Gambia, I sat among batik paintings and the bleached skulls of Hippo, Warthog, and Crocodile in the concrete-floored thatched-roof dining area and bar, fourteen hours from Dakar, highway weary, drinking chilled champagne with the trim, iron-haired directeur of the campement, whom I'd ridden with all day. I'd held a thought since at least Niokolo Koba, but probably back to seeing the first palaver tree, that Elephant of wood, a thought that at last gathered itself into inquiry.

Why was he here, so far from his place of birth, in this albeit most pleasant of places?

The directeur did not quite perform the caricature Gallic shrug.

Le virus de l'Afrique, he said, lifting his glass.

D'accord. I was fifty-four.

CHAPTER TWO

Pursuit

SIPPING RED WINE from a foil pouch carried in by the porters, I soaked fully clothed in that rarest of things, cool unclouded spring water runnelling down the flat face of a granite rock in Africa, my nursing raw blistered feet. We trekked some twenty thirsty miles that January day in 1984–my first time back on the continent after Kenya ten years before–through remote Vakaga prefecture, the geographic capstone of the northern Central African Republic, to make camp on the dry savanna beside a stony inselberg. It was my thirty-second birthday.

Where, Boo…

Behind cat-eye sunglasses beside the bare rock washed by the water, Willis & Geiger-clad Jane stood beside her husband–not Greystoke, but Walter White–also dressed in Willis & Geiger, the afternoon shade upon them like the growing of a gnomon's umbra on the face of a sundial. There was a brief interlude of sipping from their own foil pouches before Jane completed her question.

…were we thirty-two years ago?

The coronation, Walter said, without reflection, off by a year and a few months.

How's the water? my shirtless friend Carey asked, a soaked bandana knotted around his balding head.

The marvelous thing is that it's painless, I said, taking one more sip. Low on game meat–low on any meat, and vegetables, bread, coffee, tea, sugar–we ate small fish the Black professional-hunter, François Bendima–who said my name as Tome–trapped out of the creek.

At dawn the next day, we walked on–the Whites, François, Carey, the big-bearded white hunter, the wretched client from Chicago whom almost everyone else hated, the Protestant missionary–whom, one must assume believed not in hate–whose presence was something of a puzzlement, the long line of trackers and bearers, a sad horse, three sadder camels, and I–hunting for Giant eland and Central African savanna buffalo in Vakaga.

Thirty-four years later, I didn't know what became of François; but the Whites, the epitome of the sporting couple of an era passed–old Cleveland money when that, and not Silicon Valley, meant something, Princeton, Tanzania, Kodiak, the Rockies,

Madhya Pradesh, the Grand Slam of Wild sheep, hunters, anglers, private pilots, the Explorers Club, the Boone and Crockett Club, the Campfire Club, secret clubs not spoken of–were dead. Alive, though, they would have understood why I sat happily tonight not in flowing water but in the tiled, pale-yellow-painted walled dining terrace of the safari camp located just within the boundaries of Arly National Park in the far southeast of the West Central African nation of Burkina Faso. I was happy after hunting West African savanna buffalo that day for ten miles on foot–wetting my socks in my blood–through country remarkably similar to the C. A. R., its map's boundaries a smaller near replica of the C. A. R.'s. Even the sky was made sepia by the January harmattan the way it had been three decades earlier in the other country. I was happy to know there were Lion here, the last meaningful population of West African lion on the continent, with Elephant and Leopard, too. It was also my birthday in Africa once more; and in front of me was a chocolate cake, the camp's chef's baking and frosting it, piping on in white lettering, Happy Birthday Tom. I made a wish I kept to myself.

Five days earlier I flew into Ouagadougou, the bare-dirt Sahelian capital of two and a half million in the near geographic middle of Burkina Faso. I landed at night from Paris with other flights from Dakar, Algiers, and Casablanca, my fellow passengers Burkinabé who could afford travel, carrying requisite shopping bags of duty free; aid workers called to aid; missionaries to minister; along with blithe, cardiganed French tourists who must have thought this bitterly impoverished nation, without an ocean-sand beach within four hundred fifty miles, contained scenic wonders, or attractive prices.

The local fixer, a prosperously large man in an untucked shirt, met me at customs to assist in clearing my rifle. As I opened the hard black barrel-shaped case for inspection, gimmee truckers's caps, brought for the trackers and camp staff, tumbled out; and a young woman official seated at the inspection table said something to the fixer.

Give her a cap, he said sidewise. She took the new firearms-company camouflaged cap and put it on, the hang tag still attached, putting me in mind of an African Minnie Pearl at a sub-Saharan Grand Ole Opry. And with that, documents were stamped; and I was waved through. Encumbering a small taxi, we crossed the city though heavy motorbike traffic to the outskirts, to the four-star hotel built by Libyans–descended from the Libu–under the directive of Colonel Muammar al-Gaddafi, deceased.

Four friends followed. Living in winter-storm-warning country, I wanted to make certain I did not lose any hunting days to planes grounded by snow, so went ahead. For two days I holed up in my $250-a-night room, C. N. N. for ambient noise, drinking one-point-five-liter bottles of chilled water, sleeping off jet lag, coming down from the eighth floor only in the mornings for déjeuner of yogurt, fresh fruit, pieces of bread broken off from flaking baguettes and spread with beurre and berry confiture, pulpy ginger juice, and black coffee as I sat facing the floor-to-ceiling picture windows that small birds dashed themselves against, watching a parade of wedding parties–the brides in lambent-white gowns under the dappled sunlight and the grooms in festive-colored suits–posing for their portraits in the hotel's green glades.

Cities hold slight appeal for me, Ouagadougou slighter than most. From the hotel wreathed by waste ground, the city spread out, lacking definable center, just shooting axons that led to assorted neighborhoods. I like walking cities–Paris, London, Manhattan, Venice, Cape Town, etc., etc.–but not by a long chalk is that Ouagadougou.

When I came to Kenya, 1974, I saw what I took for my first true African, the stair handler when we landed at Jomo Kenyatta. It was in the early morning September gray at a mile and more above the sea; and as I stood in the plane's doorway, below me was the airport worker, his clean-shaved ebony head above a green ribbed turtleneck sweater. The sclera of his pitiless downturned eyes was red around the irises from wood smoke, his open earlobes hanging, exact long vertical paired cuneiform wedges scarring each cheek. That he seemed the first genuine Black man I ever saw said far more about me than him.

John Fletcher, of Ker, Downey & Selby, met us, my friend Bill and me, inside the terminal. The glimmer of all the old varnished British woodwork stood out, as did John's head of tightly curled blond hair and visibly broken nose. He was soon apologizing for the recent closing of licensed Elephant hunting in the country–where it would never open again as poaching, under the aegis of the Kenyatta first family, swelled to a tsunami. The Kenyan professional hunters had gone so far as to approach Princes Philip, Duke of Edinburgh, and Bernhard of the Netherlands, founder of the World Wildlife Fund, Elephant hunters both, to no avail.

We collected our baggage and my rifles–Bill carrying a camera–and drove to the New Stanley Hotel in the shadow of the Kenyatta International Conference Center tower–I was sensing a theme to Nairobi. John said that the locals called it Jomo's Erection. Checking in, we went out to the dark cool gunroom of the Kenya Bunduki to rent a 12-gauge over-under for a month. Then John took us to lunch for me to eat the first dish of curry in my life, experiencing nothing short of an epiphany. Afterward, we had to go to an East Indian jewelry store across town. We, Bill and I, took a cab–when we told John where we were going, his head pulled back as he said, There?

There was a cluster surrounding our bargain flights from London to Nairobi, purchased through a Vancouver discount-travel agent. That agent had an agent in London, with whom we meant to rectify a discrepancy in the payment. That agent, in turn, directed us to the jeweler, his agent in Nairobi. When we began seeing roads lined with tin-roofed houses and dukas, we understood Fletcher's apprehension. We stopped at the pencil-written address. Outside the locked armor-glass door, a glowering giant in a blue overall uniform and jump boots, fingers laced, forearms on his knees, sat, cradling a truncheon. He eyeballed us as we were buzzed in.

Inside were two East Indian jewelers. I told one why we were there. He presumed mild bewilderment, or maybe it was simply feigned indifference. At last, with some reluctance, he led me into the back office–making Bill wait out front–where he drew open a wide wooden drawer banked with leaves of banknotes colored like autumn foliage, filling a paper bag with banded stacks of Kenyan shillings, though the disputed transaction was made in Yankee greenbacks. Oh well, I could spend them all in country. As we were buzzed out onto the street and into the waiting taxi, the seated giant with the truncheon watched as we went.

Dinner and drinks that night, hangovers next morning. We went to the zoo and bribed a keeper to milk a large Forest cobra for us. A hustler named Ben latched onto us and wove a tale of his parents forced to drink blood, swear an oath, then be murdered by the Mau Mau. It was a good story, for the money. Beers at lunch, and I ended up pissing in what I took for a public urinal, which turned out to be the outhouse behind someone's house, an irate Black woman yelling out her back window at the white man in midstream. We returned to the hotel to dwell upon our iniquities.

The last morning in Nairobi, we packed to leave, when the screams of a woman carried through the raised window from the street below. We looked out, and a white man was helping a distraught white woman onto the curb while a Black man stood nonplussed in the crosswalk. From almost nowhere, a crowd of Africans converged upon the lone man.

The phone rang. We stepped back from the window, not watching the rest of it, and I answered the call. Fletcher was downstairs. Hanging up, I told Bill, It's time. Then, all the winged monkeys of Oz flew through the window, flapping around the room like flags snapping in the wind. The inexorable breaching horror of the dislocation of being into Africa for the first time, clutched us simultaneously, sending us into a tizzy. We didn't want to go, but we had to leave.

The monkeys, blessedly, did not follow out the lobby door into the beaming of the high-altitude morning light on the street, John's green Land Cruiser pickup, the canvas top on tubular metal frames and bows over the bed in the back where there was an added rear bench, all John's kit under the cloth cover, the safari-company's name on the door, waiting at the curb. His Kipsigis driver, Joseph, in his green K. D. S. T-shirt, took our luggage and my gun case and packed them into the vehicle. There was another, very young hunter there, too, gathering his clients into another car of another safari; and I remember the polish of the smooth Rhino-horn bracelet around his wrist and his eagerness, compared to Fletcher's all-in-a-day's-work mien.

We got into the Land Cruiser, the canvas seat coverings smelling of old animal fats and amino acids, lingering from the extended cartage of wild-animal carcasses, and drove out to the safari-company warehouse where we linked up with the lorry with all the equipment and the crew of men. It was south, then, away from Nairobi and the buildings named for Kenyatta, toward the Rombo country outside Tsavo West, and seeing in the first hour the first lone Giraffe in swaying stride. Late, there was a camp place by a small river, where Fletcher crouched and nozzled gasoline from a jerry can down the holes across the ground, dropping in matches in the dusk, wanting like St. Patrick to drive out all the Cobra–Forest or otherwise–flames bursting upward to cast diabolical light on his cheekbones and nose. The morning and the city then, at last, seemed far away.

The first panic of Africa is the most remarkable, but its vestiges are always there whenever you come back. After two days in the Libyan hotel room, I finally left to dine with the safari-company owner who disported a name that was in the leadership of Burkina Faso for more than a generation and who inherited the safari company from his father–his badges of rank a gold watch bulky as an ingot and a high-mileage Mercedes. Though he spoke impeccable English, we shared the meal with his head translator, Larry, a good Moslem according to the safari-company owner. We ate in a traditional Burkniabé restaurant with a tile floor, under slow-turning overhead fans and in sandy-cyanic fly-specked fluorescent light, my meal Guinea fowl, a most excellent sauce, and a sticky ball of plantain fufu to pull apart by hand to pick up the dark meat, then stir it in the sauce and carry to the mouth.

After the restaurant and dinner, I sat under the marquee on metal poles that ran along the side of Avenue de l'Aéroport opposite the terminal, in a plastic chair on packed dirt in the blandly cooling night, the dusty-smelling day's warmth ebbing from the ground. Motorbikes crossed and S. U. V.s made turns off the road into the airport, the avenue patrolled by uniformed troops carrying shopworn Belgian assault rifles. I sipped a beer and ate cashews freshly toasted. The safari owner beside me drank beer; and Larry, the good Moslem, had a soft drink in a bottle, as the peddlers came to the table. I was reading a book about the varied life of Colonel Patterson of the Tsavo Lion, and a hospitable stranger began discussing it with me in serviceable English. He had never seen a Lion, of course, but–Wait, let me show you.

He walked off and came back in a moment with assorted items of jewelry. One was an outsized Lion-head ring that he alluded to as gold: a police-property report would probably characterize it, without further forensics, as yellow metal. Larry purchased it. The peddler showed me a heavy bracelet of twisted strands of copper, brass, and iron. It contained particular powers and could be mine for ten thousand Communauté Financière Africaine francs.

No, no, I said.

What would I pay?

I did my best to come up with a discouraging figure.

Five thousand?

Too little, he said, and walked away again, trying to appear affronted. In a little longer time than he'd been gone before, he returned.

Five thousand.

I obviously overbid.

Among the last of the passengers from the Paris flight, my friends came out of the terminal and crossed the tarmac drive under mercury streetlights, the fatigue of their long trip from America plain. Clasped around my right wrist was the copper-brass-and-iron bracelet.

In the night we drove through Ouaga–more pronounceable that way by white people–hemmed in by the motorbikes, some ridden by sharply dressed, very attractive young women, all the bikes like anadromous fish belly splashing up a shallow streambed. On the unpaved shoulder of the jammed boulevard, new shoes for sale, aligned in hundreds of pairs, awaited shoppers. At the Libyan hotel, a mile west of the U. S. Embassy with no other buildings between, we drove into the sally port built of square steel bars where the security guards halted our vehicles and wheeled a parabolic mirror under the chassis before letting us through, taking our rifles and ammunition and locking them in the arms magazine until we departed before light the next day, too early for breakfast, ahead of us nine hours on the road.

At the table two nights later, after the first full day of hunting, I faced the birthday cake. It had been dark for some hours, astronomical sunset and sunrise coming without gradation, as abrupt as stalks snapping, the way they always came in Africa; and the night air felt somehow globular, with the bush sounds starting. On the plaster walls folk-art murals illustrated the wildlife in the safari concession, each labeled: Buffle, Hippotrague, Hyène Tachetée–who whooped through the compound at night–Cob Defassa, Bubale, Phacochère, Cob de Buffon, Guib Harnaché, Céphalophe, Crocodile, Léopard, Lion, L'éléphant. The cloth covering the table, printed with fuscia bands, was cleared of the plates on which Buffalo was served, dessert plates replacing them. Blowing out the birthday candle, and looking at the others around the table, the impression of a safari into senescence seemed inescapable.

Lance and Brent, both hunters from Arkansas, straddled either side of middle age. The other hunter was Pam–Lance her nephew; Brent related by marriage. I knew her from earliest childhood–it was in her late father Roy's paneled den that at age four I first saw a Buffalo head, a red Dwarf forest buffalo he took in French Equatorial Africa, the effect on me instant and indelible. Pam was a year older than I. Often querulous, her default disposition was a certain brittle cheerfulness, of which I always begrudged her easy display. Then there was Carey.

Carey did not hunt but fancied the uncorrupted terrains where hunters wandered and who for over forty years ventured away from his Beverly Hills practice of criminal law to be a fellow-traveler with me over stretches of Africa, including the C. A. R. and Senegal–as well as the American Mountain West, Alaska, Canada, Central America, Mexico, and even the Qinghai-Tibet Plateau of China. Sicilian by ethnicity, like a thinner Francis Ford Coppola, he'd grown slightly stooped and somewhat ramshackle, but hiked valiantly the game trails all day. And I wondered what might I see, reflected in a mirror, if I cared to look.

My age was not inconceivably beginning to tell–my maturity as always, another matter entirely. Across more than forty-five years, Buffalo were what brought me to Africa; and without Buffalo, I wonder if I would have come to know, as well as could be known by me, this natal land of our exasperating species. This Arly was new country in the sense of not being where I had ever been before; and for me it was young, though this was never less than the oldest continent and continuum of human life on the planet. And after a day's hunting in Arly, finding large animals at every turn, I could only treasure it. I had honestly not looked forward to the prospect of long foot hunts under subequatorial sun; then once here, I did.

When I have thought of driving off the spleen, I've gone about a little and seen the savanna parts of Africa. What drew me used to be the east and the south of the great beetling continent–so suggestive, as many see, of the profile of an australopithecine skull; try envisioning as vividly, and appositely, the outline of Asia or Europe–but in my latter days, the center, north, and west beckoned. There was Senegal for shooting-flying francolin and sand grouse; Tunisia for driven boar in the date-palm oases where the call to salat ali 'asar came through the trees from public-address systems in the distance; northern Cameroon along the Mayo Rey—where Fula build two-story crenulated dried-mud walls and in leather scabbards, wear brass-and-steel sabers with silk tassles—for chasse libre without benefit of a P. H.–seeing an African porcupine in the headlights as we jolted into camp, the manager, Daniel, riding with us, called to stop and began chasing it with his flashlight: very good eating. Now Burkina Faso, the Colorado-sized nation landlocked in West Africa, for the one thing for which I would never fail to come back to Africa.

Robert Ruark in *Horn of the Hunter*, his story of his first safari in Tanganyika, has his young, real-life professional hunter, Harry Selby, with a mad affection for the Mbogo–Buffalo–talk about them. After stalking and stalking and facing stampede after stampede, Ruark shot his first Buffalo with his 470 Westley Richards, in his account doubling the triggers. The two barrels firing simultaneously, he and the Buffalo both went down, the Mbogo standing first, Selby mopping up. It took another 470 round from Ruark for the coup de grâce. And that was enough for him, one Buffalo per lifetime his self-proclaimed allotment.

I don't ever want to shoot another one, he told Selby. This is the only Mbogo I need this day, or any other. He'd checked the box.

You'll shoot another, Selby promised. You will always hunt Buff. It's a disease. You've killed a Lion and you don't care whether you ever take another. But you will hunt Buff until you are dead because there is something about them that makes intelligent people into complete idiots. Like me.

You are at liberty to imagine what may have been in Selby's eyes.

You'll hunt more Mbogo, all right.

Weeks later, Selby sighted a bull meaningfully larger than the first; and Ruark was crawling after Buffalo, which, he wrote, I really did not want to do...bitterly afraid...of...the big, rope-muscled wild ox with horns like steel girders and a disposition to curdle milk.

If you understand that, whether or not as colorfully embellished, you understand why you come back to Africa. Even to take a chance on where you have not been before, as long as it may hold the common denominator of *Syncerus caffer*.

Burkina Faso, the name at any rate, was for most when I told them I would hunt Buffalo there in the winter, one of those blank spaces on the earth. Lying within the grand green northern sweep of the clear-watered river of rivers, the Niger, without being touched by it, the country was once known as the Republic of Upper Volta–République de Haute-Volta–which the nation was after it was French Upper Volta, and before that Upper Senegal/Niger Colony. Ahead of European colonial rule, it was part of the Kong Empire; earlier still, it was of the Bura culture. After independence on the Fifth of August, 1960, came a catena of coups d'état, the one in 1983 led by the Guinea-trained leftist Captain Thomas Sankara, who effected the name change to words from two languages–Burkina, meaning honor in Moore, and Faso, fatherland, from Dioula, one translation into English of the coupled words, Fatherland of Incorruptible Men. The most likely association made by people to whom you told the name and who did recognize it, however vaguely, was one of profound poverty–among the poorest people in the world–and where the black flag of jihad flew.

The afternoon before the first day of hunting–after the drive nine hours east-by-southeast from Ouaga, first on good road, then around potholes, then over dirt, through security checks manned by uniformed gendarmerie with automatic weapons, the bluing rubbed down to dull steel on the barrels where the rifles were habitually held, passing impossibly crowded commercial vans looking about to pitchpole under enormous mushroom caps of baggage–suitcases, duffels, bundles, motorbikes, live chickens, tethered goats–lashed to the roofs, through the last city, Fada N'Gourma, where one pays the tax, in the city center a shattered plaster statue of a roaring Lion standing on bare rebar, through small mud-brick villages with shoeless running children, where on tables of old bare wood with incessantly repainted wrought-iron legs stood fingerprinted liquor bottles filled with gasoline so motorbike riders could pull up and take the grimy red funnel and empty a bottle of fuel into their tanks, leaving behind the requisite number of C. F. A. francs–we came to the camp.

A giant shiny-gray baobab with arthritic limbs grew just outside the woven-branch fence of the compound. On the other side of the gate was the poste de police where the constabulary lived with wives and children and a skeletal bicycle for patrol, and in front of us a collection of round boukarous built of cement blocks on concrete pads with thatched roofs, the outside plastered walls painted with wild animals and flute-playing dancers. There was the tiled dining terrace behind a low pale-yellow wall with a kitchen behind it, a bar off the side beneath a veranda roof, and a swimming pool no one swam in. Through the back fence of the compound, past a graveyard of derelict Land Cruisers and Rovers, was the open abattoir with chains and pulleys and scales and gutters where the game was brought in whole and recorded before being dressed, skinned, and quartered, the animals weighed to guarantee the local villagers their correct division of the meat, established by agreement, another incentive to involve them in the conservation of the game among which they lived. Unpacked, we took the rifles and drove out from camp, turning past the tall baobab, and went several miles until we were beyond the park boundaries in the place we could hunt and could load our magazines.

The rifle I carried was a Blaser R93 in caliber Remington 416 Magnum. When we were certain we were outside the park boundaries that afternoon, we turned the small truck, with the safari bench seat set high in the back behind the roll bar, off the dirt road and drove across the layer of black ash from seasonally burnt grass, the vehicle stopping sideways to an iron target frame set up a hundred yards away. The driver switched off the engine, and we got out with our rifles.

The local villager, Djanjoua, a father in his thirties who held a hunter's license and carried a leaf-sighted 375 Mauser on the trail, and would be my P. H., and his younger tracker Kamiri went out to the target frame and pinned bull's-eye targets to the wooden backboard. The long stems of dead grass not touched by the flames laid over like bent drinking straws, short evergreen trees growing up out of twisted trunks, and the ground dried to a hard shiny magnesium gray after the rains, reflecting the sun in a dazzle all around. The targets affixed, the two men walked off several yards from them.

Rolled-up soft rifle cases became rests on the ticking hood of the truck. With the rifle pointing downrange, I removed the covers from the lenses of the scope and worked the bolt, feeding a tipped copper-bulleted round into the chamber and setting the eccentric Blaser tang safety: push to set, then push again to release. With the range clear, I shouted out before shooting, Fire in the hole! as one did. Djanjoua and Kamiri shouted back, and although it was in French I knew they were far enough away and let off the safety.

The first shot brought back the reminiscence of recoil, making me wonder if I had shot the rifle enough before bringing it sixty-five-hundred intercontinental miles. The shot was high, so I turned down the elevation turret several centimeter clicks. I bore down; and the second cut center, the right range for African bush. One more shot from the three-legged standing bare-wood shooting sticks, lashed together with black inner tubing to form a trivet rest at the top, and I returned the unloaded rifle to its soft case.

Pam and Lance and Brent shot after that. With all the rifles on, we were ready to leave. Carey was gone.

We shouted for him. In a bit he called back. With our rifles, we looked for him. He'd walked off behind us to a nearby waterhole. His head covered by a camouflaged do-rag and wearing a bagged camo shirt and shorts I gave him from the seemingly bottomless trove of swag sent to me by manufacturers over the years, he stood looking down by the edge of the water, smoking the blackmarket Cohiba he puffed on an inch at a time–extinguishing and relighting it–over the course of a day. Pam was the first to tell him never to wander away from the rifles, which he learned many years before.

This is Africa, she scolded him affably, but still with a stern matron's declaration. These are wild animals. They do not like you.

Yeah, yeah, yeah, Carey said, waving his hand with stagecrafted chagrin.

At his feet the dried mud was pushed up in the rains into a collared circle like a soft wax seal pressed with a signet ring, raised crazing from the cracks in the sole of the Elephant's foot on the flat, the circle big around as an oversized boule covering the end of a plank table spread with a red-checked cloth. Looking in another place, I found something more, the cloven stamp of a Buffalo track. A large, probably old, solitary bull placed it there; and the slovenly wild bush rose up to it.

The Yorùbá say that when the Buffalo's life ends in the woods, the father of the house hides in the thatch of the roof. Facing a Buffalo on the trail, a hunter swears that the gun isn't even his but one he borrowed and promises that this will be his last hunt. The famed Harry Selby during his eighty-five years of hunting, never swore the rifle was not his. With his mad affection for the Mbogo and partial to the 416, his hunt ended at age ninety-two in Maun, Botswana, his dying the day after I arrived in Ouagadougou from Paris, en route to Arly. And Buffalo.

CHAPTER THREE

Taurolatry

IT WAS THE light of the totality of an eclipse, those moments when the moon's shadow draws across all the sun. Below on the surface of the earth, the air turned a fragile blue-magenta, the god's rays undulant as if underwater. I tried to discern figures in the gloam.

A sound that seemed near drew me out of the viridarium of a Mefloquine dream. Lifting the mosquito netting, I swung my bare feet over the floor. About to touch the cool concrete, I drew my legs up and felt for the flashlight on the camp table beside the bed. Switching it on, I swept the floor with the beam, then pointed it inside my slippers, prospecting for night callers. Standing, I slid into the slippers and stepped out through the flap of the tent pitched above the Songo River flats.

The August winter dark at two thousand-foot elevation was fresh on my face. Echolocating Bats swooped past; and echoing closer than it was–as it forever did–the roar of the Lion, that had woken me, came again. From the front of the tent, I looked over the bluff on which the camp sat, seeing at the salt lick below, moon-washed Elephant, mostly cows and calves with one or two young bulls, wild and unhabituated, body checking for position. Rory gave them a name: Songo Bitches. In the million acres of hunting country in the Tonga tribe's Binga Communal Lands, the Elephant confronted continuing pressure from hungry locals and avaricious outsiders; and when we were on the ground with them in the powdery shafts of evening light through the mopane, mahogany, and duikerberry trees, they were never content to let bygones be bygones. Always, they were weighing some kidney of retribution. They stuffing want to kill us, was Rory's take on it, as he watched them, smoking his cigarette and leaning on his rifle held by the barrel, three verdigris-patinated 458 brass cartridges dispersed semipermanently among the canvas shell loops on his belt.

Rory Muil suggested a younger *Star Trek* Captain Picard, leading a harder life back on earth. A tobacco farmer at heart, in these bad days of Kamudhara, the Old Man Bob, at the start of the twenty-first century, he made do–and kept his son in school, hoping to point him to a secure career in the military outside Zimbabwe–by taking hunters after dangerous game like Elephant, Lion, Buffalo. He smoked without cessation, wafting the ever-present Newberry Extra Mild to read the wind and wreathe the smoke around his head to keep sweat bees away. He did not affect an Elephant-hair, ivory, or Rhino-horn bracelet which some professional hunters, like the young one in Nairobi, wore as signals of echelon, just a Timex with a cloth strap. The only other thing he wore on his left forearm among the solar lentigos and keratoses, was a white crosshatching of scars, put there when he pushed the arm down the throat of a Leopard to stop it from chewing on other parts of his body.

They say, opined Rory in electric-generator light, brushing his hand over the forearm as dinner plates were removed and pudding was served, you don't feel pain when a Leopard's biting you.

He paused.

The hell you don't. Pass the custard, would you?

The Elephant remaining at the water, I went back into my tent and slept a time longer, until I was woken by the staff man with the tea tray. That morning we ate crusted bread and drank white coffee in the covered dining area and left camp an hour before first light. The day before, we saw road workers in gray-white jumpsuits, breaking stones with hammers. Now, in the dark, we drove over the crushed rock. The white Land Rover Defender had brush guards wrapped around the grill, a roll bar in the back, with a rifle rack welded to it, steel ladders on the sides, and a high rear bench for the trackers to spot from. The fabric covering the right-hand driver's seat and left-hand passenger's was sun bleached to the pallid azure of kapok boat cushions, and there was no door, mirror, or windshield anywhere on the vehicle. In the dark it was cold enough for a sweater, Rory calling it a jumper.

It was a long drive to Kapinda, a place known for its dagga boys. Dagga is a corruption of a Shona word for mud, many varieties of it found in Zimbabwe–dope, madhaka, dhaka: watery mud, rain-soaked earth, the mud used for mortar–and a dagga boy is an old bull who presides over the wallows, metaling his hide against insects in cooling layers of glorious mud. Usually no more than two to four dagga boys run together, or often it is just one solitary, invariably truculent individual, long outcast from the sodality of Buffalo.

We turned off the rock road onto a dirt one, headlights waggling ahead of us, internal organs pounded by the Land Rover's thrashed suspension. As the sun came up in Kapinda, we saw the mopane trees growing to the bottoms of the rocky ridges, scattering bronze leaves like ones fallen from oaks in stony Missouri autumn woods. Thickets of bushwillow–jess–still held up their green-but-yellowing foliage, long-yellow-grassed woodland parks rolling out on broad ridge lines.

The night ended and morning started, and we went to waterholes where the trackers in the back scanned for spoor fresher than nezuro–yesterday. By full daylight, we found ones that were new.

Rory had his Model 70 458 Winchester Magnum; I, a Ruger No. 1 chambered in 450 Nitro Express–N. E.–3¼ inch. I dropped the falling-block and slid the single straight-wall cartridge, loaded with a 500-grain Woodleigh soft point, into the chamber and locked up the action, setting the safety. With us went the three trackers: short dapper Tino in front; tall John with a slightly esotropic gaze, who carried the water; and Mika with his shaved head and ragged hat, holding a Tonga axe, handled with a mopane knobkerrie and with a hand-forged, glint-edged leaf-spring-steel head.

We trailed a skein of tracks we took to be those of two dagga boys. The prints were half again as wide as a man's boot, the toes scraped out by the bulls's flicking their heavy front hooves as they walked. The tracks held a sheen, no time yet for them to be blown over. The only better sign to find was fresh dung, not oxidized all brown inside yet, but bright green when scuffed apart by the sole of a Courteney boot, and still warm to the touch, with only the start of the ammonic smell of barnyard. If the matter was coarse, it told you that it was from an old bull, its teeth worn so that it no longer chewed categorically. There was dung on the trail, but we came to no additional conclusions about this shit.

The tracks wandered seemingly directionless, crossing over one another through the grazing area, then melded into what we realized was a single wandering bull's, that led us then for an hour and a half below and around a grassy hill until we were going with the wind. We fell back to circle downwind, abandoning the fact of the track to take up the speculation of where ahead of us the bull might be, Rory thinking it had moved onto the hill above us. Slowly, slowly, Rory whispered, pressing down the open palm of his free hand; and we tried to get onto the tracks again.

Cresting the level top of the hill, we began a searching traverse through the tall grass and jess. The August air was still mild and for a quarter hour the five of us marched in one another's footprints. Then Tino, in the lead, walked past a small clump of low isolated bushwillow, and John next, with Rory behind John, and I. Then Mika at the back hissed to us through his teeth.

We froze midstride and all made a slow synchronized look back over our right shoulders. The dagga boy laid motionless as we walked by, only getting to its hooves, like a rabbit out of a silk top hat, when we came upwind, our scents at last intolerable to it. Two-dozen paces away, it stood now behind a bushwillow–not bigger than the large pericón fan used in the flamenco–that it had hidden itself somehow behind, looking over it at us. Before I got my rifle to my shoulder, the bull spun and went downwind off the hill, agile as a Deer. It ran into the sun, giving off tracers of light from its deep-curled horns and heavy boss as it escaped.

Pity, commented Rory from the top of the hill, lighting a Newberry and drawing in, exhaling the curl of smoke to float like a thought balloon above his head.

Many years later, the first-quarter paring of the moon, before setting beyond the rounded ridge of the old mountains, was margined as sharp and bright as machine-stamped steel. In the December day in this other hemisphere, cirrus clouds pleated the sky. Now at night the wind broomed them away. Walking into the freezing Wyoming air, I closed my eyes and counted ten. I opened them and there were more stars, my own stars, more brilliant.

Raising the fifteen-power binocular, I found the Belt of Orion rising into the east along its trajectory across the southern sky. The three stars of the belt pointed up toward Aldebaran and at an angle above that, the open cluster of the Pleiades, where the Lakota saw the head of a Bison. Between those two coordinates tonight, only seven million miles from our planet, was a comet wheeling in its orbit back toward Jupiter. The unsteadied weight of the binocular, though, turned everything from discreet points of light into unwatchable atomic whirls. It was better to look peripherally with only my eyes, making the starlight more incandescent.

Even with that I could not find the comet. Moving down the sky I returned to Aldebaran. Its name from the Golden Age of Islamic astronomy translates to The Follower, dutifully trailing the seven sisters of the Pleiades. In the vault of night sky it is, among the Khoisan, The Male Hartebeest, its mate in Orion, Betelgeuse, a red supergiant six hundred million miles in diameter. At a diameter forty times that of our sun, Aldebaran is a Martian-colored Class K giant, a mere sixty-five light years away.

Aldebaran had other names. It was Palicium to the Romans, for the spring feast of Pales, the god or goddess of shepherds and flocks; 'Eyn ha-shor ha-semali in Hebrew, The Left Eye of the Ox. To the Chinese, Bìxiùwǔ, Fifth Star of the Net. The Hindus knew it as Rohini, one of the twenty-seven daughters of Daksha, the ram-faced son of tetramorph Lord Brahma. The Seri of Sonora saw the star giving light to the seven pregnant women of the Pleiades, birthing. Aldebaran for the Lakota laid the course of the Mississippi by falling to earth and killing a serpent slithering on the ground. Australian Aborigines knew it as Karambal who stole another man's wife and ascended into the sky as smoke when that man tracked him down and burned him alive in the tree in which he hid.

For today, Aldebaran continues on–in the constellation abbreviated as Tau–under yet another name. In the Middle Ages it was Cor Tauri, cor meaning heart. We know it now as Alpha Tauri, the maddened red right eye of Taurus the Bull, glaring across the galaxy at Orion the Hunter.

Humans for even longer than they have been that genus, may have been naturally identifying shapes of the bull in the sky. It's imaginable that Miocene *Sahelanthropus* scanned the night and saw a configuration of stars–though not of what we know now as the Bull, which had yet to assemble–resembling, to what may or may not be our most-distant known ancestor, the shape of bovines it saw around it on the African savannas of seven million years ago. Perhaps in imitation of the sky, ancient Africans created in rocks and with paint, the bovines they knew

Earliest hominin plastic art was either mobiliary or parietal. Mobiliary was transportable and could at its simplest be shells, teeth, bones, or stones minimally engraved with lines or drilled with holes for jewelry, eroded rocks often mistaken for the work of hominin. Paleolithic parietal art–Latin paries, wall–was made most recognizably as murals in caves or on large free-standing blocks of stone. Whether produced through percussion, engraving–sometimes no more than scratching–or painting, they are immovable and persistent, if not permanent, though often nearly so. The general term for this art is petroglyphic and may contend for some the most ancient human creative works.

In parietal art, the inhabitants of the Nile Valley left graven images of the North African Aurochs, *Bos primigenius africanus*, on the rock faces in locations such as Qurta, between Luxor and Aswan. Prior to ten thousand-years ago the Sahara was for some brief millennia of rainy weather the savanna home of hunter-gatherers venturing out from the fertile Nile Valley. There were to be seen by them on those grasslands, then, water-dependent species such as Elephant, Hippo, Giraffe, Rhino, large Antelope, and Crocodile along with a species of Giant African buffalo. The prominent North African rock art of that time from Ten Thousand to Seven Thousand B. C., classified as the Bubalus Period, was found mostly in the Maghreb when the majority of subjects was wild bovines, including the extinct Aurochs and the vanished Giant buffalo once listed as *Bubalus antiquus*. Thought at first to be related to the Water buffalo, it later became *Pelorovis antiquus*, considered ancestral to *Syncerus caffer*, though the refinement of its designation did not stop there.

Throughout time in Africa, genuinely superb mobiliary art relating to the Buffalo was made. Much of such art is on display in non-African museums as the result of sacking by Europeans, often through force of arms, a grievance just beginning to be redressed internationally. In New York City's The Metropolitan Museum of Art is a Buffalo bocio crafted for the nineteenth-century Fon King Guezo of Dahomey, now Benin. The bocio is a wooden carving containing medicinal packets with spiritual powers, associated with assorted daemons and deities such as the Vodun religion's loa trickster, Legba. This one, covered in silver with iron eyes and wooden horns and tail, is dedicated to Gu, the god of iron and war. About a foot high and a foot-and-a-half long, it represents the West African savanna buffalo, one of the two hundred fifty six symbols of the system of divination known as fa.

In the time of Guezo, when war was endemic in order to maintain the brutal supply chain of slaves brought down to the coast–and traded for European and American goods such as tobacco, liquor, guns, and more–the bocio was in aid of the battles fought. At such times, it would be placed in a shrine in the palace. Annually, such objects were paraded during a festivity called huetantu in celebration of the kingdom's wealth and power. Guezo also wished to be identified with the great strength and courage of the Buffalo, though you may infer a wink from the artist who eschews realism for something like pronged caricature, his bocio grinning maniacally.

Among the enduring religious traditions of the Bwa of Burkina Faso is the crafting and owning of masks to dance in at the renewal of vows, celebrating on market days, initiations, and ceremonies for the dead. The masks's spiritual powers include those of animal spirits, such as the Monkey's, the Antelope's, and Buffalo's. A Buffalo mask will be made of painted wood and raffia fibers. Putting on the Buffalo mask, the dancer wears a raffia skirt and uses two wooden canes as forelegs. Tossing his masked head, the dancer becomes the Buffalo.

He charges.

It had grown too late and too cold to stay out and hunt more for the comet. From my view of Aldebaran with the naked eye, I went to the whole of Taurus. It stood in a field of night, awaiting assault by Orion as it had for myriad years. It, and Orion, would be gone one day. I did not have to worry about that tonight.

I watched a while longer, remembering the stars and the cold Kapinda mornings.

The Zulu of the south of Africa know the stars as the eyes of the dead, watching the human world from the sky. Unable to return their gaze any longer, I stepped back into warmth and electric light. Clouds and ice crystals were moving in, making for a sun pillar of flame at dawn.

CHAPTER FOUR

Fatherland

LONG AGO, BEYOND Kilimanjaro–it has not been explained to anyone's entire satisfaction what the name means–the sun was setting. In the open back of the Land Rover lay heavy ivory darkened and checked by decades, the roots incarnidined.

Tracking on foot into the late afternoon, they found the old bull standing under yellow acacias, guarded by two younger bulls, his askari–soldiers in Kiswahili. The hunter made the side shot, red dust flying from the head, the old bull dropping. The young ones pushed into the way, trying to shore the older back up, blocking the insurance rounds. The bullet lodged in the honeycomb of bone in the top of the skull, hardly missing the brain; and the Elephant got to its great round feet. They chased it half a mile, firing on the run, until it went down again. By then it was too late to butcher out the dark-red flesh; they left the task until morning when they would return with a band of local villagers and carry out everything edible, down to the marrow in the mammoth bones. They took only the tusks that afternoon; and when they reached the Land Rover again they were very tired, happily regretful, and ready only for a long drink back in camp.

On the way to that drink, though, the professional hunter, John Kingsley-Heath, spotted a bachelor herd of Cape buffalo–with two exceptionally fine bulls in it–and it was all a bit much, actually. He switched off the engine and slid out on the right side of the battered olive vehicle, carrying his binocular. His hunter slipped out the other side, and one of the trackers in the back, without being told, handed his 300 down to him. The hunter opened the action and pushed the 200-grain Noslers into the magazine, feeding the loose 220-grain solid into the chamber, locking the bolt as the P. H. glassed the Buff. He motioned his hunter, Roy, my father's friend, to come around behind the Land Rover to his side; and crouching, they worked behind low cover toward the Mbogo.

The first rule of dangerous game is to get as close as you absolutely possibly can–then get a hundred yards closer. When the professional hunter felt they had complied with the stricture, able to identify the birds hanging beneath the bulls's flicking ears as Red-billed, rather than Yellow-billed, oxpeckers, plucking ticks, he got Roy into kneeling position and told him to take that rear bull turned sideways to them: Put the solid into its shoulder, then pour on the Noslers. It was then that Roy took note of the professional hunter's having brought to a Buffalo hunt an eight-power German binocular instead of his customary 470 double. The P. H., seeing Roy's unspoken question, lifted his shoulders and tipped his head, to say, You can handle this.

Kingsley-Heath saw everything in Roy draw in, held. Taking a breath, Roy slowly exhaled half and hit the Buffalo in the shoulder with the solid. The bull turned to face them, faltering; and Roy put two Noslers into the heaving chest, aiming right below the chin; and the Buffalo collapsed. As he reloaded–two more Noslers on top of the one still in the magazine, a solid up the spout–the second fine bull remained where it was, perplexed and belligerent, and the professional hunter urged the hunter to take him, too: Oh yes, him, too.

This bull turned also after the first solid in the shoulder and lifted its head toward them, its scenting nose high, displaying an enormity of horns. You could suppose an intelligence, animal and angry, in the eyes, and perhaps be not far wrong–but the animal, alone, knew. The hunter was suddenly conscious of there being beside him a professional hunter in short pants, who spoke with a British accent, carrying his Schott-glass Oberkochen binocular in lieu of a made-in-England N. E. Which is when the professional hunter leaned over and whispered evenly, Look–he's going to come for us.

Another held breath, half exhaled, and the hunter fired. He worked the bolt purposefully, and placed a third bullet into the bull's chest beneath its elevated chin, just the way he had on the first Buffalo, except this bull did not go down. That left the hunter with one round in the rifle. Roy cycled the bolt; and as he was about to squeeze off the shot, he mused about whether there would be time afterward for him either to find any cartridges in his pocket and reload, or to make a run for it. Now, though, there was a wounded Buffalo to be gotten onto the ground; and all the hunter could be concerned about was holding his rifle steady until the trigger sear broke, the hammer sprung forward and the firing pin struck the primer, crushing the small measure of explosive lead styphenate and tetrazine between the primer cap and anvil, sending a jet of white-hot gases through the flash hole into the slow-burning propellant powder contained within the brass cartridge case, igniting it and firing a bullet out the barrel and toward the bull–and the Buffalo lurched forward with a bellow, falling, stretching out its black muzzle on the ground.

Standing, the hunter and the professional hunter moved toward the two downed Buffalo, the two remaining bachelors running off. Roy's rifle stayed loaded, the safety off, until they found both bulls dead. He opened the action and unbolted the last round in the rifle, pushing it back into the magazine and closing the empty chamber.

In the dwindling light they saw that one of the first bull's horns, the horn that had been turned away from them when the hunter first shot, was broken off in recent combat, a splintered stump all that remained. It had been a magnificent bull at one time, but at least the second bull's horns were perfect matched sweeps of polished black horn almost fifty inches across the spread. And there, both men stooping to squint, glinted a burnished, round half inch of metal buried in the boss covering the bull's head like a domed helm.

The professional hunter scratched the exposed surface with the blade of a pocket knife; and they saw it was not lead but steel, a ball bearing fired from an ancient muzzleloader, maybe a Brown Bess, for which flints continued to be manufactured to that day. Whoever the native hunter who carried the musket was, he relished Buffalo meat, and Buffalo hunting. What became of him after he shot and failed to kill with his quixotic firearm at a far-less-than precautionary range, was a story that must beg an ending.

In the city of Downey in Southern California there are no green hills, no hills at all worthy of the name, the average elevation just over a hundred feet above mean sea level. No tall buildings rise. The greatest heights are the tops of leafless plane trees that I looked up into, standing on the playground of the elementary school, feeling, when I should have been too young to feel it, the despair of raw January daylight.

As the marine layer burns off by late morning in the June gloom, the air above watered lawns fills with a cobwebby humid haze never happened upon elsewhere. For thousands of years Uto-Aztecans dwelt here. While not as a whole identifying themselves as a single tribe, they were recognized by the name of the circular willow houses they built, Kizh. Food plants were acorns, yucca, roots, tubers, and berries, jimson weed for their apothecary, with fish and game including Mule deer,

Pronghorn, Black and Grizzly bear, Rabbit and Hare, birds, Steelhead trout, and for Kizh along the coast shellfish, Dolphins, Elephant seals, and Whales. The Spanish came and took the land, transmuting it into ranchos, followed by Mexicans and Americans. Oranges, a domestic fruit in China for thousands of years and introduced into Spain by the Moors, were brought in the 1860s by former California Governor John Gately Downey, son of Roscommon, to the place that would be named for him; and my father kept a few Valencias scattered on the half-acre lot he bought to build his house on in Downey when I was an infant–orange trees can live for more than a century, so they could have gone back to John Downey's plantings. The home was for a family that was a ship without a tiller.

Downey had no especial culture of its own, not that of the Kizh or Mexicans or Irish, certainly not Black. The closest ethnic group was the Okies who lived in neighboring South Gate. They came out of the Dust Bowl when South Gate was an industrial town, the Purex plant there along the Rio Hondo when I was four still showing the camouflage painting–green groves on corrugated-steel siding–that had been applied during the War, to shelter national household-cleanser production against enemy bombardment–no, that is dishonest; the fear then among my father's generation in Southern California was not chimerical.

In the 1930s and '40s, and almost up to August '65, South Gate could have been Tulsa in 1921, or New York City in the far worse Draft Riots of 1863. A white gang, the Spook Hunters, was said to roam the streets on the qui vive for any Black man inadvisedly crossing into the town out of adjacent Watts. Maybe the lingering reputation motivated my father to settle in Downey with South Gate as an illusory cordon sanitaire to the west against his own apprehensions. Why not move deeper into some whiter enclave such as Orange County or West Los Angeles, which he could have afforded? Perhaps because Downey for him was better than South Gate but not so conspicuous a statement as Beverly Hills or Laguna, life less entangling when you choose not to rise visibly above yourself.

Downey produced Karen and Richard Carpenter, The Blasters–Dave Alvin wrote a 2017 song he twanged with Jimmie Dale Gilmore, "Downey to Lubbock"–and the serial Freeway Killer; but what it had for an aesthetic was for the most part cruising at Harvey's Broiler. A Googie-era drive-in coffee shop, it was built on what had been a poultry ranch, just this side of the South Gate city limits at Firestone Boulevard and Old River School Road–Firestone for the tire factory to the west and Old River for the old course of the San Gabriel that ran past until shifting in the flood of 1867. In the 1960s it was at the heart of Kar Kulture. But cars were not what made things run.

Lying on a coastal lowland with a Mediterranean climate–wide spaces and skies, fair weather–Greater Los Angeles a century ago was the ideal region for giving birth to the aviation industry, and later aerospace. For all the giants that came to be in the area–Lockheed, Hughes, Douglas, Rockwell, Northrop–scores of smaller companies subcontracted with them to the point that a tenth of the workers in L. A. were at one time in the business of air and space.

My father and his brother, and their mother, owned one of those lesser companies, Calmec, California Manufacturing and Engineering Corporation. Grandfather took over the company in the 1920s from a fellow oil-tool salesman he'd known in Mexico back in the Teens. The company was a machine shop with two lathe operators in a small Pueblo Style building along the west bank of the Los Angeles River before it was channelized. The original owner simply wanted to be done with it because too many Irish profits, he said, slipped out the backdoor. So, according to family legend, he gave it away.

While my father could be overcome with seasickness on a windless day on a koi pond, his father shipped before the mast on square riggers across the Pacific out of San Francisco, wearing a wool sweater like one he'd seen in a picture of Jack London, redolent of *Martin Eden*. He once got as far as Yokohama, then sat on the dock for weeks until his ship secured a cargo with which to return. In 1904, at age 26, he worked his way to second mate on the 185-foot Andrew Welch iron sailing barque, serving for two months between San Francisco and Hawai'i. According to his papers, his seamanship was rated V. G. by the Welch's master; but in a short time he was in Columbia, a vanished town a mile north of Goldfield, Nevada.

After a month, writing to a Dear Friend Maino on the occasion of the friend's marriage—and also calling him, your royal fatness—he told him, The company I am with owns quite a few properties hereabouts but have not yet started active operations. Until they do, I have no settled occupation but knocking about the office or taking little prospecting trips when I take a notion. Pay going on and three square meals a day coming along regular and a warm bed to sleep in and still I ain't satisfied. This is too lazy for me and I am anxious to start at something or anything.

He composed the letter on his company's office typewriter, retaining a blue-lettered carbon.

He continued, From what I think, you may not expect me in San Francisco for the next two years.

The next year, Goldfield hired Virgil Earp–maimed in Tombstone by shotgun blasts into his back, ambushed by Cowboys after the gunfight at the O. K. Corral–to be deputy sheriff, Earp dying of pneumonia nine months later in the town. It was less than a year after that that my grandfather left by stagecoach to hasten home in a search for his mother and younger brothers and sisters while the City still burned after the quake. He was back in Goldfield in time for the 1906 lightweight title fight between Oscar Battling Nelson and Joe Old Master Gans–forty-two rounds, ending when the referee could no longer overlook Nelson's intransigent fouling of the Black Gans–whose mother before the fight famously told him to bring home the bacon. In Goldfield my grandfather married a plain Iowa-born girl with Missouri roots and without religion who had moved west with the railheads as her father took successive positions as a station master for the Denver & Rio Grande. There is no smiling photo of her, not even when, just out of her teens, she married my grandfather. They were gone from the town in 1907 when Jack London came to visit his old landlords from Dawson City, the two brothers, mining engineers, chasing one last pay streak.

Selling oil tools–bits, Kelly drives, Kelly bars, Kelly bushings, rotary tables, crown blocks–the high tech of the day, he was in Vera Cruz, or so the story went, when U. S. Marines and Navy Bluejackets landed in whaleboats on the orders of Woodrow Wilson in response to a diplomatic slight. Trinidad and Tobago, Venezuela, Gallinazos flocking the garbage on the beach under the palisades of Lima–photo albums of black-and-white snapshots on crumbling black pages, images stayed as much as captured: bullrings, eight men in straw hats with a dead anaconda stretched to full length, self-portraits of a man in a cap at the rails of many steamships, ship's menus, the visit of Spanish royalty in Colombia. My father remembered torrents in Panama where they lived when he was a toddler, his mother learning kitchen Spanish and men with 22s shooting Green iguana out of the tall amarillón trees, to eat. He remembered, too, his father coming in at nights to their later home on Hobart in Los Angeles, bruised and bleeding, knuckles swollen, some broken, no word of it ever spoken in the house.

For the company he was given, my grandfather had to travel, selling. My father went with him in the summers, too young to have a license yet still spelling him at the wheel on routes out of Cheyenne and Odessa, learning that the farmer in the Model A truck ahead would swing out wide before a turn, thinking he was still driving a team and wagon. Before dawn one day, they left a Western town, meant to head west, my father trying to persuade his father that they were, instead, diving east, which my grandfather would have none of, until the sun was in their eyes. Another time, before they got home, my grandfather lay in the back seat, contorted in pain, my as-yet unlicensed father driving, getting back in time for a ruptured appendix to be diagnosed and a last-chance use of the new sulfa drug to save the old man from peritonitis. While the two were on the road, my grandmother kept the books back in the shop, often having to get to the bank to put in money before the two payroll checks could be cashed. Having ridden constantly herself as a girl–I see her, holding her seat on a colt rearing like the insignia on a blued pistol–she one time tried to get her two sons on horses, only for them to show their abject terror by pulling leather–hanging on in desperation with both hands around the saddle horn–shaming themselves in her eyes for the rest of her life.

Not knowing quite what to do with my father, they sent him to a military academy for a time, where he learned to eat white rice, cinnamon, sugar, and milk for Sunday breakfast, and back home, slick'emed haired, posed for his photo in uniform with a Sam Browne belt and shoulder strap and polished cavalry boots, on the lawn in front of a California bungalow. My uncle, several years older than my father, learned engineering at Cal Tech where as a student he nearly flunked out while he was a standout football player in the leather-helmet days, before being blinded in one eye by the sport. He met Einstein, he said. It was told that the company survived the 1937-38 recession by pirating oil tools for Pemex after Mexico nationalized its petroleum industry, and other American companies were ordered by descendants of Rockefeller and Doheny not to sell the country spare parts. Then there was the War. By the time my grandfather died—my barely remembering him as an old man in a wheelchair, wearing stained trousers—the War had turned Cold; but there was the Space Race, and later Vietnam, to profit from as well.

Every man thinks meanly of himself for not having been a soldier, or not having been at sea, said Dr. Johnson, who was never the one or did the other. My father, with a father who saw green water wash over decks and a brother who lost an eye hitting the line with a football, and an unsmiling mother who thought less of him for having, among many things, a fear of horses, tried, after dropping out of U. S. C., to experience one adventure by working on the construction of Grand Coulee Dam in the last days of the Great Depression. On the way to Coulee, he stopped at his paternal aunt's row house a block from Golden Gate Park; and her sharp-creased, cadet-sized Navy hospital–corpsman husband—reliably every Saturday playing eighteen holes on the public links and drinking a fifth of Jack Daniel's, attending Mass faithfully the next morning—kept him awake all night in the living room with the Atwater Kent radio turned off, describing in Dantesque detail the chronic ravages of venereal disease. My father straggled home in six months, by his every later indication still an angst-filled virgin, eighteen hundred dollars in his jeans, grown allergic to the hexavalent chromium in the concrete he shoveled into the formworks.

My father had superior teeth throughout his life, but was a deaf man, or at least profoundly hard of hearing, from at least high school on. The examining physician at his first draft physical at the opening of World War II took his blood pressure and asked what was wrong, kid, didn't he want to be in the army? My father said he had extreme difficulty in hearing. The doctor asked if he could hear thunder and classified him 1A. They never called him up.

There was no war for him, no desire to seek out any adventure after Coulee–though dumbfoundingly, in his late 40s he made two hunts to the frozen Bering Straits for Polar bear, the first with Roy when Roy's usual hunting partner, his big Dutch-American friend, Bogert, who was called Bob, broke his leg and could not go, not killing on the first, but going again by himself the next year, goaded to prove to Roy, and his own sons, that he would not back out always, returning with his Bear, entranced by the sea ice, and never wanting to go again–and he circumscribed his travels by journeying only to places he could reach by automobile on the highway, unable to turn loose of the means of escape in the shape of an ignition key.

He perversely mortified his flesh by eating open-faced ketchup sandwiches, yoghurt without fruit, baker's chocolate, whole peeled lemons, drinking Postum, yet waxed obese. He advertised his conductive-hearing loss all his life through a conspicuous brass-colored body-worn hearing aid clipped to the outside of his shirt, a braided cord running from the amplifier to the earpiece, near enough to the wearing around his neck of a placard, announcing, I am deaf. His otosclerosis could be corrected by a surgical procedure known as stapedectomy; and he prepared many times over the years for the operation with the finest otologic surgeon in the country, always finding a reason for putting it off, afraid in truth of what it would be like to hear, to abandon his steadfast impairment. At the end of his life, he had the surgery, belittled into it not least by his elder son. Weeks later, he was dead.

Before that, my father without a degree or a direction he could or wanted to articulate, was a legacy at Calmec. He was acknowledged by default, to be a skilled machinist and production manager. Yet he never felt even a constituent of his own family, which resolved into the cadre of his parents and older brother and the brother's alcoholic golfing wife and an only daughter. Awkward, supremely unclubbable, phobic, begrudging, fundamentally humorless, alone by degrees, by turns hair-triggered and passive-aggressive without forewarning, his unselfconscious literary protagonist of choice being that instrument exquis of cultivated revenge, the Count of Monte Cristo, he presented a frequent stumbling block for the business, being fired and taken back again and again. His wedding, to a woman who hid her greater age and Eastern European descent–she told him she was Norwegian when her parents came from Buda and Pest–was a predictably sour affair, officiated over by a Methodist minister when the parish whiskey priest's first question to the couple, when they met him in the rectory to discuss the nuptials, was, And who is the Catholic party, and my father stood and walked out, refusing to be wed in her faith. The marriage from there proceeded apace into ugly fiasco for husband and wife, a disaster for two sons.

With some frequency, navy-blue-uniformed police wearing polished shields entered his bedroom, illuminated only by the cathode-ray television screen, where he reclined, fully clothed even to his shoes, an unrestful Gautama Buddha lying on his side on the bed, to question him about the charge my mother lodged over the phone when she dialed zero–when younger, I was drawn into his room when he went to work so I could lie on that bed and smell the odor of his head pressed into the pillow; years later, from the cabinet where he kept the 303 Enfield Jungle Carbine, the civilian AR of 1965 when he bought it, I took the rifle and loaded one full-metal-jacketed round and sat on the foot of his bed, the windows curtained, before unloading the rifle and returning it to the cabinet.

The police had him stand, escorting him to the dining room where my mother sat flushed, lacquered blond hair unkempt into a leaning mow, screaming in impotent outrage, You bull! You dirty bull! over and over as if it were her vilest epithet, when he was the antonym of almost anything taurine, other than oxen. He stood silent, grim, suppressing the alarm as the handcuffs ratcheted melodically behind his back, the officer asking my mother if they should remove him to jail, she not answering, only resting her brow in her hand, fingers splayed in an elegant, rehearsed theatrical gesture, my taking this as the accustomed way of all families as my father was released from custody.

When I was a small boy, my father saw that my mother dressed me with my belt buckle on the right side. Predictably, he tore it, his voice loud, from the loops and put it back correctly, pulling it tight with the buckle on the left, the way a man was supposed to wear it. Born sinistral, I was instructed at the supper table when I was four or five, that this was a right-handed world–I still struggle to visualize in what way this plays out–and he faulted my mother for allowing me to hold my fork in my left. The inexorable fight followed, and my father, as my mother shrieked incoherently behind the slammed bedroom door, sat on the sofa along the back wall of the front room as I sat silent on the other sofa across from him, he comforting my younger brother with his blond hair and blue eyes, and told me I was responsible for it all and that he'd make me use my right hand, which resulted in mixed handedness, mild dyslexia, cross-eye dominance, and only a hint of a stutter.

One day I came home from high school and found my mother lying on her back on the couch, a rumpled handkerchief across her eyes, white-cloth surgical tape bandaging the bridge of her nose. She would not speak. When my father came in, his right hand was bound in white, done by a physician. He wanted me to know that when my mother and he battled their way into the children's bathroom in the afternoon, he reached out in rage, after breaking her nose, and tore the small curtain off the bathroom window, gashing his hand open badly on a sharp edge on the back of the traverse rod. There was no discernible remorse, or unaccountably even any glozing for his actions, only the bathos of the inflicted Kong, clinging to the zeppelin mooring at the top of the Empire State Building as another wave of chattering biplanes stooped.

The necessary things–according to him–that he told me were always some reflexive variation on a theme of don't. Among the undertakings he counseled against was letting a woman before marriage connive me into making love with her, ensnaring me. Another was attempting friendships with employees—assuming I would be one day an employer—while he tried to do that himself, without noticeable success, never sensing the air of imposition it spawned among those employees. He had at best one good friend, who was in fact not in his employ.

Roy was the chief engineer for another aerospace job shop, somewhat larger than Calmec. Perfectly middle class, he saved his money to go on hunts–for his first time to Africa, he cashed in his wife's life-insurance policy. He lived in a house in Downey, too, smaller, on a street corner across from a middle school. He'd married young, had a daughter, divorced, as a single father took the girl when she was a toddler on the road with him on his motorcycle, found his job in Southern California, married again. His second wife painted and gave birth to Pam, only about a year older than I. Roy's father had been a barber who moved the family to New Mexico for his lungs, where my father's friend learned to hunt. There was a monochrome photograph of him at 16, looking like the tough Depression kid he was, a curl of hair on his too-salient forehead–he is hatless because he never met anyone with a head as large as his, except for a Navajo he said he knew, and recalled that he may have had some sort of learning disability, until he came to California and met my father. In the picture he is leading a saddle horse through black timber, a big Mule-deer buck hitched between pommel and cantle.

His house had a sunken den paneled in hardwood with a hardwood floor and a stone fireplace. It smelled of unfiltered Camels, later pipe tobacco. There was the Mule deer's head on the wall, the head of a whale-tailed bull Elk, a pair of Elephant tusks with a bullet hole though the base of one, from French Equatorial Africa. There would be a glass of bourbon with ice on the wooden coffee table in front of the big leather couch when my father came over.

In the room was another photo of Roy in his 30s, in color. The picture was new when I was four. Looking into the camera, Roy sits in the tall green grass of a baï, a few-acre clearing in the equatorial forest. He has found a broad-brimmed hat that fits, and he could do with a shave. Beside him is a red seven-hundred-pound bull Buffalo, *Syncerus caffer nanus*, the Dwarf forest buffalo. He is lifting the head by one of its horns.

The head of the Buffalo in the photo, mounted from the shoulder forward, hung on the wall of the den. The hide was the ochre of wild bulls on cave walls. It was creased around the neck, veins represented beneath the hide. The muzzle was square, black, and hairless. Where the hair slipped from the hide on the lower chest, an extra patch of tanned skin was stitched. The glass eyes held, as they only could, a fixed stare. The fringed ears showed the tatters made in them in life. The ebony horns of the bull came out from its forehead and swept back flat to defined symmetrical points. They were exceptionally long for the subspecies, and the bases were broad and ridged and grew close together.

In a photograph of an animal there is a finite impression: what the photographer saw in 1/125th second, and how he interpreted it in f-stop, focus, framing, and printing in an image no more than atoms deep. Motion photography adds only duration, a sequence of exposures projected onto a flat screen and through a persistence of vision producing a false sense of unbroken animation. Even though scientists have yet to find a serviceable substitute for physical skins, skeletal remains, pinned insects, whole animals and parts both dried and embalmed in fluids for accurate, comprehensive study of holotypes, there are nonetheless people–who like all humans, resort to varying degrees of hypocrisy in their lives–demanding of them, and certainly hunters who bring taxidermy into their homes, to answer the question of, Why can't you please please please settle for a picture?

A video or still image of an animal, seeming to do no harm to that animal–other than perhaps shriveling its soul–ought to suffice, it is said. Museums under sentimental cum totalitarian-spirited pressure move steadily toward withdrawing wildlife specimens from their public exhibits, turning increasingly to audio-visual displays that strive to substitute so-called interaction for corporeality, a Cinerama Dome in place of the Galerie de Paléontologies et d'Anatomie Comparée–which still draws in thousands due to dry bones's behaving as strange attractors, as they have throughout the existence of our species. Why should not, it is said, a hunter, too, by forsaking both weapon and a compact with ethical death, restrict contact with wildlife to that through a lens?

At the age of four, seeing the Red buffalo hanging from a D-shaped ring from a heavy nail driven into the paneling, a magical article to find in a place such as Downey–something never to be found in my father's house–I learned to view animals three dimensionally, unlike a photographic image that provided no more than a discreet aspect. Maybe if I had never seen that Buffalo head from all its sides, or had not seen it until later when I possessed a less impressionable awareness, I would not have become incorrigible. But with that sight something slouched toward birth; and after that and until I was old enough to make it possible, I knew I would have to see a Buffalo myself, one alive and outside a photo. And hunt it.

Many years later, a friend brought back a thin Nairobi phonebook from a trip to visit the country's national parks. Paging through it with an object, I found the address for Ker, Downey & Selby Safaris–with whom Roy hunted in Tanganyika some time after his first safari in French Equatorial Africa, and Ruark with them too–and wrote them a twenty-one-year-old's idea of an arch letter inquiring about a hunt in Kenya. I asked my father if he wanted to come, and he said yes. I knew he would say that. He always did, at first.

The price of the safari for me came from a small inheritance from the estate of my sailor-salesman grandfather–all those long miles of peddling to go up in rampant sport–maybe the only money I would ever see, which with the intervening years of episodes in Africa from then to now, became far more than a self-fulfilling prophesy. The safari was arranged for a year from September. It took my father till the spring.

I always knew he looked at me, in the only word for it, askance. I was a disappointment without his ever being able to articulate to me, and most of all to himself, what it would take to make me acceptable to him. Love, or what he may have thought love to be, was one thing. Liking a son was another. He would say he was putting things dispassionately; but he was a nail who longed to be a hammer, in order just to be one, finding thin satisfaction in pounding down whatever smaller nails he could. He told me it was necessary for me, as an eighth grader, to know that my being excited for having been accepted into Jesuit prep school, for which he wanted me to take the entrance exam to begin with–swayed by the Sisters of Notre Dame at the local parochial school, that I had a future, which no one had ever said about him–made me a braggart. I wanted to stand out, he said; and that to him, it took me such a great deal of time to realize, made me the worst possible kind of nail. As long as he inoculated his words by calling them candid or frank–for my own good–he said it should make them anodyne. He, of course, never took anything said, and some never said, to him as intending anything but injury.

Not good at emotion–the ones he was most deft at being depression, anxiety, and tamped-down rage, all of which he indulged in an harrowing, thin-lipped hush–he would offer self-justifications almost without affect. With his hearing aid clipped to his shirt, he told me that–though he was not talking to me, not actually, my being simply the wall of a canyon from which his words could echo–he would not be able to go to Africa with me because of his hearing loss. If the professional hunter said something to him in the field at a critical juncture, he would not be able to understand it. It would be for everyone's safety if he did not go, not realizing that I already knew that unless you were utterly deaf, which he was not, you could hear even the slightest sound against the background silence of wild country. He presented the reasons that suited him; and I saw, not for the first time, a coward. Still, I came late to that game, the fact of it not hidden as long for many others with lesser stakes. He simply pulled leather too often for it not to show.

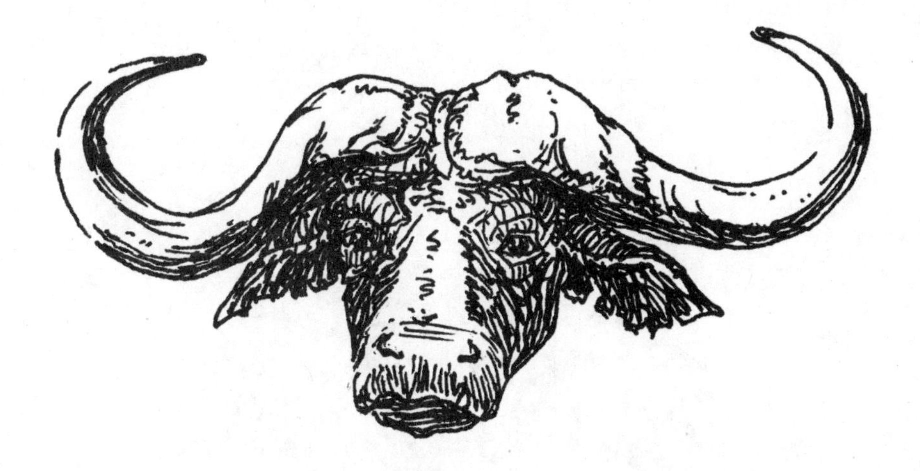

You know your father's fundamentally a coward–unruly nature his deepest dread–and you wonder what you are, never a soldier or sailor yourself. In the Rombo country below Kilimanjaro between Tsavo West and Amboseli were Lion, Leopard,

Elephant, and still in those days Black rhino, with Spitting cobra on the ground and Eastern green mamba in the trees. For nights, alone in my tent, I listened to the sounds that kept me awake in interminable hypnogogic horror.

For that to begin to change, it meant reaching Block Sixty A on the Soit Ololol Escarpment above the Rift, where we exchanged dry savanna for verdant pasture, trees, and dense bush thickets in which Buffalo lived. Trailing the herds of dagga boys to the edge of the thickets, the P. H. John Fletcher would halt and take stock, and in a few seconds decide we would follow the Buffalo in.

I remember how it felt. At first it was a spring over-tensioning deep in a clock-works. Then it verged on cataclysmic uncoiling. Concerns with regard to bowels cropped up. Only if we got close enough to the Buffalo, whom I could never see, and they crashed away, telling me it was over, would it subside.

It was the claustrophobia of the cover, the knowing that Buffalo could be just behind a scrim of leaves, feet away, but still not knowing. Wondering if there would be time to make a shot, in the stopping place, with no room to run or anything to climb and nothing between me and a bull but my dubious skill at arms. It was also about being untaught in Buffalo, even if I had learned its track. I needed time with Buffalo in the bush. Seasoning. All that mattered till then was never letting the fear grow so sizable I could not contain it. So that I never pulled leather.

On my wall now in my home in Wyoming, I look at the head of that Red buffalo I first saw in Roy's den almost seventy-years ago. It is not a photograph, but the head itself, sent to me by Pam after her father died. It was what a photograph could not be. Seeing it, itself—hide, pelage, horn—makes all the difference. Has made all the difference. It was what caused it all to begin.

If I knew another, less banal, way of saying it, I would; but I wouldn't have wanted it to have begun any other way.

CHAPTER FIVE

Bovinigenesis

HE CALLED IT Bob's Circus.

We drove through the dark toward it, returning from another day's hunting Water buffalo on twelve hundred-square-mile Goodparla Station, the Southern sky's stars filling the inexhaustible territorial night. I listened to the gamelan clang from old leaf springs and shackles on the undercarriage as we traveled over the rough ground that we felt more than saw. Below the billion and a half-year-old sandstone of the Arnhem Land Escarpment, Wild pigs, Brumby horses, Feral burros, and tens of thousands of Buffalo ran; in the daylight there were freshwater Johnstone's crocodile adrift in the billabongs and flocks of Galah flying between stands of trees, Cockatoo wings beating rose-gray, rose-gray, rose-gray. This winter, in August, we were the last hunters, the last hunters not Aboriginal.

Bob Penfold, the professional hunter, told me this was where, twenty years before in the 1960s, just a little to the north near the then-fading abattoir at Mudginberri, he hunted Buffalo for the commercial meat market. The other day in the supermarket in the new uranium-mine town of Jabiru–the largest stork in Australia–stretching out his hand for a box of Weet-Bix on the cereal shelf, it came to him that when this was all only pandanus swamp, here was the exact spot where he killed the biggest Buffalo he ever saw.

He lived in those days, in his words, like an animal, shirtless, shoeless, eating nothing else than what he caught from the water or shot on the wooded savanna, carrying a 375 to take only three-year-old bulls to sustain the herds, making head and neck shots to limit wastage, running shoeless up behind the downed animal, reloaded rifle in one hand, long knife in the other, flicking an eyelash with the blade to make sure the bull was dead, then using the knife to bleed the carcass at once. Six bulls to make a four-ton load on the trailer, five loads a day delivered to the slaughterhouse, nights back in Buffalo camp spent reloading cartridges and changing burnt-out clutch plates. The old-time Buffalo runners in the American West remembered the creak of stirrup leather and the smell of prairie fires. Bob remembered Land Cruisers's diesel engines's clattering over at first light and the smell of burnt smokeless powder drawn through the air in the tourbillion of the bullet in a line to the dead Buffalo bull as Bob came up to it after the shot.

Into sight came the colored lights, powered by the portable generator, strung across Penfold's tent camp: Bob's Circus.

The Buffalo here were feral, and the land of this station was to become another part of expanding Kakadu National Park. So while the uranium mine stayed, the Buffalo–and other feral animals–would within a few months all be dead, shot by rangers armed with black guns, firing from helicopters's flying relentless grid patterns, not one of the animals on the ground left standing. That was why we were making the final hunt for non-native animals by non-native gubbah–government, the name for all whites–men. After this, it would be nothing other than cull for Boar, Brumby, Burro, and Buffalo.

Of the six seasons of the Top End, this was kurrung, hot-dry. Before daylight the heat burgeoned in the evanescent cool at the dusty level of the ground, and the sable motifs of Buffalo took shape among the scattered timber. Finding them was easy. Finding the one to be the last one hunted was hard.

It was midday when we saw the old, hairless, rubber-ball-black bull, the one we both knew was right, on the edge of a dry floodplain that was chaff yellow and the gray of baked mud. It stood in a tea-tree thicket along the bend of a sandy creekbed, its neck weighed down by the noonday and the burden of horns. As we neared, it lifted its stolid head. Bob stopped the truck and looked at the black lunar crescent of horn for a long time with his binocular, until the bull drifted into deeper cover, watching us as it went.

We slid out of the truck, pushing the doors behind until they latched softly. I hunted with one of the 458s Bob had custom made, barrels shortened, bolt handles lengthened for surer racking. Before we started the stalk, I chambered a five hundred-grain soft nose and set the safety. I got up to a tree, the Buffalo still watching; and against its bark, I braced my hand under the rifle's fore-end. Then the Buffalo spun, trotting deeper into the thicket, broad horns laid bright along its back.

Bob and I circled two hundred yards around the edge of the creekbed, downwind, working back to the bull. The air smelled of baking heat and eucalyptus. The Buffalo was a hundred yards distant on the other side of the wash, walking through the brush, the bottoms of front hooves lifted up. Looking for a shooting lane, I found one a foot wide; and as the bull moved into it, I rested the rifle on another tree. The Buffalo's shoulder filled the opening. I fixed the crosshairs on it and pushed off the safety.

There was risk with any animal this size, and only more so if not shot right. I kept out of my mind any thought of following a blood trail or having to peer beneath thick brush to find what might be on the opposite side, as I pressed the trigger.

Just before the soft-nosed bullet reached the Buffalo, a twig tip snapped in the opening I shot into. You think you cannot see a bullet in flight, but I saw the flashing of the gilding metal on the jacket of the five hundred-grain projectile as it tumbled the last few feet. Upset, the bullet keyholed when it struck the bull; and in that instant, I did not know if it would penetrate deeply enough or not. There followed an interregnum between cause and effect, lasting one second but seeming uncountable.

From a standstill, the Buffalo hobbied forward, its forelegs giving out, the chin and square snout driving into the sandy earth. The bull rolled like a galleon keeling, its short legs thrust out. Already working the bolt, I sent the penny-bright empty spinning in the air, feeding another round into the chamber. Resetting the safety, I ran toward the bull, ready to fire again if it tried to stand; but it was already dead. All the same, Bob and I came up from behind with care, flicking the eyelash. From the ground, the waxing crescent of ridged black horn canted to a width of the headboard of a double bed. I cleared the round and worked the bolt, extracting the live cartridge and pressing it back into the magazine. I slipped the bolt forward, locking it into the empty chamber, and set the safety.

I suppose something could be said about songlines and dreamtimes. But those belong to the original people. I do know, though, that for the original people what was hidden inside was as real as what was outside, as in every caterpillar there lives a moth or butterfly. Nineteenth-century British hunter-explorer Frederick Courteney Selous said that the Ndebele, with whom he hunted, called the African buffalo Izinkomo ka M'limo, God's cattle. Here was a different Buffalo in a different land. Perhaps it was still God's cattle within. Or at least a demigod's. And it wouldn't have to run in the end, trying to elude a helicopter's narrowing gyre.

In line with fundamental Biblical genesis, all types of horned cattle, wild and domestic, come from an original kind, created by God. They descended from this baramin that was transported on the Ark of Noah. The diversity we see today in the tribe Bovini–genera *Pseudoryx*, *Bubalus*, *Bison*, *Bos*, and *Syncerus*–results from chromosomal rearrangements that according to creationist scholars are designed mechanisms that provide the variability that allows animals to adapt and survive in a sin-cursed environment: Although because it fails to hybridize with other Bovini–as does the Indochinese Saola, *Pseudoryx*–the African buffalo would seem to fall outside the *Bubalus-Bison-Bos* monobaramin in creationism's exegesis; though that may be simply more evidence of the Buffalo's being uniquely the cattle of God.

There is life, domain, kingdom, phylum, class, order, family, tribe, genus, and species, as we remember from our high-school biology. Since we remember nothing of the sort, we start by stating that life is what it says, a physical unit that shows biological processes. From there the Biblical and the evolutionary narrative of the Bovini's descent part ways, perhaps.

From the evolutionary standpoint, it pleases us to think of the origins of mammals in forest scamperers, such as the shrew-like one hundred sixty million-year-old Eutheria, the Good animal from the supercontinental Pangaean Triassic, restrained from growing bigger than modern house cats until the death of the Dinosaur with the crashing into the earth of the comet Chicxulub. But double that time frame and you have the Synapsids, the proto- or stem mammals who in that time, and for fifty million years, were the largest terrestrial vertebrates on earth. So much for the humble beginnings of class Mammalia.

The order Artiodactyla, the even-toed ungulates, reaches back more than fifty million years to the early Eocene epoch. With the end of the Dinosaur at the start of the Tertiary Period came the radiation of mammals around the planet. Ancient Tragulidae, like the hoofed hornless Chevrotains of today that can be less than two pounds in weight, were the common ancestor of giraffids, cervids, and bovids, which began to diverge from other mammals around twenty six to twenty eight million years ago. The suborder of Ruminantia, whose three- or four-chambered stomachs digest vegetation continuously, is the next category into which the Bovini fall, followed by the infraorder Pecora with bony growths projecting from their craniums. Through fossils, Bovidae trace back to eighteen, perhaps twenty, million years to Early Miocene Epoch paleontological finds in Pakistan of the genus Eotragus, Dawn goat, the size of an East African Thomson's gazelle. Based on molecular comparison of genes, though, Bovidae were, in some protobovid form, here certainly earlier.

Bovids, the most recently evolved hoofed mammals, divided again between the clades–taxa of species with common ancestors–of Aegodonts and Boödonts based, in the condensed version, on the complexity of their cheek teeth, Boödonts's larger, taller, and more primitive, Aegodonts's flatter and more advanced. The latter includes the true Antilopini and Caprini while the former is the Spiral-horned antelope and the bovini, Boödonts evolving in Eurasia and Aegodonts in Africa, the two interchanging as continents adrift joined and parted; glacial periods advanced and retreated; sea levels fell and swelled; and land bridges came and went.

The most distinguishing anatomical characteristic of the Bovini is horns, which often also appear attached to religious, mythic, and artistic figures, as we've seen. Horn is said to represent a complex interaction between the soft tissues and the underlying bone. A horn consists of live bone core, known as ossicone–Giraffe horns are permanent, hide-covered ossicones–that in Buffalo begin with faveolated–honeycombed–bases that bulk up and upon which the horn covers ultimately meet to form the boss. Seldom surviving in the biostratigraphic layers, the covers are sheaths of keratin, one of the family of fibrous proteins–scleroproteins–that are as well the main structure of scales, feathers, hair, hooves, and talons. Collagen, giving ligaments and tendons their elastic strength, is another, while other scleroproteins help construct sponges, corals, the flagella of bacteria, and spider's silk.

Wild and domestic cattle horns–which are almost never shed: among the Bovidae, the Pronghorn antelope is the only one that sheds its horn sheaths annually–are mostly smooth and unannulated–exhibiting no growth rings–and without keels–sharp anterior, posterior, or sometimes both, ridges. Horns can grow throughout an animal's life with new keratin added at the bases as the older keratin, which can be worn down, is pushed out by the growing core. Those that curl or curve, do so through the physics of outer edges growing faster than inner. What they are for, exactly, remains unresolved.

The Darwins, Erasmus and Charles, arrière-oncle et petit-neveu, some sixty-five years apart, shared the idea that horns are armaments with which males contest with other males of their species, the winner with the presumably larger horns, passing the trait on to its spawn. Other naturalists believe cranial appendages developed on places on the head where the scalp was subject to injury. Or they might have been for defense against predators and tied to changing nutritional conditions, or cues identifying sex in dimorphic species. More theories: luxury tissue for pure adornment or a handicap for attracting females, which because of the energy invested in growing it shortens male lifespans, males being in general dispensable once the delivery of spermatozoa has been accomplished; therefore, their dying early increases feed available for cows, calves, and juveniles. The other question is what purpose horns serve for females who have them, the case with all the Bovini.

It's thought that horns on females may make them appear more formidable when they group together to protect their young and one another from predators–and can ultimately be used as weapons. Horns can also benefit females who find concealing themselves problematic. Big wild cattle can't conveniently sneak off, especially in savanna landscapes where they are conspicuous. So, they brass it out by looking like aggressive bulls. A third, maybe most intriguing notion is that by females's having horns, young bulls, often targeted by mature ones and driven from the herd by misuse before they become potential rivals, can instead blend in among the crossdressing cows and advantage from more growing time before having to go out into the world on their own.

Bovini in their wild numbers are among the greatest engineers of geomorphology in the natural world, and in herds of domesticated species probably the major despoilers. Domestic cattle in the non-native form of cows in North America, have been responsible for widespread overgrazing and riparian-habitat destruction. The feral Water buffalo introduced from Asia are considered by the Australian Government's Department of Sustainability, Environment, Water, Population and Communities to be a major environmental disaster in the wetlands of the top end of the Northern Territory, causing soil erosion, channelling of floodwaters, increased intrusion of saltwater into freshwater habitats, and destruction of wetland vegetation. Hence the rationale for culling. Yet wild, native Bovini are sorely missed by all the lands they once inhabited.

Natural wallows of the North American prairies were only enhanced by visits from American bison, in the wet or dry seasons. The result of one-ton bovines rolling in them was to compact the soil, enlarge the dimensions, and by depositing hair, body oil, and skin debris into them, make them drain out slower. Thanks to Bison–domestic cattle doesn't wallow–waterholes could hold rainfall and snowmelt longer and support a prosperous variety of wildlife and plants. The U. S. National Parks Service estimates that on the five hundred thousand square miles of the Great Plains, as many as five wallows of varying sizes could have been found per acre, meaning possibly more than one and a half billion across the habitat. And these would have supported a far greater diversity of birds, amphibians, insects, and wetland plants than what remains today when the ghostly waterless outline of an old wallow may be all there is to lead the imagination back to the drifting scenery of once massive herds of Bison streaming against the evening sky.

The most-mourned bovine on the continent of Europe is the Aurochs, *Bos primigenius,* first-born cattle. For some six hundred thousand years, the Aurochs and other large herbivores shaped the environment by browsing, grazing, trampling, and breaking the soil with their massive weight and sharp hooves, nourishing it with their dung–the ecological value of bullshit has defined the natural heritage in Europe for thousands of years, says one group of writers on the rewilding of the continent. They provided predators, humans figuring prominently among them, with fresh flesh, and scavengers with carrion. Nothing wasted, their scraps and skin were food for Dermestidae beetles; and their disarticulated skeletons, as well as fertilizing the soil, were when ingested, an essential source of phosphorus and calcium for a broad spectrum of animals, including those of their own tribe. And of course, we were attracted to their horns as arts material, utensils, totems, and trophies. For millennia, Aurochs was a keystone species in European nature, its feeding and other activities and its byproducts converting closed-canopy forests into open grazing land for long intervals between the land's returning to forest to repeat the cycle. Beneficiaries of the presence of Aurochs's were as manifold as Frittilaries, orchids, Partridges, Griffons, even lavender.

If you imagined the archetype of all the Bovini in its most nearly idolized form, it would be the Aurochs. The debate continues over whether it evolved, as long as eight hundred fifty thousand years ago, in India or Africa, possibly descending from the Indian subcontinent's *Bos acutifrons,* the most ancient *Bos,* or even the African *Pelorovis olodowayensis,* and spreading primarily to the west and north, though it would ultimately inhabit the whole expanse of Eurasia. When Gaius Julius Caesar trooped his legions into the Hercynia Silva of Gaul, he encountered the Aurochs, which he called the Uri and admiringly described as a little below the Elephant in size, and of the appearance, color, and shape of a bull. Estimates of shoulder heights in bulls run between six and six-and-a-half feet, with weights from the Late Middle Pleistocene of as much as one-and-a-half metric tons. Domestic taurine cattle are thought to derive from the Aurochs. For a domestic bull standing on the shade side of an Aurochs, the sun would have been eclipsed.

The Aurochs's horn, pale or yellowish white and turning to black at the tips, is described as a stretched spiral. Each was estimated to be as much as seven inches in diameter and potentially more than 40 inches long. The horns curved in, a bull's more dramatically than a cow's–conceivably to lessen the chance during dominance contests between males of either's being seriously impaled. A mature bull's hide, based on old descriptions, was sooty black while at birth both sexes were chestnut, with females remaining that color into adulthood–in Poland, where the last Aurochs lived, the shade of red was called płowa, fawn. A two-finger-wide gray dorsal stripe ran down the bull's back, and its chin was said to be white.

Like African buffalo, Aurochs cows, calves, and juveniles herded together, bulls staying mostly apart for the greater portion of the year, rendezvousing to breed. Wallowers in the way other wild cattle are, they largely favored lowland fens, as far as the Nile Valley where pharaohs hunted them from chariots.

Accounts of Aurochs's meeting and attacking people even on horseback, and hurling horse and rider into the air on its horns, then goring either or both to death, are well founded. Yet where after centuries of overhunting and ouster from its native range by domestic livestock and land clearance by farmers, the species was granted much-too-belated protection in royal enclaves such as the crown Jaktorów Forest, the Aurochs grew far more–perhaps excessively–tolerant of human presence. It was done in, at last, by our species's mismanagement, poaching, and the ultimate corruption of gamekeepers tasked by Polish King Sigismund III with guarding the species, the final one, a female, dying off in 1627.

Next in the historical order of Linnaean classification, Bison are represented today by two closely related species of shaggy beasts: the European bison, *Bison bonasus*, Wisent in German, and the American bison, *Bison bison*, Tatanka to the Lakota and Cuhtz to the Comanche who along with other Plains tribes fashioned their culture around the gigantic herbivores that lived with them in the millions. There is speculation that Bison might be placed in the *Bos* genus; but enough differences exist to suggest a genus of their own, *Bison*, it and *Bos* estimated to have separated from a common ancestor more than a million years ago. Wisent bulls can stand more than six foot at their high withers, be nearly ten feet in body length, and weigh up to two thousand pounds. A record horn spread, measured across the outside curves of the horns, comes close to three feet. Wisent have fourteen pairs of ribs, American bison, fifteen. While Wisent are longer legged and on average taller, the largest American bison could stand a half-foot more at the withers and almost two feet longer, weighing as much as an extra two hundred pounds. Its horns, though, are shorter and less massive, pointing more upward than the inward-curving Wisent's and often hidden in the American bison's longer curly scalp, its hair also longer and thicker over the forequarters and down the upper forelegs. Both species's males use their horns to batter other males during mating contests.

The population figures on the American bison, both Plains and Wood subspecies–*B. b. bison* and *B. b. athabascae*–were, as late as the nineteenth century, legendary. Another perspective is that the original range of the Bison on the North American continent amounted to almost 40 percent of the land and encompassed twenty-two separate biomes from semi-desert to boreal forest. Now, the only place remaining where Plains bison have lived wild through their entire existence is Yellowstone National Park. Suspected of being extinct, some two hundred relatively pure Wood bison were discovered in a remote portion of Wood Buffalo National Park in Alberta, in 1957.

The three subspecies of European Wisent, the Lowland, *B. b. bonasus*; Caucasian, *B. b. caucasicus*; and Carpathian, *B. b. hungarorum*, were shot into extinction by the late 1920's, many for rations during World War I. All that exist today, free-ranging in old-growth woods and numbering close to five thousand, were from the reintroduction of captive animals trapped before disappearing from the Białowieża Forest on the Polish-Belarusian border. There is today a pure Lowland-Białowieża subspecies and a hybrid Lowland-Caucasian.

One animal, however, yet remains to be described, who surpasses all others in dogged ferocity when once aroused. This is the Buffalo.

Those words are taken from Sir Samuel White Baker: credited with being an English explorer of the Nile, military officer, naturalist, engineer, abolitionist, international big-game hunter, and author–and for all that, a racist, jingoist, imperialist, and too-often callous slayer of animals to the point of frequently being rebarbative–writing in the *The Rifle and Hound in Ceylon* in 1853. The Buffalo is the wild Water buffalo of Asia.

The Buffalo is, Baker tells us, about the size of a large ox, of immense bone and strength, very active, and his hide is almost free from hair, giving a disgusting appearance to his india-rubber-like skin. Although Baker does not mention, their having them, wild Water buffalo wear off-white stockings and carry twin cream-colored chevrons on their necks. Bulls have also achieved extreme weights above twenty five hundred pounds.

Baker continues, He carries his head in a peculiar manner, the horns thrown back, and his nose projecting on a level with his forehead, thus securing himself from a front shot in a fatal part. This renders him a dangerous enemy...Should he succeed in catching his antagonist his fury knows no bounds, and he gores his victim to death, trampling and kneeling upon him till he is satisfied that life is extinct.

Baker describes the haunts of this animal as the hottest parts of Ceylon, now Sri Lanka, in the neighbourhood of lakes, swamps, and extensive plains, the Buffalo existing in large herds. They wallowed in the soft mire, passing two thirds of their time in water, so that they may be almost termed amphibious. The Water buffalo Baker hunted, though, may not have been native or even entirely wild, such Buffalo halting north of the Godavari River across the waist of the Indian subcontinent, and those on Ceylon likely feral descendants of domestic stock, having been imported many generations before Baker encountered them.

Bubalus arnee, the wild Water buffalo, is believed to have diverged from the Bison and Wild yak three million years ago. During an interglacial period in the Pleistocene another species, *B. murrensis*, inhabited river valleys in what are now Germany and the Netherlands, along with Straight-tusked elephant, Merck's rhinoceros, and European hippopotamus, until that animal was frozen out by glacial ice. *B. arnee*'s distribution at its peak reached through the wetlands of India from the central to the northern parts, then possibly as far as the Euphrates River, back throughout present-day Myanmar, Thailand, and Indochina, and down the Malay Peninsula and possibly Sumatra, Java, and Borneo. No other wild Bovini has more spectacular horns. In 1955 a bull hunted in India carried horns spreading thirteen-feet eleven-inches between the tips across the forehead and along the outsides of the curves.

Two types, the river and the swamp, were domesticated around five and four thousand years ago, respectively, the first in India, and from there going west as far as Italy as dairy and draft animals, while the other, tamed in China, was distributed east and south from the Yangtze to Assam. Domestic breeds are counted in the scores, with the animals themselves in the hundred millions. The last purely wild Water buffalo may exist in the few thousands, scattered about in pockets of their historic range.

To find the largest herd of Banteng, *Bos javanicus*–thought to be comprised of three subspecies–whose historic range included Java, Bali, Myanmar, Thailand, Indochina, and Borneo, you need to look in the Northern Territory of Australia where feral Water buffalo also live. Having been brought there some hundred eighty years ago, thousands of Banteng now range freely on the practically uninhabited Coburg Peninsula.

Based on fossils, *B. javanicus* evolved eight hundred thousand to nine hundred thousand years ago in East Java. Major George Patrick Evans of the King's Royal Rifle Corps, who pursued Tsaing, the name for the Banteng in the dry Irrawady forests of colonial Burma, now Myanmar, offered his description of them. Writing in *Big-Game Shooting in Upper Burma*, published in 1911, he asks us to imagine a massively built Hereford, or a miniature Gaur–informally called the Indian bison–though the Banteng is by no means small. A bull, which like so many others of the Bovini tends toward solitariness outside the breeding season, can stand at the withers as much as seventeen hands, some extreme specimens growing over six feet in height. For so large a beast, Evans wrote, its hoof is very neat, while its legs are short and sturdy to support the huge body, which can weigh close to two thousand pounds.

Banteng carry a large white patch on the rump and white stockings. The subspecies of Java has a darker pelage than the ones Evans hunted in Burma. While cows's hides in Evans's words are bright chestnut, an old bull may, he said, be red, but it will be a dull, yellowish red, the shade of a withered leaf, or the red of aged brown canvas.

Old bulls, Evans wrote, of a dirty grey colour throughout, are occasionally met with, and these animals always possess magnificent heads. He continued:

> The horns are unlike those of the bison [Gaur]. They stand out at right angles to the skull, turning upwards and inwards somewhat abruptly. They are usually shorter in length than the horns of a bison, and smaller in girth. In colour they are very similar, and are deeply corrugated when they belong to an old bull. Good average horns measure about 24 in. in length, with a girth of 14 in., and a spread of from 25 in. to 30 in. Anything over 25 in. is a very good head. Occasionally tsaing with enormous heads measuring over 30 inches, with a girth of 18 inches, are shot.

This was prior to 1911 when the species was more untouched. Whatever its physical characteristics today, though, it is doubtful that the Banteng's instincts have ameliorated much from when Evans would say, After many years' experience...under all sorts of conditions, and at all seasons, I have no hesitation in declaring an old bull to be the cutest, wariest beast that ever roamed the jungle. What this amounts to, in my words, is a shadowy Whitetail that can and will kill you on a whim.

It is hardly possible to exercise too much caution when following up a wounded beast, wrote Evans, who hunted with a side-by-side 450/400 shooting a 40-caliber solid-nickel or soft-nosed four hundred-grain bullet propelled by sixty grains of cordite, considering it the lightest effective rifle for heavy Burma game. As with many other Bovini, Banteng, per Evans, share an unpleasant habit of occasionally turning off...and then retracing their steps for a short distance in thick cover, keeping parallel with the original track. They will then watch the trail from cover until the hunter following the spoor passes. Which is when the Banteng rushes out and charges him from behind.

Once found widely in South and Southeast Asia–its range reduced by more than four fifths–the Gaur, *Bos gaurus*, though called the Indian bison, is genetically much closer to the vanished Aurochs and the Wild yak, *Bos mutus*, than to either of the *Bison* species. In size, it vies with the Wild yak as the largest extant Bovini. Bulls can stand six and a half to seven feet at the withers, almost eleven feet from nose to rump, and weigh more than two thousand pounds; weights over three thousand have been asserted. A distinctive dorsal ridge, formed by spinal processes, mounts above the back on males; and the dewlap is wide and draping. Black bodied, white stockinged, with a strange high-crested forehead, the Gaur carries often pale-jade horns shaped like those of some acromegalic American bison, the Gaur's having been reported to reach more than forty inches in length and fifty-six inches across the outside spread. Their hides secrete their own insect repellent. Look into the eye of a Gaur, and a milk-blue eye looks back.

The adult Gaur's one credible animal predator is the Tiger. When threatened, a Gaur performs several stiff-legged bounds, bringing its forelegs down hard on the ground, making loud thumps, before escaping without making any more noise than the sound of its hooves trotting through the foliage of the forest.

Because of the Gaur's dewlap and thick neck, taking it by the throat and asphyxiating it is very difficult, as is overpowering it by leaping onto its heavy-muscled back. So a Tiger will attack on the ground from the rear and bite through a Gaur's hock to hamstring it. The Gaur, though, is also capable of killing the Tiger with its horns or hooves. Gaur and Tiger have been found lying together, having died in combat.

Looking like a Water buffalo calf, the Anoa of Indonesia's Sulawesi and Buton Islands is an example of insular dwarfism–island species that grow smaller than their mainland counterparts. Two species, the mountain, *Bubalus quarlesi*, and the lowland, *B. depressicornis*, are recognized, the former reaching up to more than three hundred pounds, the latter as much as twice that, while continental wild Water buffalo can weigh three to four times as much. The lowland's hide has sparse dark-brown hair, while in the mountain subspecies the hair is lighter and thicker. The lowland also carries patches of random white on its front and forelegs. Record horns, when the animal could be hunted legally, had only to be seven-and-a-half inches in length, though some twice that were measured.

More than forty thousand years ago, on the stone walls of Sulawesian caves, ancient artists painted animal-headed humans hunting Anoa; their descendants hunt them today. The endangered species is killed for the usual reasons: raiding gardens under the cover of darkness; meat that is said to be considerably tastier than deer; and the unusual–its horns hung in a house, project a protective power against santet, black magic. Not that the Information Age goes unacknowledged: Illegal trade in Anoa meat has purportedly been carried out on Facebook.

Along with vying for the largest extant wild Bovini, *B. mutus,* the Wild yak and the Gaur may be the two of their tribe, along with the African buffalo and, of course, the two Bison, that might conceivably today be sustainably hunted within their home ranges, if foolish, petty bureaucracies and governments under the sway of virtue-signaling, faux animal-sentimentalists, could be persuaded to recognize the value of managed hunting to prevent habitat loss and poaching, to the benefit of the species.

The Wild yak is the shaggiest of shaggy beasts. It has a brushy horse tail; and its long guard hairs over a thick wooly undercoat are dark-brown to black and can like a pleated ball gown almost touch the ground. Described as possessing a large and compact body with short, strong legs, huge is what the Wild yak is, a bull potentially capable of exceeding twenty six hundred pounds, making the domestic yak not a thing like it.

The domestic yak's Latin name is *B. grunniens,* the grunting or groaning bull for the sounds it produces. When it was determined that the Wild yak made no sound, it received the species name *mutus. Grunniens* gives milk to humans, and is renowned for its butter, and can be used as a pack and saddle animal–the American explorer, sculptor, taxidermist, scientist, and hunter, James L. Clark, made famous his riding yak, Pegasus, in his tellings of his expedition into the Pamirs in the 1920s to hunt *Ovis poli,* the Marco Polo sheep.

No other Bovini lives at anywhere near the elevation of the Wild yak, whose habitat can be at up to twenty thousand feet; by comparison, the highest survivable human permanent habitation today is believed to be a mining village in southern Peru, three thousand feet lower. The Wild yak's wide, lyre-like cow's horns are as much as forty inches long, and nearly that across the outer spread. Nineteenth-century Russian Imperial geographer and explorer, Nikolay Mikhaylovich Przhevalsky, classed a wounded Wild yak bull as authentic dangerous game. As he trekked what another writer called the bleak and scanty pastures of the empty North Tibetan desert–hoping to reach Lhasa; dying before achieving it–it would have been staggering to see, then, the great, long-haired bovine, Drong in the language of the plateau, in its possible millions.

Another exemplar of insular dwarfism is *Bubalus mindorensis*, the Tamaraw. An animal of the uplands and the size of the Anoa of the Sulawesian lowlands, it is essentially another miniature wild Water buffalo, yet the largest endemic mammal in the Philippines. Adults tend to be grayish black in overall color with gray-white rings around the eyes and slashes under the jaws and at the base of the neck. The triangular horns grow flat from thick bases back toward the shoulders in a V, the tips turning in. With the head raised, the Tamaraw's flat horns, which with a bull can reach about a foot in length, won't impede passage through tangled scrub.

Indigenous peoples such as the Mangyan, traditionally hunted the Tamaraw with poisoned arrows, spears, dogs, traps, and by surrounding them with fire. Theodore Roosevelt III while Governor-General of the Philippine limbo colony–a concept of one historian, for lands governed by the U. S. that were not official colonies in the way English or French ones were in Africa and around the world–hunted Tamaraw, earning the name of One Shot Teddy for his marksmanship.

In the 1930s a combination of high-powered rifles–used for hunting but also by ranchers to kill any Tamaraw they saw among their herds–logging, slash-and-burn kaingin farming, and an outbreak of rinderpest contracted from domestic cattle, drove the animal's population down to no more than five hundred, prompting the enactment of some desultory protective ordinances, in time for the occupation of the Philippines by the Japanese, followed by MacArthur's promised return. Having fallen to fewer than two hundred at the turn of the twenty-first century, two decades later thanks to intensified conservation initiatives, the Tamaraw is successfully breeding in the wild and could number as many as six hundred.

The most chimeric of all Bovini, the Kouprey, *Bos sauveli*, may be thirty years extinct, if it ever existed to begin with. Not even recognized as a–potential–species until the late 1930s, and awkwardly similar to two other Bovini, Gaur and Banteng, with which it shared–shares?–a putative range in Vietnam, Laos, and Cambodia, it has for decades been considered by some, a zany inadvertent cross between various wild species, including Water buffalo and perhaps even domesticated Zebu cattle. Whatever it is or was, the Kouprey impresses.

Up to six foot high, a bull has white lower legs, its hide gray with black or brown parts and well-developed dewlap, more distinctive than the Gaur's, while the Banteng lacks one. The body mass of bulls is estimated to be two thousand pounds, length without the tail, over seven feet. Its most identifiable feature is its cattle-like horns, spanning to forty inches on the outsides. On mature bulls, the ends become splintered into what one twentieth-century hunter called pom-poms. This may be from the Kouprey's rubbing them on trees or the ground; or as the above hunter noted, the bull's inexplicable habit of horning termite hills as it passes them.

Non-native Kouprey hunters were next to nonexistent, accounts of their hunts even more scarce. François Edmond-Blanc, international hunter and son of a great French breeder whose horses won multiple times the Grand Prix de Paris, left Saigon for eastern Cambodia at the beginning of March, 1939, with the professional hunter and taxidermist, A. V. Pietri, to collect a complete specimen of the Kouprey for what he wrote was to be serious scientific study. At that time, the only mounted head was of a Kouprey taken in Cambodia by the veterinarian, a M. Sauvel, for whom the species was named, and given to a Professor A. Urbain, who did the naming, for the Muséum national d'Histoire naturelle. Malheureusement, the cape skin of a domestic bull had to be pressed into service to cover the skull, the original it may be assumed having rotted in the tropic swelter in the field, though the professor was responsible for a live calf being brought back to the Zoo de Vincennes in Paris, where it posthaste died.

As Edmond-Blanc hunted in the open forests of eastern Cambodia, he learned that the native people of the area called the animal the Kouproh, as opposed to the Kouprey–describing the latter as being of a species like the calf Professor Urbain brought back. The difference seems to have been in the horns, the Kouproh's turning slightly more inward and being more greenish gray than the Kouprey's off white. Was the Kouprey, though, no more than an immature Kouproh?

We do not know! wrote Edmond-Blanc.

In that spring of 1939, he trailed for seven hours through 95°F heat and stifling humidity, an adult Kouproh-Kouprey bull. At the end of the wet season, few muddy pools of water remained; but the lone animal Edmond-Blanc pursued stopped at every one to wallow. Always rare, only a few hundred *B. sauveli* may have been alive at the time. When Edmond-Blanc finished his long stalk, there was onc less.

Identified in 1937, the last Kouprey was reported seen in the wild in the late 1980s. While it's hard to imagine a Bovini so large, eluding scientific classification for so long, it's even more problematic to comprehend how so rare a species could have survived at all into the late 1980s in the killing fields of Cambodia, as is claimed. It has been learned from D. N. A. studies that *B. sauveli* is its own species, not a hybrid of others. Research has discovered that somewhere around a million years ago, the Kouprey passed genetic material into what is now recognized as the Cambodian subspecies of Banteng, and not the other way. All that remains for absolute proof of the species is finding where any of it may still exist.

The only Bovini more enigmatic, and more newly discovered, than the Kouprey is *Psuedoryx nghetinhensis*, the Saola. It is said that no biologist has seen one alive in the wild: Identification came in 1992 from two skulls, one from the kill of a native hunter and another found in the Annamite Mountains in the newly established Vu Quang National Park along the Vietnam-Laos border, making it the first new large-mammal species to be identified in half a century. Argument followed its discovery about whether it should be classified as a bovine or a caprid. One writer said that of a dozen features characterizing Bovini, *Pseudoryx* possessed none, therefore placing it in the Caprini. The proof of its bovinity rested finally on a preponderance of molecular studies.

The most reliable data on the behavior of the solitary Saola may be summed up as: little is known. Its name comes from the Tai language of Vietnam, meaning spinning-wheel post horn for its straight oryx-like horns, thus the genus name. Those horns may grow to twenty inches in length, while the animal stands about three foot at the withers and weighs more than two hundred pounds, still considerably smaller than the Anoa or Tamaraw and so the smallest of the Bovini–and probably the most primitive, reputed to have begun to diverge from other species a nearly implausible thirteen million years ago. The medium-brown animal sports white stockings and white patches on its face, neck, and rump. Scientists have depended almost entirely upon the knowledge of local hunters such as the Ka Tu to learn the behavior of the Saola. It lives in wet forests up to twenty five hundred feet elevation, requiring salt licks and springs while feeding on arums along streams. Pursued by natives's hunting dogs or the wild predatory canid, the Ussuri dhole, the Saola goes to water to escape. Population guesses swing from seventy to seven hundred fifty, the species threatened by the usual suspects. Besides being one of the most recently found large mammal species, it could be the quickest to trudge from discovery to extinction.

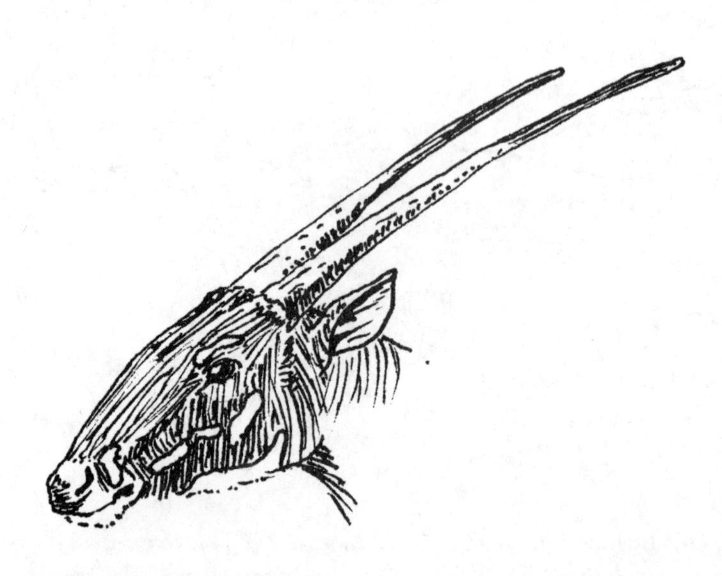

Walter White was a Tiger hunter, and there are, like the Aurochs, none anymore–Tiger hunters, not Tigers. Hunting with the famed shikari Rao Naidu in Madhya Pradesh in the 1960s, he took a name Tiger, identified for its infamy as a cattle killer, far more than ten feet between the pegs. When he killed it, entire villages came from the surrounding area to see, to bear Walter on their shoulders, and when they could, to pilfer claws to concoct philters and whiskers to grind up for mechanical poisoning, the little pieces, when sprinkled into food, becoming like slivers of glass causing gastric bleeding.

When one summer I first walked into the room where the animals were in Walter and Jane's home by the lake in Cable, Wisconsin, a few years after we returned from the Central African Republic, there was a full-body mount of the Tiger stretching its clawed paws–artificial replacements, perhaps?–into the air, permanent snarl affixed. It was not the tremendous cat that I saw, though.

On the far back wall hung the head of a bull Gaur, green horns and blue eyes, that Walter had taken on the same hunt in India. I think he knew I didn't look at the Tiger the way others did. He may have known that in the presence of the Tiger–a predator like us–I felt minor shame for Walter, and maybe he felt some himself. I didn't feel that about the Gaur.

He saw where I looked.

If you had to choose…?

He did not answer. He did not have to.

CHAPTER SIX

Syncerus

THE GREENEST HILLS of Africa rose above the River Mara.

That late September in 1974 on the Soit Ololol Escarpment in Kenya's Block 60A, the short rains were almost here, the first cloudbursts falling on bare outcrops, swelling the air with petrichor. In the morning heavy dew bent the tall grass blades, soaking pants legs through to the knee. Now it was the afternoon coming on; and from the high ground we saw Buffalo below on the parkland scattered with low brushy trees, like verdant talamh féaraigh in Kerry.

John Fletcher, tangled blond head hatless, nose beaked where it was broken in a mess-hall fracas during the Mau Mau Emergency when a regular British Tommy Atkins sailed a dinner plate into his bloody colonial face, wore shorts and once-white scuffed low tennis shoes and no socks, and a dark-green pull-on raglan jumper spangled with moth-chewed étoiles. He carried his scoped Remington 375 and I my Winchester. Behind us Mmaku had Fletcher's dulled-blue William Evans 500 with leaf sights. We had the wind and switchbacked down the slope, our feet sliding on the slick grass, the Samburu tracker, Mketi, ahead.

On flat ground, into the wind, we moved low toward the herd. Clouds scudded across the sky like a child's white blanket shaken out over an adult bed, blue clear air beyond the folded-back western edge. A hundred yards before the Buffalo, rain showering more, Fletcher lowered himself onto his bent left knee, tucking his right leg under him, buttressing himself with his left arm around his Remington, recoil pad planted on the ground, holding his binocular with both hands cupped around the objectives to shield them from drops of rain. The forty-odd Buffalo fed; then the wind swirled, and forty-odd heads lifted.

Buffalo are often described as pig eyed, with deep set, little, mean eyes. These give-or-take eighty eyes were not little or deep or mean, in the sense of cunning, but large, purposive, and glaring. Wet from the shower, their hides sheened like the black vulcanized slickers of old-school beat cops, their horns and black snouts backlighted. Fletcher glassed across the phalanx, then back, then stood.

We'll back out, he said.

As we took steps backward, the herd grouped, pushing forward, their eyes on us, trying to decide not so much what we were but what we meant. After twenty-five yards, we turned our backs on them and started walking, looking behind as we went. The Buffalo bunched tighter, and we walked faster. Fletcher went to Mmaku and traded his 375 for the 500. He breeched the double as we walked, checking the chamber for the thin flat-flanged-brass bases of the twin cartridges with the copper primers pressed into the centers and loaded with 570-grain solids. Assured, he closed the action, sliding the checkered safety on the tang, returning it to safe. He glanced over his shoulder. I followed his eyes back to the Buffalo, then dropped to my waist into a Warthog hole, stuck like a cork in a bottle, water showering down.

The Buffalo moved, the sun from behind flashing off their wet hides and horns. Fletcher and Mmaku and Mketi were stopped, looking from me to the Buffalo. Fletcher turned to face the herd. With his trigger hand, he stroked his thumb over the sights, making sure the long-distance leaves were down, moving his thumb onto the safety again, not taking his eyes from the Buffalo.

Mketi took my Winchester. He and Mmaku used their free arms to pull me out, coated in mud from the waist down. Feeling the layering chill of the matope through my pants, I took my rifle. We didn't wait but went on, the sun in descent at our backs, away from the Buffalo that started to mill, mixing in a sort of pedesis of random particles in a medium of rainwater and the declining afternoon light, the parkland in front of us against the lowered gray sky, greener than some final earthly elysium, the air cleaner, my glee overt and approaching absolute.

Out on the Safaris, I had seen a herd of Buffalo, one hundred and twenty nine of them, come out of the morning mist under a copper sky, one by one, as if the dark and massive, iron-like animals with the mighty horizontally swung horns were not approaching, but were being created before my eyes and sent out as they were finished.

That is Isak Dinesen's story of the dateless genesis of African buffalo. There are other, less lyrical but as imposing, tales of its descent.

In the codex of geologic time, Aegodonts and Boödonts divided about twenty five million years ago; and somewhere in Asia south of the Himalayas, as some paleontologists maintain–though others cite a location more generally in Eurasia–the Bovini originated, evolving from the ostensibly most primitive bovid, the ancient Eotragus, already well in existence as early as twenty million years ago. Though numerous, all the bovid reliquiae does not connect like Ezekiel's dry bones into an unbroken lineage down to the African buffalo. Along with the taphonomic evidence, hypothesis, and downright conjecture, is called for.

A paleontological record, necessarily gapped, is more about discontinuities than cogent narratives; for all the interregna, it can be determined that the subfamily Bovinae–the tribes Bovini, Boselaphini, and Tragelaphini–further evolved away from the greater Bovidae family some nineteen million years ago. The true Buffalo, the Bubalina–today, the extant Water buffalo, African buffalo, Anoa, and the Tamaraw–and the Bovina–the *Bos* and *Bison* genera–were separating ten million years back, Bubalina proceeding to diverge into *Bubalus* and what became *Syncerus* between eight and nine million years ago, ancestral *Syncerus* migrating into Africa.

Due to a dearth of African fossils from ten million to seven million years ago, it is not possible to pinpoint when the bovine first entered the continent, other than that the earliest record of an undescribed one comes from seven million-year-old finds in the Toros-Ménalla Formation in northern Chad, perhaps not coincidentally coeval and colocated with what was thought to be the initial, named attestation of hominins: Sahel Man, *Sahelanthropus tchadensis*. Better known, however, than when bovines came to Africa, is what they sought.

Author Peter Hathaway Capstick's first, most popular, and cheerfully fabulist African book was titled *Death in the Long Grass*. In Capstick's lore, that grass was a locus of bad ends for man and animal. For the ancestors of *Syncerus*, though, the earliest long grass of Africa offered the right place, right time, to pioneer new habitat.

C_3 grasses–C_3 referring to the three carbon atoms in the compound produced in the plant by photosynthesis–evolved during the Mesozoic, which began about a quarter billion years ago. The cooler, wetter conditions in the CO_2-rich atmosphere of the time let the grasses–cereals such as barley, oats, and wheat, and pasture and lawn grasses–flourish: One of the few C_3 grasses endemic to the torrid zone is bamboo. With the decrease in the level of carbon dioxide around thirty million years ago, along with a drying, warming climate, came the evolution of C_4 grasses–four carbon atoms.

Inexpertly put, C_3 grasses transpire moisture far more profligately than do C_4s, better suiting the latter to the increased-arid conditions. The change to C_4–switchgrass, corn, sugarcane, Bermuda grass, millet: You might think of C_4 as a warm-weather grass and C_3 as cool, or if you like, C_4 as rum and C_3 as scotch–is said to have transformed the biosphere. Much of what we now call sub-Saharan Africa became tough, weedy grassland and savanna at about the same time as bovines entered the continent, and hominins were considering giving bipedalism a whirl across the more open topography. This led, long before we acquired domesticated dogs or horses to assist the chase, to cursorial par force hunting, made possible by our exceptionally persistent stamina, if unremarkable footspeed.

Mega-anna-old bovine molars from paleontological digs show signs of better adaptation to the more physically and metabolically rough and bulky C_4 grasses. The molars display thick enamel ridges, heavily coated with cementum. They are also significantly larger, higher crowned, with more occlusal–chewing surface–complexity than those of their less-advanced boselaphine relatives. Yet with *Syncerus*, dentition does little to inform the two key words surrounding its African origination: probable and puzzling.

Around five and a half million years ago, the first bright-line ancestor of *Syncerus* appeared in Africa in the form of the genus *Ugandax*, the name based upon craniums and teeth found, unastoundingly, in Uganda, as well as Ethiopia. A largish bovine, it carried shorter, primitive horns that grew close together and swept back. A possible descendent, intermediate to *Ugandax* and *Syncerus*, was *Simatherium*, similar in size to *Ugandax* with apparently longer horns growing obliquely backward and tilting upward. Once classed in *Syncerus* as *S. acoelotus*, *Simatherium*–said to mean the Turned-up beast, perhaps in reference to the upright horns–is now given as the better attribution by paleontologists. *Simatherium* is considered by some, though, to be a stage in the evolution of *Pelorovis*.

Pelorovis, Monstrous or Prodigious sheep, the translations of its Greco-Latin generic epithet, is linked to *Simatherium*; and as *Simatherium-Pelorovis*, is considered along with *Ugandax-Syncerus*, to be one of the two lineages of Bovini living together in Africa during the late Pliocene and early Pleistocene epochs. At one time, two species were identified as belonging to *Pelorovis*: *P. oldowayensis* and *P. antiquus*. The former, found at Olduvai in Tanzania, was close to the modern Cape buffalo in estimated weight, though longer limbed. The most noticeable differences were in the *P. oldowayensis's* skull, elongated and similar to that of the *Acelaphini* such as the Hartebeest and Topi, and long horns that grew out and down in mirrored circling curves, somewhat like those of the Urial sheep.

The other *Pelorovis*, *P. antiquus*, the Giant African buffalo, originated at the same time as *P. oldowayensis*, two and a half million years ago. The nineteenth-century French geologist, Nicolas August Pomel, studied the relics of *P. antiquus* in Algeria and presented the image of a Bovini challenging the North American *Bison latifrons*, the Giant long-horned bison, as the largest ever to exist. *Antiquus*'s body length stretched to ten feet, while it stood over six at the withers. The weight of a bull may have reached two metric tons, almost forty five hundred pounds, while its horn cores spanned nearly ten feet; with the additions of keratin sheaths, ephemeral in the geologic strata, that width could have been double in life.

Pelorovis oldowayensis, vanishing eight hundred thousand years ago, is now believed to be connected to the origin of *Bos primigenius*, the Aurochs. From Ethiopia, *oldowayensis* may in some more refined version approximating *Bos*, ramified into Eurasia, its fossils coetaneous with Acheulean stone tools–from the Middle Pleistocene archeological finds in the type site at Saint-Acheul France–carried by *Homo ergaster*–working man–meaning that the human and bovine could have walked out of Africa, stride by stride, perhaps beginning as much as one point four million years ago. *P. antiquus* looked like what it was, a brazen exaggeration of its near relative, the African buffalo, *Syncerus caffer*, so much like it that its genus was changed to *Syncerus*, making it *S. antiquus*–it is considered now even more closely allied, so that it is classed as *S. caffer antiquus*. *S. c. antiquus*'s size may have been its final undoing.

Much larger than the shorter, lighter, smaller horned, more adaptable *S. c. caffer*, *antiquus* dominated the terrain until environmental conditions militated against its continued survival, or at least survival that was not without change, perhaps through transposition into *S. c. caffer*. As the gigantic specimens were in the process of vanishing, though, they also demonstrated intransigence, remaining in eastern and southern Africa until twelve thousand years ago. In North Africa, *antiquus* may have lived until three thousand years before the present, long enough to be hunted by Berbers with zaġāya, the spear.

Among the Berber Kabyle of Algeria, the belief is that all game animals originated in the primordial Buffalo, Itherther, perhaps the product of an ancestral memory of the Giant buffalo extant during the rainy phase, seventy five hundred years ago, that has been called North Africa's lush-prairie period. A bull, Itherther, came like an imago from beneath the earth with a female calf, Thamuatz. The two mated, begetting a male that then drove off Itherther and bred with its mother, then its own infant daughter. Wandering alone in the mountains, Itherther had only to think of Thamuatz to ejaculate. Its semen ran into a natural rock bowl. The Sun took the fluid and from it created all the game animals the Kabyle hunted.

Paleontologists offer a date of a million six hundred thousand years in the past for the emergence of the Buffalo on the continent. With a boatload of binomial names down through the years, there are presently no more than five scientifically proposed subspecies: *S. c. caffer*, the Cape buffalo, found from southwestern Ethiopia and throughout East and Southern Africa; *S. c. nanus*–dwarf–the Forest, Dwarf, or Congo buffalo, also the Bush cow, inhabiting areas of Central and West Africa that transit between dense forest and savanna and receive fifteen hundred millimeters of rain per year; *S. c. brachyceros*–short horned–the West African savanna buffalo of the Sahelo-Sudanian band of savanna and gallery forests tracking rivers from Senegal, northern Ivory Coast and Benin, southern Burkina Faso, the far south of Niger and locally in Nigeria, as well as northern Cameroon, and restricted regions of the Central African Republic; *S. c. aequinoctialis*–equatorial–the Nile buffalo of the northern C. A. R., southeast Chad, the northern Democratic Republic of Congo, southeast Sudan, and western Ethiopia; and *S. c. mathewsi*, the Mountain or Virunga buffalo, sharing habitat with the Mountain gorilla in Rwanda, Uganda, and the D. R. C., though *mathewsi* is not entirely recognized as a separate subspecies. The single climatic condition that most Buffalo need for survival is an annual rainfall of at least ten inches, *nanus* needing far more.

The contention of the taxonomic lumpers is that the subspecies of Buffalo are just two, *S. c. caffer* and *S. c. nanus*. Subsuming *brachyceros* and *aequinoctialis*, *nanus* may represent one of two separate lineages of Buffalo, West and Central African. East and Southern African take the form of *S. c. caffer*, the two lines–*nanus* and *caffer*–diverging as much as four hundred forty nine thousand years ago, *nanus* considered to be the primitive ancestral form for all Buffalo. Others theorize, though, that a drying environment starting about two hundred twenty thousand years ago, brought on a contraction in rainforests, to be replaced by savanna. It is estimated that more than a hundred thousand years ago, Savanna buffalo migrated west from their likely evolutionary omphalos in what is now the Central African Republic, not as a primitive species but one to become a more advanced forest dweller. Beginning approximately one hundred to two hundred thousand years ago, Buffalo grew further in population and farther in habitat, expanding east and south, to occupy in time their present historical range.

The Buffalo is credited as being the most massive bovid in Africa, though the Central African giant eland, *Taurotragus derbianus gigas*, may in fact rival it in size. Buffalo are uniformly broad headed with short skulls; wide, wet muzzled with a keen sense of smell; large eyed with seemingly good vision for spotting predators–they are said to be able to spy Lion at over a half mile–carrying fringed ears that droop down; the neck is thick to support a heavy head, the legs stout, front hooves larger than the rear to support the bulk of the trunk. Adult bulls have a tufted penis and can appear to have a chin beard. Females have four teats. While sharing all those features, the African buffalo is one of the most motley species of megafauna in Africa. In size, the color of pelage, and horn shape, the Buffalo taxa can be more different than same, although *nanus* may exhibit fewer dissimilarities across its subspecies than do other Buffalo. An adult Forest bull can weigh seven hundred pounds at the extreme, stand four foot, and be seven foot in head and body length without the tail. The hides of calves are copper, a rufous shade in cows, while bulls may span the spectrum from reddish-brown to black. The Dwarf buffalo's horns are the smallest, sweeping rearward along the plane of the forehead for flatter travel in jungle habitat, record horn length along the outer curve being greater than twenty inches–and up to twenty-eight–spanning across the outside as much as two feet.

Buffalo segue from *nanus* with a steady increase in body and horn size, through *brachyceros* and *aequinoctialis*, to the largest of the Buffalo, the Cape, *S. c. caffer*, a bull capable of reaching a short ton in weight, over five feet at the shoulder, and nearly ten feet from muzzle to rump, its hide black, often ashen, and covered in a fraction of the amount of hair found on domestic cattle. World's record horns, taped across the outside span, can exceed sixty inches.

The most emblematic marker of *S. c. caffer*'s horns is that boss, which does not always develop in the horns of the other subspecies and is not found on horned cows. Among Cape buffalo, horns grow laterally outward, curving down and up to pointed ends. In males, the horn boss, which is an evolutionary feature from the Late Quarternary, only a half to one million years ago, may start to appear at around age three to five; but it can take another four to five years to achieve hard horn grown completely together, fusing into a casque over the top of a Buffalo's head. Beneath the boss, and the brow like masonry, the honeycombed frontal bones absorb the impact of cracking blows from other bulls during skirmishes.

Bulls establish hierarchy through displays of dominance, triggered very likely by their endocrine systems. Confrontations can amount to no more than threat posturing between the bulls by presenting their horns–heads up, muzzles down–an unequal, submissive male retreating of its own accord or being bogarted away. Other times, a subordinate bull will approach a dominant one with its head low, parallel to the ground, placing it between the hind legs of the superior animal and bellowing throughout the ritual of acquiescence. Calves behave like this to prod their mothers into letting down. If there is not a clear difference between two bulls, combat may ensue. Most times, the contest is one of sparring by twisting together locked horns. During matches such as these, bulls are observed to engage in an average of seven bouts, each lasting about ten seconds. Matches mostly end in the contestants returning to unperturbed grazing. The clashing of bosses is rare, but it can be serious enough to leave one or both of the bulls dead. Other causes of death not related to predation are falls from cliffs, being stuck in mud wallows, and even strikes by lightning.

Leopard may attack and kill young Buffalo–though calves are well protected by cows–while Painted wolves and Spotted hyenas avoid herds. Buffalo remains can be found in Hyena scat, but this is usually the result of their scavenging on carcasses left by Lion. Aside from humans, the adult Buffalo's only predator of consequence is Lion. They can chance upon a Buffalo, or hunt one on the fringe of a herd. Solitary males are a preferred target. Cows exploit this by pushing males and weak animals to the outside of the band. Maybe it can be said of outcast Buffalo, as Philip Larkin is said to have spoken of himself, I have no enemies. But my friends don't like me.

The strategy in the open for Buffalo against predators is strength in numbers. Buffalo in herds in dangerous territory trust in mature cows to scan not only ahead in search of threats, but to stop to watch the back-trail for over a minute at a time; and if not liking what they see, they trigger stampede. Having top-speed bursts of fifty miles per hour, a Lion still finds it a challenge to run down a Buffalo over an extended distance, when the Buffalo may be sustaining a pace of thirty-five miles per hour. So the Lion seeks out places for ambush, while the Buffalo is alert to the terrain, such as choosing not to drink from waterholes when–often at dawn and dusk–Lion could be lying in ambush near them. In an attack, Lion try to get a Buffalo down, which with a full-grown bull in good health, is difficult enough that a Lion can end up roosting, bewildered, on a Buffalo's back, wondering what is to be done next. If a Lion is hanging onto it, a Buffalo has several stratagems–to be discussed in more detail–for shaking off its attacker. When bayed up, it can even kill an assaulting Lion that becomes incautious. It is always the Buffalo's game in dense cover.

Buffalo appear to enjoy physical contact with their species, resting like a very large, very scary hamperful of puppies. Mating seems keyed to placing calving in the rainy season. When a cow is in season, an adult bull who is tending, or consorting with, it, and which will have been tasting its urine and showing flehmen–the curling of the upper lip to waft the scent to its nostrils–tries to lay its chin on the base of the cow's tail, at which point for the most part the cow walks away. Eventually, the cow accepts the advance, which is when a bigger, more assertive male often butts in to seal the deal in a quick mount and a flash of ejaculation. If another bull attempts intromission, the cow will run off, making Buffalo females at least serially monogamous.

Gestation among African buffalo runs around three hundred forty days, somewhat longer in the Cape subspecies. Healthy, full-term calves can weigh up to a hundred thirty pounds at birth, those of the Dwarf forest buffalo as little as ninety. The herd will leave a cow to tend to its newborn, of which the female will be highly protective. A calf will stand within the first ten minutes after birth; and usually, by the end of the first day, it is able to walk slowly with the cow to rejoin the other Buffalo. A Buffalo cow's beestings–the colostrum–is some of the richest milk of all the bovines, its nursing calf putting on as much as a pound per day. Reddish is the predominant color of calves, while the Forest subspecies for the most part, remains red throughout its life. Weaning may take half-a-year; and maturation is a comparatively slow process, during which the cow trains its complete attention upon the calf. Young Buffalo may bond with calves of their own cohort and remain together into adulthood. A result of what is no doubt taken as an affecting image of a fraternity can end in a pair of inseparable Buffalo chums being killed together by Lion.

Sexual maturity is reached around three-and-a-half years of age. A dozen years is a generous lifespan for most Buffalo, though some live into their twenties, and in captivity have come close to reaching thirty. By fifteen, many Buffalo are geriatric. While males are targeted by predators far more than females that are in their prime, females in senescence stand a 25 percent greater mortality rate than younger cows. Not only do individual Buffalo have average life expectancies, so too do herds, some existing longer than fifty years, across three or four generations or more, some numbering twenty animals, others, sixteen hundred.

From data collected from collared Buffalo near Tanzania's Greater Ruaha River, home ranges can be between thirty and two hundred fifty square miles. Besides that, within home ranges two other types of movement are recognized: migratory and dispersal, which should be self-explanatory. Another recently described category–and there may be more–is that of expanders, who take in their dry-season range in the wet, but also travel beyond it to woodlands without permanent water courses, without dispersing into them. The two limiting factors upon the Buffalo's range are rain and grass. With enough of each, they can live almost anywhere, up to thirteen thousand feet elevation.

The population of Buffalo in Africa at the end of the nineteenth century is retrospectively estimated at three million. Then came the great epizootic, rinderpest, and human-population increase and land cultivation. Number estimates today range from four hundred to nine hundred thousand still inhabiting nearly the whole of the continent below the Sahara. With Wildebeest and Elephant, Buffalo make up the bulk of the large herbivore biomass in Africa.

Walking through the rain on the green Kenya escarpment, the matope washing from my clothes, the solid weight of the rifle in my hands, I didn't have the need to estimate the biomass gathering at the broad of my back. I didn't have to look back to feel its substance, measured not just in pounds but on the scale of sight, scent, and hearing focused on us.

So we walked on, not needing to look back.

I looked back.

CHAPTER SEVEN

Arly

AT THE VERGE of a green sward, on the fourteenth successive morning of hunting African buffalo in Kenya, I screwed the pooch on my chance to kill cleanly the first bull I ever tried to take. It was the smallest-bodied of three dagga boys, old, close to hairless, sightless in one eye, its horns sweeping out nearly forty-five inches, much farther than either of the other two's; and when I fired–low, near the heart, but not near enough–it trundled in a slow circle as the two younger bulls at an oblique angle ran past, visible in the fringe of my scope. I shot again, in the just wrong place, and again; and John Fletcher fired the right barrel of his 500, that I never heard; and the Buffalo went down. I finished it on the ground. When the bull lay dead and my rifle empty, I knelt beside it. I'd been to touch the great death. It wasn't.

We went on hunting Buffalo to my last day on safari, Fletcher looking for an even better bull for me, and me looking to make up for the first hunt, hoping there was still time.

The Spanish philosopher José Ortega y Gasset in his treatise, "Meditations on Hunting," wrote, A person who has never seen a good bullfight cannot understand what the mediocre and awful ones are.

I will add that like bad bullfights, bad hunts exist only at the expense of the good, bad hunts evincing, as Ortega y Gasset wrote, that in the human order...the depraved, the stupid, and the trivial are tenacious parasites of perfection, and not to be fretted about. It is always a question of whether the good are worth the bad, as in that, Ortega y Gasset again, if there are so many bad writers it is because there have been some good ones.

The good hunts are what you go back for.

The last morning of hunting in Kenya we flushed a bushbuck, and I had the briefest instant to make the fastest running shot I ever made and took the sturdy, aggressive little antelope through the heart as it stretched into full flight in the thick green grass. I was desirous to try another Buffalo before leaving.

In the evening, John and I and my photographer friend Bill out alone, the trackers back, breaking camp, we found the herd. The Buffalo drifted in and out of the forest all the gray highlands afternoon with us following–a bull's cloven print, looking not so big around as a silver salver, distinguishing itself from the others. It seemed that we lost the herd for good, until a small boy, no older than four or five, dressed in an un-dyed shuka knotted at the shoulder, carrying a smooth stick for herding, appeared out of the bush before us, asking in Maasai if the mzungu wanted a Buffalo.

The little child led us along a forest trail to the skirting of the trees, where he pointed across an open glade to the bull. The Cape buffalo bull, its tight boss doming high above its head, stood in the herd of a dozen or fifteen other animals in the near-ing dark, only a few yards from heavy cover, in which in no more than half-a-dozen running steps it would be completely concealed. Fletcher, for one, was uncomfort-ably aware of this. He remembered too well how badly I killed my first bull; and though saying nothing, he knew how much the Buffalo undid me. If I wounded this bull, now, and it made it into the bush with the light going, and the second rule they give you for dangerous game being that you follow all wounded animals in…

Fletcher, his mind turning, looked at me. There was no denying it was a good bull, and the trackers and camp staff always wanted more meat to take home, and there was still light, and–and oh, bloody hell!

We knelt at the hem of the trees, and Fletcher whispered to me, Relax, now. Keep cool. Take your time. Are you ready? Are you right?

I cut my eyes toward him, then back to the Buffalo. The Yorùbá have a verse about why the Buffalo lacks emotion, even fear, toward humans. They say the Buf-falo does not care about hunting amulets or a hunter's trade musket; it carries on its head horns sharp as knives, which is all it needs. I wanted this bull to have no feel-ings for me, or even to know of my existence. It was good enough for me to know of it, without its knowing of me at all.

Where, I whispered, easing off the 375's safety so it did not click, do you–want me to shoot?

John Fletcher stared at me harder, then whispered only, There, in the shoulder.

You can see where a Buffalo's shoulder socket bulges under its hide; and a bullet of sufficient size and velocity entering its body there will travel through to where the spine dips down from its humped back to become its neck. That was where I laid my cross hairs; and when the 275-grain soft-point Nosler hit there, moving at over twenty six hundred feet per second, the bullet broke the shoulder, then went through its spine. The bull was down, chin out among the short blades of grass, bellowing its death song. The rest of the herd wheeled, their eyes clear, wide, and uncattlelike, the smell of the bull's blood in their nostrils. I finished the bull with one more round to the neck, where it needed to go, and the herd was gone, vanishing as quickly as that bull could have vanished if my shot were at all wrong.

In the photo in the last light, the little Maasai boy stands beside me as I kneel behind the bull. He has his stick on the ground like a moran with his Lion spear, his eyes dif-fident but unafraid, showing above the fold of the shuka he holds, covering his mouth.

That last night in camp, while the staff jerked long strips of Buffalo meat over the campfire to carry back to their wives and children, John Fletcher, Bill, and I sat in the dining tent and ate hot oxtail soup and steaming slices of boiled Buffalo tongue and drank too much of the last of the champagne and cognac, and laughed too much. We finished breaking camp at dawn and returned to Nairobi along the trails that went through the grass.

My first hunt in Africa ended in Buffalo. And something, more, began.

Almost forty-five-years later, after sighting in the rifles the afternoon before, and the first night in Arly in Burkina Faso, I was awakened from sleep on the hard-foam mattress with sheets under a light blanket, in the boukarou, an hour before shooting time. In the low-walled dining terrace we tore pieces of baguettes–the crusts lightly charred from the wood baking oven–with coffee, butter, and fresh fruit, the chilled papaya with wedges of lime to squeeze, brought out of the dark to the table beneath the overhead fluorescent light, Pam not eating any of the fruit–nor a tomato or liver, all of which, in her words, slimy. Knowing what she did enjoy eating was a process of elimination–certainly not bleu cheese or cracked black pepper due to painful childhood dietary memories, or real food in general, it seemed. Even in Africa, where clean water tasted better than it did anywhere else, she suffused hers with festive squirts of dyed sugar-free artificial flavor enhancer dispensed from pocket-sized plastic bottles.

Finishing, we assembled our rifles, binoculars, sweaters, and gloves from our quarters–Carey bent like an interrogation point on the bare dirt between the huts, his face illumined by the blue butane flame for his Cohiba for the day–and walked to the four drubbed mini trucks with raised seats in the backs, diesel engines tappeting, where the professional hunters and trackers waited. We drove out of the compound, the black silhouette of the baobab looming ahead as we turned out onto the road toward the hunt.

Each truck traced its own route through the hundred twenty thousand-acre concession. Once beyond camp, past the park boundary, Alassane braked, switching off the engine, and pointed to my rifle for me to load the magazine. When I closed the bolt over the full magazine and on the empty chamber, Alassane started up again; and we went on. It remained dark a long time while we drove, the air cool like the first summer morning at home when it feels that fall is coming. The sun rose swiftly out of the rim of the horizon behind, throwing the shadow of the truck far out on the dirt track. Seeing the inky trunks of the stray short gnarled trees, glissando notations rising from the sandy soil, I remembered the turbines in the desert.

My mother's youngest sister came out from Lorain with her immigrant mother close behind, the older woman leaving her husband to be with her favorite. The daughter drank in old-man's bars in L. A., went home with many, married some. In the end, she lived in Downey, her mother then living in Northern California in her only son's home. One morning, before I left for high school, the phone rang. It was a stranger in my aunt's apartment. They met in the Zebra Room in Downey the night before. She suffered from diabetes. The stranger, adrenaline pumping through his hungover brain, alibied like crazy, saying he found my mother's number in my aunt's address book. When he'd woken, she was dead beside him. No signs of foul play, if you did not count an entire lifetime.

Another parental sibling. Another death. The long white vanes turned on the hubs of the nacelles, sweep oars rowing in synchronized rhythm in the August wind draining down the pass. We were just east of Whitewater on the interstate, the temperate-zone twilight elongated, my driving my father in his Oldsmobile to his dead brother, the last of his birth family. Just hours before, his brother stood in his golf-course condominium; and something tore or bifurcated, and he died in a snap. Now, my father was betrayed. His brother had arrogated the death he wanted: abrupt, instant, first. Get out as early as you can.

My father said all that, bringing up every coral-encrusted miserere from the seafloor of his thalamic brain, all the outrage of being desolately, desperately, distraughtly hoodwinked, defrauded, suckered, bamboozled, victimized, preempted.

To listen to it was like chauffeuring Dutch Schultz in extremis: A boy has never wept...nor dashed a thousand kin. Yet the subtext was manifest. The dead man should have been he.

No longer was there a living party to whom to attach his grievances–though it would not arrest his project of searching for others, responsible or not. None left who knew the particulars of his saga and could number and recite chronologically each of his lifelong failings–arrived at by family consensus–which gave him strange succor, as close as he got to feeling cared for. No one else to kindle fulmination in him, which gave his life savor. This was one more thing to envy, the last, his brother's taking what he might have succeeded him in. With the premature death of his brother that day, my father was a spacewalker blown out a hatch, untethering from the umbilicus, hurtling through the accelerating expanse of dark energy and dark matter.

At the condominium, night appeared beyond the windows as we waited inside beside my father's brother's widow–a brief second marriage that seemed good, after the earlier, longer one that had not. We stayed while my uncle's wife's adult children from her first marriage were en route.

As we listened to the abruptly widowed talk, my father's actual emotions were incommunicable. So he mangled himself into bromides in lieu of speaking his mind. Then my step-aunt in the kitchen slumped, clutching the edge of the sink to support herself, and crying, as if it had all just become decided, We were so happy.

Who knew how that rang in my father's dampered ears.

The dawn sun behind us into the floury Burkinabé sky cast a flat light. We drove for miles before coming to a T, yellow flowers like crocuses growing on the ground. To the left the black trees, turned to gray in the gauzy air, went off south on the spreading long-grass savanna. Right, the road passed into a narrow saddle between twin monadnocks, upright stone pianos set atop talus cones.

We turned toward the saddle, shea, Roan-fruit, and Isoberlinia trees lining either side as we drove on the dry sand surface. From the back of the mini-pickup, Djanjoua, the professional hunter, drummed on the cab roof. Alassane braked, and we all climbed down to the ground. Djanjoua pointed to other dust above the stand of trees to the west. Taking the rifles, we chambered rounds and set the safeties. In the 416's chamber I had a 350-grain tipped copper bullet, 400-grain solids underneath in the magazine.

Doves called. A breeze brushed, the air like a hot bath turned tepid. We were an entourage–Djanjoua, me, the translator Thomas, the tracker Kamiri, and my non-hunting hunting-trip companion Carey; but we moved quietly. First, over the tops of the short trees, there was only the dust to see. As we got closer to the dust, I turned down the power ring on my riflescope to close-range magnification.

We heard the Buffalo now–cows lowing, bulls grunting. Nearer, we saw them drifting away, two dozen together, hides in shades of black and red and brown, herded together. We were looking for a bull of a size and age we would know, when the breeze freshened and shifted.

Without hesitation or the lifting of their heads, the herd ran forward in hobbyhorse gaits, horns striking sparks of sunlight, tails whisking limply like ribbons. We followed a short way, but they were soon beyond us; and we turned back to the truck, unchambering our rifles when we got to it. Climbing in, we drove into the draw between the buttes, which would become the iconic cenotaphs of the hunt. Pressed between the paired buttes, we passed a fire ring with cottony ash stirred by the wind, surrounded by a ruffle of plucked Guinea fowl plumage, evidence of fête, Guineas to cook, domestic chickens, especially black ones, to sacrifice. Coming out of the draw, we turned out onto another sand road that went among scattered trees where Hartebeest ran.

Western roan antelope, posed like short-maned horned horses cast in bronze, materialized across the savanna, watching us before we saw them. I wanted nothing but Buffalo, though; and Djanjoua scanned out over the hood of the truck for their tracks crossing the soft soil of the road. Late in the morning he tapped on the cab roof. By the time the truck stopped, we passed over the tracks. We got the rifles, chambered rounds, set the safeties, and started following the hoofprints.

The long bent straw-colored grass was sparse where we trailed. We got to where it had burned and saw the round cloven tracks in the soot. We walked for several hours, Carey with us, stopping so Kamiri could hand us the liter bottles of water he packed. Leaning on my walking stick, I took swallows, not all the way warm yet, quitting before I drank too much. We went on.

Three hours later, we'd crossed a wide tract of savanna, without sight of a Buffalo. We came out on another road where somewhere down it the truck was waiting, having driven around; and Kamiri jogged off to bring it back to us while we waited in the shade. That evening, undressing to shower for supper, I sat on the edge of my bed. I untied my boots and took them off. Looking down at the black ash on my shins and on the tops of my white socks, then at the blood from walking, soaking through the toe of one of the socks, I smiled.

Pam took a Roan early on that first day. After almost forty years of hunting Africa, she had never found one. Within hours of starting to hunt in Burkina Faso, she had gotten an old bull, its hide rough and muddy, the horns thick, heavy, and blunted with age, a perfect animal to have taken. That night, I blew out the birthday candle.

The next day, Pam had the first Buffalo, an old caked dagga boy with horns more than two feet across the spread, which would place it somewhere up in the records book for Western savanna buffalo. It was brought in whole; and before the skinners dressed it, they cut parallel slits in the back hide to make a loop. Inserting the hook of the electronic scale, they hoisted the doubled-up carcass, drawing the clanking chain hand over hand through the pulley with ratcheting like handcuffs locking up. Before the bull's nose was off the concrete slab where the butchering would be done, the red numerals blinked out at the maximum of six hundred kilograms. Lowered, then chained by the hind hooves and pulleyed up again, the Buffalo's paunch was opened into a rusted red wheel barrow to catch the offal: tympanic plash and borborygmus hubble-bubble before the flies came. At supper we ate fresh liver, though Pam ate none.

Lance and Brent both had Buffalo by the next day, and went on for Roan and other game–Brent, his first time in Africa, meant to hunt everything. All Pam wanted, now, was a bushbuck, and concentrated on the draws and thick cover where they might be found. I went on after Buffalo.

At dawn the herds fed out of the park, working their way back to it as the day went on; and we tried to be where they were coming out. Hunting for them, we went down to the Arly River, with the park on the other side, and from the steep bank watched a bloat of Hippopotamus, ear-flicking heads and wet-washed backs, folds of enflamed flesh around jowls and monocled eyes, blood sweat on the skin, protecting against the sun, rumbling and bellowing, floating in the flowing water the greased color of graphite. But there were no Buffalo.

Before we left the area, Djanjoua set fire to a large patch of tall dead grass, the concession being burned piece by piece as the season went on. As the flames mounted, Djanjoua, tall, camo shirted, hatless, rifle balanced over his shoulder, did what humans, as far back in time as we have existed, did in the presence of fire. He stared into it, in the waking dream a blaze induces. Pulling himself out of it, he came back to us.

We drove the roads in the early morning, often passing between the twin buttes, sometimes turning a different way on a different day. Sometimes we returned to camp for lunch and an hour's rest, but on most days we walked. There always seemed to be Buffalo tracks to follow and often fresh manure–judging when the Buffalo came through by the green when scuffed by a boot–even if we could not find the animals themselves. Cotton-pennant-white Cattle egrets lifted from the backs of hidden Buffalo; but the herd would be gone when we reached there. In walking, though, we saw what could not be seen from the road or the truck.

We found new tracks of Lion. One late afternoon, we were at the far end of the concession, near the park boundary. Djanjoua saw a Lion track at his foot and realized where we were. He spoke to the translator, Thomas.

We have to go, Thomas said.

Why, I asked.

This is where the Lion hunt after the sun is down.

During the days, we did not walk where Elephant were, or even drive up to them. We passed them when on their hind legs, they stretched two stories into the trees to pull down green feed with the tips of their trunks. The Elephant we saw were almost all tuskless, which is perhaps why they were there; and some were true giants, battleship colored in the argentine morning, ears fanning gently like turbine blades, moving not as if ambulatory but under full cloth sail. That kind of Elephant was the exception, almost all the others even down to the juvenile ones–or maybe especially the juveniles–exhibiting irreconcilable aggression, without doubt well founded. Charges were inaugurated; and if we did not drive off in the truck, the Elephant would have carried through.

One evening on the drive into camp, past the Elephant, Thomas and I were together in the double cab of the truck. Thomas had a question.

Tom–

Yes?

There was a pause. Then–

Can you tell me why–Tom–it is that your President calls my country a shithole?

He was in a way, I am sure, smiling, somehow slyly.

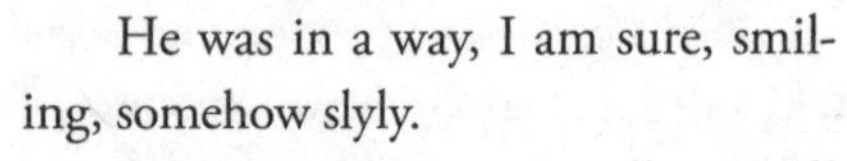

Being a white man's really not all it's cracked up to be.

Licensed Elephant hunting ended just before I came to Kenya, when I thought I wanted to hunt one. Since I could not, I settled for stalking up to a herd of cows and calves to photograph them, performing as per Ortega y Gasset, a plausibly ethical mannerism of the hunt. We were within yards, a tricky wind coming at us for the moment. John Fletcher gave a brief tutorial on shot placement. After I exposed several frames we backed out, staying low. Forty yards from the herd I stood and turned toward the Land Cruiser. Within a step, John Fletcher spoke out loud.

You should, he said, run.

She was a tusked cow, mounting far over John as he took his 500 from his gun-bearer. She came on, slaty against the sun, ears back and head down. And John stood there, steadfast, a deadline a measured distance in front of him.

I ran. I wanted to yell, Stop, lose our scent, change your mind.

There was no shot.

I reached the vehicle. Every Elephant I met in Africa took immediate exception to me.

CHAPTER EIGHT

Toxin

IN THE C. A. R.'s February days, the boundary between sallow sky and dry savanna was inappreciable, one tone of yellow transuding into another. Shifting sixty miles north from where we safaried on foot, to the French company's Koubo camp, we found grass-walled boukarous for sleeping, on the cloth-covered dining table small glass shaker bottles of red pili-pili peppers steeping in white vinegar, a hand iron heated by coals of wood embers to press clothes, and at our disposal rattling vehicles for transportation. We hunted in the rivershed of the Chari, the main river–that strange river, wrote André Gide of his travel on it in 1926, that turns its back upon the sea–feeding landlocked Lake Chad. Beside the camp ran a small clearwater creek; and across the daytime air, the sand-painting wind drew amber streaks. There were, here, Lion and Giant eland.

Morning after morning, ahead of the heat, Walter White dogged the Eland. He pursued cloven tracks around the rocky hills, sometimes for ten, fifteen miles on foot, able never to overtake them. Returning in the afternoons, he was too beaten to go back out; and he let me hunt for Roan and Buffalo with his professional hunter, François Bendima of the Banda tribe–who was young and did not tire–while he, Walter, rested in camp.

With François, there was a long stalk for a very good Buffalo bull, interrupted by one of the trackers, Alamine, The Torch. At all times, The Torch clamped a wooden match between his white teeth; and he rode facing rearward in the open back of the white Land Cruiser pickup, removing the match to snap it on the striking surface on the cover of the box, illustrated with the red-trunked Le Boxeur. Flicking it flaring behind as we drove the two-track roads, he ignited fluttering orange tongues in swaths of tall dry savanna grass to clear the soil for green growth, then replaced the match between his teeth with another from the box, every quarter mile flipping out a newly lighted allumette.

In the small herd of bulls we followed, one was uncommonly good. These were Central African savanna buffalo, smaller horned and bodied in comparison to the Southern Cape buffalo. Toward the end of the stalk, we had Alamine wait behind, fewer people standing a better chance of closing with Buffalo. As we crept up on the bulls, Alamine, thinking we were farther ahead, sauntered into the herd, scattering them like a busted covey of glandular-giant quail, guttural noises and the hollow sound of hooves on the ground. C'est la vie was the light in which I chose to interpret the incident, trying to appear as nonplussed, possibly even pococurante, as possible–while unable to shake the memory of a meter of sweeping Buffalo horn, hastening away.

Another afternoon in the straw-strand harmattan air, François sighted a long line of grazing Buffalo, copied out on the savanna as if illuminated lettering across the xanthous page of some vellum manuscript. We halted the Land Cruiser and got down with our rifles to stalk, looking to find if the herd held any good bulls.

On foot we arced around the Buffalo for a mile or more, getting into position where we could look them over without spooking them. François's chief tracker, Tchekel, led, then François, me, Alamine carrying my 375, and the water bearer Amath behind. Ahead of us arched a naked spine of rock where an old dead snag stood, a bony finger indicating skyward. Climbing to the crest, we saw the Buffalo close in front of us, feeding in a cloudy mob.

For less than a minute we watched them, when Alamine pushed past me, spitting out his match, hissing words in Sango at François. Then all four Africans flew away off the ridge, including Alamine with my rifle, while I stood, uncomprehending. For one second, as I swiveled my head, I could not discover what was surely about to kick me, bite me, claw me, or trample me, before a furious swarm of African bees flooded out of the hollow honey tree and launched themselves at my face.

For a large man I ran rather credibly, overtaking and passing François and the others within a hundred yards. At two hundred a small band of Hartebeest looked up with a start as one white and four Black men bore down, howling, flailing, their arms about their heads: A sight unlikely seen since the era of par-force hunting several millennia past, sending them racing off on half-a-dozen independent paths. At three hundred yards the Bees with their venom-injecting stingers, relented; and I discontinued my flight, miraculously unstung, while the others totaled up their welts.

I assumed that would pretty much be that for Buffalo for the day.

Au contraire, said François, rubbing the back of his neck. They have paid no heed to our capering.

So we sneaked back toward them–this time I my own gunbearer–and closed to within ten yards of the grunting, feeding herd. Evening was coming and the Buffalo seemed gentled in it. On our hunkers, we watched them for several minutes at disquieting close range, Tickbirds pecking their hides and the huge red and black animals tossing their heads and flicking their ears at the ultimately welcome annoyance. They went on, paying us no heed, but the herd held only one young bull, who was walking up on us, its head lifted and hard eyes showing the whites, knowing something was there.

Squatting at François's side, I tugged at his sleeve and drew his attention to the bull Buffalo that looked about to trod on us.

Too small, François dismissed it, tossing his hand as if swatting a walking stick off a trouser leg. In the end François stood and shooed all fifty of the wild bovines away, simply dispensing with them.

As we made our way back to the Toyota in the dusk, François, the trackers, and I began to giggle contemporaneously as we remembered the Bees. The residual fear siphoned off, and now it was pretty hilarious if you thought about it. We thought about it.

I teased François, noting that for someone who seemed to harbor hardly any anxiety about being in the proximity of big, potentially obstreperous bovines, he certainly did let a few insects get the better of him.

Well, Tome, François explained, smiling with sang-froid, you can shoot ze Buffalo. You cannot shoot ze Bee!

Africans are the earliest, longest hunters of Buffalo, because hunting was the first organized task of humans; and African is what humans were before anything else. Over all those millions of years, we proceeded from vulnerable limb-clasping simians to ground-dwelling bipedal predaceous hominin, not in a monotonic movement but one which paleobiologists speak of as the result of faunal pulses. Evolutionary change was made in stages across diverse times and the ascension and recession of varied habitats and dominant species, all of which we seemed to suit ourselves to with fluency. Periods of peak disappearance and appearance alternated, including the vanishing of ancestral relatives of *Syncerus* and the rise of the present genus. C_4 grassland extended; forest cover shrank; and we took to walking.

Imagine innocuous winking arboreal frugivores cum insectivores–the latter taste as Endnoted, presumably inaugurating our Family *Hominidae*'s casual attraction to psychomimetic fungi propagating with the bug life in bovine dung–witnessing their wooded enclaves dwindling. Yet they remained oriented toward trees and their produce. Before, they could swing limb to limb through an unbroken canopy, in order to reach different, less exploited groves. With the widening of clearings, though, their reach exceeded their grasp; and they climbed down to the opening landscape and felt the earth more and more beneath their progressively plantigrade feet. That is one possibility. Another might be our recognition that the main chance lay on the savanna, waiting to be seized by certain cheeky monkeys, such as we.

We already possessed opposable thumbs–as do Waxy tree frogs, so something less exceptional than we might want to congratulate ourselves for having. Georges Bataille, French philosopher and intellectual provocateur, called the rigid big toe the most human part of the human body, unlike any corresponding element of the anthropoid apes whose hallucis are prehensile. The former prehensility in our feet, though, according to paleontological evidence, did not impede our going about on two legs. The surest sign of upright walking is not the nature of the digit but the location of the foramen magnum, the large oval opening in the occipital bone through which the spinal column exits the skull. Set further forward in human than in quadruped skulls, it permits the hominin head to be propped up more vertically and with less muscle exertion, aiding in a more erect posture and leading to the identification of bipedalism in fossils. The big toe's evolutionary loss of opposability enhanced the foot's ability to absorb the impact of two-legged running and walking. In the grand scheme of which came first, being upright preceded a rigid big toe.

Hind-legged ambulation opened an entirely new world for the rude primates which we still largely were–not that we may be all that much improved now. The speculative assets, to be cataloged elsewhere, were many. Incontrovertibly, it gave us two suddenly free, independent hands to do with as we wished.

The late Valerius Geist, an ethologist like his own late friend Konrad Lorenz with whom he did his post-doctoral studies, wondered–if only to his slight amazement–how we ever, once we lit on the ground, survived among the great predators. Our physical strength hardly registers compared to that of any one of the other large apes. The human bite generates something just over a hundred twenty pounds of force; a Hyena, a thousand, while our canines have been diminishing for a million years. We had, and have, indifferent night vision and a loss in climbing ability when there were in any case fewer trees to which to retreat. Slow, skeletally spindly, covered in thin hides; diurnal, fat, toothsome, prone to deep sleep, snoring, with infants who cry aloud; putting into the air scents of childbirth, menses, wounds, and bodily waste; our diverging editions of *Homo* seemed to have more ways than not for calling meat-eaters down onto them.

Our universal fear of the pestilence that walks in darkness did not arise ex nihilo. Humans have every reason to harbor a lingering dread of the terror by night, which from their earliest days is when they were recurrently slain and eaten by other animals. The light of day was not much better.

Out of that dread, we developed several modes of protecting ourselves. Among the most basic: As a whole, we can, before we can speak, recognize predators for the natural-born killers they are, even if we can see only portions of them; and this is a rudimental element of our genus: distinguishing good animal from bad–bad for us. In its more fraternal expression, it's what E. O. Wilson–also late–the stellar myrmecologist who fathered the concepts of sociobiology and biodiversity, would have likely identified as biophilia, a term he popularized: the innate tendency to focus on life and lifelike processes, to affiliate with living nature. In the case Wilson puts forward, the result is a form of grace. For early humans, the focus on many animals was not, out of the striving to survive, one of affection, but of the horror, the horror.

Besides alertness, selection of terrain was another defense. The margins of shallow lakes and ponds, and along streams and rivers, made certain that at least one direction would be secure from silent approach. The bodies of water were also sources of novel aquatic foods. According to Geist, another type of food new to *Homo* and useful in the dry season, were geophytes–underground roots, tubers, bulbs, and corms. As well, there was bone marrow, brain, and burrowing animals and ones that den in tree hollows. The means of getting at these, after our discovery of them, were to dig, root, and stab. And for that we needed a pointed tool, a stout stiff sharpened stick.

In the mid-1920s, the Australian anatomist and anthropologist, Raymond A. Dart–along with finding the fossils of the nearly three million-year-old *Australopithecina* Taung Child in what he believed to be a kitchen-midden lair in what is now the North West Province of South Africa–arrived at another conclusion. Waxy frogs be damned, opposable thumbs not only let us, when we were arboreal, perform pullover shoots through branches, like other primates and trapeze artists, but when we were once reliably terrestrial, they let us specialize in twirling weapons about ourselves. So, advancing from limb bones of ungulates, used as cudgels for bludgeoning, we–in paleolithic divergence from Isaiah's exhortation to beat spears into pruning hooks–extended our killing reach with digging sticks converted to hand spears and then to javelins. We took game at a distance increasingly long and safe, foregoing placing our own bodies in direct contact with prey as other African predators were compelled to. This acquired skill meant, as Dart saw it, that the game these proto-men hunted were neither small nor slow but huge and active, all the way up to the size of Elephant and Rhinoceros–and Buffalo.

Somewhere in the African Middle Stone Age, researchers contend, projectile technologies and elaborations began. Five hundred thousand years ago in Africa, *Homo* was using the exacting Levallois technique of preparing lithic cores by knapping, creating a tortoise core–for its domed profile and the scutelike appearance of the flaked surface–from which a plano-convex, already-sharpened point was lifted from the striking platform with, ideally, a single, precise blow.

From the Klasies River Mouth Cave on the Tsitsikamma coast of South Africa's Eastern Cape Province, was excavated an embedded stone fragment associated with a projectile impact mark in the approximately one hundred thousand-year-old cervical vertebra of a Giant African buffalo, confirming that Buffalo were customary prey, never too big or daunting for us to hunt. The paleontological evidence of another stone-point wound in Buffalo bones from the Middle Stone Age of about Thirteen Thousand B. C., indicates the Buffalo's being a preferred species in both eastern and southern Africa, despite the risks posed in hunting it. In parts of Africa, such as Zambia, in the present, successful Buffalo hunters achieve an elevated status.

It is not certain whether that wound was inflicted by a spear–thrust or thrown by hand–or a dart from a spear thrower or arrow from a bow. Throwers and bows, appearing sixty to seventy thousand years ago, or even earlier, turned projectiles from simple–propelled by human-muscle strength alone–to complex–involving mechanically delivered projectiles. They also made approach hunting–stalking in open country sometimes no closer than forty meters to be in range–possible. Yet we retained other methods.

We never wholly abandoned tree climbing, upper branches making ideal roosts for ambush, as hardwoods Whitetail hunters still implicitly acknowledge. Persistence hunting, practiced by the Khoisan today in spite of some scientists's discounting as apocryphal its practice, meant the pursuit of game animals that while faster than humans in straight-line bursts, could not match us in extended endurance contests as we ran, tracked, and walked them down into exhaustion. With enough bodies, we could pour onto an animal in a horde. The ultimate object of the hunt is to disadvantage the prey so it may be brought to hand. And the most refined instrument for disadvantaging was, and may still be, arrow poison.

Over four thousand years ago, in the First Intermediate Period–a time of fluid transition between the Old and Middle Kingdoms of Ancient Egypt–a poison arrow was placed in a tomb; and certainly Africans have been hunting with such arrows far longer, only the organic decay of wooden shafts destroying the evidence. Poison is the single most important advance in making Africans into the paramount hunters they were, and are. In A. D. 1447, the efficacy of African arrow poison was first italicized for *Homo sapiens europaeus*–Carolus Linnaeus's formal name for whites–by Nuno Tristão, one of the favorite pilots of Infante Dom Henrique, o Navegador, of Portugal. On his fourth voyage to West Africa, Tristão offered irrefutable authentication of the potency of native toxins by falling under flights of coated projectiles, he and over a score of his crew killed emphatically by them.

Hans Dieter Neuwinger in *African Ethnobotany: Poison and Drugs*, makes the case that no other arrow poisons are so varied, daedal, and shrouded in mystery as those of Africa. He goes on to write that preparation varies from the boiling of seeds in water for simple extraction, to extended and time-consuming rituals and sacrifices, oath-taking, commandments, taboos, and secret ceremonies, to which outsiders and white men had hardly any access up to the end of the Second World War. The concocting of arrow poisons is usually carried out in almost sacramental mystery, the absolutely essential element for their success, to quote Neuwinger, the support of higher powers.

Plants form the bases for most African hunting poisons, though some animal parts such as the venom sacs of serpents, may be added as garniture. In earlier times, the Kikuyu of Kenya, according to Neuwinger, did use a toxic white-and-reddish frog, kiengere, *Hyperolius marmoratus glandicolor* Peters, not as arrow poison but to salt the feed of European settlers's cattle. When the frogs were ingested, the cows's stomachs swelled, their mouths foamed, and they died directly, the settlers's punctually burying the carcasses, the Kikuyu's soon after exhuming them surreptitiously, to eat.

Approximately three-quarters of African hunting poisons are derived from the A. P. S. plants–the genera *Acokanthera*, *Parquetina*, *Strophanthus*–the Big Three. While some banes can be squeezed out by merely wrapping a plant in a fiber net and twisting it like wringing wet laundry, *Acokanthera* toxin–ouabain, a digitalis-like compound–requires a lengthy, clandestine boiling of the plant's wood, leaves, roots, and seeds into a thick paste. This substance is never handled with bare hands but is traded in poison-cigar packages made from bound maize leaves. Poison is usually applied with a leaf or stick, not to the arrowhead, where the hide may wipe it away when the animal is impaled, but on the shaft, a hunter wrapping the coated portion in strips of hide for safe handling. The shaft may also be notched to increase the chance of its breaking off when the animal bolts, keeping the ouabain in the body.

South American arrow, or blowgun, poisons are based on muscle-paralyzing curare. An animal with curare in its bloodstream eventually suffocates from the inability of its diaphragm to contract. Most African hunting poisons work as heart glycosides, bringing on swift cardiac arrest. A curare-poisoned animal could conceivably be resuscitated with artificial respiration until the toxic effects wore off. For arrow poisons, there is seldom any treatment or antidote, for either game or human.

Arrow, and other, poisons in different potencies and modes of administration also perform pharmaceutical and ceremonial functions. Before going after game, hunters in the interior of Congo wash themselves in the macerated bark of a small forest tree, *Annickia chlorantha*, a fish poison, believing that by doing so they will see abundant prey and shoot well. Pygmies carry portable net presses on their hunts, letting them access *Parquetina* anywhere in the forest at any time. The vine's extract, nigrescigenin, is a powerful, chloroform-containing cardenolide. Shot from an arrow into the blood stream in larger dosages, it causes the heart to clench itself to death in minutes. Taken per os in measured amounts, its medicinal effects, put decorously, include genital stimulation, earning it a name in one West African language, said to translate as, make old women cry.

H. s. europeus always harbored official suspicion and bureaucratic contempt for African arrow poisons–and, never more than thinly veiled, despisement for poison makers and users, past and present, not so much for what was done to animals, but for what it enabled Africans to do for themselves. The colonial ideal seemed to be–as with America's intentions through the reservation system for indigenous people of this continent: Kill the Indian in him, and save the man–to turn Africans exclusively into peasant farmers to grow crops to feed the mills of Manchester or to collect the rubber of the Congo for the wharves of Antwerp. And that could not be accomplished if Africans still had access to the res nullius–something not in the exclusive possession of any individual–of wild animals living on their land, and to the liberty that hunting conferred.

By the time of the Belgian Free State, British East Africa, French West Africa, and other territories under foreign domination, the concurrence was that Africans must not be permitted to hunt. Yet the colonists had no interest in making hunting universally proscribed, which would fetter them and white sportsmen traveling to the continent from overseas, as well. To preclude Africans from the hunt, therefore, a potent myth had to be prepared–like brewing a toxin.

First, it was established that firearms, especially modern rifles, were ultra-humane weapons for hunting–and they are when used by a practiced, insistent marksman. Colonial game departments would even come to mandate the 375 caliber as the minimum for hunting the larger dangerous game to ensure clean kills–or to assure critics of the safari that the welfare of the quarry was taken into consideration. Of course, the Great Powers of Europe could not for all too–for them–prima facie reasons, allow Africans to carry breechloaders; and throughout most of the continent for a period around the turn of the twentieth century, modern rifles were by international treaty banned from import for sale to Blacks. Arrow poison, though, could be formulated furtively and used silently, a powerful attraction when white and Black game rangers hunted you for the crime of wanting to live off your own land's wildlife.

Edward I. Steinhart in *Black Poachers, White Hunters*, writes that government gamekeepers considered poison cruel and unsporting, believing, or at least saying, that it caused its victims to suffer a slow and painful death and to require little skill or courage from its supposed savage users. This colonial taradiddle is perpetuated today by conservation writers who credulously parrot stories of native poachers's shooting an Elephant with allegedly crude bows and rough-hewn poisoned arrows and waiting for the animal to die a prolonged agonized death. Not even Peter Kolben at the beginning of the eighteenth century, trumped up such whoppers about the Khoisan he felt called upon to caricature. What he reported of the way hunted animals died was something otherwise:

> And having by this Time a Multitude, perhaps, of poison'd Arrows and Hassagayes upon his Back, the Hottentots let him go very freely;

> but follow him at a little Distance. The Poison quickly seizes him; and he runs not far before he falls.

An European anthropologist among the Pogoro speakers of southeast Tanzania–then Tanganyika–saw the result of the use of *Acokanthera* arrow toxin. Hippo were the hunters's prime prey; and when shot with a poison arrow, the enormous animals ran in single five hundred-yard rushes and died. Of three Buffalo whose hunting the white man witnessed, one was found dead the next day, its liver when the carcass was opened in an extreme state of decomposition. A second died shortly after being struck. The third fell and died on the spot, as if God hunted it down, striking it with a bolt from the sky.

The twentieth century white professional ivory hunter, commercial poacher, John Pondoro Taylor, author of the comprehensive–for the day–*African Rifles and Cartridges*, witnessed the use of arrow poison by the tribal hunters in the Portuguese East African territory across which he wandered. Taylor hunted so far off from other Europeans, he only learned about World War II some time after its opening, when one of his camp staff returned from a trading post with canned goods wrapped in old newspapers headlining the launching of the September campaign. In another book, *Pondoro: Last of the Ivory Hunters*, he wrote that the better poisons kill in a remarkably brief space of time.

I've seen animals, he continued, receive the arrow, run a short distance, stop, sway, and collapse. There were some that looked dead before they touched the ground: there wasn't a movement out of them after falling.

His conclusion: I was quite prepared to hunt Rhino and Buffalo with the primitive bow and arrow–particularly if my arrows were dipped in fresh poison.

As far as rude archery tackle, Africans bows go from enormous longbows–those of the Liangulu of the Kenya bush are almost six feet in length with draw weights well in excess of a hundred pounds: Elephant, Rhino, and Buffalo killers–to short bows for dense jungle, and even crossbows, used by Pygmies. Savanna arrows are elegantly iron-tipped and multi-barbed, the best quality fletched with Eagle feathers; and even plain jungle or forest arrows have wooden tips that are deftly fire-hardened.

Never recognized officially as a tribe, the Oromo-speaking Liangulu, or Waata–Watha, to some–lived as hunter-gathers inland from the Kenya coast, from south of the Tana River to west of the Shimba Hills, and were driven to effectual cultural extinction from the 1950s on, when herded into village life. They were true people of the bow, theirs going from a hundred-pound draw weight up to a stupendous hundred seventy; the English longbows at Agincourt pulled at a yeomanly seventy pounds. The Waata hunted with *Acokanthera* arrows, killing Elephant to eat, the ivory throughout most of their history being of little consequence and recovered seemingly as an afterthought.

On the hunt, the hunter applied poison to the arrow only when the game was sighted. Because the toxin's potency deteriorated with time, the Waata hunting ace, as the most expert bowmen were called, used a clean arrowhead to make a straight cut on his own leg. As the blood drop ran down, he touched the poison to the bottom of the trickle and gauged how fast the flow coagulated upward on his leg, prudently wiping it off before the poison entered his own blood stream. Stripping off all his clothing, he rubbed himself in Elephant manure and stalked, cloaked in invisibility, into a full herd, targeting one Elephant. He knew at which angle he would be concealed from the Elephant's line of sight and approached until he was within yards of his rumbling target. He then drew closer and, knowing Elephant anatomy intimately, fired up into the killing place, wanting the arrow and poison to enter the body cavity and travel to the heart, the perhaps-ten thousand-pound animal dying within the sweeps of a watch's second hand. The rest of the ace's family band of twenty or thirty came then to where the Elephant lay, to eat the meat fresh and smoke-dry the rest, living off a kill for sometimes two months before another Elephant needed to be hunted. They took the useful hide, and traded with some of the ivory with other Africans for cloth, salt, and lamb, accounted a delicacy. Caching other tusks, they eventually trekked to the coast with them, to trade with the buyers there, selling often at a tenth of the going blackmarket price, just to be rid of the superfluous ivory without letting it merely crumble to fine particles.

Absent a cash economy, the Waata squandered ivory money prodigally. The proceeds went promptly into prodigious palm-wine debauches, as colonial administrators–still with designs on domesticating these supreme hunters–looked on, appalled. And this is the way of hunting, and of life, that authorities and nature essayists qualified as cruel, unsporting, cowardly, dilatory, and torturous. Worst of all, of course, was its being distinctly African.

Poison preparation is part of a near-timeless African oral tradition, the knowledge of it drawn from the natural world and passed on through instruction and demonstration by master makers. But when an old man dies in Africa, the West African poet Amadou Hampate Ba is quoted as saying, an entire library burns. For the young, the wisdom of arrow poison dims, until in Neuwinger's words, sooner or later it will disappear on the continent. No doubt, there are those eager for that inevitability. Yet, Africans will hunt.

Because of tsetse fly around their home in the Luangwa Valley of Zambia, the matrilineal Bisa cannot, or could not, keep livestock. Therefore, their protein needs and wants are met by wild game, mostly Buffalo, Elephant, Warthog, and Impala. Muzzleloaders are probably the most traditional hunting weapons used by Africans such as the Bisa who no longer rely exclusively on bows and poison arrows–though bow and arrow have never gone entirely away, again for the reason that a killing shot is as unheard as the tree that falls in a forest when no one is there. For hunting

Buffalo, muzzleloaders are a more discriminating choice over breechloaders. Inherently shorter ranged, they are better suited for hunting single or small herds of old bull Buffalo. Culturally and for subsistence, the Bisa prefer to hunt old bulls because maleness matters and because of their larger size–and larger return on hunting effort–but also because they are abundant. No longer functioning contributors to the gene pool, they are often isolated from other Buffalo or banished to the outskirts of the large herds. A hunter can draw into closer range with them than with an animal within a muster of other Buffalo; and they are more predictable in behavior than females and juveniles. They are also paradoxically not as dangerous to hunt as cows, especially cows shielding young, mapete. Still-hunts in the dry season, when Buffalo concentrate around water, may last no more than two or three hours, extending to six or seven in the rains.

The ways of African hunters for finding Buffalo, as exemplified by the Bisa, are basically three.

Hunting from ambush is an ancient enterprise extending back nearly two million years into our hominin past. Where to construct blinds for hunters to conceal themselves is chosen by the ages and types of tracks and feces, often approximate to water sources–and sometimes sources of minerals or of especially flavorsome food–an example, as related by Taylor, to be found in the Endnotes. These signs identify places for drinking, licking, and eating, frequented by animals, both prey and predators, all of whom might be menacing. Ambush hunting from blinds operates best during the dry season, when animals are tied to wherever water is.

Another tactic: Ascertaining the direction of the movement of the Buffalo, a hunter will orbit ahead to a point to which he believes the animals are traveling, then watch for stragglers or ones outspanning to feed apart. Even if a herd stampedes, a hunter, as Stuart Marks, author of *Life as a Hunt*, saw in several instances during his field studies in Africa, will run at them at a right angle, some of the Buffalo often halting in bewilderment long enough for a hunter to get off a shot.

The third method is fast-paced still-hunting. The Bisa carrying their muzzleloaders, walk at around a mile every quarter hour, slower through thickets, tall grass, and where they suspect animals may be present. They observe more animals than they can realistically hunt; but although Buffalo make up less than 10 percent of the game they sight, they almost always stalk the ones they see.

Being a slayer of Buffalo, as noted above, is a distinction among the Bisa. To them, Buffalo are inama yakapashi, gift of the spirits, the spirits shrouding the hunter from the eyes of the Buffalo as he draws near it. They charge their muzzleloaders according to the animals they picture in their dreams, maximum loads for Buffalo–the percussion cap is affixed to the trigger guard with wax, so it is accessible to press onto the firing nipple when the hunter cocks the hammer and is prepared to shoot.

If the Buffalo is lying down, the hunter knocks his knees together to have it stand and make a larger target. Firearms are only implements, added to the way of hunting that has been ongoing for more thousands of generations than are handily countable.

Ortega y Gasset wrote of the admiration and generous envy that some modern hunters feel toward the poacher, stemming from the fact that the best-trained hunter cannot begin to compare his form to that of the sylvan actions of the present-day Pygmy or his remote counterpart, Paleolithic man. As our hunting technology progresses, Ortega concluded, it is offset by regression in the hunter.

The poacher is, he wrote, in distant likeness, a Paleolithic man, from whom our descent comes. He represents the municipal Paleolithic man, the eternal troglodyte domiciled in modern villages. Of the hunting in Africa by that man, that human, male or female–whom we indeed envy and admire–Marks tells us:

> [Hunting] is about moving through a landscape of sights, scents, and sounds; of plants known and unknown; of spaces connected by historical events and antecedents; of stories and the richness of figurative associations; of autonomy; and of community. It is about direct encounters with other sentient entities that are aware of their pursuers and capable of evasion, deception, and outright hostility. Individuals exercise and hone their skills at every stage of a process that includes assessing the behavior of their prey as well as determining the chances of trailing the prey through the tactics of searching, hiding, following signs, and stalking, which if successful may lead to butchering, preparing, and sharing bushmeat for others to prepare as food. People learn how to perform these tasks by watching and through performance rather than by exclusively listening to a teacher or reading a manual. In the bush, the many factors a hunter evaluates and upon which he makes his calculations are difficult to measure or to capture as they come with time and experience–the distillation of a glance, an impulse, an intuition of circumstance, place, and occasion.

Along other paths through the wild, we may find many of these properties, though not every one in the signal way it is encompassed by the hunt. It is only there that it all is obtainable to us to the degree to which we can approach the spirit of municipal Paleolithic man, whom many of us wish we might somehow be.

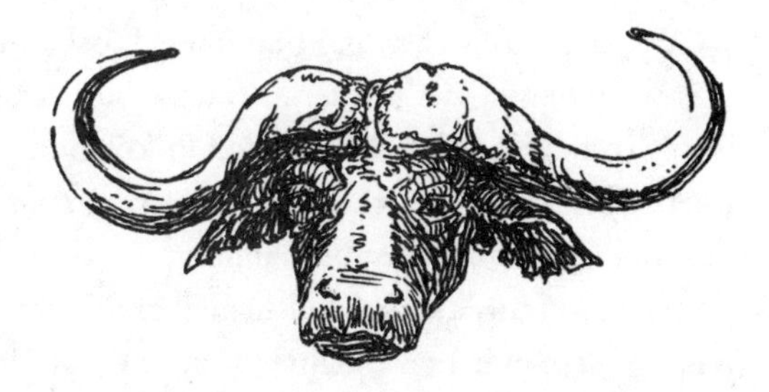

This early in the year of 2014 the grass grew more than head high in the lamido of Rey Bouba; and where we hunted was in the select burned-over patches, tussocks standing upright on the ground like a scattering of clown wigs, black solid-ash blades long and intact, not yet blown apart or crushed under hooves. In the wet season millions of worms cast up mounds the size of Titleists; and in the dry the mounds hardened into a feature of the landscape called kiibi, making walking toward the sunrise over them an ankle-busting trek like stumbling across a field of so many…Titleists.

I tried to keep up with Daniel Sodea. Not a professional hunter–none is required in the north of Cameroon because of lingering French colonial laws–he is a much younger man than I, small, neat, a fine dresser in an olive-drab forage cap, and with two wives. He wouldn't touch a gun, yet was from the Gbaya, the foremost hunters in the country.

Another of the Gbaya in the camp along the Mayo Rey River, was Amadou Davide. In his sixties, rangy and more youthful looking than that, he was the last of the Python hunters. As with poison making, young men no longer desired to learn from him, to take up his occupation of hiking four days from the village to reach Python country. There Davide searched for Aardvark burrows appropriated by female Rock python. Binding dried Antelope hide around one forearm and with a bundle of burning grass in the other, Davide bellied into the burrow to face a twenty-foot, two hundred-pound serpent coiled around its clutch of up to a hundred eggs or live hatchlings. Davide let the Python bite onto his wrapped arm and dragged it out to the surface, killing it, taking the skin, and drying the meat. While he salted and cured the snake hide, destined to be turned into yippee-ki-yay buckaroos by some El Paso bootmaker, he lived off Python eggs, raising to a considerable height the bar for manliness.

Daniel and the other tracker, Victor, shaven headed in blue-vinyl shoes and shiny worn black sports jacket, floated over the jagged ground, gray scale fluttering up with each step, the ash a perfect medium for showing what had been here and when. I clopped along.

We hunted away from the Hilux truck, feeling the day's heat expanding around us as we walked, unbraiding lines of tracks and assigning identities: Loder's kob, Sing-Sing waterbuck, Harnassed bushbuck, Warthog, Western roan, Lelwel hartebeest–from yesterday, last night, an hour before, minutes ago. Then wide ovoid cloven tracks coined in ash, heading toward rocks and the long grass.

We followed the Western savanna buffalo into the dawn along intertwining tracks through black fields cobbled in kiibi; and I numbered my steps, wondering when my last walk in Africa was to arrive, and if it would be this. It was a feeling, like the kiibi under my boots, but somehow inside, behind the heart.

Buffalo trails divided and Daniel and Victor caucused. I looked up. An Abyssinian roller landed on the limb of a wait-a-bit bush, head alert, breast and coverts blue as open flame from a gas jet. Daniel turned, and it flew. We picked a trail and went on.

Side-hilling, we passed a salt lick hollowed gray into the slope. Moving through rocks, I saw a Buffalo track in the ash, big as a Cape buffalo's, with it the track of a smaller askari. We rambled over low rises now, climbing higher from the flats, the wind favoring, the rises able to conceal a Buffalo on the other side. In a quarter mile we came to Elephant grass higher than our heads.

Tight together as tied shocks, the grass made it impossible to see more than a few square inches of bare dirt under foot, much less the fully recognizable track of a Buffalo. Pushing into it ahead of me, Daniel was swallowed within a step. If the bull and its askari went to ground in here, lying up after feeding through the night, they would be facing their back-trail, counting on the wind blowing from behind to warn them about that direction. Upwind, we would come on without any scent; and the Buffalo might not differentiate the soughing in the grass from our moving through it, so we might walk on top of them before either we or they knew. Unarmed, Daniel would have to leap aside for me to face a charge with my 375, borrowed from the camp, the synthetic stock broken and taped together; and I was none too pleased with the possible scenario. We turned back.

The thicket covered half a football field. Circling it, we hunted for the trail to see if the M'bana, the Fula name for Buffalo, were still in the tall grass. On the far side, the tracks came out and moved uphill into the rocks.

We followed into a flat of rocks and gravel. The Buffalo were hours ahead of us; now their tracks were lost over hard ground. Breaking off tracking, we rounded the hill, going back to the truck.

The numbered steps climbed to higher sums in my head. Bleaching on the trail was the skull of a doe Djama thirga, Bushbuck. One hundred thirty seven paces more was a rack of long thin brush limbs, lashed together with twine of twisted grass, mounted on a frame of heavier charred posts over a bed of white ash. Here the meat of wild animals was smoked, to be eaten and shared out by the natural-born hunters of the game, whom others call poachers.

CHAPTER NINE

Gore

AT THE END of the year, the rains were coming. In the heavy air along the border with Botswana, the old dagga boy was alone in the tall trees at midday, its horns respectable enough for Sandy to reckon that we could do worse than to use one of our permits. The bull moved off when we began the stalk, but halted out ninety yards from us, showing me the point of its left shoulder–the same target that a Giant eland gave me in teak woods in the C. A. R., two years earlier, though much longer than that by the striking of a secret interior timepiece. I got a rest on the sticks, held on that point, and expecting the Buffalo to collapse with the shot, let off the safety and squeezed the trigger.

The shot yanked the bull, and it began to run. My first mistake was that I didn't hit heart or bone. The second was that we did not give the Buffalo time to lie up, but rushed after it before it could stiffen, jumping it a few hundred yards into the brush and pushing it away before I could put a solid in.

For an hour-and-a-half we followed a trail of blood drops, like burst beads of salmon roe. From behind every bush, tree, or tall termite hill, I knew the Buffalo was going to loom up, the anger in it burning.

Early on, Sandy whispered to me to breathe through my nose, not my mouth, to prevent dehydration. There was no telling how long we would be out here, and we went off without water. The next thing he whispered after an hour of my waiting to be murdered, or at least severely walked upon, was, Oh yes–be alert. He fairly twinkled from behind his full Canadian beard when he advised this.

Alert? Be alert? I am the Alert Man from out of the pages of Ortega y Gasset, not the least bit drowsy.

Then a lone bull was directly ahead of us in the direction the blood spatters led. Two hundred yards out, it walked slowly with its head down; and neither Sandy nor I hesitated. It got away once already, and we could not let it get away again. We both raised our rifles and fired simultaneously. Then, as reliably as iron ducks popping up in a shooting gallery, Buffalo come out of the grass and brush everywhere and charged off, the wounded bull falling behind.

What the hell?

Making a wide orbit around us, the herd, fifty or sixty strong, slowed, then halted in a milling knot, trying to fix on from where the shots came. The bull was moving laboriously, and I crept up to a sapling to take a rest against it. I held the crosshairs on the knobby part of the shoulder, and the 300-grain solid sent the Buffalo's legs out from beneath it, its head twisting up and its heavy black body collapsing as the herd galloped off.

Here was a dead bull Buffalo, but was it the right dead bull Buffalo? It certainly looked right when we got to it, but we only counted three wounds after firing at it four times, including the first shot. A flyer? To make sure, we went back to the place where we shot from, when we thought it was alone, and traced the blood trail. Its logical conclusion appeared to be none other than the dead Buffalo, with blood leading to it and none continuing on with the herd. The puzzle pieces seemed to lock into place.

I said that we should make one more cast, one last sweep to see if there were any other sign of blood. So we did; and in the opposite direction from that taken by the fleeing Buffalo I heard the tracker, Enoch, bent low to the ground, uttering distinctly what could have been only the Shona equivalent of Uh oh.

It looked as if the wounded Nyati had led us into the herd and passed through, trying to lose its tracks among all the others. We three stared at the blood and one another. It was impossibly hot and there was no water and we had been chasing that Buffalo hard now for three miles or more. We had one on the ground that was a good one, and no one would be the wiser. Except us.

As we trailed after it from there, the wounded Buffalo's tracks never slacked. At each increasingly infrequent, red-rusty, dime-sized drop on the ochre dirt, I considered what I was feeling. Regret for the bull, to be sure. Remorse for not having killed well. What else?

In hot pursuit of an animal said to run both ways–away, but also toward–particularly when injured, my most sensible emotion should by rights have been, my thumb lying moist against the ridged spur of my 375's safety and my eyes bored ahead, one of outright witless nightmare. Yet I could not honestly say what the true chord being struck was.

I assuredly had no desire to be maimed or killed, but in a rather baffling manner I delighted in this. I wouldn't intentionally have created the situation–as much for the animal's sake as my own and Sandy and Enoch's, not to mention a matter of dignity–but now that I was in it, all the more prosaic concerns of life were swept off. In this existential state of freedom, the only obligation was to stay tuned for the abrupt manifestation of something large, black, horned, and infuriated, and to kill it when it showed. Yes, I was enjoying this, certainly more than I ought. Though that is not the word, somehow. More than enjoying, it was about doing. Or being. Being what?

We were losing the light. By its trail, the bull was skulking through a grove of trees; and we found where it stood long enough to bleed onto the ground a pool of blood the size of a saucer. It might be lung blood; but that might mean it was hit in one lung only, probably the left from the angle of the shot; and one lung gone might not be sufficient to bring the Buffalo down for miles more. Or it might be hit high in the shoulder, that shot probably not fatal. It had gone on from here, but we had to go back to quarter up the other bull and fetch the Land Rover to load it in and carry it back to camp. As we walked out, Enoch broke off green leafy branches from the bushes he passed and with one hand looped the long grass along the trail to mark the way back to the spoor when we came again in the morning.

We dismantled the dead Buffalo as you would a Deuce Coupe in a chop shop on the edge of town, and stacked the parts–protein-rich quarter panels, meaty fenders, and fleshy front hood–into the Land Rover, filling it so we had to ride on top of the Buffalo. In tropical Africa the sunset has no denouement. Darkness comes like MacDuff's sword on Macbeth's neck. As I rode back in the night, seated on the polished horn boss, every jolt of the rutted dirt track was transmitted through to me; and I wondered what I lost or gained out there on the trail. The Land Rover bounced hard, and I held onto the curved horn tips for dear life.

We planned to go out late the next morning to give the Vultures time to soar on the midmorning thermals into the blue sky and orient to the position of the Buffalo on the ground. We wanted to find it down and as we approached to see the Vultures around its carcass lift up in flapping wings that would have the dry sound of newsprint fluttering in the wind. We did not want to believe that the bull could still be going on. It went on.

For four hours we trailed it, past dry pans where the baked mud was as white as newly cast aluminum billets; through thorn-bush coverts where the Buffalo could lay up and run through us when we stumbled over it; and finally into a bedded bachelor herd, Sandy, Enoch, and I bellying to within fifteen yards, our belt buckles scooping dirt. We glassed the Buffalo.

One bull was sheer enormity, over forty-five inches across the spread of its horns; but neither it nor any of the others showed any wounds. So we stood; and the bulls stood with their shining-black scenting noses high, peering at us in the simmering shade the trees made, then ran. In a few hundred yards they joined a breeding herd with a hundred Buffalo in it. We drove them all ahead of us, watching for a straggler, until having crossed wide Buffalo land of timber and savanna, we reached the tar road; and the Buffalo trotted across it and into the forest on the other side. There was no more spoor to follow.

The Department of Parks and Wild Life–as their shoulder patches read–was notified of the dead bull and the wounded one still at large. Both, as they should have been, were marked down against my two permits. Then Sandy had to leave, and another P. H. came. The rains broke, and the green became unbearable.

Human lives ended by wild animals in Africa are a statistically fanciful quantity. The mosquito as a vector, as we know, is the most deadly complex living organism on the continent–Africans evolved sickle cells to combat the chronic malaria carried by mosquitos–followed near at hand by the tsetse fly. After that come venomous serpents, then Crocodile and Hippo, which may tally, respectively, one thousand and five hundred souls per year. Around the same number of deaths as brought about by the Hippo are ascribed annually in Africa to Elephant, Rhino any longer too insignificant on the scale of population to constitute much of an imminence, though at one time they were ominous and implacable. Lion take their toll, as well, while Leopard attacks seem relatively restrained. For Buffalo, the usual number subscribed to is two hundred fatalities per year, though the methodology for arriving at that figure would seem relaxed at best. Never-the-less, Buffalo can and do kill people, never pleasantly and not always when they are wounded, being defensive, or feeling cornered. Sometimes, they merely kill.

The usual shape, if there is one, of a Buffalo attack runs along the lines of what happened in 1965 to Glen Cottar, an East African professional hunter whose grandfather Charles came to Africa from Oklahoma to hunt in 1910 after reading Theodore Roosevelt's *African Game Trails*, returning to plunder ivory in the Belgian Congo and ultimately to found his own famed safari company–that passed down through each generation to his great-grandson today–before his being killed by a Rhino he was capturing on film. In the high savanna in Tanzania between the Serengeti and the Maasai Mara, Glen Cottar's client, who overcame a childhood case of polio although it left him with the need for a cane, made a good hit on a Buffalo with his magazine rifle. The bull ran as the client fired three more rounds into it before it vanished into thick cover, none stopping it.

Because of his client's disability, Cottar left him behind as he with his tracker and skinner trailed the widely spaced small droplets of blood–hardly heartening spoor–through the bush; he would have wished for puddles showing that the bull was stopping and bleeding out. Finally finding the Buffalo, Cottar fired his borrowed 500/465–his own double out for repairs–but the bull ran on. The Buffalo was jumped more times and more shots fired. Thinking he had the bull ready to finish, Cottar walked toward it without reloading a fired right barrel, when the Buffalo came out of a thick stand of bush. Cottar shot pointblank, and then was hit.

As Cottar yelled at them to grab the buffalo's tail, the skinner and tracker dematerialized. The Buffalo came with its forehead on the ground, driving Cottar back as the man fought to prevent being horned in the torso, which left his legs vulnerable, torn muscles hanging in strings out of slashes in his inner thighs. At one point, as the Buffalo battered him, Cottar looked over at the hoof planted beside his head and couldn't help but think of those curio lamps that the taxidermy establishment Rowland Ward of Piccadilly made out of wild-animal body parts. The bull halted its attack; and somehow, Cottar found a tree and pulled himself into it with his arms alone, his legs no longer functioning. Glancing up, he saw the skinner already high in the branches, and called out to him to drag him up.

When the two men were side by side in the tree, Cottar looked down and saw the Buffalo standing below, bleeding heavily from its nose and mouth. The tracker had gotten away and brought back the safari car. The disabled client got out and put three more rounds into the bull, eleven in all, before it died.

While Cottar lay on a makeshift bed in the back of the safari car, pumped with as much morphine and penicillin as could be found in the first-aid supplies, his wounds cleaned rudimentarily in the field, they sped by trails and tracks and roads across country toward Nairobi, thirteen hours away, coming to a camp that night where Charles and Anne Morrow Lindbergh were on a photo safari, Lucky Lindy offering to fly Cottar to the hospital in daylight; but the Land Cruiser pressed on through the dark, getting Cottar to the medical attention that saved his legs and possibly his life. Two dozen years earlier, Glen's father, Mike, Charles's son–like father, like son–killed a Buffalo in a mid-downhill charge, the momentum of the body sending the Buffalo bowling into him. Mike Cottar got up laughing, brushing himself off; but years of blackwater fever had swollen his spleen, which the deadweight of the Buffalo ruptured. He died a short while later.

Buffalo charges seldom result in uniform injuries. There is an entire suite of possible traumata. Though drawn from a report on attacks by domestic Water buffalo in rural India, the wounds would be commensurate to those exacted by the horns of African buffalo: violent and goring in various shapes, sizes, and directions, they may also lacerate, be crisscross, or penetrate body cavities, or without entering the body, result in contusions and fractures. And end often, it seems inessential somehow to add, in death.

Many woundings are located in the lower body because of the character of an attack with the horns. Alarming mirrored French curves, Buffalo horns end in points that appear to be the prime weapon; and the Buffalo does seem to relish hooking into a body and lifting it high with the tremendous muscles of its neck, then flicking it off like an annoying insect, the predator, Lion or human, going spidery into the air, losing all equipoise and alignment and any bodily force, the only force the force of gravity. And of Buffalo.

It may be surprising that horn wounds are as routine in India as they are, except when it is recalled that sacred cattle roam unfenced across the subcontinent. There is less wonder that the injury, known as a cornada in Spanish, is common in Latin countries with the tradition of the corrida. So it is from there we gain most of our knowledge of such wounds.

A puncturing laceration, whether from a domestic bull or Wild buffalo, can be made anywhere, including the head or even intraorally–wounds have been made through the upper palate. It can also be simple, with a single trajectory, or have multiple channels if the victim on the horn is turned as he is lifted, the horn creating stellate wound patterns, worse if the horn point is splintered. The key to treatment of wounds plain and fancy is locating and probing all the channels and making sure they are properly debrided and cleaned. Live muscle and vein ends will be reattached; or if needed, available, and possible, repairs may be made with endoprostheses, artificial arteries and veins. Some goring wounds are classified as sheathed: Fatal injury can occur internally without insult through the outer skin–Mike Cottar's fatal injury might be classed as among that type of goring. The greatest danger of being gored in the leg or groin is a tearing of the femoral artery, from which a person can bleed out in seconds; in the field, overall mortality is high with this type of wound. One technique taught to the military to stanch such bleeding is to apply a hundred twenty pounds of pressure, using a knee or balled fist, to the distal aortic or iliac arteries in the lower abdomen.

In May of 2018, a South African professional hunter and his client took a Buffalo bull along the Levubu River in Limpopo Province. As they cleared the brush to get the vehicle in to load the carcass, another bull, assumed to have been with the dead one, though not wounded, came out of cover unexpectedly and drove toward the professional hunter, tearing open his femoral artery with the point of its horn, the man bleeding to death in moments.

Bleeding out may be the classic scenario of death by Buffalo. Buffalo, of course, don't kill with their horn points alone, but with the flats or the boss as well.

While the horn points may prompt the highest intimidation, the rest of the horn–the flats and boss–is capable of causing injury by battery that results in death as decisively as that by goring. The full initial impact of the boss of a charging Buffalo replicates being struck by a small car in crosstown boulevard traffic. Then, when the person is on the ground, a Buffalo can continue pounding its forehead and boss into the body, or use its hooves. And what would a Buffalo charge be without litigation?

Along the Mara River in Kenya, a fifty-year-old American woman tourist was walking outside a safari car, stretching her legs during a game drive–really a drive in a vehicle to view wildlife. According to the lawsuit, a Buffalo classified as rogue–meaning a dagga boy, which is no more rogue than any other old, solitary bull–was known to frequent that region of the river; but the tourist, as told in the March, 2011, edition of *Plaintiff* magazine, was never informed of this. Nor that the armed game ranger was armed with an unloaded, inoperable rifle, while another staff member carried conspicuously a Maasai spear, though he had never thrown, let alone hunted with, one, and was in fact the camp dishwasher.

As they all approached the Mara, the Buffalo appeared, charging up the river embankment and struck the woman in the chest, causing a pneumothorax–releasing the air from the lungs into the pleural cavity, the resulting pressure collapsing the lungs. A third member of the staff, without a gun that did not shoot or a spear he did not know how to use, and unlike Glen Cottar's tracker or skinner, grabbed the Buffalo by the tail; but it still succeeded in goring seriously another woman tourist in the thigh. Air evacuation was called after the attacks, but the first woman was dead by the time the plane landed. The second one survived. The dual actions brought against the tour operator–in San Francisco where the travel package was sold–were for damages for personal injury and wrongful death. It just shows that even without hunting, Africa with Buffalo is a tough town. Though probably not as tough as civil court in Baghdad by the Bay.

That, and in sufficiently numerous other ways, is how people are killed by Buffalo. Buffalo have their own ways of being killed.

No Buffalo is born to die of natural causes or senescence. Before they grow old enough for organ failure, or to grind their teeth down so far as to be unable to feed any longer, they will almost always die earlier because of, first, disease, then malnutrition and predation.

Out of territoriality, Elephant and Rhino can, and do, kill Buffalo with their tusks and horns, not infrequently tossing the bovines the way the bovines toss a human. Hyena clans or a Leopard may be able to cut a calf out of a herd by shear audace, but that can pose a spendy risk to the predator. Lion are the only wild animal that consistently hunts Buffalo with success, which does not mean that many are not crippled or killed in the pursuit.

Buffalo do have means of defense: Remaining in herds, choosing their ground, watching back-trails, protecting their rears and flanks by pushing them against trees and brush and facing Lion head on, scraping clinging Lion off on thorn bush, and stampedes are avenues of survival. The Buffalo's sense for the scent of the Lion is acute, and the Lion's roar echoes for miles. While Lion spend more than 80 percent of their time asleep, Buffalo ironically catnap, sleeping only a few hours in a day and night, devoting so much of their time to grazing. They will come upon sleeping Lion and attack them unprovoked, trampling the ones they can, cubs earning particular attention before they grow into adult-sized predators. Semi-aquatic, Buffalo move through water where Lion are reluctant to travel. The birds that feed off their parasites provide a D. E. W. Line for Buffalo by flying off their backs if they see something coming.

Because breaking a Buffalo's neck is such a strenuous undertaking, Lion will take it by the muzzle or throat to suffocate it, but also to forestall its making distress calls that bring the herd back to its aid. Taking a Buffalo by the muzzle or neck can be, though, particularly inauspicious–for the Lion–because of exposure to the never-to-be-ignored horns. The conventional method is to come at a Buffalo–preferably a lone bull, absent a herd with which to contend–from behind and to go for its back legs, trying to strip the tendons and get the Buffalo down. The siege can last hours, and the Buffalo can still escape, especially if other Buffalo are drawn to its relief. If a Buffalo is brought to ground, though, Lion often first go for the external sphincter, fastidiously licking it clean before biting into it and pulling out the alimentary canal, starting with the cloaca and moving upstream. The abdominal area is then opened to access the vital, and if not dainty, lights, heart, liver, and kidneys. It is reported that Lion may eat in a single serving a hundred pounds of meat apiece.

One of the most monstrous wounds–at least the sight of it–that a Buffalo can receive is one inflicted by another. Gorings of Buffalo by Buffalo occur, but that bauplan–building plan–of the bovine makes these not common. Clashes amount mostly to crashing bosses. Sometimes, though, from out of the cracking of horns and the dust, a Buffalo emerges with a horn snapped off through the bone core, leaving a stump on one side–as on the first bull Roy killed many years ago in Tanganyika.

A break on the core bleeds in a way disconcerting to see: spouting out for feet through the air like water from a high-pressure nozzle. It seems impossible for a Buffalo bull to have enough blood in its body to survive such a wound, or to tolerate the presumably exquisite pain. But it can appear indifferent, at least. Such an injury may cost a bull any future chance of finding a cow to accept it for mating, but otherwise it carries on. A Buffalo with one horn can go on fighting when cows are in season, and break off the other, too. After more years of wear, the hornless boss takes on the look of a rugby scrum cap, and that is what it is called. Some think of a Buffalo with a boss like that, because of the story it tells, as the noblest trophy.

Buffalo are at last killed by humans's using, for the most part, poison or bullets. We can conjecture about the misery of poison death; from the evidence of humans who have been brought close to dying from heart failure, oxygen runs out and organic processes–regulating hearing, sight, sentience–shut down. Exsanguination heads down the same path. Is a bullet wound overwhelmingly painful in and of itself?

Ernest Hemingway, who knew the pain of wounds from shrapnel, bullets, and broken bones, assessed in *Death in the Afternoon* what a bull might feel in the ring: All wounds [punctures from pics, banderillas, and the sword] he receives are in hot blood, and if they do not hurt any more than the wounds a man receives in hot blood they cannot hurt much.

Bullets well placed in a Buffalo, that do not fracture bone, which can hurt instantly and wrenchingly, likely do not hurt greatly, either, not at first; and if lethal, death will occur before real suffering sets in.

My uncle, tall, wavy iron hair, rimless gold-temple glasses–an ocular prothesis with a glassy thousand-yard stare in place of the eye blinded playing football at Caltech–golfer, business executive, trim while my father went to fat–soft, so very soft–did not know guns and asked to borrow one from his brother so he might learn to shoot–this was August, 1965, in Southern California, so conclusions are permitted to be drawn.

My father, exercising a sporadic opportunity for power, refused, citing his concern of some accident occurring and costing his brother his one good eye. My uncle instead purchased a rifle and a pistol for himself, buying what he had seen: a 30-30–Thuddy-thuddy–Winchester Model 1892 lever-action rifle and a 380 Walther PPK–Polizeipistole Kriminal–semi-automatic pistol. John Wayne and James Bond.

Later, after he died with probably no more agony than a Buffalo shot straight through the heart, his widow summoned my father and me again and presented his arsenal. My father got the rifle without a notion, quite, of what to do with it. I was handed the PPK which, of course, was something I wanted from the time of *Dr. No.*

Twenty-five-years later, on New Year's Eve, I sat alone in my armchair in my den and had the pistol in my hand.

If you don't recognize the bent whim, there is no adequate explication or apology–it was de rigueur, for instance, for some of my friends and me never to attend a revival of the director's cut of *The Wild Bunch* in a theater unless we were carrying, illicitly, 1911 pistols in our belts beneath our shirttails. There are just times when it suits the mood to heft a pistol in your hand. After all, that is what it is made for. This time the PPK was loaded with 90-grain hollow-point Federal Hydra-Shok ammunition that met F. B. I. testing standards for penetration and expansion.

Along with the loaded magazine, the chamber was charged. I had the knurled hammer locked back in the single-action position, for whatever reason or no reason whatsoever. It was time to let the hammer down and put the pistol away. Holding it in two hands, pointed at the floor, I held the hammer back with my left thumb and with the right forefinger I pressed the trigger, releasing the hammer–there is a proper technique for this, and that was not it. Before I eased the hammer the entire way down, the knurl slipped from under my thumb.

The gunshot was somehow concrete, as if it fabricated the squared sides of a sonic cube. I smelled the smoke and looked for the hole in the carpet; but then I realized that when the gun fired I felt a numbing blow to my inner left thigh. There was a small hole through the pants leg, blood beginning to well into the fabric. Taking my pants down, I found the hole, small and stippled. The blood ran down my leg and over my sock into the Crocs slide I wore. I went to the bathroom and took a towel and wrapped it around the self-inflicted gunshot wound and pulled the pants back up. Then I woke my wife, sleeping through it all, upstairs.

Fifteen minutes later, the sliding glass doors of the hospital emergency room opened, and I announced that I was shot. As I said, this was New Year's Eve; and this situation made for an exhilarative interlude for the staff. There was still no real pain, just a stunned feeling. On the gurney, I had my pants cut off with scissors while the emergency-room technicians and doctors worked on stopping the bleeding, calm voices assessing injury. Two sheriff's deputies arrived and asked me pointed questions, which I answered judiciously. Later, one returned to the house with my wife to see where the shooting occurred and to unload the PPK for her.

At the velocity of a thousand-feet-per-second at such close range, the bullet blew to flinders, tracing trajectories through the flesh of my thigh without tearing the femoral artery. In the dimmed I. C. U. room, all the light emanating from monitors, sounds of beeping and pumps cycling, there was pain. By then, there was also morphine and, best, intravenous liquid acetaminophen, but disappointingly only once every eight hours. After the first pint of blood was transfused, it was deemed necessary to administer a second due to the volume of loss.

During the days in the hospital, the cleaning, debriding, and bandaging went on. There was no attempt to probe for the bullet fragments–sterilized in the firing and by friction through the air–or stitch anything up as over time the wound spread farther and farther as the skin and flesh around it necrotized. I was not allowed to walk to the bathroom to shit but had to strain at the stool on a portable toilet beside the bed as nurses flittered about.

I was released with a portable wound vacuum tube under the bandages to assist closure. At home, the faint shade still showed in the carpet where the blood had been shampooed up. Now the pain was dull and consistent, and there was an odor. I went for changes of dressing every few days, then every week. The wound nurses were positively giddy to have a gunshot to treat, its being a rare diversion from ulcers and sores–I gave each of the two winsomely striped socks in gratitude for the light moments. There was another debridement procedure under anesthesia. Finally, the wound vac was taken away and then came the last bandaging. I could not have any more prescriptions for opiates filled, despite asking.

The four-inches of wide scar tissue slants down the inside of my lower thigh, following the bullet's path, looking like a satellite photo of the Mississippi Delta's Southwest Pass, fringed by mudflats and banks, as it flows into the Gulf below New Orleans. I thought about the scars on the hides of Buffalo, clean white hard patches and long streaks from the horns of other Buffalo and the teeth and claws of Lion. What did Buffalo feel when horned and bitten and clawed? How bad and long was the pain after? I thought about how a bullet might feel in comparison. I knew about a bullet.

Late in the afternoon on the first day of hunting in the Binga Lands, after we gave up tracking the runaway Buffalo in Kapinda, Rory Muil stamped on the Defender's brakes and leaned out, looking at the sandy dirt. He kept swiveling his head, uncertain about something. I looked to the left. Ten yards away, two bulls stood, gazing at us. One wore a bell. They had weeks ago wandered away from the small herd of one of the trackers in camp. Now here they were, standing contentedly in the jess beside the dirt vehicle trail where they made their hoofprints.

From his posture, Rory seemed on the verge of speaking–talk something he budgeted–when I said, Um…

Rory sat up, staring at me from behind his wraparound sunglasses. I tilted my head toward the cattle.

Oh hell! he shouted in disgust. Shoot the bloody things!

Instead we roared off, leaving them to go on dodging Lion, as they seemed to be doing with some success, thus far.

The second morning I heard the camp waiter when he drew back the flap in the dark, bringing me hot tea with milk. I drank, sitting on the edge of my bed. We left in the dark, returning to Kapinda.

By eight a.m. we were on another set of tracks of a band of dagga boys. We stayed on them for three hours, often losing the trail and ranging out until we picked it up again. Eventually it led back in a wide inebriated circle to the road from which we had taken off, not far from where we left the Defender.

We returned to the vehicle and ate chicken-and-mayonnaise sandwiches while Rory charted our future course. The wind freshened, gusting from the direction in which the Buffalo tracks went. We finished the sandwiches, checked the rifles, and began following again. We didn't need far to go.

For half a mile we walked through head-high bushwillow and tall grass, Rory absently breaking off a dry stem to twirl in his ear. Then everything stopped.

At first it was Tino who halted and pointed, crouching. Then Rory halted and leaned far back to see where Tino pointed. Rory gestured to me to get low. My legs felt like Portland cement when he motioned me toward a bare willowbush and to look–there.

Forty yards from us, in the shade at the base of the heavy trunk of a thickly leaved mopane was a gray-black canyon boulder, with the gleam of curved horn growing from it.

Can you see them? Rory asked in a whisper.

I saw one horn, then a gray face with deep wrinkled rings around the eyes, the eyes turned toward us, then saw more boulders jumbled near the first. I slipped the 450 through the branches and got down on the scope.

Not him, Rory whispered, meaning the one looking our way. The best is on the farthest left, broadside.

That farthest boulder, I now saw, had a rump and withers, and a head with a profile reminiscent of the portraits of certain medieval pontiffs wearing a papal triregnum.

I see him.

He's lying down.

Yes.

Rory paused, glassing him, then said, In the middle of the shoulder.

I eased off the tang safety and lowered the crosshairs onto the bull's shoulder.

Got him?

Yes.

Sure?

Yes.

All right.

I took a breath and breathed out half.

Maybe I should have made the bull stand, but the bullet seemed heavy enough for a lying Buffalo, even with its meat and muscles bunched. The big rifle rang and in the scope I saw four bulls–including the one I'd fired on–up and running, short-tailed broad rears vanishing, no time for a second round before the bulls were gone. I had not heard the echoing impact of the bullet, but maybe we were too close and it was covered by the gunshot. I levered out the empty case and slid in another 500-grain Woodleigh, this time a solid, raising the falling block on the single-shot. I set the safety.

Rory ran to the left behind me, craning to see where they went.

Did you have a good picture? he asked, looking at me sharply,

Yes.

All right, he said, exhaling. Let's see.

We waited five minutes, then went to the tree where the bulls had lain. There was no blood. Rory and the trackers studied the ground.

I thought I had a good picture, I said, weaseling, worried because the ground around the tree was dry.

Rory looked at me.

No, he said, reading my thought. It won't have started here.

It started ten yards away with one small spatter, already dried on the dirt. We moved forward, following more drops. They turned steadily into bright red splatters of blood. Everyone was solemn, searching the trail, but looking up, too, watching ahead. Then Tino, John, and Mika all spoke out in conversational tones. They pointed. I moved up and saw the gray-black shape on the ground ahead. Rory and I circled toward it, rifles up.

The bull went two-hundred-fifty yards without a bellow, and lay, legs collapsed beneath it, its muzzle pushed forward on the ground, in repose. Lung blood trickled from a disproportionately small hole in the shoulder. We walked up, and I backed Rory as he extended the muzzle of his 458 to the bull's open eye. When the muzzle touched it, the eye did not blink.

As we unloaded our rifles, Rory looked back at where the bull came from, in his mind tracing the tracking, the stalk, and my–for a change–decent shooting.

That's the way to hunt buffalo, he said with blunt satisfaction. At least at the shot, I hadn't behaved like a ninnyhammer.

Tino, John, and Mika sharpened their spring-steel Tonga axes and knives on stones on the ground and worked hard for most of an hour, cutting the bull in two. Rory drove the Defender in from the road and somehow we managed to winch up and wedge in every edible–and some not so–scrap of the Buffalo.

We made our way back to Songo Camp from Kapinda, the long trip lengthened by the heavy load. When we came in late that afternoon, we swirled to a stop by the skinning-and-butchering shed. The camp staff came out and saw the horns and hooves rising from the back of the white Land Rover, and offered a discreet round of applause. Which embarrassed me to the point of blushing.

To cover the rush of feeling, I stood from my seat and lifted my hat, giving a stage bow.

Thank you, thank you! I called. You're too kind. I'll be here all week. Don't forget your waitress. Try the veal!

No, make that dagga boy.

CHAPTER TEN

Plague

MY FOOT PRESSED into the sandy soil, the grains scouring the sole of my boot, the heat radiating upward. We trailed the skidding track of a dragged right hind hoof across the open jess to a dry creek bottom where the prints played out on the rocks. From the track, it was a dagga boy that had certainly been caught in a snare–double strands of twelve-and-a-half-gauge fence wire–and pulled free.

Three days before, hunters went down to the big river, the Sengwa, to spear another Buffalo. With wire tangled around its neck and head and horns, the Buffalo had still not succeeded in strangling itself to the hunters's satisfaction. As the spearmen approached what they took for an ensnared animal, adrenaline surged in the bull. Snapping the wire–with a tensile strength twice its bodyweight, the sound like a ricochet–the Buffalo butted, gored, and stamped the first man into the ground while his collaborators shagged off. Then the bull walked off, sporting its garland of wire.

Here, a mopane grew out of a wide, dense clump of bushwillow. We spread out around and above it, hoping to pick up the trail again. Tino was in the creek bottom when a pair of Oxbirds rose out of the bushwillow. Everyone, and everything, froze. Rory Muil and I were on the creekbank above the bushwillow. Rory slid to my side. More birds flew.

If it charges, he whispered, his eyes on the bush, it's coming, and we'll have to grab it.

He held up his free hand–the one not wrapped around the barrel of the 458 Model 70 with worn bluing and iron sights–and closed it on the air as if trying to capture a gnat in flight.

Do you know where it is? I asked, looking down at my 450 N. E. 3¼-inch Ruger No. 1 to check the position of its safety, and to make sure it was really in my hands.

Haven't a clue.

The Buffalo was twenty yards away, lying deep in the bushwillow at the base of the tree, watching. It took a quarter hour to verify that, as we jockeyed side to side and back and forth to get a look. The best that could be seen, with a binocular, was an eye and a sector of curved horn.

This Buffalo should have been gone by now, Rory said, his hushed voice sounding tight.

Do you think there's fear in a handful of dust? Imagine a bush, yards away, where a dagga boy's waiting, having resolved not to run.

As long as we stayed downwind, the bull wasn't going to show itself, so we crossed rapidly the rocks and dimpled sand of the creek bed and circled upwind of where the Buffalo lay on the opposite bank. As our wind drifted into the bushwillow, and we waited with our rifles, we heard the shuffling of dead leaves as the bull got to its knees, then its graphite-black sheen moving.

The young dagga boy walked out, black muzzle and face, lumped boss, pleated neck, shoulder proud, front legs ending in the polished black lacquerware of overlarge cloved hooves—lethal weapons in their own right and emblem of the artiodactyl—packing a rear hoof ringed above by a bright-blood ligature wound. Its hipbones showed, hunger having wasted its body; and it had been fortunate not to have been taken by Lion, as of yet, as must always be added. It moved in pain under the slanting late-morning sun, holding us in a level stare, reconciled to whatever came next, as it drew off. We watched it go. It could still survive and in time mend, maturing into a bull that did not run, facing the possible accusation of roguery. The sun trajected upward, the air moving warmer. Rory consulted his Timex and said we ought to make our way back to the Land Rover before the day grew too warm.

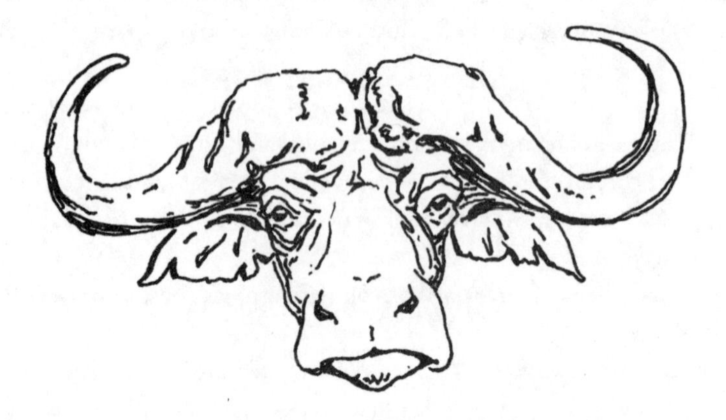

The record of humans driving the American bison near to extinction in the nineteenth century is shamefully notorious–when the Texas Legislature proposed in 1875 to enact protection for their shrinking numbers, Little Phil Sheridan, though the official record is lacking, is said to have made an infamous address, imploring the lawmakers not to save the Buffalo, the Indians's shaggy commissary, but to aid the Buffalo runners: Send them powder and lead, if you will; but for the sake of a lasting peace, let them kill, skin, and sell until the buffalo are exterminated.

For that other species of Buffalo, the African, near extermination at the turn of the twentieth century was brought on by a different agent.

Death for the African buffalo could come from hundred eighty-pound female Lion hunting for the pride, or a pair of great males, specialists in taking down Buffalo bulls. There could also be a 500-grain solid from a N. E., or arrow poison that stops the heart. Another source, though, might be a virus, smaller by a factor of fifty than a human red-blood cell.

Viruses leave no fossils; but they have been here since at least the origin of eukaryotic cells almost three billion years ago, and may have had a role in creating that life by infection with viral D. N. A. Although infections have always existed, hunter-gatherers as a whole, living in troops ideally of thirty to fifty and naturally socially distanced from others by home ranges that can cover as much as five hundred square miles, do not experience epidemics, let alone pandemics. It is agrarian societies and industrial cities–civilization–that foster them.

Alongside parasitological malaria, bacterial diseases such as the A. D. sixth century Plague of Justinian–ten thousand dead each day in the streets of Constantinople–the fourteenth century's Black Death–extinguishing as much as 60 percent of Europe's population–and to this day persistent waves of cholera–brought about by drinking water polluted upstream with human sewage–have through iteration upon iteration, scourged humankind. As devastating or more, though, have been viral ones.

The Spanish flu infected a third of the earth's population, resulting in the deaths of one in ten who contracted it. Nameless and innumerable have been the outbreaks of smallpox: Called the speckled monster, variola is said to have claimed a billion human lives before the last case was seen in nature four decades ago. It destroyed entire empires–the Aztec and Incan being two. Other viruses altered history, as well.

The absence of immunity cost Napoleon tens of thousands of his soldiers to yellow-fever in just months in the Saint-Domingue expedition, ending his campaign to retake what is modern-day Haiti from the revolt of its slaves, strapping the First Consul with the need for exchequer, and leading to, when we were looking only to acquire New Orleans, our purchase of the Louisiana Territory–never Bonaparte's to sell, or ours to own, but no matter I suppose–and all that came out of that, in the making of a country. Woodrow Wilson's bout of Spanish flu affected his diplomatic undertakings at Versailles that then produced a treaty so punitive that it not only drove Germany out of all it's colonies in Africa but impelled it toward World War II, and as many as eighty five million additional corpses. Now we have Covid and, what the shit? monkeypox.

The debate continues over whether or not viruses constitute, strictly speaking, a type of life. Viruses do not replicate outside a host but pass protein and genetic material into the cells they infect, appropriating a cell's functions to have themselves reproduced–submicroscopic bodysnatchers. New viruses assemble in the cell, then burst out, killing it and infecting other cells. The art lies in not annihilating all hosts. It would be a very dull pathogen not to lay something by for the future, and in this way the viral molecule is seen as operating within the web of life, if never quite part of it.

Viral plagues are not restricted to our species. Others, such as the African buffalo, have had their own onslaughts of disease that have held as immense significance for people, history, topography, and other wildlife as any human pandemic we have endured. It may have been a particular virus, one that replicated by passing its R. N. A. into host cells, that at the end of the nineteenth century nearly erased the Buffalo, and shaped the Africa we knew for much of the twentieth.

From the evidence of ancient papyri, the virus was present among domestic cattle in Africa since the days of the first Egyptian pharaohs, but waited millennia to destroy, then remake, the continent. Nor were God's cattle spared His wrath, suffering exceedingly from the disease.

By the time of Moses and the pharaoh Thutmose IV–Thutmose III, the hunter of Rhino, begat Amenhotep II who begat Thutmose IV–the Lord's anger had been in Egypt for over fifteen centuries, long enough for Jehovah to say unto Moses that at a set time His hand would be upon the cattle of the field of the Egyptians, severing between them and the livestock of Israel. And on the Egyptians's beasts, but not those of Israel, fell a grievous murrain, all the cattle of Egypt dying. And this was the Fifth Plague, deber in Hebrew, which would be later called cattle plague–that plague probably the one labeled in German, Rinderpest, in that language with a capital R.

Evolving with ancestral Bovidae in Pleistocene Central Asia, rinderpest was, most simply, a form of measles found in animals–the virus in the family Paramyxoviridae, genus *Morbillivirus*–to which humans were resistant. For a clade of other animal diseases, rinderpest was the archaevirus from which they descended. Contagions ranging from cetacean morbillivirus to canine, feline, and seal distemper, and peste des petits ruminants–sheep and goat plague–came out of mutations of rinderpest as probably did human measles, too, spilling over from animals–like the most-recent coronavirus, officially S. A. R. S.-CoV-2. In the case of measles, it leaped from cattle into cattle-keepers, likely in the A. D. eleventh or twelfth centuries, though as was said, humans never contracted rinderpest itself. In Europe, rinderpest was known from before time became history–it was ascribed to being brought in from Central Asia thousands of years ago by the nomadic warriors of Scythia, drinkers of mare's milk and smokers of cannabis, who had a winged-bull deity like the one the Assyrians's called lamassu. In the A. D. eighteenth century, alone, rinderpest destroyed two hundred million head of cattle on the continent. By comparison, the fourteenth–century Black Death in Europe killed a quarter as many humans. Rinderpest in cattle, as well as in wild even-toed ungulates such as Kudu, Eland, Roan, Oryx, Wildebeest, Giraffe, Warthog, and other African artiodactyls, and perhaps most dramatically, Buffalo, was one of the most fell infections ever on earth. When it reached populations without a previous history of contact, the disease went through like flame through a magician's flash paper.

Symptoms manifested themselves within as few as three days of exposure. There was fever, anorexia, salivation, and–in the words of C. A. Spinage in his monumental, and scattered, *Cattle Plague: A History*–weeping mouth and urogenital ulcers, plus discharges from the nose and eyes, constipation followed by profuse diarrhea and a loathsome stench, frequently blindness, dehydration, and death, often no more than a week from the onset of the fever.

When it began its progress south into greater Africa at almost the opening of the A. D. twentieth century, it had already been labeled in a compound of Greek and French, Phlogoso-gangréneuses, a gangrenous inflammation; in French typhus contagieux and maladie contagieuse sur l'espèce bovine; pesta bovina in Italian; in Russian tchouma reina–a reference to vampires–and in English Great Gall–because of the gross distention of the gall bladder visible beneath the hide on the side of an animal–mountaine evil, heart soft, Hungarian sickness–in recognition of one of its waves of infection coming with the Huns in the fourth century as they swept across the steppes into Europe before the time of Attila–flying fire; and Louis Pasteur thought it to be an organized germ. When it reached its pinnacle in sub-Saharan Africa, it had many names–the Hausa in Chad, the largest single ethnic group on the continent, called it sannu, a word for an expression of sympathy; chinpumba—Zambezi cattle fever—in what is today Mozambique; sadoka, possibly from a word of the Swahili Coast for a sacrificial offering; mubiamo in Kiswahili, some saying that may not be a standard word of that language but one created for it; and to the Maasai, ol-odua, their word for bitterness. There were even names for the effect of the disease on the world in which the humans lived: among the Borana Oromo in southern Ethiopia, ciina, the end of everything; in the Transkei masiligame, let us all be equal, because it spared neither poor nor rich; and the Maasai, two-thirds of whom were estimated to have died of starvation in its aftermath, calling it enkidaaroto, destruction, and also emutai, finished off completely.

As with many diseases seen for hundreds or even thousands of years, its mechanism of transmission remained nonetheless an interminable riddle. Spontaneous generation was the initial theory: Air was filled with germs, in the sense of microscopic seeds and sprouts, that developed when they fell on the proper medium. Aristotle believed Eel arose spontaneously from mud and rainwater. Shakespeare, for one, wrote of Crocodile growing like bullrushes out of the mud of the Nile, likewise in Hamlet's words, For if the sun breed maggots in a dead dog… The process was named panspermism, the seeds of all things, including rinderpest, wafting on the wind.

Other notionalists held that contaminated dung and urine carried it, but proof of its transmission through befouled bedding was never substantiated. The clothes and shoes of cowherds tending sick animals were pointed to, as was their hair which would be tied up in bags in the hope of halting further spread. The vapors from tallow candles were blamed. Raw wet hides, skinned from infected animals, were charged, as was uncooked meat, both indictments having some substance. Ophthalmic moths and head flies, attracted by the moist rheum from the eyes of sick animals, actually did transmit the virus in turn to uninfected ones.

Though on some humid nights capable of traveling more than a hundred yards, like smoke in particulates, the virus mostly carried short distances on aerosol droplets of exhalation–aerosolization–or excreta, sprayed or rained from one infected animal onto another in close contact. The virus could live actively outside a host, but just briefly, the fragile pathogen destroyed by natural conditions such as dry and damp, heat, light, ultrasonic waves, acid or alkaline environments, or rapid evaporation. This was to be learned in time; before then, witchcraft was not to be discounted.

Between the 1300s and 1500s in Western Europe, when otherwise inexplicable human deaths were attributed widely to sorcery–chance or fortune going uncredited–hundreds of women, and a smattering of men, identified as witches, warlocks, and wizards, were tried as the culprits. And the mysterious deaths of cattle from plague did not escape attention, either. Scores of those accused of casting spells on cattle were burned, beheaded, strangled, or variously otherwise executed, often according to the directory of Malleus Maleficarum, *The Hammer of Witches*, authored by a Dominican prior and soi-disant inquisitor in Germany. One warlock was both strangled and burnt for infecting with enchanted stones water drunk by livestock. As late as the 1890s crucifixion was carried out in Hungary on a woman accused of bewitching cattle in their stalls.

Prevention, rather than retribution, was practiced by putting pins in boiled cow hearts. Among other nostrums were the bleeding of cattle, purging, administering magic herbs, as well as concoctions of beer vinegar, wine vinegar, swollen crab's eyes, saltpeter, virgin honey, and hell-broth water. In Barbados in the eighteenth century, murrain, which would not have been rinderpest which never transited the Atlantic, was treated by the administration of a half gallon of rum punch to a suffering animal. For rinderpest, need-fires were ignited. In the Western Isles of Scotland, the custom was called Tin-egin: Eighty-one married men rubbed two large planks together to create a glowing ember. When the resulting bonfire died down, cattle were driven through the embers to be purified.

Away from the enlightened West, outbreaks in Russia saw men and cattle locked away while the village women carrying burning splinters circled a naked widow with a horse collar around her neck, the women visiting each farmyard, chanting, Ai! Ai! Cut, hew the Cow-Death! If a cat ran in front of them, it was recognized as a daemon or a familiar of the necromancer who brought the plague; and it was destroyed. In other villages old women in black petticoats and soiled shifts carried a black cock three times around a fire, then threw it into the flames, alive. Or they simply rode on broomsticks. Recourse to Orthodox prayer and procession was near universal.

Until the refinement of a vaccine, marginally successful means of prevention were found in a turn to folk remedy by soaking wool in the bile of infected cattle and placing it under the skin of an animal or under its tail–a rudimentary form of vaccination–or to do no more than to create better living conditions for livestock, especially during shipping. Up to the nineteenth century, cattle onboard vessels often went without water, ventilation, or free from impossible filth. Improvements in these meant less importation of the disease; but for Africa they came too late. The rinderpest that laid the greatest waste to the continent was a product of nineteenth-century colonial military adventurism.

Though the destroying angel had been for centuries in the nominal Africa of Egypt–so different from the rest of the continent, at least by its own lights–killing millions of head of cattle there over that period, it was not until the late 1880s that a more transmissible entryway into the continent was provided. The Italian Vincentian monk Giuseppe Sapeto, following the unification of Italy in the 1860s, pursued dominions in Africa for his country. At the opening of the Suez Canal, he was instrumental in having a shipping company purchase land from the Danakil tribes, establishing a coaling station on the coast of what is now Eritrea, the Red Sea's Greek name that the Italians applied to the country.

Umberto I's troops landed at the port of Massawa–Massaua in Italian–to support Regno d'Italia's new colony. It was in 1887 that almost-certainly-rinderpest-infected Indian cattle came with reinforcements. Ethiopians believed the Italians introduced the disease intentionally to serve the project of imperialization—they even named a specific Italian, one Andreoli, as the source of the introduction–but it probably had more to do with incompetence and negligence on the part of the autorità coloniali on the coast that let the contagion spread into the highlands as the Italians moved into them. By 1889 there were reports of starving Ethiopians boiling and eating the hides of cattle killed by rinderpest. A missionary advised the famished to study religion, to which they responded by showing him their dead cattle, barren ground, and vacant houses, pointing to their empty bellies rather than passages of Scripture.

Within days of contracting the disease, paralyzed cattle were incapable of grazing and died. Cattle fatalities reached 90 percent in some places. The herding of domestic cattle is at least five thousand years old in Africa with many tribes said to be almost exclusively dependent upon their animals's beef, milk, and blood for food. Others counted on oxen to pull their plows and turn the soil. Rinderpest in extinguishing that cattle was closer to the proximate than intervening cause of unimaginable hardship, famine, and brute death for such people. Somalis were said to die of apathy because they could not become accustomed to a diet without milk and meat. Discovering his herds dead overnight, a wealthy Somali stabbed himself to death.

In 1891, there were reports of rinderpest in Dori in the Mossi Empire–to become French Haute-Volta, then Burkina Faso. This was on the northern limit of the range for African buffalo; and they remained uninfected, at first. The disease was also then in Sudan, in the heart of the Mahdist uprising; so a definitive tracing of its route of transmission there was unobtainable by Europeans. It is thought, though, that by the start of the 1890s rinderpest, along with going west with domestic livestock, was moving with migrating wildlife herds down the tributaries of the Sobat River and crossing out from the southeast of southern Sudan into Kenya and Uganda.

Among the Maasai around Tanganyika's Ngorongoro Crater in 1892, the women were, according to the report of a German explorer, reduced to walking skeletons, out of whose sunken eyes looked the madness of hunger, children resembling deformed frogs rather than human beings, [and] warriors who could hardly crawl on all fours.

For them anything was food, it was said, dead donkeys a delicacy. With the mortality rate for cattle as high as it was, not just herds but entire herding cultures vanished. The Murle of the plains of southern Sudan ended the initiation of young warriors because it required large sacrifices of cattle, a monster known as Mainlorien, the size of a mountain, stalking the country and destroying the herds. Among other peoples who traditionally paid the cost of brides in cattle, the disappearance of the herds ended an institution and could lead to revolt against the governing foreign powers seen as being at fault. Traveling implacably south at an estimated five hundred fifty miles per year, the disease reached the Zambezi by 1893, where it stalled for three years until fording the river in 1896. From the Zambezi it was transported south at one to two miles per hour by full spans of sixteen susceptible oxen, drawing Cape wagons.

By the early spring of 1896 rinderpest was across the Limpopo and as far as Mafeking in the Transvaal. The British authorities sent African traditional herbalists, labeled witch doctors, to their protectorate of Bechuanaland, now Botswana, to see the disease for themselves, to impress upon the local people its ravages, the need for regulations to prevent its spread, and even try their hands at a cure. While the herbalists were there, twenty-seven cattle died in their presence, while seventy-seven survived and were declared cured: All seventy-seven died within seven days of the departure of the herbalists, who blamed red-water, lamsickness–botulism–and a combination of all the other diseases of cattle, according to Spinage. In a futile effort to keep rinderpest back, the Cape of Good Hope Government ordered herds of suspect cattle shot, a dual line of fences strung, and patrols of mounted police, empowered to halt the movement of livestock south of the cordon, deployed.

From Mafeking in April, the contagion was in Vryburg in May and Kimberley in September. In 1896 all travelers going south into the Cape were required to be disinfected. For Europeans this meant only their clothes, while for every Kaffir–the word employed–the program involved full-body dipping in disinfectant, all of his clothes washed, and any milk, meat, or cattle products in his possession incinerated.

When he was at least middlingly dry, he received a pass and in the words of the Transvaal Veterinary Surgeon, he went on his way as if nothing had happened, no indignity inflicted, no resentment fostered. The last stand against the disease was a thousand miles of barbed wire stretched from the border with the southwestern corner of Bechuanaland east to the Indian Ocean. All of it held rinderpest back for six months. Wild African buffalo were already dying in what would be almost uncountable numbers.

Forty species of African wildlife could contract rinderpest with varying degrees of acuteness. Across the almost four million square miles of African habitat affected by the disease, the initial outbreak of the panzootic–the animal form of a pandemic–that began in the 1890s, killed as many as an estimated two hundred twenty five million wild herbivores. Next to domestic cattle, though, the African buffalo was most vulnerable to fatal peracute infection. Because of that vulnerability and its ubiquity across Africa, its gregariousness, and considerable mobility when driven out of its sedantation by drought, the Buffalo has been called the most important wild species in the epizootiology–defined by the *Merriam-Webster.com Dictionary* as the sum of the factors controlling the occurrence of a disease or pathogen of animals–of rinderpest in Africa. Buffalo, unlike desert species such as Gazelle, are highly water dependent, which means in dry conditions they were more likely to visit domestic sources of water frequented by cattle infected with rinderpest; and during the time of the disease's outbreak, drought, often called simply the thirst, was common, as were plagues of locust–if it's not one thing, then it's another for Africans.

The explorer, mercenary, colonial administrator, and British Army Captain Frederick John Dealtry Lugard left Mombasa on foot in August 1890 to pioneer a routeway to Uganda and to build forts and enter into treaties with the native tribes he encountered on the way. With him was a guide who had been through the same country the year before and reported seeing mingi mingi–many many, literally thousands–Buffalo at the time. All Lugard saw were Vultures that had so many carcasses lying on the ground on which to feed that, said the Maasai left alive, they forgot how to fly.

An accounting of the toll on African buffalo more than a hundred twenty five years ago, can be at best anecdotal. Sir Gerald Portal, intimately involved in the establishment of the Uganda Protectorate, even though he died of typhoid a few months before it was declared, wrote in 1893 of the Mau forest in Kenya:

> Three years ago the magnificent African buffalo roamed in tens, and even hundreds of thousands over the Masai [sic] plains and the Mau mountains, over, in fact the whole of what is called British and German East Africa; but now a traveller may wander for months in all the most likely or inaccessible places, and see nothing of the buffalo except his

> horns and whitened bones scattered over the plains, or lying literally in heaps near tempting springs and cool watering places.

In Rhodesia, now Zimbabwe, H. F. Varian, the eventual chief engineer of the Benguela Railroad, said that buffalo that once numbered in the thousands along a tributary of the Pungwe River, were reduced to a hundred by 1896. Where before they fed out into the open during the day, they now never left cover other than at night.

John F. Burger, the Afrikander professional hunter and author of that hyperbolically titled 1947 Buffalo book, *Horned Death*, saw his first Buffalo as a boy when he trekked with his family across the Kalahari to Rhodesia after the Second Boer War–not living herds gathering on the savannas, but thousands of carcasses felled by rinderpest. The Irish-born James Stevenson-Hamilton, the first game warden of South Africa's Sabi Nature Reserve, that grew into Kruger National Park, reported that after the disease, the remaining Buffalo in the North-East Transvaal were one group of twenty, which remained in the densest part of the Sabi bush. Surveying along the Chobe River where Buffalo abounded before, Stevenson-Hamilton found that the disease made a clean sweep of them. Across sub-Saharan Africa at the turn of the twentieth century the story was the same.

In time the disease burned out as herd immunity spread. By 1910, Theodore Roosevelt on his historic safari reported that the panzootic of the 1890s led to years of the Buffalo's ceasing to exist as a beast of the chase in East Africa; but that during the decade prior to his arrival, the animals's increase had been in his words, rapid, he finding substantial herds to hunt.

The fact is that after rinderpest the African buffalo never entirely recovered its old numbers from when in miles-long enjambments, it was seen heading to water. But its herds did rebuild from the near-extinction. If allowed to reproduce unimpeded, it can, and did, grow its population by as much as 15 percent per annum. It took years, but Buffalo returned to robust populations.

Spinage, though, could conclude that upon Africa no other single disease, human or animal, had as much effect, with such wide and diverse ramifications. The long-term economic outgrowths of the disease were far more destructive to African society than the immediate starvation and impoverishment. On the scorched earth left in rinderpest's wake, the stage was set for even more widespread colonialism over the continent. Imperial officials actually saw rinderpest's benefitting the labor market, as in South Africa where from what were before rural, independent peasants and hunter-gatherers, the hungry and destitute Zulus became a migrant proletariat in thrall to the gold-mining Randlords of the Reef–Witwatersrand. Yet while Spinage suggested that the panzootic did not cause but merely revealed, and exacerbated, forces already at play, the English science writer, Fred Pearce credited—if that's the right word—rinderpest with helping create the brutal social divide between Black and white that prepared the ground for the apartheid upon which industrialized South Africa proceeded through most of the twentieth century.

Driven down by the cattle plague, the population of Africans, and of livestock on the continent entered a trough at about the turn of the twentieth century from which it was estimated not to emerge until the 1940s. The geographer Jared Diamond, *Guns, Germs, and Steel,* elsewhere wrote that the most far-reaching effect of germs–meaning human, not bovine–in recorded history was to aid the European conquest and replacement of Native Americans, Pacific Islanders, and Aboriginal Australians. In New Guinea and Africa, he went on, local diseases and differential susceptibilities enabled native peoples to resist European invaders, for a time. At contact with the Portuguese, the Khoisan may very well have had an at least temporary virological edge. It was *Rinderpest morbillivirus,* the bovine germ–along with gunpowder–that unlocked thoroughly the treasure cache of Africa for looting by colonists.

With so many of the native peoples of Tanganyika and Kenya and much of the rest of eastern and southern Africa dead or incapable of opposition, Germans and British had African lands served up…on a plate, in the words of Pearce.

There was another, though, more lasting condition that has continued long after the ending of recognized suzerainty, a condition rooted in delusion.

The discovery of topographies empty of Africans persuaded Europeans, and Americans such as Roosevelt Twenty-Six, that the continent was a wide pristine wilderness as yet untouched by people, when such habitat was existing then for only a decade or two from the time of the depopulating wrought by rinderpest. What Roosevelt and others saw was unrepresentative of the millennia of human manipulation that Africa had undergone. For one, much of the supposedly virgin forests were second growth at best, harvested through history to make charcoal to fire iron bloomeries for metal for implements and weapons. The reality of the five thousand-year pastoralist African tradition–significantly enhanced by hunting and gathering that has never gone wholly away–was one of co-existence between wild animals and humans, their fields, and their grazing stock.

Not only did rinderpest sweep that away, it may have also brought about another unintended consequence in the winged form of the savanna tsetse fly. It is a conundrum, a which-came-first story.

With the ending of the African herding life, and the wiping out of grazing animals, domestic and wild, the thick natural brush, the nyika, grew back. That part is known. But that either made conditions ideal for tsetse flies or, with the death of Buffalo, swept them away. In 1908 Selous contended that the fly was killed out with the Buffalo, and seventy-five years later it was determined that Buffalo urine was in fact a powerful attractant for the fly. Others, though, pointed to the regrown bush as perfect tsetse habitat. And with the fly and trypanosomiasis, sleeping sickness, carried by its bite, the reintroduction of livestock was infeasible.

It was rinderpest and its by-products that were the calamities that shaped so much of the wild land we know in Africa. On the skeletons of Africans, white conservationists based magical thinking about an untouched continent of lands empty of human life. In the now-open country upon which wildlife not only swiftly recovered but absent competition with people swelled–some imperiously called the tsetse fly the best game warden in Africa–those Great Powers of Europe, often with an eye to the big-game hunting possibilities, sought to impose the incompatible model of the United States's Yellowstone National Park, which really had been pristine wilderness–though even there, the semi-nomadic Sheepeater Indians hunted Bighorns when the park was established. With that–willfully?–wrongheaded assumption began the enterprise of the vast African wildlife-park system–Kruger, Etosha, Hwange, Kafue, Tsavo, Ngorongoro, Serengeti–all to greater and lesser degree coming to adhere to the 1960 dictum that the German zoo director and public conservationist, Bernard Grizmek, applied to the Serengeti, No men, not even native ones, should live inside its borders.

Harumph.

Not only have Africans and their cattle been removed from lands where for generations uncounted they lived as grazers and intermittent hunters. Their traditional hunting methods, branded, as we've seen, as cruel, have been outlawed; yet even with modern weapons, not to be adjudged barbarous in the hands of Europeans and virtually unobtainable by rural Africans, they are not permitted to hunt to any significant degree. Where this has led, and continues to lead, summed up by Jonathan S. Adams and Thomas O. McShane in *The Myth of Wild Africa*, is to parks that are surrounded by people who were excluded from the planning of the area, do not understand its purpose, receive little or no benefit from the money poured into its creation, and hence do not support its existence.

Overwhelmingly, unlike the template of North American national parks–supported by the largest economy in the world–African ones fail, again and again. During the pandemic the tourist system supporting African parks and preserves essentially collapsed, though it has never been very successful at any time. Where the system succeeds in Africa is where parks and preserves are buffered, buttressed really, by being surrounded by hunting-safari camps.

Park boundaries are artificial or political constructs–sometimes the products of corruption–seldom related to the natural ranges of wildlife. Safari-hunting camps, into which the animals are free to roam from out of the parks and from which to return, expand crucial, and finally undeterminable, habitat boundaries—to put it plainly, the larger the better. The operators of those camps also collect invaluable wildlife data and patrol against poaching–especially during the vulnerable wet season–before the poachers have the chance to make their way into the parks. Hunting safaris outside their perimeters are what ensure the value of parks as refugia from the modern world or perhaps even history, for the animals that the safari operators, and the local Africans they employ and who interact with the wildlife almost daily with or without benefitting from them, want very much to conserve for the very selfish motive of exploitation–sustainable exploitation, if you will, of which vital protein is no small part–a modern form of the old African co-existence between people and wildlife.

Animals for hunting represent a concrete asset for local Africans. What happens without hunting, and with only tourist parks, can be seen in Kenya, which ended safari hunting in 1977, and has now even outlawed wingshooting. Since then most wildlife populations have fallen by two-thirds, the ones worst hit being Wildebeest, Giraffe, Gerenuk, Grant's gazelle, Warthog, Lesser kudu, Thomson's gazelle, Eland, Oryx, Topi, Hartebeest, Impala, Grevy's zebra, and Waterbuck, many of the same that survived rinderpest, and that flourished when comprising the bulk of safari big game, their post-hunting numbers fallen to levels that threaten their existences as species in the country, people now the worst panzootic.

According to Pearce, rinderpest was arguably the greatest natural calamity ever to befall Africa. In time an effective vaccine was developed; and after thousands of years of pitilessly destroying animal life, and in so doing ravaging on an incredible scale the life and culture of humans, and too often bringing out the worst in us, rinderpest became in 2011, following smallpox in 1980, the second viral disease to be certified as eradicated in the wild.

The white bones of Buffalo will never again lie scattered across the plains because of it. The Africa it bequeathed, though, does not promise an indefinite destiny for the African buffalo or any other animal or human on a dozen-million square miles of earth that grows too hot to the touch beneath the open sky of the continent.

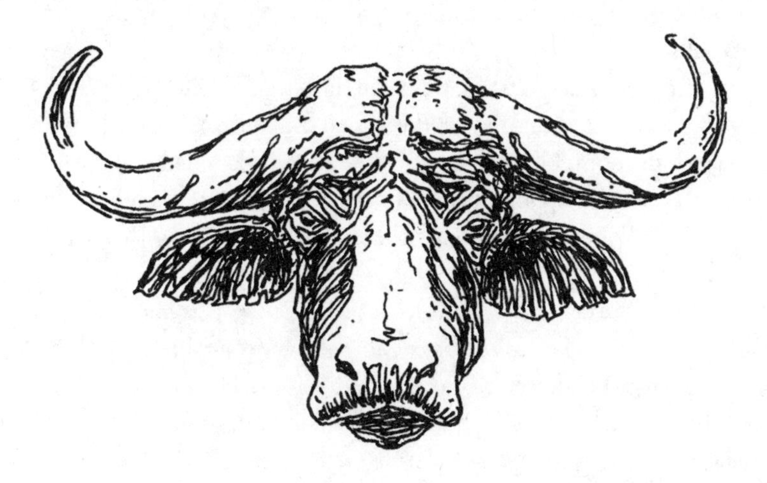

We are born into the plague of family.

Fifteen years after he lay dead in a humid August night, she died, too. And in the August following her death, I returned to the continent I loved, to find a lame Buffalo with Rory Muil.

Before going back to Africa, I went to the empty single-storied house under the flight path–the salmon-satin bellies of jumbo jets overhead, engines, hydraulics, and actuator noises screaming across the sky. The house was stucco walled and roofed in uncoursed rough rock like a rubble field, or a field of kiibi, all the exterior painted an acid shade of psychosis avocado that she fancied. It was the house of my first memory, unsolved forever, of a face, gargoyled, boo, meant to surprise and frighten me, coming out of the darkness over the bars of the crib in which I lay, my awaking to the sight. I never determined whose face it was, male or female, or what it meant, except it was never not something fearful in my remembering.

In the storage-freezer room off the concrete patio–where I once hid myself to offer childish orisons for the resurrection of a yellow Easter duckling, slaughtered by merciless affection–were cardboard boxes of cancelled checks and other papers. I went through them, transferring them into a black trash bag. There was a name-change document from a court in Lorain, Ohio, from the war years of the 1940s, in which my mother made her mother swear that her given name was not the Magyar one with which she was christened, but the French one that meant the same, pearl. There was a sheaf of sheets torn from scratch pads. Across them, she scrawled her frenzied invective, directed at him and at so many others, whomever she felt monstrously wronged by at the moment and toward whom she felt that way all her life. They were stapled together with the letter from the attorney, who described them as evidence of a marital issue, not anything warranting involuntary commitment. It was my father's seeking my mother's institutionalization for lunacy, a nineteenth-century word for what would have been a nineteenth-century proposition: clapping her into the madhouse.

I went to the barbecue kettle standing on three legs and lifted off the lid. Removing the grill, I leaned it against one of the legs on the concrete beside the lid. Returning to the storage room, I got the legal name-change document and sheaf of papers and attorney's letter. Dropping them onto the grate at the bottom of the barbecue, I soaked them in charcoal-lighter fluid, the smell of kerosene. With a butane candle lighter, I set the fire.

As the paper burned, the top sheets curled seriatim, turning black and edging ashen white. I looked away to the place on the lawn where he lay in that Downey night, on the lawn beside the Mister Lincoln tea-rose bushes, her pride, his final gesture laying the pillow he brought from his bed onto the dewed grass and his head upon the pillow.

When the flames burned down, I used the end of the lighter wand to stir the embers into smoldering dust. I put back the grill and covered the kettle with the lid. In the storage room, I added more papers to the trash bags. There was a rented roll-off dumpster in front of the garage. When there were no more papers to put in the bag, and no more that needed burning, I twisted the top of the bag and tied it into a knot, carrying it out to the dumpster. Later, a moving company came to take my first Buffalo head, the one from Kenya, and ship it to my home in Wyoming, California which had meant something to me into my bones, meaning now nothing at all.

CHAPTER ELEVEN

Tracks

THE PUGMARK WAS infixed in laterite-red dry clayey ground. Hunkering, I touched my finger to it. First, I shivered. Then, I smiled.

There were no Buffalo here, because now, this first time in Africa in Kenya, we were in the arid Tsavo land and not yet come to the green Mbogo country higher up. The next afternoon, the day after seeing the track, we found where the Leopard hoisted the carcass of an Impala doe into a tall tree near the Njugini River. The trackers built the blind twenty yards from the tree, weaving a flat curtaining screen from brush they cut with pangas. At dinner in camp we had peppered slices of roasted Impala from the more-than-decent buck I killed that morning, feeding on what the Leopard was feeding on out in the night.

Before dawn, Jbwani entered my tent with the tea tray. I ate an English breakfast with the broken-nosed John Fletcher under the whishing gas lamp in the large olive dining tent. Thirty minutes afterward, the darkness siphoning from the sky, John, his gun bearer Mmaku, and I dropped from the Land Cruiser and crawled to the blind as the Toyota drove off. The Maasai herded cattle and goats in this southern Rombo country, where, across the border in Tanzania Kilimanjaro hunched above the horizon, its square top unbelievably white in the sun, as Hemingway wrote; and as we sat motionless in the blind, we did nothing about the ticks–detecting us by our breath, our heat, or our shadows–that we knew were drilling their hook-covered mouthparts into our skin. John had his 375; I had my 300; and Mmaku had John's 500 N. E. double, loaded with 578-grain soft-noses. No ruling has thus far been handed down, specifying what constitutes too-much gun for going in after a wounded Leopard, the object being not simply to administer a finishing shot, but to slam and bolt a door between you and it if it charges.

When in first light minutes later, a Leopard walked around the edge of the blind and stood two-dozen feet from us, staring off in the direction in which the Land Cruiser drove, I was the first to see it. I moved only my eyes but was able to make out with inerrant clarity, the black rosettes charred into the golden hide, the small-flat-eared head, short sloped muzzle, pugnacious chin, and how the lithe, feline line of the body was broken by loose white fur and skin hanging along its belly. It came to evaluate what went on. Mmaku beside me did not see it until I touched his leg. He whispered breathily across me to Fletcher.

Chui.

Do not move, John confided in a strangled whisper.

Move? I would go on sitting here, watching this first Leopard I ever saw in the wild–who, because we were motionless, could not identify us–until ticks made me into a dry husk, tumbled off by the wind. Then the Leopard snapped its head toward us, perhaps registering the flick of an eyelash; and I stared into depthless *Panthera* eyes. The cat froze a full minute before crouching and whirling, the long dry grass brattling as it went away through it.

We saw the Leopard an hour later, stretched out on the limb bearing the Impala.

She-leopard, John said after glassing for a few minutes through his binocular. And there's a cub. I drew back the muzzle of the 300. For the next two hours, until the Land Cruiser returned for us, we watched the cat in the tree, its big cub tucked near it in the crotch of the limb.

Before the vehicle returned, a Fish eagle, marked like a Bald but with the white plumage bibbing the breast and draping the nape and mantle, gyred over the Impala as the She-leopard watched. The Eagle dropped, wings rayed, talons agape, stooping toward the antelope; and the She-leopard sprang. It reached the far end of the branch that bowed deep under its weight, one front paw sunk into the carcass, the other stretched out, claws unsheathed, swiping at the empty air as the Eagle beat its wings, feather tips flexing, and sculled away upward, rising back to pride of place.

In very little time, the Eagle spiraled in again to the doe. And the Leopard, having retreated back to the limb crotch, flew out once more to the hanging Impala, extending to the limit of its reach to bat at the air as the bird flared, over and over, repeating what had been repeated between the two from times before humans were ever here to see.

I came to Africa to hunt. If I never hunted, I would never have been here to see.

I like to shoot a rifle and I like to kill and Africa is where you do that, a callow Ernest Hemingway wrote to *The New Yorker*'s "Paris Letter" writer, Janet Flanner, before he turned thirty-four in 1933.

And that is why, in 1974, when I was twenty-two, I went to Africa for the first time; and because I did not want to become my father, who could never go because he would not. But by going there for that reason, I arrived at others for returning for more than forty years, and would return again, happy, this day.

In his letter, Hemingway continued, Like to get very tired too with nothing connected with my head and see the animals without them seeing you.

That was something with which I concurred.

Spotted hyena came though Arly camp one night, with low bays rising to long notes like ones played on a steam calliope. I woke gradually and lay in the bed, feeling chilled and warmed simultaneously by the calls sifting through the thatching of the round roof of the white-washed-walled boukarou. I knew that everyone else in their beds in the blackness of the camp listened, too. The Hyena voices were a strange amalgam of caniform, feliform, something purely hyaenid. Having vocal Hyena at large across the grounds at Arly was a certification of our presence on the continent of Africa.

Some hate Hyena for their supposed miscreation. Hemingway branded the Hyena a devourer of the dead, trailer of calving cows, ham-stringer, potential bit-er-off of your face at night while you slept, sad yowler, camp-follower, stinking, foul, with jaws that crack the bones the Lion leaves, belly dragging, loping away on the brown plain…

So far, so good, I'd say. For Hemingway, though, he had to compose his own signature fate for them, shooting every one he saw.

Robert Ruark was scarcely more measured when he contended that Africans are not given to jokes, yet for them the one never-failing source of mirth is the Hyena–Fisi–a ridiculous animal who could be called a dirty joke on the entire animal kingdom, he wrote.

And one wondered, what had Hyena ever done to them?

Never mind Hemingway's near moony adoration of the big, indolent, and frankly not terribly bright Lion. Or Ruark's gratuitous mythicizing of the Buffalo. The imagined conduct of the Hyena leaves some appalled, while for the Painted wolf they express fondness, practically unrestrained Gemütlichkeit, without ever witnessing their general behavior. Amid mosaic habitats of savanna and woods, Painted wolves adopt lower-endurance tactics, compared to open grasslands where they hunt in packs like hounds; and as brutish as hounds, they chase their prey to exhaustion, set upon it, tear it apart, and consume it while the animal is often very much still alive. Side by side, the Hyena's hunting may look positively demure.

If it must be said, Hyena pups are born with, as a mechanism for survival, opened eyes, erupting incisors and canine teeth, and are capable of killing their litter mates, and often do. In some respects, that possibly ought to represent a facet of their innate charm. If not, it may be the case that if you cannot intrinsically love the Hyena, you may not be fully capable of loving, or recognizing completely, what wildness is. You have to love the zealously ugly Hyena, White-tailed gnu, Warthog, Crocodile, old scrum-capped lone Buffalo bull–and apprehend their beauty—in order to love Africa concomitantly.

The doctrinaire definitions of wilderness emphasize uncultivation, uninhabitedness, and being uncrossed by human pathways, exemplifying the planet's record of life or geologic processes, the active course of evolution, phenomena of superlative beauty, and provide biodiverse habitats for rare and vulnerable forms of life. Meeting these descriptions are summits, rivers, falls, canyons, soaring forests, vistas, nacreous sunrises, vermilion sundowns, all sights to behold, never meant to be places for humans to live.

There is more wild beyond that insufficient prescription. Like Hyena, the rest of the wild is far from splendid, magnificent, inspiring, enchanting, glorious, panoramic. It is often, instead, sere, scrubby, harsh, raw, bleak, stinking, sulfurous, unsettling, and not necessarily absent the human species, if that species inhabits it in a perceptibly accommodating way, with or without wireless communication. It will be plainly identifiable as wilderness to the common viewer, even if not up to supercilious standards set by bureaucracies such as the United Nations Educational, Scientific, and Cultural Organization for world natural-heritage sites–U. N. E. S. C. O. a body of Mandarins that relish dismissing the average person's more earthbound, pedestrian notions of nature. As with Hyena, it does not have to be a wonder of the world to be something singularly sublime. Being undomesticated is frequently all that it takes.

The Hyena went away. I went back to sleep.

The days in the Arly hunting zone took on a welcome correspondence. Buffalo tracks were cut, and we moved on the trail. I wore my Blaser 416 on my back with a double sling. Djanjoua led. His military camo shirt was untucked, and he carried his iron-sighted 375 over his shoulder as he always did. As he walked, he broke off green twigs from a plant he knew and peeled them down to the moist cambium to clean his white teeth before throwing the sticks aside.

Kamiri held back, then came up with an armload of brindled baobab seed pods he picked from the ground. Formed like small footballs, their woody husks were covered in soft hairs. Kamiri broke them open, and we took out the white cube shapes of the seeds. They felt and tasted like la pavlova in the mouth. He also showed us small trees that grew tart little yellow fruits we ate whole, his telling us the name was Roan fruit, the big antelope loving to feed on them.

We saw Mongoose, Ground squirrel, Savanna hare. Tracking Buffalo, we saw birds. The Helmeted guinea fowl flushed in wide bands ahead of us, often flying over herds of Roan. I only ever shot them in Africa by stalking or when they could be driven; and a drive never amounted to more than one flight overhead, the birds's hitting the ground again when they had flown over and then running, uncatchable, into the brush. The ones I took in Kenya, though, cooked slow, made the best curry–here in Burkina Faso, I did not know Pam's opinion of Indian food; but I suspected she might not care for it. The male Dove displayed for their mates, puffing out brown-pink breasts and calling. If we walked too close, they flew up with their wings stretched full and tail feathers fanned like winning hands of cards. Other birds were Lapwing, dark-plumed Ducks, Hamerkops around water, and Double-spurred spurfowl that I hunted one sunset with the camp's over-and-under I borrowed, in sight of black-striped Desert crocodile basking beside a large pool on the sandy shore, sliding into the water as the light left. I was able to kill a few birds, until a herd of juvenile Elephant came out of cover and challenged us to leave. We left. The cook in camp cooked the spurfowl not in a curry but too quickly, making them tough and dry, though I ate them, never-the-less–I had killed them. Other nights at supper there was Buffalo, Roan, and Hartebeest, all fine to eat.

We found fresh sign but no Buffalo as the days went on, which at first passed by uncounted. The land made easy walking. Hours passed as I dreamed my way through the rhythm of the trekking, yet alert to what was to be seen. I saw all the other game I did not mean to hunt, out after Buffalo alone. Somehow, animals that are not being hunted know your intentions and are less apprehensive. Again, you could not know that, unless you hunted other animals before.

Even when it was still morning and there was a cool breeze on the dry grasslands scattered with trees, the sun pressed onto my shoulders and neck like a yoke hung with heavy pails. The light came down as if through glass panes in a greenhouse, intensifying the heat. As the walking went on, each step turned into an attainment, like pulling a boot out of sucking mud. If we were close enough to camp at midday, we went back to rest on our beds for an hour or two. That let us return to walking in the afternoon.

One of those afternoons when the sun was just beginning to sink and the shadows were black under the trees, Djanjoua halted and gestured for me to come up beside him. He pointed off several hundred yards. On the trunk of the tree, enveloped in the shade, a long shape came down headfirst–that head flat eared, short muzzled, a chin like a boxer's–a tail curled behind. Jumping the last feet to the ground, landing on four paws, its dark back visible above the tops of the dead grass, it walked away, slowly and unconcerned, vanishing before it came into full sunlight. We were not the only ones hunting in Arly

We walked back to the safari truck as the afternoon lengthened. The return drive headed us into camp in the dark. As we went, my unloaded rifle setting on its butt on the floor between my feet, I began to feel aswim. The top of my skull throbbed; and I wanted to sleep, but couldn't in the warm, dusty vehicle. We drove over the saddle between the buttes; and I saw the fire ring circled with feathers. I knew the distance to camp, and all I thought of was getting there.

We turned at the inky bulk of the baobab into the entrance to the camp, coming to a stop in the open dirt yard of the compound. I got out and was at once vertiginous as I reached back for my rifle, having to take hold of the windshield pillar to keep myself up. I asked the translator, Thomas, if he could help me to my boukarou.

The noise of the generator was coming from across the yard as I opened the door. I stood there, steadying myself on the door handle. Thomas was behind me with my rifle, and I turned back and took it with my free hand. I switched on the overhead light in the circular room and leaned the rifle on the stand of rattan shelves against the wall, as the blades of the ceiling fan began to turn. I asked Thomas please to bring me two bottles of cold beer from the camp bar.

As I waited for Thomas to come back, I sat on the edge of the bed and tried to make things achieve a balance again. Thomas brought the two beers, and I said I would not eat supper. He left, and I drank. Putting the empty bottles on the concrete floor, I undressed, turned off the light, and lay down to sleep.

That night, there were no Hyena; but from a few-hundred yards up the unpaved road, from the village of mudbrick houses around a galvanized lever-action hand-pump well, the djembe drumming and singing began at midnight. From the distance, it echoed clear in the night air, mournful and ardent and all too alive. I slept and woke, and it went on. It continued to first light, passing through the dawn above the roofs of the boukarous. A knock came at the door, and I tried to sit up. Everything was tilting, still, and I called out that I was not going hunting that morning. And a rounded African voice said, All right.

There was light through the metal louvres over the windows when I woke again. I felt leveled when I stood. Showering, I dressed in fresh-laundered clothes and walked outside. It was midmorning, gray and cool. I went through the opening in the woven-branch fence at the back of the compound and toward the abattoir. Between the fence and the shambles, wrecked Land Cruisers and Land Rovers were scattered and piled, now little more than exoskeletons stripped of parts. Wheelless on the ground, the Land Rovers sat with their cracked windshields winking, square fenders extending beyond the grills like the paws of a sphinx.

A Roan, a morning kill, was in the round-walled abattoir. Kicking-foot young boys sat on the top of the high brick wall, watching as the chief skinner, having weighed the heavy antelope, and his assistants hoisted it up to dress and skin. I remembered something I had in my boukarou and went back for it. Returning, I gave the new, packaged diamond-steel sharpener to the head skinner. He nodded and took it out, dropping the wrapping onto the concrete pad of the cleaning floor. He ran the skinning blade across the sharpener.

Two of the trackers who came in with the Roan leaned against the wall. One saw a folded packet of white paper fall out of the packaging. He picked it up and it laddered down like a long transit-transfer ticket. On one side was printed a compendium of safety instructions in atomic detail. On the other, the same list, in French. The tracker who picked up the paper walked back to the wall and leaned against it alongside the other tracker. He read at first to himself, then started reading out loud to the other tracker. They both began laughing until the first tracker let the inane precautions, written by attorneys, flutter away from his hand like a length of ticker tape from a downtown office window. No more proof was needed that all mzungu were obviously crazy. The head skinner with the newly honed knife, punctured the bloated paunch, gas hissing out as if from an open jet.

I walked to the terrace for lunch. Pam was there, and Lance. Pam's translator came past. She asked him what the drumming had been all night. The translator told her it was from the village. Could he, she asked, make sure it didn't happen anymore?

The translator looked at her a moment. It was for a dead person, he said. If she wished, she could go over and ask them herself to cease commending the soul over the frontier dividing life from death…

In Kenya we found another tree where a Leopard with a much bigger track hung its kill, and built a round blind by another tree across the clearing. The first afternoon we stayed in the blind till long past sunset, waiting for the Land Cruiser to return to take us back to camp. In the darkness, we heard, hidden, the male Leopard in the tree, feeding, separating the joints of the Impala with a sound like the twisting of a leg off a roast chicken. Back in camp, Fletcher said we could have used a light. He knew other professionals who did. But that was not how he hunted.

Still in the dark in the morning, up an hour earlier than the day before, Fletcher and I and Mmaku walked in the last mile to the blind, without flashlights, being as soundless as we could. I could not see what was around us, which made the land the biggest place in the world, and the closest. Then we were at the blind. We sat motionless in it a long time, the dark unchanging until the light came up in the equatorial way: not there, there. Watching, not seeing the Leopard coming through the grass around the trunk, I saw the form of the cat leaping into the tree. Then it was out on the limb where the carcass was wedged. The head was larger, squarer than the female's. I slid the rifle forward slowly. In the crosshairs I picked one, individual, black spot to aim at. I let off the safety and placed my finger on the trigger.

As the rifle came out of recoil, I saw the Leopard not jumping but falling down the trunk. Moments later, out of the blind and by the bait tree, Fletcher looked down.

Good job, lad, he said, pleased. Or relieved.

I looked at the rosettes and golden fur and tried to see the answer in the pattern of the hide, knowing there was none. Except that now I knew I would not hunt Leopard anymore. Not like Buffalo.

CHAPTER TWELVE

Mzungu

THOSE DAYS, GIVEN over to the next Buffalo in the Binga Communal Lands, were a knot of old tracks, no tracks, blown stalks, wrong bulls. In the middle of the bush, Rory Muil's tracker, John, kicked off the ground an outsized patinated, forty-year-old Rhodesia and Nyasaland penny center-holed for stringing, the reverse stamped 1961, the obverse festooned with Elephant gamboling. He gave it to me, and I threaded it onto the wind-string through the crown of my hat, for luck. No speedy enhancement of our fortunes was afterward forthcoming, however.

Fastening on Buffalo as the tracking persisted, we grew indifferent to the bounding away of Kudu or the gray apparition of a rare Southern roan, galloping. This did not mean we were insensible to the surroundings. We felt thorns; we saw in the cool breeze, leaves flittering on trees. Once, Rory picked up a small Leopard tortoise, tucked in like a clutch purse, sleeping soundly under the grass, exhibited it, then placed it back considerately in its cover. Snowy flashes on the ground came into resolution as scattered white bones of the broken skeleton of an Elephant, too heavy for scavengers to drag off. Trailing Buffalo, we came onto the wide sandy beds where Elephant lay down on their sides, a sunken pillowed place for the head, with a lesser impression above it, where a tusk furrowed the ground.

The Buffalo knew where to lead to divert us from the track: unbroken dry shoals of quartz pebbles, tall thickety grass, shelves of flat bare rock, across raucous acres of fallen leaves–Like walking around in a crisp factory, Rory said, taking a fatalistic drag on his Newbury, his turn of phrase reminding me of Floyd Thursby's covering the floor of his hotel room in crumpled newspapers in *The Maltese Falcon*. Buffalo were Floyd Thursbys of the African bush, no more so than when all the trackers halted in silent unison, the pause pregnant, their looking and listening, before taking up the trail again.

For six days we hunted that way. I recognized, by then, without hesitation, the gallimaufry of prints by species and age. By the fifth day, I was altogether premonitory, telling Rory we would find the dagga boy on the seventh. He had no quarrel.

At first light on the seventh morning, we looked for Buffalo on a high grassy flat where, the evening before, we saw tracks heading; but they moved through and away already, only Klipspringer clipping ahead of us off the kopjes. It was over a dozen hard miles back to Kapinda where the stands of mopane trees grew up to the bottoms of rock spines, the bushwillow jess was thick, and long-straw-grassed woodland parks rolled out over broad ridgelines. We started out.

The air warmed as we drove in the open Land Rover. Reaching Kapinda at midmorning, we hunted tracks along dirt roads not to be trusted, expiring without warning. We found large round hoof prints, two dagga boys running together.

Pulling into the shade of a tree, we got out. I took my soft case down from the rifle rack welded to the rollbar behind the truck cabin, unzipped it, and slipped out the single-shot 450 N. E. Sliding in a snap cap, I levered up the falling block and dry-fired at fifty, then thirty, finally fifteen, yards, selecting as a point of aim in the crosshairs of the scope a unripened monkey orange or dying leaf, the power ring turned down to one-and-three-quarters magnification, holding steady through the squeeze and the hollow hammer fall. Ejecting the cap, I pocketed it and chambered a 500-grain soft-nosed bullet, loaded to twenty one hundred-feet-per-second velocity, and set the safety. I took a long drink of water from one of the canteens John carried in his day pack. I handed it back. We began to walk.

I came to think of Kapinda and dagga boys as analogous to monkey oranges. The fruit hung under spiked leaves from the branches of a small evergreen, its turquoise peel ripening to aureate. The pulpy flesh is quite edible and by all accounts succulent; but it encapsulates numerous seeds, the way a pomegranate's does. *Strychnos*, its genus, alerts one to what it contains, buried in the seeds: poison. Hidden in the wild and beautiful Kapinda country, like the seeds in the monkey orange, was *Syncerus caffer caffer*.

The tracks of the dagga boys crossed the usual dubious terrain. We lost and found the trail again and again until on a tall ridge, we tracked into a keep of battlemented rocks. The sign showed the bulls were just ahead, not hurrying, likely bound for bed.

Wind, above all else, kills Buffalo. It is also what keeps them breathing. Now, the wind squirled to their benefit. There was a percussive crashing, three-quarter-ton mule deer bursting from Great Basin sage cover, unseen. We stopped and hunkered in silence into the rocks; and I imagined the Buffalo somehow stotting like mule deer, or as in the hunting poem of the Yorùbá, those butterflies of the savanna, flying along without touching the grass. When we no longer heard them running, we began tracking again, slowly, slowly.

A quarter-hour later, Samuel, Rory's head tracker, spotted the old dagga boys feeding among the mopane on flat ground below the rocks where we were. They had not been irreparably spooked. And in fact, all seemed forgiven.

How far, Rory asked, can that rifle shoot?

Not that far, I answered, seeing where the Buffalo were.

Two hundred yards?

The Buffalo were well beyond that.

One hundred, I said. Less.

Rory calculated. We had the wind up here and saw the Buffalo well. Going down, we would lose sight of them and did not know how the wind was. A low ridge, mounded with large rocks, branched off and ran close to the Buffalo. Making a wide circle, using the rocks as landmarks, we could go down, then climb that ridge and get inside a hundred yards, if all went according to plan. Rory knew I did not want to try a shot at sniping distance with a N. E., or with any other rifle, with Buffalo. There was a greater sense of security in getting up close, even glint-of-the-eye close, rather than endeavoring to fell a Buffalo at a venture.

Rory made the call. We crept away from the rocks; and out of the Buffalo's sight. Standing, we, worked our way down. I stumbled more than once, fighting the tension that was excitement rather than dread, assuming each time that I had started the bulls to run again. That could not be known, though, till the end.

On the flat ground, moving toward the low ridge and landmarks, Rory asked what I had chambered.

Soft.

Solid, he whispered.

I opened the chamber and took out the single cartridge, reloading it with a solid, easing the block back up.

Coming to the low ridge, we left the other trackers behind; and Samuel, Rory, and I climbed, moving along the crest. We navigated by a black-and-white rock hollowed by wind. Looking over the other side of the ridge, I saw a black shape standing beneath the low sweeping branches of a mopane. I reached out and touched Rory, and he whistled softly to Samuel. We stopped.

Lining up three trees, we used them to conceal us as we worked closer. At the last tree at sixty yards, on a slight slope, cover played out. The tree provided no rest for a shot. I slid out from behind it to have the Buffalo in sight. Setting the fore-end of the single-shot rifle in the leather covered cradle on the top of my hiking staff, I turned the scope magnification up to four power and found the Buffalo in the sight. Its head was in the branches and leaves.

The bull angled to its left toward me, a blocky rump, swayed back, great bellied, the real weight carried in the bulked shoulder hump and forequarters that were unobstructed. As I looked among the foliage, I saw a solid boss and the long curve of horn and that telling glint: The Buffalo saw not something, but some thing where I stood, its waiting on the wind to tell what that some thing was.

The bull's left ear flicked and drooped, and below its tattered fringe was the base of its neck and its chest. I whispered across to Rory that twigs were in the way; and he mouthed back that there was not enough to upset the bullet; all quite thin stuff.

I looked back through the scope and saw he was right. I found a place that looked open, on the bull's chest under the ear.

Just below the tip of the left ear, I whispered across.

That's a good place, came the almost unhearable reply.

I held longer, making sure that what I was seeing in the blackness in the scope was the bull's chest. I slid the safety on the tang forward.

The barely audible caution came from Rory: Don't shoot unless you're absolutely happy.

Happy, somehow, seemed not to the point. What was the point? Not that there was time to analyze that, but I knew this all was what led to happy, if... If not, it could be the unhappiest thing in the world.

Before the wind turned, my finger, as if in monosynaptic reflex ahead of consciousness, pressed the trigger.

The rifle fired and the bull spun out from beneath the tree in a splintering of limbs. It ran widdershins in a half circle, bringing it fifteen yards farther out along the line of fire. Partly covered by the mopane's trunk, the Buffalo held its head–Roman nosed and domed by the heavy tight boss–high and scenting, searching from where the blow struck. The other dagga boy behind pounded past and wheeled into the wind, drawing the wounded bull with it. This all happened much faster than the telling; and as it did, I levered open the action, the long, straight-walled brass case ejecting, and pulled another solid cartridge from the loops on the neoprene sleeve on the stock, chambering it. The two bulls went straight away across the open toward another, lower ridge, to a gap at the end. Behind and to the side, I heard Rory firing one of his sprinkling of verdigris cartridges from his 458, missing, the dirt beside the Buffalo spuming up. Offhand, I threw the crosshairs onto the wounded bull in the rear, at a hundred yards now. The rolling, tidal recoil of the rifle hardly registered; and I saw that the second 500-grain bullet broke the Buffalo's left hip and traveled on into its body cavity. The Buffalo seemed to absorb it, the two bulls going out of sight beyond the ridge.

I reloaded once again, set the safety, picked up my hiking staff, and started off the ridge. Then through the gap, I saw the bulls, hard noon sun on horns and bosses, out of range, running from sight. As the first got away, the second lurched to its right. Its head torqued downward, its body dropping, the dust rising from where it fell out of view behind the lower ridge.

We covered quickly the two hundred yards between the place from where I shot to where the Buffalo dropped, hearing a mourning bellow as we jogged.

He is dead, Samuel pronounced, performing a solemn nod.

Over the ridge, the bull lay on its right side, its back to us. It bellowed faintly, wobbling its head above the ground. A third solid, in the back of the creased neck, and the head bent down, the bellowing ended, the left hind leg stretching out, then levering down slowly.

Pale-green cambium plugged the rough texture of the boss from the Buffalo's butting and rubbing against tree bark. The horns were worn back to where the thickness carried out to the blunted tips. The high withers and back had hair only in patches. The first solid cut the aorta; but the Buffalo ran, no matter what. As they do.

In childhood, Joseph Conrad embraced an obsessive attachment to charts and atlases. Rather than star-gazing, which led to the borders of the unattainable, he became addicted to poring over maps, which brought the problems of the great spaces of the earth into stimulating and directive contact with sane curiosity, as he said. Calling himself a contemporary of the Great Lakes of Africa, at least as they were introduced to people in Europe and the Americas–long known already, of course, to Africans–he came to the defense of the atlas with which he grew up, an 1852 edition that neglected to represent not only the lakes, but even the boundaries of Tanganyika, Conrad sedulously sketching on the page in pencil the borderlines of the new German colony.

In the perhaps final essay he wrote, published in the *National Geographic* in 1924, the year of his death, Conrad said of his atlas that the heart of its Africa was white and big, which may have meant something other than what he supposed.

From well before the time when the Romans used to say, according to Conrad, some new thing was always coming out of Africa, the vasty cartographic blankness of the continent–for white-skinned people rather than for Africans–generated both a nearly irresistible tug toward trespass, and boundless avariciousness for what were thought to be unclaimed treasures.

Whether or not D. N. A. analysis casts doubt on the predominantly African origins of the ancient Egyptians and the Berbers of North and Saharan Africa–always remembering that to be human is to be incontestably African for nearly four and a half million years–making them interlopers on the continent, is not a subject into which I am prepared to risk inquiry. To anyone else so inclined, bonne chance. The ancient Berbers did hunt the *antiquus* Buffalo; and the pre-Hellenistic pharaoh Thutmose III combined hunts with his many campaigns out of Egypt proper. Conquering Nubia to the Fourth Cataract of the Nile, he found the opportunity to kill with his bow and arrow a Northern white rhino. If the climate of Nubia in the mid-fifteenth-century B. C. was habitable for Rhino, could it not also have been for Buffalo, such as the Nile? Did Thutmose see Buffalo, or even hunt them?

Whatever the case was for Egyptians and Berbers, the immediate origins of the Phoenicians, Greeks, and Romans lay unarguably in somewhere other than Africa. In the earliest portion of the Vulgar Era, two Romans, the Grecophile Claudius Aelianus and before him, Pliny the Elder, wrote of Theres Aithiopikos and Libyes, the wild beasts of Ethiopia and Libya, the aliens's name then for, as we know, all of Africa. Respectively, they wrote of Tauros Aithiopikos and the Tauri Silvestres, the Ethiopian or Forest Bull, basing their histories on the narratives–implausibly first-hand–of travelers returning from the distant continent.

A fabulous creature, no doubt, it was said by Aelianus to be the king of beasts to the Troglodytai–cave dwellers–with the courage of the Lion, the speed of the Horse, the strength of the bull, and is stronger than iron. Pliny described this largest of bovines as having a tawny hide as hard as flint with the hair turned backward, an open mouth that gaped to the ears, blue eyes, and mobile horns, that was carnivorous and hunted all other wild animals and could only be caught in pits, where it always died game. As with Flaubert and etymology, a little Latin and ingenuity makes it a short step from Tauros Aithiopikos to imagining *Syncerus caffer*.

Hunting in Rome was not as culturally significant as in Greece, but the Roman demand for wild African animals ran deeper. Emperors and patricians with ambitions perceived a crucial need for bloodstained wild-animal spectacles in the coliseums to galvanize the plebeians, tens of thousands of beasts being killed over time. So extreme were the entertainments and the industry that mounted them, they attracted pasquinades such as that in *The Satyricon of Titus Petronius Arbiter*: The wild beast is searched out in the woods at a great price, and men trouble Hammon [the Carthaginian god Ba'al Ḥammon] deep in Africa to supply the beast whose teeth make him precious for slaying men.

In the century plus from 19 B. C. to A. D. 90, Romans conducted various overland expeditions into sub-Saharan Africa, some reaching nearly to the Senegal and Niger rivers and Lake Chad–legend has it that caligae-ed cohortes praetoriae sent in A. D. 61 by the Emperor Nero, transited the equator and found what is now Murchison Falls on the, now, Victoria Nile. Along with scouting for potential conquests, the missions were in the cause of securing trade routes for, and the sources of, gold, ivory, carbuncles–red gems–and slaves, without having to enter into partnerships with Africans; but these schemes proved in the end uneconomic. It is difficult to imagine, though, that the legionnaires would not have encountered Buffalo somewhere.

From the fond wish to find a white, or at least Christian, kingdom in the Conradian vacancy of Africa–a kingdom offering the hope of coming to the aid of the troubled Second Crusade–materialized the twelfth-century legend of Prester John. Originally a chimera of Central Asia, by the thirteenth century the monarch was associated with a continent-wide empire of non-Africans, webbing out from medieval Abyssinia. Keen to discover him, the Portuguese christened this region Terre do Preste. His realm, properly dismissed as fantasy by the late 1600s, could not have helped but to contain Buffalo.

While the Buffalo of the Cape of Good Hope were being hunted by Dutch Calvinists by the seventeenth century, Buffalo in other parts of Africa on the west and east coasts were likely hunted by Europeans for centuries prior. Henry the Navigator in the early 1400s started sending vessels south of another cape, Bojador, on the west coast of Africa, into oceans harboring sea monsters and running to the rim of the world. Before the close of the fifteenth century, the Portuguese doubled the continent and came to the Mozambican shore, commencing a long colonial initiative lasting into the latter half of the twentieth, ending not at all well. And they would have found Buffalo waiting there.

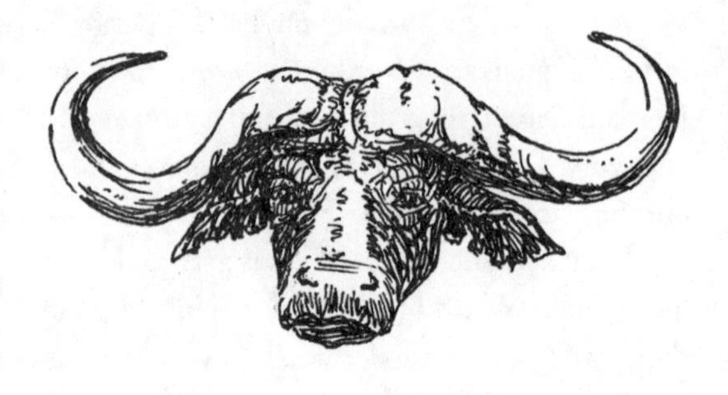

Until the eighteenth century, Europeans, Arabs, and even Indians who traded on the continent did so primarily from the littorals. As long as they kept to there, accepting the commerce that came to them from within the continent–even if were trafficking in bondage–they probably remained after a sort, comprehensible to Africans. As they began penetrating the interior, though, they became less explicable. The Bantu from Congo to Madagascar could find only one ideal word for these bewildering people traipsing through their lands. Mzungu has its roots in Kiswhaili for spinning around and dizziness, referring to what is regarded as the perchance aimless, and assuredly pointless, wanderings of non-Africans, the natives of the continent seeming to know concretely where they are and where they are headed. The paradigm of the way of the mzungu is the safari.

As anyone who has opened a *Lonely Planet* guidebook to Africa knows, the word safari derives from safar, the Arabic infinitive of to journey, with safariya the noun for traveler, the words drawn from the mzungu travels of Arab traders in the African bush. The one to blame or credit for the inception of what we know today as the wildlife safari would be William John Burchell, though other Europeans did explore Africa before Burchell.

The Scot James Bruce spent the years 1768 to 1773 along the Nile and in Ethiopia, searching for the source of the Blue Nile–already visited, independently, some time before by two Jesuit missionaries, one Spanish, the other Portuguese. Bruce came back with tales, many receiving unmerited derision–such as that of Abyssinian soldiers slicing steaks from the rump of a live cow, then closing the flap of hide with skewers or pins and sending the animal on its way to be further lunched upon another day. He did not, though, return with any floral or faunal specimens. Burchell made up for that.

Born in 1781 in Fulham near London, the son of Matthew Burchell, a nurseryman, William apprenticed at Kew Park, later the Royal Botanic Gardens. In 1805 he sailed for what became Napoleon's penal St. Helena to go into a partnership chandlering the global ship traffic making through port at the island. He also anticipated the arrival of his fiancée, Miss Lucia Green, from England, all the while collecting plants. Lucia arrived, but now enamored with the captain of the ship that transported her, jilting Burchell with, as he put it, all the levity and a gaiety of a girl going down a country dance.

Along with his betrothal, the business partnership foundered and Burchell became the island's schoolmaster and official botanist. In 1810 he departed St. Helena for Cape Town. There he had a trek wagon of his own design constructed to withstand rough travel and loaded it with barter goods: clothing and blankets for his own Hottentots, as he nominated them; arms, powder, and shot; fishing hooks and line; tools and utensils; water casks, victuals, and dry goods; medicines; reference books; stationery and prepared canvases for painting in watercolors and oil; unassembled packing cases made of deal; and the colors of the nation of England, and set out into Africa in June, 1811.

Perhaps no country in the world can boast of possessing a variety of wild quadrupeds as Southern Africa, wrote Burchell, ungrammatically, in 1822 in his *Travels in the Interior of Southern Africa*. It nonetheless took until 1812 and crossing six hundred twenty five miles of land from Cape Town to Bloem's Fountain, for him to see his first Buffalo.

He thought Buffalo a misnomer for the animal known as Naari by the Bichuana–an obsolete tribal name for the Tswana–the animal's seemingly cardinal distinction, he wrote, being that two charges of powder and two balls now obtained for him a waggon load of provisions. By his 1815 return to the Cape, he traveled forty five hundred miles around southern Africa and collected sixty three thousand geological, anthropological, botanical, entomological, ornithological, and animal specimens. He executed five hundred illustrations, as well as finding time for astronomical and meteorological sightings and measurements. Among the specimens were a hundred twenty animal skins from eighty separate species, along with skeletons.

Large-mammal collections in the early 1800s were a rarity due to scientific collection being, according to Jane Pickering, author of the paper "William J. Burchell's South African Mammal Collection, 1810-1815," expensive, time-consuming, difficult and sometimes dangerous–as safari hunting can still be. John Edward Gray, head of the zoology department for the British Natural History Museum, described Burchell's South African specimens as the first in Britain.

The omnium-gatherum was dispersed between the British and Oxford University museums, Burchell coming to lament the British's, and Gray's, handling of its share–collections tending there toward a sad state, according to Pickering, and much more limited than similar ones in Paris.

Burchell complained that the museum made no attempt to preserve them by even a bit of camphor…I found these skins swarming with live moths and maggots and the hair dropping off.

More than half failed to survive. Those at Oxford fared better, and the collection includes assorted Buffalo horns and frontlets on wooden plagues.

Never marrying, Burchell continued traveling and exploring, spending five years in Brazil, his journals from that time unhappily missing. As he aged, his life became circumscribed by depression. At age eighty he was enfeebled; at eighty-two he shot himself under a tall cedar in front of his house. Not dying directly, he concluded the task by hanging himself amid the plants in his garden.

Years before his end, Burchell fabricated the template for the mzungu safari so that all later ones should be described as A. B., After Burchell. As Burchell taught lessons to St. Helena schoolchildren, Sir William Cornwallis Harris, the next to be adjudged an African great white hunter, was being born in Kent in 1807. At fourteen he entered a military seminary, and at sixteen joined the army of the Honorable East India Company in Bombay as an engineer with the rank of second lieutenant. In a score of years, he advanced to major. In 1836 he was, by the military medical board, invalided to the Cape–whose sovereignty transferred to Great Britain under the Anglo-Dutch Treaty of 1814, apparently without bothering to ask the Khoisan.

Cornwallis Harris evidently contracted shooting-madness at a tender age, and on the voyage to Africa struck up a friendship with a notable shikari with whom he planned an expedition. On landing, he consulted with a naturalist who returned from up country, then set out with the shikari from Algoa Bay on the Eastern Cape, striking out toward the Orange River. For nearly two years, he and his compatriot safari-ed, reaching the kraals of the king of the Matabele–known now as the Ndebele–and the southern tropics, before turning back to the Cape.

Cornwallis Harris encountered, and hunted, many Buffalo. He marked the bovines's inseparable attachment to wetlands by writing of a chain of lakes along the Mimori River, that contained a herd of Wild buffaloes, whose formidable heads, resembling masses of rock, were protruded from the water amid waving sedges, the whole of their bodies being immerged.

According to a biographer of Burchell's, of the pioneering Cape travelers such as Kolbe and Sparrman, not one other could match Burchell's glittering literary style in his *Travels*; and no one else could touch Cornwallis Harris's talent in the painting and sketching of African wildlife, as proven in his vibrant studies of Buffalo.

Returning to India, Cornwallis Harris put down his adventures with his own illustrations, in *The Wild Sports of Southern Africa: Being the Narrative of an Expedition from the Cape of Good Hope, Through the Territories of the Chief Moselekatse, to the Tropic of Capricorn*. In the 1840s he came back from a mission to the Abyssinian highlands where he concluded a commercial treaty with the ruler of the region of Shewa, an achievement for which he was knighted. In October, 1848, near Poona, India, at just forty-one, he died from one out of that imperial macédoine for poorly understood ailments, labeled fever.

In districts long-since cleared–that is a refrain found continuously in chronicles of mzungu safaris in the nineteenth century. Game was steadily rolled back to the north, to wilder and wilder reaches, particularly into fly country where riding and draft animals could not be employed due to the presence of African trypanosomiasis, necessitating long lines of porters in place of beasts of burden for reasons often related to the greater economic worth of domesticated-animal, rather than human, life. The all-encompassing response to this from the mzungu who are the principal cause, has been the soothing contentment of lamentation.

In the fatalistic, misanthropic romanticism of an *Out of Sydney Pollack*, is repeated the willful error made over and over by mzungu, as spoken by the actor Robert Redford to the other actor, Meryl Streep, in the line, There's country there you ought to see…it won't last long now.

It is the fallacy that a fragile wild Africa is there to be estimated and esteemed truly only by the elect eyes of empathetic white people, despite their seeing the continent–where billions of Africans have lived for epochs, and will live still for epochs more–as in passing, always as something passing, when it is they–we–who are only passing through.

The frontier of African wildlife receded because many, though not all, who followed Burchell and Cornwallis Harris were butchers–while even at that, the actions of mzungu settlers rather than safari hunters were far and away more detrimental. Yet all those who trailed Burchell and Harris probed relentlessly deeper and deeper into the Dark Continent, ad verbum, often leaving in places an aftermath of desolation.

Whether Samuel Baker's effect upon the continent was favorable, or the contrary, remains a matter of debate. It is assumable that he would have shared the sentiments about Africa that years later Hemingway advanced in his letter to Janet Flanner. As well as a killer, Baker was an ardent anti-slaver and hierophant of empire. He felt deeply that, as he wrote in the introduction to his *The Albert N'Yanza, Great Basin of the Nile and Explorations of the Nile Sources*, the primary object of geographical exploration–along with, though he never comes out and says so in this exact way, that the places previously unexplored by mzungu were where the best hunting ought to be–is the opening to general intercourse such portions of the earth as may become serviceable to the human race [sic]. The explorer is the precursor of the colonist; and the colonist is the human instrument by which the great work must be constructed–that greatest and most difficult of all undertakings–the civilization of the world.

Rule, Britannia!

The son of a wealthy sugar merchant, banker, and ship owner, Baker was born in Worcestershire in 1821, one of seven children, including his scandalous younger brother, Valentine. It is conceivable he began hunting in the Scottish Highlands, chasing stags with hound and knife. Completing a civil-engineering education in Germany, he planned bridges and railways in Romania, before marrying his first wife in 1843, the couple going on to have seven children, three of whom died in childhood. With another brother and their wives, both sisters, Baker went to

Mauritius to oversee his family's plantation. In 1846, he moved to Ceylon to found a successful agricultural estate of his own, spending the next eight years hunting on the island.

His wife, Henrietta, died of typhoid in 1855. Baker was thirty-four. He consigned his four surviving children to the care of one of his sisters and returned to drafting Romanian infrastructure. While hunting in the Balkans with a maharaja, they visited, as a caprice, a genuine slave market; and Baker saw on the block, the teenaged girl–some say no older than fourteen–who would, someday, become his second wife. From the Hungarian family of Finnian von Sass–over time, she went by no less than seven names–Florence survived the Turkish massacre of all her direct relatives in Transylvania and in 1848 as a child, was taken into slavery in the Ottoman Empire. Baker freed her in dramatic fashion–runaway carriages in the night–and Florence was with Baker, as she would always be, on his expeditions, even martial ones, as he started out in March, 1861, seeking the Nile's origin.

Before me, untrodden Africa, Baker wrote, against me–the obstacles that had defeated the world since its creation; on my side–a somewhat tough constitution, perfect independence, a long experience in savage life, and both time and means which I intended to devote to the object without limit.

There was also a race underway, between Baker going south by river and Captains John Hanning Speke and James Augustus Grant moving overland from Zanzibar, both expeditions in search of the Source. While Speke and Grant were sent out very publicly by the British government, Baker did not presume to publish his purpose.

Baker spent a year on the Sudan-Abyssinian frontier, hunting and learning Arabic, the lingua venditoris servi of the interior, which he felt compulsory to study if he were to forge his way upriver. In June of 1862 he came to Khartoum at the confluence of the White and Blue Niles. Six months later, he had three riverboats–two large barges known as noggurs and a decked vessel with comfortable cabins, that he called a diahbiah–with forty sailors, along with cooks and servants, and forty-five men armed with double guns and rifles, donkeys, horses, and camels, stores, and rations for four months, and set off for the island trading station of Gondokoro–also the site of an abandoned Catholic mission and the end of the navigable river. As head man, a German carpenter–an excellent sportsman and an energetic and courageous fellow, perfectly sober and honest, wrote Baker–was hired. Alack, he died of what was almost certainly tuberculosis within days of their setting out.

A few weeks later in the Sudd–where, per Baker, the marshes were frightful and the windings…tedious and melancholy beyond description–a half-hour before sunset, the diahbiah being man-hauled by the crew on the deck pulling on the high reeds, a Buffalo was sighted on a patch of dry ground. Baker's men, famished for fresh meat, implored him to shoot; and climbing onto cargo stacked on the poop to spot the animal, Baker made a hundred twenty yard shot with his No. 1 Reilly rifle, the bull dropping at the report. His men stormed up the bank to the Buffalo, one of them holding it by the tail and another dervishing on the carcass, brandishing his knife, when the carcass resurrected and charged through the crew members, disappearing into the grasses and falling, the men said, into a morass.

Too dark for them to follow, the crew returned to the vessel, chagrinned at neglecting to hamstring the animal when the opportunity presented itself. In the morning, the groans of the Buffalo could be heard, and now forty men with firearms and edged weapons went out. They seemed to wander in the knee-deep swamp for an hour; and Baker tried calling them back by beating on the boat's drum, when he heard yelling and the discharging of guns. At three hundred yards through his spyglass, he saw the men clustered on a white anthill, keeping up a dropping fire at some object indistinguishable in the high grass, he wrote. The shooting halted, and the men came out not with Buffalo meat, but the dead body of Baker's best choush–a Turkish attendant–Sali Achment, surprised and trampled into the mud by the wounded bull. Only weeks into the expedition, and two key members of his corps were already dead; but at least there was meat. The crewmen, burying Sali Achmet in an Arab grave that is an improvement upon those of Europeans, in Baker's estimation, by being basically a sealed crypt, went back to butcher the Buffalo.

There was more disappointment a month later in Gondokoro–a perfect hell and nest of robbers, to Baker's eye–just northeast and across the Nile from today's Juba, capital of South Sudan. On the fifteenth of February, the rattle of musketry at a great distance, Baker recalled, blazoned the approach of the two white explorers, Speke and Grant, the former looking excessively lean but in reality in good tough condition, while the latter was in honorable rags, his knees visible through his trousers. The gala saluting by Baker's men resulted in the shooting of one of his donkeys. Ushering the pair to his diahbiah for rough fare, and the almost statutory cups of tea, and gaining the intelligence that they had found the source of the ancient river, Baker claimed to feel with all his heart, pride in their being his own countrymen, though he now considered his own expedition terminated. They would all sail back down the Nile in Baker's boats–when Speke and Grant showed him their map with another of Conrad's white and big hearts.

The two believed there existed a great lake in the upper Nile system that they had not found. They heard it called Mwitanzige, the locust killer because the insects were said to die in attempting to fly across it. They delegated Baker and Florence to crack the code.

A little over a year later, when on the march Florence fell into a week-long coma, brought on by coup de soleil, sunstroke, and recovered–Baker could not attempt to describe the gratitude he felt at that moment–the glory of our prize burst suddenly upon me! he said.

Riding an oxen to a hilltop, he saw lying far beneath him a grand expanse of water, a sea of quicksilver–boundless on the horizon on the south and southwest, glittering in the noonday sun; and on the west, at fifty or sixty miles's distance, blue mountains rose from the bosom of the lake to a height of about seven thousand feet above its level. In a memorial to one loved and mourned by his gracious Queen, and deplored by every Englishman [sic], he named the waters Albert N'Yanza, which with Victoria N'Yanza that Speke and Grant saw, gave England title to the two Sources of the Nile. They had then to hurry back to Gondokoro in order to find the boats to return to Khartoum and ultimately Britain, barely having time en route to pass by and name Murchison Falls–after Sir Roderick Impey Murchison, then president of the Royal Geographical Society–the falls the Romans may have seen.

There were more expeditions and travels to Africa for Samuel and Florence, some in official capacities for different governments, often with military aims. As well, they hunted the Rocky Mountains, the French Alps, Cyprus, India, China, and Japan, coming full circle to Ceylon near the end. On the way, Baker was great good chums with, and traveling companion to Egypt of, Albert Edward, Prince of Wales; yet in spite of his naming that lake after her late consort, Baker never found favor with the head of the House of Hanover–it goes without saying, there was the sketchy business of Valentine, and the always-lingering question about whether Baker's marriage to Florence was ever entirely solemnized. That design for living, his nascent progressivism, coupled to his jingoism, made him an idiosyncratic admixture of Victorian and modern. He died of heart trouble in Devon in 1893, Florence, as whenever he looked up, there; and there, in his mind, new territories, still promised.

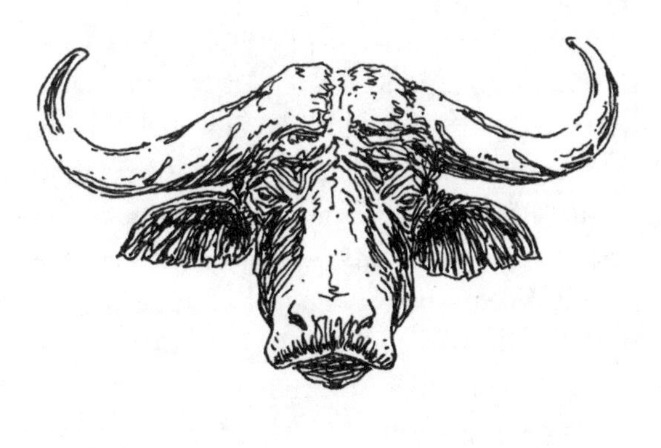

Frederick Courteney Selous came from that British class of nineteenth century masters of their fates, produced by the elite public schools, who were destined to elevate to the officer corps in the Imperial army; and who, as per one writer, kept to the military convention of marrying later in life while focusing earlier on soldiering and big-game hunting. Shooting in England, then concerned most with formal marksmanship and artificial custom–think Bisley and driven Pheasant–lacked the genuine satisfaction of the more physically testing, virile, and fraught hunting of wild big-game and birds across the pink bits of the map. This is the colonial convention that Selous bestrode like a Colossus.

Born a Londoner in 1851 to an old Huguenot family, Selous was the son of the chairman of the London Stock Exchange, still spelling his name Slous. Slous was a noteworthy chess player, Frederick's mother a published poet, twenty-five-years younger than her husband. Attending Rugby, the boy slept in only a nightshirt on the floor, toughening up for the type of wilderness life he foresaw for himself. He played the school's eponymous game, as well as cricket, and the sports of tennis, cycling, and swimming–while skating on the lake in Regent's Park at seventeen, he was one of two hundred plunged into the water when the ice broke beneath them, and one of some hundred sixty to come out alive. And, of course, he rode. His fitness regimen also extended to trekking, marching, and forever hunting.

On the Fourth of September 1871, I set foot for the first time upon the sandy shores of Algoa Bay, with £400 in my pocket, and the weight of only nineteen years upon my shoulders, he wrote in 1881.

Selous judged it would be easier to make a definitive start on safari into the interior, not from the coast but rather from the Diamond Fields inland, where at Kimberley was a hole filled with gems with a city being thrown up around it. He engaged a bullock wagon for him and his three hundred pounds of impedimenta. Travel was only at night to spare the oxen the hot sun–as the animals rested, Selous with an immense amount of hard walking, did a good deal of shooting in a small way, he said, for Klipspringer, Bushbuck, and Mountain reedbuck. The journey required weeks to come to the land of blink klippe–bright stones.

For the next few months, Selous with another mzungu, traded in Griqualand, waiting for the best season to decamp for the veld primeval. At the end of April 1872, his and two friends's ill-equipped safari crossed the Vaal River and trekked towards Kuruman, two hundred miles northwest of Kimberley, where Selous knew they should strike the main wagon track to the interior. In August the safari came to Matabeleland–the same country in which Rory Muil and I hunted far later–and sought out the Ndebele king, Lobengula, the chief of, it was said, a savage and barbarous people, and secured permission to hunt in the king's realm.

Most of the ensuing two decades were taken up in hunting the then-remote, for mzungu, regions from the Transvaal to the basin of the Congo. For Selous, the raison d'être for his hunting was the accumulating of species for museum and private arrays, making consequential scientific discoveries and observations in geography, natural history, and ethnography, while remaining on amiable terms with African natives, such as Lobengula.

From early in his wanderings, Selous began transplanting experience for accepted wisdom. He often heard that all other animals at a waterhole gave way to oncoming Elephant. On a burgeoning-moon November night in 1873, tented near a vlei of fresh rainwater west of the River Gwai in Matabeleland, he saw a large herd of Buffalo come down to drink. Almost as soon as they reached the water, thirty Elephant cows and young began to approach to drink, too, passing close to the fires of Selous's encampment, turning to peer myopically into them as they fanned their ears and walked in straight-legged strides.

At the border of a thin mopane forest, a hundred yards across open ground from the Buffalo, the Elephant, no doubt exceptionally thirsty, respected the distance, until the Buffalo, that may or may not have been aware of their presence, finished drinking. It was only after the Buffalo fed off into the forest on the other side of the vlei that the Elephant came down, lining out like those Songo Bitches to take long drinks by way of their trunks, slaking their thirst.

Selous for the time and place, unlike a latent psychopath such and W. D.–D as in Darth Vader–M. Bell, Karamojo Bell of the thousand tusked Elephant, and more than eight hundred Buffalo kills, shot a rather ordinary hundred or so Elephant and by his own tally some hundred seventy five Buffalo as he went, to feed his entourage.

Selous took up the white man's burden, fighting in savage wars of peace–though in the Second Boer War, which he opposed, his sympathies were with the Boers–did indeed marry late–a canon's daughter more than twenty years younger, who gave him sons–was a guide in the hire of Cecil Rhodes; in his light clothing and putties–attributing his slender deliverances from incensed wild animals to the mobility such garb afforded him–rakishly swept felt hat–when not covering his head with a superannuated cricket cap from his days at Rugby–and Vandyke, cutting the figure upon which such fictional adventurers from Allan Quatermain to Indiana Jones were fashioned; was a friend of, and mentor in all things African to, Theodore Roosevelt.

In World War I, enlisting by a circuitous route at age sixty four, Selous fought against Imperial German Army Major General Paul von Lettow-Vorbeck, the Lion of Africa, to fall in 1917 to the bullets of a sniper–von Lettow-Vorbeck, with rather progressive attitudes toward Black Africans, at least in time of war, apologized, it is said, to the British for Selous's ungentlemanly death–and was buried in what is now the twenty one thousand-mile square Selous Game Reserve in southeastern Tananzia.

Selous decried the potential vanishing in his lifetime of White and Black rhino and Cape buffalo from South Africa, blaming it on the proliferation of firearms purchased from the Diamond Fields by Black Africans. The calamity he saw, as he wrote, was that when these highly specialised and most interesting creatures have completely disappeared from the face of the South African veld, there will be no living species of animal left alive in that country that resembles them in the remotest degree.

Writing in 1908 in his *African Nature Notes and Reminiscences*, though, Selous was much more sanguine about the conclusive extinguishing of the Blaauwbok–Bluebuck–and Quagga. In some curious conservation formulation, while putting upon the Cape colonists the entire blame for the extermination, ongoing from the seventeenth century, of these two species, he found it less distressing, due to the existence of other similar animals such as the Roan antelope for the Bluebuck and the Zebra for the Quagga, than the threat to the Rhino and Buffalo posed by Black Africans with guns.

Most of Selous's reserve is now Nyere National Park, after Tanzania's first president, Julius Nyere; and more than five hundred square miles is slated to be submerged behind a boondoggle dam on the Rufiji River in Stiegler's Gorge–the Swiss engineer, whose forename seems to have gone unrecorded, who in 1907 first surveyed the gorge for its hydropower prospects while dabbling in hunting Elephant, which got him killed–the waters to reach close to where Selous was buried beneath a wild tamarind tree. Verifying that the government contract is mightier than the gun.

Other hunters, other Buffalo, populated parts of Africa other than the south and east.

Dr. Cuthbert Christy, choleric hunter-explorer-naturalist-doctor-bureaucrat and opponent of Africans governing Africans, spent long years hunting the continent's game from a decidedly, by his standards, lofty perch, every beast he killed, he took pains to claim, being required for museum purposes or as food for his camp, or in the case of Elephant, for the sake of the ivory.

Well, when you put it like that…

Dwarf forest buffalo may have meant the most to him. Pondoro Taylor called Christy the foremost authority on the little Forest buffalo of the Congo and across to West Africa, Christy's book, the name escaping him, a mass of information on these Buffalo.

Christy likened the Dwarf forest buffalo, for its ability to escape beneath the densest jungle undergrowth, to the Rat of the forest; but hunting it took infinitely more skill and forest-craft than hunting the black races of Buffalo in bush or grass, and he knew of no hunting, unless perhaps that of Okapi or Elephant, which requires more concentration. Or offered quite as much danger.

It was late May of 1932, after many encounters over several decades with the Dwarf buffalo, a sixty-nine-year-old Christy, looking decades younger and still called a most difficult and irascible man, had his last meeting with one along the Aka River in the Belgian Congo, hunting Elephant as part of a wildlife survey for the colonial authorities. Coming onto the bull Buffalo, Christy fired at sixty yards, launching the animal into a charge. It struck him and gored the femoral artery in his right thigh–again, the sticking place in the human for the horn of the Buffalo–as his native hunters rushed in to kill it.

Christy was carried back to his camp, runners sent to cover fifty miles for medical help. Before they could return, Christy's condition worsened; and he ordered the natives out of his tent. It is said he died in agony, by himself, without the sight of Black people in his presence. The Dwarf buffalo was that first African buffalo head I saw on the wall of my father's hunter friend, imprinting so much on me.

Effectively unrecollected in our time, Paul Belloni Du Chaillu was one of the most celebrated–and most controversial and oppugned–explorers, zoologists, and anthropologists of the nineteenth century. Much about him remains undetermined, including his birthdate and race. The nearest to a concurrence is that he was born in 1831 in the French territory of volcanic Île Bourbon, today Réunion Island, four hundred thirty miles east of Madagascar in the Indian Ocean. He was the unacknowledged son of a French trader, and accused slaver, forced–due to his revolutionary sympathies at the time of the overthrow of Charles X–to clear off the island months before the birth of the child to a mulatto woman, making Du Chaillu in the agonized racial calculus of the period a quadroon, all of which he took pains to obscure, seeing that as in some ways imperative.

His biological father, Paul, returned to Réunion in 1840, leaving for a position as a trader in Gabon some six or seven years later, Paul fils with him. The younger Du Chaillu seems to have been in Paris in 1848 for the révolution de Février, turning against the country of France after the killing of protestors by the municipal guards and the rising opposition of the reactionaries, leaving again for Gabon, where he studied with both American and French missionaries. Arriving in the United States in 1852 with a cargo of ebony and a modest assemblage of preserved birds and animals, which drew the attention of the Academy of Natural Sciences in Philadelphia, and by extension the Main Line, Du Chaillu accepted a position teaching French in a seminary for young women in Carmel, New York–where he had favorites; and with looks with a touch of homuncular charm, and that accent, found favor, too.

The year after his application to become a naturalized U. S. citizen was denied–and would never be granted despite his sincere desire to be an American, his lacking an official birth certificate the presumptive cause–but with no necessity, then, for a passport for travel, he sailed to Gabon once more in 1856, where he spent the next three years in pursuits real or fantastical, depending on who judged.

While most of the country was covered in equatorial forest, there were also savanna and baï, where the Dwarf forest buffalo–called Niaré–came out to feed. Du Chaillu thought these animals beautiful–and they are, with reddish-brown coats, dark-brown forelegs, swept-back scythed polished black horns, black muzzle, large eyes, and outsized white-tasseled ears–seeing in them something more antelopian than bovine. He confessed a great partiality for the Buffalo, their meat in particular. While Selous would write that he never thought it necessary to make his will before attacking a herd of Buffalo, Du Chaillu recounted one cat-whisker escape after another from these dwarves. Among the first Buffalo he hunted–as was the case in many more hunts after, according to him–a bull he shot and wounded, charged. Turning away, Du Chaillu found his foot snared by a tough root with the Buffalo snapping the thick vines in its path as if they were threads. With only a single loaded barrel left in his rifle, Du Chaillu brought the sturdiness of his nerves to that of a rock; and leveling at the animal's head, he held fire to the last second, till the bull was at five yards, his shot turning the Buffalo into a mass of dead flesh, almost touching his feet.

He relished each time he came into country where he might hunt Niaré, and behold ever more wondrous occurrences. Using charcoal, he applied blackface–not in minstrelsy, but because he contended that nothing caught the eye of a wild beast of that country so quickly as a white face; and you wonder if recording that was to deflect questions about his race–and hunted frequently at night under the stars.

Beneath the shelter of an enormous anthill along the walk of the Buffalo, he lay down in the sombre light of the forest, remaining on stand for several hours and negligently going to sleep, not knowing for how long. He snapped awake to an unearthly roar of an animal in terror and torment.

Hurrying through the trees toward the sound, Du Chaillu came to the edge of a baï; and he saw a short way across the opening, scudding across the plain, a bull Niaré with a Leopard crouched on its neck, teeth and talons sunk in. The Buffalo reared and tossed and ran and bellowed trying to rake the cat off on the trunks of trees. Du Chaillu thought it was going to fall; but gathering itself, it made one more frantic rush. As it went by, Du Chaillu fired at the shape of the Leopard without result. The conjoined animals went out of sight, in time the bull's roars ceasing. Anyway, that was his story.

Not shy about embroidering his narratives, Du Chaillu met with the Fang, or Fãn, people to whom for centuries were readily ascribed tales–promulgated by mzungu with ulterior motives–of cannibalism, reciting allegations of their robbing freshly dug graves of rival tribesmen to eat the corpses. He admitted, though, that he retreated when a dead body that was purchased elsewhere was about to be dissected, he in fact not viewing the proceedings. When in 1861, he published his *Explorations & Adventures in Equatorial Africa; with Accounts of the Manners and Customs of the People, and of the Chace of the Gorilla, Crocodile, Leopard, Elephant, Hippopotamus, and Other Animals*, the greatest controversy was aroused.

Du Chaillu's descriptions of the Gorilla, called Nguyla by the estuarial Mpongwe with whom he traveled in Gabon, were echoed seventy years later in the behaviors seen in the Eighth Wonder of the World, *King Kong*. In Du Chaillu's estimate, the two fiercest and strongest beasts of the continent were what he called the Crested lion of Mount Atlas and the Gorilla. Along with charging the Fang with necrophagy, he echoed the luridnesses of male Gorilla getting native women into their clutches and rather than killing them, forcing them to submit to their carnal desires without otherwise injuring them, then permitting them to return to their villages. When at last Du Chaillu met the king of the African forests, the animal filled the woods with a tremendous barking roar resounding like thunder. It stood to confront him, unfazed, with fiercely glaring large deep-gray eyes, immense bodied, huge chested, with muscular arms, beating its breast with its fists, like pounding on a bass drum. It advanced on the humans, and at sixty yards they fired, killing it.

Du Chaillu's high-society supporters adored the stories in *Explorations & Adventures*, which went on to sell an estimated one hundred thousand copies. Authorities like Burchell's nemesis at the British Museum, John Edward Gray, though, attacked those stories vociferously in letters to *The Times* and scientific journals. He criticized Du Chaillu for everything from claiming the discovery of bird species already known to reputable ornithologists, serious acts of plagiarism, and just plain fibbing about Gorilla broadly. Others said he never shot a Gorilla–dead ones and body parts were available in markets on the Gabon coast for him to purchase and claim as his own. Later explorers faulted him for being too generous with his native personnel, inflating the costs of subsequent expeditions.

Du Chaillu sought redemption in a second exploration of Gabon, inviting both the American Consul in the country and the polymathic Captain Richard Burton–another hunter of the source of the Nile–then British Consul on the Spanish colonial island of Fernando Pó in the Bight of Bonny, to come along as impartial observers. They sent their regrets. Further setbacks awaited. Du Chaillu belatedly studied geography and photography in the hope of bolstering any new claims, then lost all his instruments to the sea when trying to come ashore in Fernan Vaz Lagoon on the coast of Gabon. He did travel to unmapped sections of the country, and described the small forest people known as Pygmies. When one of his men accidentally killed two Pygmies in Ashangoland, he and his safari fled, Du Chaillu unable to gather his notes and bring them with him.

His concerns about his mixed race being used to discredit him may not have lacked substance. Jules Verne made an Atlantic crossing with Du Chaillu in 1867, and dismissed him as the only ape he, Du Chaillu, looking into a mirror, was likely to have seen in Gabon. Du Chaillu then transferred his field of study to the Northern Hemisphere, centering on the whitest people there are, Scandinavians. While on a research trip to St. Petersburg in 1903, he suffered a stroke and died in bed.

There were women as well. Florence Baker struck out in the company of Samuel; but others in the day of the great European geographical investigations into the source of the Nile and the bounds of its basin, explored also, absent the aegis of a husband. One was Alexandrine Petronella Francina Tinné who at age ten upon the death of her father, became the wealthiest woman in the Netherlands. In the 1860s as the head of expeditions depicted as being of colossal proportions, she made repeated forays up the White Nile from Khartoum, being turned back by disease and finally by the deaths of two scientists, her governess, her aunt, and her mother, who all accompanied her–she carried the corpse of her mother back with her to Cairo. Whenever she could, she took it upon herself to free any slaves encountered. Intrepidity, though, carried her only so far. In 1869 at thirty-three, between the oasis of Murzuq and the city of Ghat in the Libyan Sahara, en route to Lake Chad, she died by the sword of a Tuareg brigand.

If the never-wed Mary Henrietta Kingsley read Thoreau, she read it as the woman, rather than the man, who goes alone can start today. Her father was a physician to peregrine British aristocrats, a writer and traveler in Spain, Polynesia, Japan, the Antipodes, and North America–among the folklore about him was that he was to ride with Custer at Little Bighorn, but fortuitously had his fate recast by an

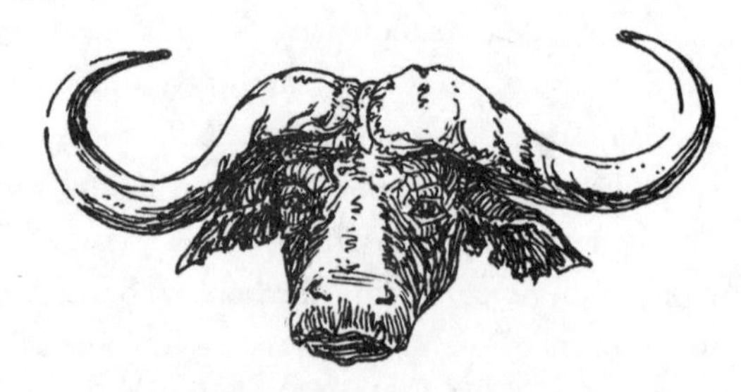

inclemency of weather. Mary, having studied medicine–her father contriving to press-gang her into being an aide in his practice–became not merely a traveler but an explorer, naturalist, and ethnographer, making West Africa her destination, meeting with hardships unlike any her father ever knew.

Born in 1862 four days after her parents's wedding, Kingsley was a spinster, as was the word then, and fundamental outsider, living at home to care for her increasingly infirm mother and father, Mary and George. She was, though, an inveterate adventurer in exotic lands through the printed page. With the deaths of both of George and Mary in 1892, Kingsley came into her share of her father's £8,600 estate, more than a million pounds today. She was free then to explore.

In August of 1893 she came to Sierra Leone to ply her way down to Luanda in Angola. In a stunningly un-British approach to exploration, she learned from the native peoples bushcraft and survival techniques that would stand her in good stead in the jungles, sparking her to travel as Thoreau suggested, except for the presence of her African porters and assistants.

Returning to England in December, she sought and secured support from the British Museum and a book deal for the account of her travels. And the next December, she set off to canoe up the Ogooué–known to her as the Nazareth–in what is now Gabon, her ambition being to collect heretofore unclassified fish specimens, observe Gorilla, and study the culture of putative cannibals.

When she came to Gabon, Europeans roundly considered that cryptic portion of the globe the White Man's Grave; but Kingsley never mislaid her equanimity. She celebratedly recorded in her book, *Travels in West Africa, Congo Français, Corisco and Cameroons,* that when importuned to wear men's clothing, as being better suited to the equator, you have no right to go about Africa in things you would be ashamed to be seen in at home, which meant she dressed at all times in a stiff black skirt and blouse, high buttoned shoes, what's been described as a perky hat, with added accents of a knife and a revolver–which she never drew–and attired like that, summited Mount Cameroon at more than thirteen thousand feet.

Her encounters with Gorilla–the Africans with her sheathed their flintlock long guns in ape hide–were always thrilling; none of the other big game she saw at close quarters, she said, gave her that feeling of horrible disgust that an old Gorilla gives on account of its hideousness of appearance. However, when she feared one of her assistants, Wiki, was about to shoot an enormous silverback, she placed a restraining hand on his wrist; and as was the case most of the time, she returned as she usually did from a sporting adventure, without measurements or the body.

She found many Bush cows, the Forest buffalo Du Chaillu knew as Niaré. One hunt with the Fang–Kingsley sharing Du Chaillu's opinion of their cannibalism–was with trained dogs and nets handwoven from plant fibers, the nets the finest she ever saw. Men and woman and their belled dogs made beats through the bush, driving the game. The animals netted were for the most part beautiful little gazelles–Ncheri, assumably Duiker–though even juvenile Bush cows were caught and were unable to break out. One Leopard, though, took its section of net away with it him, and a good deal of vegetation and sticks to boot.

After a year, Kingsley was back in England, confoundingly taking up housekeeping for her mean and small-minded brother. In 1897 she published her African book which was directly a bestseller–she was resolute in not proclaiming herself the discoverer of any topographic feature, it obvious to her that Africans knew about them all along–and she became a fixture on the lecture circuit. Her health, though, deteriorated rapidly. Yet she set out for South Africa during the Second Boer War to nurse prisoners. And there, in 1900, she died, her body at her behest buried at sea from the deck of a British warship.

Some may think of her real life, the self-reliant one in Africa, as abridged, making for tragedy or melodrama or some political lesson. For some sixteen months of her whole life, though, she found lands where she could ask questions that mattered. As she did of her assistant, Pagan:

> …I ask Pagan whether there are many gorillas, elephants, or bush-cows round here. "Plenty too much," says he…

Osa Martin might be talked about more earnestly, if she did not seem such a stagecrafted creation. She married, as we know, adventure in the form of filmmaker Martin Johnson. They met in vaudeville in Chanute, Kansas, the hometown of Osa–née Leighty. Martin, a born vagabond just returned from a long South Seas voyage with Jack London on the writer's forty-five-foot ketch, *Snark*, was presenting a travelogue with his photos–plenty too much nudity–and artifacts. He hired a girl to perform ersatz Hawai'ian and Polynesian songs and dances. When she became ill, her best friend, Osa, stepped in. Initially put off by Martin's bumptiousness, Osa wed him within a month in 1910 in Independence, Kansas, he twenty five, she sixteen.

By 1917, while filming on Malekula Island in the New Hebrides–the modern island nation of Vanuatu, cataloged today among the happiest in the world–they were detained by the Big Nambas–more reputed cannibals, their name in bêche-de-mer, pidgin Bislama, meaning numbers, for the size of the men's fiber penis sheaths–the couple having to be rescued by a British gunboat. They received a more cordial welcome when they returned to Malekula in 1919, projecting the footage they filmed before, seeing themselves proving irresistibly seductive to the Big Nambas.

Über-explorer, inventor, and the recognized father of modern taxidermy, Carl Akeley met Martin through the august Explorers Club, into which Johnson was inducted in 1921. Seeing Martin's cannibal, sic erat scriptum, films, Akeley encouraged him to go to Africa. That year, the ocean liner carrying Martin, Osa, Martin's retired-jewelry-store-owning widowed father, John, and a Gibbon named Kalowatt, docked at the port of Mombasa.

It took three days for the Johnsonses to clear their eighty-five steamer trunks through the douane and load them onto the train for Nairobi. Traveling overnight, they saw the next day their first Maasai when they were fifty straightline miles from their destination at a stop at Kiu–Kiswahili for thirst, where the Chinese-engineered modern railway now no longer stops. Though she thought the tribespeople interesting, Osa stayed apart, finding them also inexpressibly filthy and swarming with flies. Outside Nairobi, Osa and John located an eight-room bungalow with familiar flowers, to be their home base for their first time in East Africa in 1921 and '22.

In Nairobi seeking out advice, the Johnsons found themselves being counseled by Fellow of the Zoological Society, Member of the British Ornithologists's Union, Chief Game Warden Arthur Blayney Percival–elder brother of Philip who was the professional hunter for Theodore Roosevelt and Ernest Hemingway–not yet fifty but from decades in the African climate looking like kiln-dried hardwood. Arthur tantalized Martin with a yellowed notebook written by a Scot explorer in the early 1800s, telling of a crater lake, ostensibly unmapped, in the north-central region of the colony near the Abyssinian border, surrounded by an undisturbed forest sanctuary for wildlife–then curbed Johnson's enthusiasm by recommending that he, Osa, and John, should ease into expeditioning with a few short safaris before taking on such a serious journey.

For their first hunt, the Johnsons, according to Kelly Enright in *Osa and Martin: For the Love of Adventure*, consulted the Bureau of Native Affairs and Newland & Tarlton–the safari company that one of Theodore Roosevelt's other outfitters and guides, Australian-born Leslie J. Tarlton, co-founded–about camp staff, gunbearers, and head men. They bought two Ford safari cars, one new and one used, both modified to their designs, the second as a film vehicle for all the camera equipment. Neither Johnson had ever learned to drive, but the safari company taught them well enough for them to receive road licenses–though Osa was always a terror at the wheel. They had to forego a white hunter, however, the thousand-dollar monthly fee too dear. And then they struck off for the Athi River, thirty miles out from Nairobi, much farther then than it may sound now, but close enough to the city for emergency evacuation.

To feed the camp, Martin found he had to spend more time shooting game than trying to film it. A complication was that the Muslim Africans ate only halal meat, which meant cutting an animal's throat when there were still arguable signs of life, or at least the pretense of them, something Martin failed to do. Frustrated, the Johnsons started on a day's round trip to Nairobi to purchase meat slaughtered in accordance with the Quran. On the way, Martin thought to get some footage of a herd of, in Enright's book, anonymous Antelope, and asked Osa to fire a warning shot to stir them up. Osa instead aimed dead-on, dropping a big ram with her shot and was furious when Martin thought it must be an accidental kill.

On the third preliminary safari, to the Ithanga Hills, northeast of Nairobi, their head man, Jerramani, led them down a mysterious ravine and onto a sleeping gaggle of Buffalo. Closing to within a hundred feet, Martin began to crank; and the Buffalo awakened, getting to their hooves. Humans's and animals's eyes–the Buffalos's, of course, Martin said, blood-red balls of fire–met. Two hundred years and more of the European lore of the brute Buffalo kicked in; and the Johnsons fled helter-skelter back up the ravine, Jerramani sauntering behind, shaking his head.

Martin was not as much of a hunter–or really a hunter at all–as a tramp royal, who could not use one bed too long, as the saying went, equipped with a portable Akeley Motion Picture Camera; and Osa was in any case the far better shot. Not unaware of her attractiveness in front of the lens–smiling for the camera, you knew she was gonna love it–and at pains to project herself as the dutiful wife who not only cooked and cleaned on safari, but fished, gathered, and hunted, she proved herself with experience a dab hand at woodswomanship in Africa, and sometimes without Martin's being quite aware, the captain rather than the subaltern. She bristled at the chorus, chimed over and over, that wherever she went, it was no trip for a woman; and the male officialdom of exploration did dismiss or ignore her, at least while Martin was alive.

One day, a wandering Dorobo–a derisory term in the Nilotic Maa language for hunter-gatherers who did not keep cattle–taking it for an easy meal, tried to shoot an arrow into Kallowat in the tree where it frolicked. Apprehended, he made amends by leading the Johnsons to a Leopard. Again, Martin wanted Osa to shoot and miss in hope of capturing a charge in the camera; but once more, she hit the animal. Then seeing it was injured, she quickly finished it, causing Martin to lose his temper over missing out on what he was sure would have been boffo footage.

Martin mobilized some of the staff to drive Buffalo toward him. Osa had her rifle, but Martin told her that if the Buffalo charged and got too close, she should use her hysterical scream to turn them away. Instead, as the Buffalo came on, Osa dropped two in front and the herd swung off. When she killed a black-maned Lion, and the staff, gunbearers, and head men all went mad, Martin appeared to bask in Osa's glory. And why not? For as he said, after all, she was his woman.

Before the end of their first African sojourn, they found the lake of legend in the caldera of Mount Marsabit, naming it Paradise. For the next decade and more, the Johnsons, increasingly better financed and equipped, came back again and again to Africa, on one expedition bringing three national-competition-winning Eagle Scouts–assuredly for a merit badge no longer presented. Sensing a sea-change in the tastes of movie audiences, the Johnsons insisted more and more that the animals they killed were taken in defense of life.

Whatever.

By their last African adventures, they added flying to their driving skills and came with personal Sikorsky amphibious planes, in which they traversed the length of the continent, filming from the air, flying later in Borneo, logging more than sixty thousand air miles. Then while on a nationwide lecture and radio tour, they crashed on a commercial flight in bad weather into a mountain above the San Fernando Valley. Martin was killed. Osa had a broken leg and back injuries, but continued the tour from a wheelchair. Within months she was leading an expedition to Africa for Darryl Zanuck for second-unit photography for 1939's *Stanley and Livingstone*. There followed silent lecture films, ghost-written memoirs, children's books and stuffed toys, a line of women's active wear, and early television. Somehow, none of it worked.

Still wed in her heart to another man, she made a bad marriage to her agent who stole from her. Petitioning for an annulment, she drank, drank more. Later, she cohabited with her lawyer, described as a degenerate gambler, still thinking of herself as, literally, the Queen of the Jungle, and Mrs. Johnson. Osa was found in 1953 in her New York City apartment, lying in an empty bathtub where she fell, dead of a heart attack.

In the early 1920s, there were, relates author Françoise Lapeyre, a score of women hunter-writers, either travelers or colonists, keeping busy throughout Africa. Vivienne de Watteville was born to be among them.

Her father Bernard Perceval de Watteville, born von Wattenwyl, was from a noble Swiss family and moved to London to study landscape painting, destroying every canvas he started. He found his serious passions only in fishing and, according to Vivienne, practicing ski turns or hunting Bongo.

He married Florence Emily Beddoes who gave birth to Vivienne in the Shropshire village of Hopesay in 1900, then died at Christmastime in 1909, of cancer, binding father and daughter in mourning. Bernard soon enough, though, put Vivienne in the care of his mother and cousin, Alice; but his imprint upon her was ineffaceable. She felt the inception of a life of adventure when Aunt Alice, as she was called, escorted her into the Hardy Brothers tackleshop at 61 Pall Mall in London to be fitted for her first pair of waders.

Bernard withdrew Vivienne from boarding school in summer to travel with him for a spot of friluftsliv in a far-off forest in Norway where he leased two lakes, a mountain, and an icy trout stream where she bathed each morning. Knowing her distaste for Norwegian food, Bernard kept her fed with wild fish and game. She called him Brovie, brother. He called her Murray, my boy, as he rolled twin cigarettes, handing her one. She later rolled the cigarettes for them both and grew into a long-faced young woman with bobbed hair.

Bernard's birth in Switzerland seemed to exempt him from fighting in the Great War; and in 1914, he went off on his own to Rhodesia to stay for two years. When he learned the country well enough, he organized his own safari. He returned with heads and horns, donated to the Naturhistorisches Museum Bern. Receiving a commission from the same museum for a large collection of animals for planned dioramas, he returned to Africa in 1923, bringing Vivienne.

With a sheaf of permits, they safaried across Kenya, Uganda, and the Belgian Congo for a year and a half without a professional hunter. Vivienne did the skinning and preserving, sometimes by matchlight; Bernard did the shooting–missing everything at the outset, he became proficient through on-the-job training–taking all the Big Five, along with Giraffe and thirty types of Antelope, including a Bongo after seven weeks of hunting in the Aberdare Mountains. With the now-endangered tribe of Pygmies, the Echuya Batwa, there was an unsuccessful hunt for Mountain gorilla in the Virungas. Then there were Lion.

The cats penetrated the thorn bomas around their camps and attacked pack animals–a Leopard ate Vivienne's airedale. A canvas bathtub was, in the mistaken belief it was edible, snatched off by a Lion impelled by intense hunger. Bernard shot nineteen.

The last came on the Congolese shore of Lake Edward on the thirtieth of September, 1924. The officials would not allow the hunting of an Okapi, so another Lion would have to do. While Vivienne remained in her tent, shuddering with spirillum fever–sometimes called Rat-bite–Bernard went out alone to check baits. Finding a Lion on one and wounding it, he chose to follow Hemingway's later dictum of shooting yourself out of the trouble you shoot your way into–as de Watteville did with Buffalo–tracking the Lion into a bed of tall reeds. There, it caught him, knocked him to the ground, but left him.

As the Lion went off, de Watteville stood and fired on it, provoking the Lion to whirl and attack once more. It got him down and tore into his chest with its claws. Somehow, de Watteville got a killing shot into the animal. In its death spasm it clenched his chest, and de Watteville had to pry loose each claw, one by one.

Hours later, Vivienne heard her father's voice as he reached camp, saying, A lion got me. How he made it back is anyone's guess. His leg muscles were torn half out, his arms in shreds, a hand lost. Vivienne closed and patched what she could, administering raw crystals of permanganate. She sent one of the Africans on a futile days's run for the nearest doctor. Her father before the scoriations had time to turn black, died that night and was buried.

One of the species most sought by the Bern museum and not yet collected was the Northern white rhino. For the next two months, Vivienne, to fulfill her father's mission, ably led the safari, taking up her father's rifle and providing for the workers. In Uganda–enrolling in an exclusive fellowship including Thutmose III and, as shall be seen, Theodore Roosevelt–she took the White rhino without her father. It stands in the Bern museum today.

De Watteville wrote of the safari in *Out in the Blue*, enchanting Edith Wharton. Conceding that her experience of Africa was represented by a library lampshade for a mountain tent, a garden for a wilderness, and her Wildebeest stealing down to drink being two astute and arrogant Pekingese, Wharton wished de Watteville to write another book, but one in which nobody wants to kill an animal, and they live happily ever afterward!

De Watteville obliged with *Speak to the Earth: Wanderings and Reflections Among Elephants and Mountains*, the outgrowth of her private dream to go into the wilds unarmed and, in some unforeseen way, to win the friendship of the beasts. And she spent a year around and on Mount Kenya, not firing a shot, though one Lioness, part of a pride of man-eaters well known to the Maasai of the Namanga Hills along the frontier with Tanganyika, was shot by Mohamed, a government askari, as it prowled among the tents one night–a few nights earlier, thinking her terrier, Siki, was barking at Hyena, de Watteville left her tent to frighten them off, and walked within arm's length of the bulking silhouette of a Lion in the dark, holding herself together sufficiently to rush at it with stamping feet and yelling, until it bound away with a snarl.

Climbing one day to the false summit of a mountain with Mohamed, Asani, her camera bearer, and Muthungu, the water carrier, she and the men became lost on the way back to camp. With wholly fictitious confidence, de Watteville said she knew the way and plunged into the forest with wingèd speed as night was coming on. She outpaced the three as she flew down the slope, drawing out of earshot of them. Noticing a good deal of Buffalo spoor, she halted, waiting for the men, and especially Mohamed's rifle, to catch up. It was then that a djinn spoke to her imagination, asking what she would choose to be for the next seven minutes.

Oh, please, she said joyously, a Bongo!

And she sprang away into the thick foliage, leaping fallen trees, doubling through tunnels of green stuff, her horns laid along her striped and chestnut flanks, the men now her pursuers, a maze of paths through the jungle revealed to her. At last she came out above deserted Maasai huts–framed like lobster pots–that were a landmark. With the men reaching her, they all reached camp in the cataclysmic African sundown.

For two months she lived with a gramophone and Beethoven in the idyll of pure nature in a hut on Mount Kenya, even planning to build a house of her own at its foot–until a wildfire showed the other face of nature to her and drove her away. Unlike an Edith Wharton, de Watteville recognized there is nothing sentimental in nature, in which the mate or the cubs of the dead Lioness would return to eat her écorché carcass, as per course.

In spite of her promises, intentions, and dreams, de Watteville could not mask the sheer carnality of her human nature, as when she took the hide from the Lioness:

> The lioness was in poor condition, but I took her skin. As I sat under the shade of a thorn tree with Mwanguno [a WaKamba with filed teeth] and Asani, the skin spread between us, and I heard again the ring of the knives on the whetstones and the boys' droning talk, I felt anew (in spite of all my theories) the thrill of the taxidermist in handling the beautiful, supple skin, and the joy of working on the delicate tissues: cutting with the blade of a small penknife to divide the skin between the eyelids, the outer and inner lips, paring away the cartilage inside the nose, and turning the ear.

With an everlasting itch for things remote, from Africa she moved to a gîte on Port-Cros in the Îles d'Hyères east of Toulon in the Mediterranean, the population today twenty. There she confronted her demon of the freedom-complex and married a soldier-diplomat, Captain George Gerard Goschen, moving back to Shropshire to raise effectively on her own two children–one named for Kenya's Tana River.

She may have always thought that the beasts saw her–as Hemingway was sure they did not see him–and concluded that she was some extraordinary kind of animal with no real motive at all, as is the way of the mzungu. At fifty-seven, looking back on a life and seeing its satisfactions, Vivienne died, not unhappily, of cancer, as had her mother.

Vivienne's Northern white rhino, in the diorama in the Naturhistorisches Museum Bern, is paired in front of a Southern white rhino from another expedition. Both animals no longer have their natural horns but wooden cutouts. According to the head curator of the Department of Vertebrates, when I contacted him, the real ones were removed some years ago due to a wave of thefts and raids on museums and collections from England to Austria by organized gangs who sold them to Asia. Lapeyre, often spotty with her facts, may have gotten one thing correct when she wrote that the corridors of such dioramas still offer the visitor a magical stroll, yet are threatened by the risk that museography will someday retire them to the museum of museums.

Coming to Vivienne de Watteville's aid in planning her Mount Kenya expedition was Denys Finch Hatton. Saying his name summons that of Karen Christenze

Dinesen, later the Baroness Karen Christenze von Blixen-Finecke, known by the nom de plume Isak Dinesen and Tania or Tanne among her set on the margin of the most sybaritic and wicked expat colony in history, Happy Valley. And then there was Peter Beard.

Finch Hatton was the first of the three to reach East Africa. Another P. H. who earned legend status, Frank Maurice Bunny Allen, who began hunting in Kenya in 1927 at age twenty-one, and went on until hunting was closed in the country in 1977, dying at ninety-five, said Finch Hatton was one of the first great white hunters–leading a commentator to riposte, but surely he was thinking of Finch Hatton's reputation and not his achievement. Finch Hatton would also likely be the last white hunter portrayed, in a favorable light, by a bankable Hollywood film star–that list of actors including Harry Carey, Gregory Peck, Stewart Granger, Clark Gable, and finally Robert Redford. As John Wayne was, at least by the historical record, nothing like Temüjin, Redford was as far as one might get from Finch Hatton: too old, even if he didn't look it; shorter; a nominal juvenile delinquent instead of the third son of an earl; his alma maters Van Nuys High and the University of Colorado where he bobbled a baseball scholarship by getting drunk, Finch Hatton an alumnus of Eton and Oxford, where they didn't care what, or how much, you drank; Redford with a full head of luxuriant hair, Finch Hatton's Somali moniker around Blixen's farmworkers, Bedar, the Bald One; and one might presume, Redford not being gay.

In the movie, *Out of Africa*, the affair between Finch Hatton and Karen Blixen was scuttled by Finch Hatton's taking up with a thinly veiled Beryl Markham, libidinous daughter of British settlers in Kenya, horse trainer, flyer, and the claimed solitary author of the memoir, *West with the Night*, over fifteen years younger than Blixen. In 1986, Markham identified Finch Hatton to her biographer, as homosexual–or technically bisexual. Finch Hatton's closest attachment was not to any woman other than Blixen, but to Reginald Berkeley Cole–played in the film by Michael Kitchen–whom his relatives in England knew to be Uranian and who came to Kenya after the Second Boer War and founded in Nairobi the white-settlers's Muthaiga Club, where he knocked back a chilled bottle of champagne every morning at eleven a.m., dying of heart failure at forty-two. According to Linda Donelson, author of "Karen Blixen: The Quintessential Dane," the rupture between Blixen and Finch Hatton, was brought about because of a Viking sense of loyalty.

Finch Hatton, in Africa from at least 1911, did not take up professional hunting until 1925 when he was thirty-eight. That is also the year of Cole's premature death, and when Finch Hatton moved into the newly divorced Karen Blixen's home,

Mbogani. By 1931, he'd flown his de Havilland Gypsy Moth biplane into the ground after taking off from the airstrip in the southwestern Kenyan town of Voi at the edge of the Taru Desert, killing him and Kamau, his Kikuyu servant.

Earlier, in 1928, the Prince of Wales was coming out on safari with him, and Finch Hatton was distraught. It wasn't the hunting but the organizing, accommodating, and tolerating of what would approximate a military campaign with a future monarch surrounded by a cavalcade of retainers, colonial nawabs, and spouses. Finch Hatton concluded that he should select as his aide-de-camp, for his bonhomie as much as for his hunting instincts and talents, the husband Karen divorced, Bror von Blixen-Finecke, who was also Karen's distant cousin. For Karen, this was an unpardonable betrayal.

Bror would not only be bringing a new Baroness Blixen-Finecke on the safari, but Karen would be precluded from joining it. According to Donelson, in the Viking tradition to which she saw Karen Blixen adhering, a person stood with his family to the death. With Bror and her, now joined as enemies, she could not understand one of her new family, Finch Hatton, so callously inviting Bror. She made a scene.

Finch Hatton, always a favorite in his birth family and unaccustomed to complaint, was unsympathetic, even asking Bror again to be with him on a second princely safari two years after the first, then refusing to loan Karen the money he promised to help her stay on the farm in Africa, at the foot of the Ngong Hills, and taking back the ring he gave her.

If it needs retelling, there was in Denmark Karen's unrequited desire for Bror's twin brother, Hans, Swedish military officer and Olympics bronze-medal equestrian, the first of her beloveds to crash, in 1917, in a plane from the sky. Before Hans's death was her and Bror's immigration to Kenya in 1913 to become coffee growers, their marriage in Mombasa, and her contracting syphilis from him while ministering to the ailments of her Africans. Ultimately unsuccessful as farmers, they later gained fame in other endeavors, Bror as a hunter, Karen, of course, as a writer of Romantic tales. She was introduced to Finch Hatton at the Muthaiga Club in 1918, but they would not be recognized as a couple for another seven years.

There is something about safari life that makes you pack up all your fears and woes, and as Dinesen wrote, to feel as if you had drunk half a bottle of champagne—bubbling over with heartfelt gratitude for being alive.

By safari, she did not mean, at least not for some time, going out to watch wild animals. It meant for her, hunting and killing them.

But my old friend Uncle Charles Bulpett had told me, she wrote, the person who can delight in a sweet tune without wanting to learn it, in a beautiful woman without wanting to possess her, or in a magnificent head of game without wanting to shoot it, has not got a human heart.

When Karen came to Africa, she could not live without getting a fine specimen of each single kind of African game.

She did grow punctilious about shooting except for obtaining meat for her Natives, thinking of all hunting for any other purpose an unreasonable thing, indeed in itself ugly and vulgar, especially when the quarry was Elephant or Buffalo, which she believed lived a hundred or fifty years, respectively. Lion, though, remained irresistible until nearly the day she went out of Africa.

A Lion on the plain bears a greater likeness to ancient monumental stone lions than to the Lion which today you see in a zoo; the sight of him goes straight to the heart, she wrote. Alighieri cannot have been more deeply amazed and moved by the first sight of Beatrice in a street in Florence.

Sure.

For Blixen a Lion hunt each single time is an affair of perfect harmony, of deep burning, mutual desire and reverence between two truthful and undaunted creatures, on the same wave-length.

I, apart from Blixen, can say, though, that for most who have done it, Lion hunting may be the first hunting they cease to pursue if they come back to Africa, and not due to reasons of danger or fear.

Flying over Africa with Finch Hatton was the most transporting pleasure of Blixen's life on the farm. Even short flights with him were like the Prophet's soaring through the Seven Heavens with the Archangel Gabriel. One day, Finch Hatton carried her off from the farm where she was hosting a tea party for Lady Delamere, an early British East Africa settler, to see the Buffalo feeding.

> Upon one of the long rounded green ridges which run, like folds of a cloth gathered together at each peak, down the side of the Ngong mountain, a herd of twenty-seven Buffalo were grazing. First we saw them a long way below us, like mice moving gently on a floor, but we dived down, circling over and along their ridge, a hundred and fifty feet above them and well within shooting distance; we counted them as they peacefully blended and separated. There was one very old big black bull in the herd, one or two younger bulls, and a number of calves. The open stretch of sward upon which they walked was closed in by bush; had a stranger approached on the ground they would have heard or scented him at once, but they were not prepared for advance from the air. We had to keep moving above them all the time. They heard the noise of our machine and stopped grazing, but they did not seem to have it in them to look up. In the end they realized that something very strange was about; the old bull first walked out in front of the herd, raising his hundredweight horns, braving the unseen enemy, his four feet planted

> on the ground, suddenly he began to trot down the ridge and after a moment he broke into a canter. The whole clan now followed him, stampeding headlong down, and as they switched and plunged into the bush, dust and loose stones rose in their wake. In the thicket they stopped and kept close together, it looked as if a small glade in the hill had been paved with dark grey stones. Here they believed themselves to be covered to the view, and so they were to anything moving along the ground, but they could not hide themselves from the eyes of the bird of the air. We flew up and away. It was like having been taken into the heart of the Ngong Hills by a secret unknown road.

She then had to go out of Africa.

She returned to her family in Denmark and remained. Her writing led to her repeated nomination as a Nobel laureate in literature, as she subsisted on oysters, grapes, royal jelly, dry biscuits, pillowy clouds of tobacco smoke, and harsh laxatives until her living profile came to look acutely like that of the mummy of Rameses II. Nearing an emaciated death, she blamed the lingering effects of Bror's syphilis and the corrosive effect of the medicines used, in fact, to cure her. Others assumed anorexia nervosa. The real cause: complications from ulcer surgery.

The last thing left in nature is the beauty of women, so I'm very happy photographing it, Peter Beard told the British newspaper *The Observer* in 1997. It was he who in his book, *The End of the Game,* paired his stark photographic profile of Karen Blixen, in her seventies, with the mummified one of the nineteenth dynasty pharaoh. Yet he never found her anything but beautiful.

The story of Beard–a once-young, forever strange, intense, patrician, kinetic ex-pat American adventurer, naturalist, photographer–began in New York City in 1938. He came from old money on both sides of his family, yet never had quite enough to keep him in the style he preferred. In private grade school, Beard won his first arts prize for his photo of his dog jumping up for a ruffed grouse perched on a windowsill. He was hypnotized by wild lands and wildlife from before he could remember, collecting antlers and mounted heads obsessively. His schoolboy friends included Michael Rockefeller, son of New York Governor and future U. S. Vice President Nelson, likely eaten by headhunters during an expedition to New Guinea in 1961. At about that time the mythology of Peter Beard in Africa commenced.

It's best to step back a little to when he first set foot on the continent. At seventeen in 1955, with the great-grandson of Charles Darwin, he went to South Africa, Zululand, Bechuanaland, Portuguese East Africa, Madagascar, and Kenya to photograph wildlife with a Voigtländer camera. Beard reportedly said that during that trip he realized that America was not where he should have been born. Nonetheless he entered Yale and studied pre-med before switching to art history. At the end of his junior year he sailed for Kenya with a copy of *Out of Africa*, which exposed him to a world, principally vanished, of which he very much wanted to be a part. For the book and its author he could hold no greater reverence.

I am unsure of the sequence, but he did go to extraordinary lengths to arrange an audience with Blixen in Copenhagen. He would come to call her an unseen support for him, tirelessly stirring in him the need for his photographing Africa, the old white Africa being reduced to a residue, and the traditional Black Africa beginning to be supplanted by men wearing watches. Then he went on to Kenya and entered legend.

In 1961, Beard got to meet the original cast from the time–Blixen's–that he saw as a golden age in East Africa: Philip Percival, J. A. Hunter, Ewart Cape-to-Cairo Grogan. It would be actually hard to name anyone of notoriety, in Africa or elsewhere from the 1960s onward, whom Beard did not know. Along with assorted Roosevelts, Kennedys, du Ponts, and Mellons–in his exhaustive book, *African Hunter*, James Mellon thanked his old friend and companion in Africa for the many photos Beard gave him–there were the Rolling Stones and Fleetwood Mac; the artists Andy Warhol, Francis Bacon, and Salvador Dalí–who thought Beard was, somehow, his dead brother, the painter's shadowy, ghostly Ben Day-dot portrait, *Portrait of My Dead Brother* from 1963, bearing some resemblance to Beard–the Beales of *Grey Gardens*, supermodels including one of his serial wives, and writers like Truman Capote, William Burroughs, and Terry Southern.

In Nairobi, Beard lodged in the New Stanley Hotel where he came down to breakfast with, when they were in town, professional hunters such as John Sutton, Glen Cottar, and John Fletcher. Beard soon met Dougie Collins, a P. H. with a touch of the rogue and a former district commissioner in Somaliland. He helped Beard buy a rattletrap secondhand Land Rover and an old 9.3 Husqvarna from an Elephant-control officer who perched at the Long Bar in the New Stanley and just happened to have a medium caliber for sale. Collins and Beard headed into, then, the remote Northern Frontier District to explore every square mile; and en route, not far north of Nairobi at Ol Donyo Sabuk–the Mountain of Buffalo–Beard hunted his first big-game animal in Africa: a Hippo cow he shot for two-tons of meat for the safari and nearby villagers. Today, the spot is marked by apartment complexes.

Beard was not after trophies, though he would take a Leopard with a 375 whose broken stock was bound in rope. He and Collins hunted for food, or just to hunt. Out of meat, Beard made a snap shot at an Impala and only wounded it. As he chased it to finish it off, he put his foot into a Warthog hole and broke his ankle. As he lay on the ground, the Impala fell dead; and two young Turkana boys suddenly materialized. Instead of coming to his assistance, they set to eating the raw kidneys out of the Antelope.

After three months, Collins pushed on to return to Somaliland while Beard found a job doing game-control on a cattle ranch in Laikipia, hunting Zebra, Lion, and Buffalo. On one Buffalo cull with dogs, he with his 9.3 and his partner Bryan Colman with a 577, both ended up slammed to the ground by wounded animals, a dazed Colman, lying on his back, getting off a lifesaving shot into the heart of a charging cow.

Beard began to work and photograph in Tsavo National Park, and to see the certain end of the game. Eventually he documented the annihilation through starvation of up to thirty five thousand Elephant that overpopulated and overgrazed the parkland, as the government did nothing to curtail the apocalypse. His aerial photos of silent Elephant bones scattered across the ruined habitat are perhaps the most impassively telling conservation messages in the later twentieth century. He had been moving to the conclusion for some time; but this is what confirmed him in his bleak opinion, that on earth, humans were the main disease.

In Africa, Beard the artist had ready access to his favorite medium: blood... better than any ink or paint, he said.

From boyhood he kept the most fantastic and detailed diaries and journals–a habit his mother instilled in all of her sons–filled with photos, clippings, shells, animal parts, marginalia, and memories and observations put down in a cramped longhand in India ink, fresh blood slathered on many of the pages and left to dry. When an old mill on his New York property–purchased when the owners, Arthur Miller and Marilyn Monroe, put it on the market–burned in 1977, the fire consumed all the early journals he began at age eight. He started over.

In the mid-1960s, with Alistair Graham, a zoologist contracted by the Kenyan government, Beard spent a year on the fly-blown shore of isolated Lake Turkana, surveying Africa's largest remaining Nile crocodile population. Caking themselves in mud, the two floated out on inner tubes to the Crocs–when hunting at night, they targeted the eyeshine they detected in their flashlight beams. Overall, they shot, skinned, and necropsied just shy of five hundred in the year, living off the lake's two hundred-pound Nile perch that were either speared or killed with a 357 Magnum pistol.

Also in the mid-1960s Beard acquired forty-five acres of raw bushland near Karen Blixen's old farm, calling it Warthog Ranch for all the *Phacochoerus africani* living in and around it. When he was in Kenya, Beard sat beside the fire at night, woke up under canvas in the morning, and worked on his journals through the day. And there was the sex.

It was also at Hog Ranch in 1968 that Beard apprehended a poacher, a worker on a neighboring ranch, caught with a snared Suni. Beard told him to lead him to all his other snares; and when the poacher denied there were any more, Beard struck him with his fist, ineffectually he said, then bound him to a fencepost with his own snare wire, stuffing a leather glove in his mouth as a gag and telling him he could stay there till his memory improved. Then Beard went to town to lunch. When it began to rain, one of Beard's employees released the poacher.

Eighteen months later, the police appeared and arrested Beard on charges of assault and wrongful confinement. Found guilty–the verdict possibly influenced by Beard's imperial sentiments, or his having gone to lunch while the poacher remained tied to the fence–he was sentenced to Kamiti Prison for nine months and twelve strokes to his bare buttocks with a rattan cane. Ten days later, under international pressure, Beard was released, unlashed, his conviction set aside. At that point, having had to live for spells on Zebra meat in the N. F. D., his teeth turned brown from drinking the alkaline water from Lake Turkana, and his head shaved in Kamiti where some prisoners refused to eat or drink in order to avoid having to venture into the execrable toilet facilities, he was ready, for a time, to go out of Africa, himself.

In the U. S., where he was now in great demand as a fashion photographer, Beard's life entered a long chapter of Twenty Four Hour Party People. Already precarious marriages crumbled under the weight of nearly endless model-perfect other women, more than a few genuinely famous models. At Manhattan's Studio 54, waterhole and wildlife took on meanings entirely different from what they had in Africa. He could stay on the track of recreation as long and hard as he tracked Buffalo through wait-a-bit bush. The stories, so many, do not lack for phantasmagoria. Everybody seems to have another, ever more outlandish one to tell or to be Googled. Even the polite ones take a Beardian turn.

Terry McDonell, my erstwhile editor at *Sports Afield*, remembered a Beard, with whom he worked when he was editing *Esquire*, who was kind as well as charming, and very generous when flush. Beard's house—the one he bought from the Millers—was the last at the tip of the peninsula in Montauk, New York, the end of America, the open Atlantic a surrogate for savanna; and McDonell visited him there once with his two sons when the boys were attending Buckley on the Upper East Side, where Beard had been that prize-winning student. Beard was basking rather like a large ectotherm on a wide flat rock when they came upon him.

He was very cordial, Terry said, and advised his sons to quit school before they were ruined. The boys were nine and seven.

In between exhibiting his works, on assignment for magazines, discovering the world-famous model–destined to be David Bowie's widow–Iman–his saying she was herding goats at the time when she was in fact, walking quietly down a street in

Nairobi when this unsettling mzungu in a sarong started stalking her—locating new drugs to ingest, he knew he had to return faithfully to Kenya, even as the curtain descended on what he longed for.

Going back, Beard was increasingly anguished by what he saw as the summation–development, the decline in wildlife, crowds–yet still finding the wild and beautiful, if in only the most meager remnants of what he once knew. Not all of Africa welcomed him, though; and some inhabitants found their own ways of lodging complaints.

In 1996, a herd of Elephant cows and calves was crossing out of Tanzania into Kenya to raid shambas for cabbages. The villagers who grew the cabbages chased the Elephant off their food plots, often with gunshots. They say Elephant never forget, and they, like the Irish, certainly never forget a grudge.

Beard was helping a friend open a safari camp, taking photos, when the herd, fifteen strong, came over a hill and sighted them. The lead cow made what seemed a pro-forma bluff charge. Beard and the others, all unarmed, ran a short way and stopped. The cow retreated, then charged again, this time for real. Everybody ran, scattering; and Beard realized the Elephant was singling him out, and that it was faster than he. After a quarter mile, Beard tried to take cover behind an anthill; but the cow just trampled over it, and Beard grabbed one of its legs and hung on. They danced that way until the Elephant threw him off. It then drove a tusk through his left thigh, leaving a hole large enough to put a hand into.

The cow tossed him against the anthill, then brought its head down onto him, Beard's feeling like he'd been hit by a fallen elevator. The rest of the herd came up and snorted and sniffed around him–it was actually almost worth it, he said, for the experience–but otherwise let him lie until the hunting car drove in and sent them off. His pelvis and ribs were fractured, he was bleeding from his thigh and internally, the sheer impact of the attack shocked the optic nerve so he was temporarily sightless, and he was four hours by road from a hospital. When they brought him in, he had no detectable pulse. After being stabilized, he was air-evacuated to a New York City hospital where he was operated on for ten hours to put in place seven titanium plates and twenty-eight screws to reconstruct his pelvis.

Later, Beard would say about it, I just felt like an idiot.

Truthfully, you have to suspect it may have been one of the capstones of his life.

I first heard the name Peter Beard from John Fletcher in Kenya in 1974, somewhere in achingly green Block 60, when I didn't know I was at the end of the end.

Sitting in the dining tent before dawn, John told me I ought to read his friend's book. Then I would understand where the country and its wildlife were heading. Back in Nairobi, I looked for a copy of *The End of the Game* in bookstores, but found only Beard's, at the time, newest book, *Eyelids of Morning*, about the Crocodile survey, his photographs accompanying Alistair Graham's words.

Beard's *Eyelids* photographs were gleefully erotic, outrageous, and grotesque, yet with something quaking about them–one of a Crocodile is now crossing interstellar space on the N. A. S. A. *Voyager* probe. They also reflected Graham's harsh textual view of sentimental conservationists who fondled a fantasy of communion with a baffling nature.

When I finally found a copy of *The End of the Game*, I thought it must be the most poignant, saddest book I ever read. If you read it, you will understand.

In 1900 there were one million three hundred fifty two thousand Kenyans, six people per square mile, the population density today of Wyoming. When Beard first saw the country in 1955, it was a still practicable, for land and animal, thirty-one per square mile, totaling almost seven million. Sixty-five years later, the main disease numbered nearly fifty four million, two hundred forty people per square mile, growing by two each minute. In 1977, Kenya outlawed safari hunting–and of late, bird hunting, as well. Since then, wildlife has fallen 70 percent, with many big-game species, once abundant in the country, racing toward extinction. Peter Beard could have told you, as far back as *The End of the Game*, that this would be the case.

It's not pleasant to consider humans a pathogen, and Africans undoubtedly don't think of themselves as such on their continent. It's not, though, about what Peter Beard may have believed, and to a certain extent did. What matters was what he saw, and recorded for us to see, before it ended. Virtually nothing he cherished about Africa was correct; but it was genuine, unlike what is fed to tour groups or the viewers of wildlife documentaries.

Karen Blixen said that hunting is ever a love-affair; only, in general, the infatuation will be somewhat one-sided. In a letter to a friend, Beard wrote, of the woman he idolized, that her writing tells us that nature is the most important thing in our lives, and the closer people and animals are related, the more meaningful, genuine, authentic, relaxing, and life-enhancing it will all be. Perhaps he was conceding that after all we can rise, if merely accretively, above the status of viruses.

Beard, it must be said, was, like so many mzungu before him, an unblushing product of privilege. He wrote, I came to Africa because I wanted to break free, to set sail. I came for fun, to fulfill my dreams, to learn something new from something old.

In March of 2020, suffering from dementia at eighty-two, Beard, as mzungus do, wandered off from his house in Montauk into the woods. A massive search was launched and eventually suspended. For weeks many wanted to believe that this was some ultimate prank of Beard's. Others hoped his body would never be found, unrecoverd like the bodies of so many other adventurers and explorers. After nineteen days it was discovered, appropriately, by a hunter.

Peter Beard understood that the love of nature, like Karen Dinesen's desire for her cousin Hans, may only be unrequited. We can merely bow to the natural world and acknowledge that it is not moved in anywise by us, and that the love is forever one way. It was nature, the wild, without affection or malice, that at last killed Peter

Beard as he lay in the forest. Probably, in some briefly well-lighted frame of his flickering mind, he would have had it no other way.

At the turn of the millennium, the tall young woman, exhaling tobacco smoke, looked over the red embers of the fire into the night beyond.

Don't, she said softly, drawing on her cigarette, the flaring glow irradiating her face as if caught in some far-off nuclear flash. Move.

I sat in a low-slung canvas folding chair on the far side of the fire. Days earlier in Victoria Falls, Mosiatunya, The Smoke That Thunders, I saw what one aspect of Africa had come to in fifteen years. The Vic Falls of old Africa was hot tin roofs, stunned yellow-blue-green *Platysaurus* lizards appliquéd to whitewashed walls, one very colonial hotel in which to take a sundowner of an afternoon, and Africans in shiny black pants and tire-tread sandals squabbling in broken English over who was to handle the bags out to the dented Land Cruiser. It was the point of arrival for ruddy safari clients and Katherine Hepburn doppelgängers underneath Tilley hats, carrying dog-eared field guides to the birds of Southern Africa.

The new airport's decor was pastel, arcade ceilings and indirect lighting; earthtone knits and silk shirts replacing black pants and line-dried white cotton shirts. Basket-weave faux Gucci loafers supplanted honest sandals. The English was decidedly unbroken, as was the French, Italian, and Japanese being spoken into cell phones held in front of chins. There was a saying once about Africans, now used roundly, that white men had all the watches, but they had all the time. Now they had all the watches, too, on every wrist tributes to Rolex, if not quite the bona fide article. Mercedes vans idled in the white zone–For The Immediate Loading And Unloading Of Passengers Only–waiting to collect their khaki-clad, adventure-traveling charges come to Game Drive, Whitewater, Balloon, Honeymoon, all capitalized verbs, on three- to five-day excursions. Cooling my heels for forty-five minutes in the airport in another of many Augusts in Africa, witness to the mindless celerity of time, I searched for a bush pilot to effect my escape from the intolerable that was the new Africa.

The tented camp was in a grove of shady winter thorns along the river where tasseled phragmites reeds grew. In the canvas chair, a tall beaded glass of gin and tonic in one hand, hearing Hippos in the Lower Zambezi making throat-clearing noises and the distant roaring of Lions from across the water, I thought how this was still the best part of the Africa I knew, the old, human-animal-paced Africa, where what mattered was not how many Leopards you saw in how many days, the number of rivers you ran, or miles you trekked, but the Africa that didn't have to produce any adventures at all, which from the lookout of Vic Falls appeared to be the part being x-ed out, turning the Dark Continent into every other place where tourists went for prompt, if not instant, gratification. The thing of it was, you didn't have to look, for Africa to happen. It would happen on its own, in its own time. In Africa, even this new one, words still had material meaning. Run meant that. As did Don't. Move.

I did not move, only watched the woman's eyes watching over my right shoulder. She and her husband managed the camp. On approach in the bush plane, we waited for Cape buffalo to clear the dirt landing strip before touching down. A few days earlier, a herd of a hundred fifty Elephant shambled among the tents, upsetting not a single object in the camp. In my case, earlier in the day as I was on the river, casting for Tigerfish, a tusked Elephant in the reeds took to balling up clots of mud with its trunk and flinging them at me. Elephants and me.

Wuzzit? I wanted to croak at the woman now. She was tilting her head to get a better vantage.

Crunching came from behind. Turning my head with incremental purposefulness, I looked over my shoulder at the gathering black figure fifteen feet away. The Buffalo bull fed on the seed pods fallen from the winter thorns, working its way into the firelight. The woman went on smoking; and I cursed myself for being sunk into the chair, as composed for flight as a stupefied aardvark supine in the depths of a Karoo borehole.

When the bull came fully into the light, it lifted its head and fixed us with one huge round white-rimmed eye, causing the planet to grind to a standstill on its axis. Then it dropped its head and went on moving and feeding until the darkness subsumed it, and the earth began its rotating again.

That was interesting, I said, letting out my breath.

Funny thing about them at night, the camp manager said placidly, taking another drag and breathing it out through her nose. If this were the day, we'd be quite dead now.

I manipulated myself out of the canvas chair, drank down the gin and tonic, and set the empty glass with the ice in the bottom on the table beside the chair. I picked up my torch, as the British call it, and walked to my tent in silence, not switching the light on.

CHAPTER THIRTEEN

"Gentlemen . . ."

AS I WALKED from the fire ring to my wooden-floored tent, the Lion on the Zimbabwe side were more distant than their sound. When I saw the canvas roofline against the black mercury of the river, I could see also, bedding on the grass in front of the tent's entrance, a small herd of bachelor-bull Buffalo. I stopped. In my hand I had only the unilluminated flashlight.

For some minutes, I just breathed. The Buffalo made no sounds, some of them sleeping, others with their horned heads up. I stepped back without turning, feeling the ground underfoot, not daring to trip. I scribed a large circle around the tent and the Buffalo that were turned upstream, into the wind. I came to the flap on the back of the tent, boosted onto the wooden platform, and went in.

Crossing the tent without lighting the lantern, I looked through the net flap and over the levee of kohl Buffalo to see the rain fall and the lightning transpierce the ground across the Zambezi, hearing the Lion mingled with thunder. I undressed and drew back the thick blanket on the camp bed. I lay down as the roaring of the storm, and the Buffalo's silence, went on. When I awoke at first light the clouds had rolled back; and it was quiet except for bird song and the cold drip of water onto the fallen leaves, the Lion done hunting, the Buffalo gone off.

His preferred honorific was Colonel, and the Colonel found the Kamiti a queer little stream coming out of the north on its way to the Nairobi. For most of its course it flowed through a nearly impenetrable swamp of twenty-foot papyri, and along its edge he, always the ornithologist, watched the male Wydah hovering, black-pennant tails flagging the female, and listened to the trilled honking of the then-populous Gray-crowned cranes. Within the swamp lived a herd of a hundred Cape buffalo, veiled from view.

Since arriving in the British East African Protectorate, the same year slavery and witchcraft were outlawed there, he came to know the Buffalo as near-intertidal animals with tremendous strength to let them push through water and mire that reached to a man's hip. The old bulls here were sparsely coated in black hair spackled in mud, their massive horns rising into great bosses at the bases, meeting with the years to cover the forehead in a frontlet of horn. Their weapons, besides horn and hooves and muscle, were secreting and obduracy.

If Buffalo did not seem as prone to charge as Elephant, they were more dangerous when they did, the Colonel said–Rory Muil in Zimbabwe stopped Elephant charges by shooting a relatively harmless 458 hole through a flared ear, which delivered the message. And as formidable and swift as a rushing Lion was, it was also easier to stop or turn than a Buffalo, leading many hunters to esteem the latter as the most deadly of African game. The Colonel believed that where less problematic prey, such as Zebra, was plentiful, not even Lion would meddle with Buffalo. And though Buffalo are never temerarious, they are fast learners: Where persecuted, they do not stand their ground in the open but retreat deep within the most shadowy tangles of cover and nightfall, prickly circumstances for any predator, hominin or Lion.

At dawn, having made camp along the Kamiti the day before, his son, their pair of professional hunters, and he, with a local Boer farmer and three strong, large dogs, headed out for the buffalo ground. He and his son carried their heavy double rifles, while the lead professional hunter had a 577, and the other two, magazine rifles. Within two miles of walking they sighted Buffalo at the edge of the papyri.

There were four bulls, white-handkerchief Cattle egrets roosting along their spines. In the morning light the bulls's bodies glistened, their upswept horns silver. Holding to the line of the tall sedges, the hunters stalked to within a hundred fifty yards before the Buffalo saw them, lowering their heads.

The biggest bull stood out from the other three. The Colonel had the right of first blood. Leveling his double, he struck the bull on its tough hide and through the lungs. They expected the Buffalo to gallop back into the swamp after that, but instead in a piece of huge good luck, he wrote, they turned out in front of the hunters into the open plains. Now his son shot a second bull, and the Colonel fired into a third.

At this point firing became general; and the bulls ran until the first, which had, most importantly, no other bullet than the Colonel's in it, fell. The three remaining Buffalo grouped around the carcass; and the hunters went at them, anticipating a charge. With many yards still between them, the Buffalo turned back toward the swamp.

Because the distance was long, the Colonel exchanged the double for his Winchester 405 lever, and leading one of the bulls, tumbled it onto its back, hoofed legs kicking. In a moment, though, the bull regained its feet and followed the other two, all wounded, as the hunters ran at an angle to them.

Two of the Buffalo lay down in the tall grass at the fringe of the swamp, while the third, the one that had fallen and gotten back up, faced the hunters and came for them. The Colonel had gone back to his heavy rifle and took the bull before it reached them. The other two animals stood and moved into the cover, separating to the right and left, leaving the hunters to choose which to follow. Up till now, the hunt had lasted no more than minutes from when the Buffalo were first sighted. By other measures, it had taken more than half a century to arrive at this place. And this was not his first hunt in Africa.

Born in Gramercy Park in 1858 in the house that was his grandfather's gift to his father–at age six, with his younger brother, he watched from the window of his grandfather's house, the Grand Review of Lincoln's funeral procession being drawn down Broadway–he had doctors morosely prophesying his death from respiratory conditions and nervous diarrhea by the age of three. With a weak heart and what would prove poor vision, he had to face his parents's attempts to shelter and cosset him, to which his disposition seemed mutinous from the outset, his forever seeking occasion for risk taking. Once spotted as a tyke, dangling from a second-story window, he led his mother to conclude that were it not for the intervention of the Lord, her son would have perished long before.

Though often bedfasted, he was powerfully drawn to the environment even in the then-wilds of Manhattan or the woods around the family summer home on Long Island, loading his trousers pockets with curious and colorful living creatures and specimens, transferring them to his bureau drawers which became menageries for small mammals, reptiles, insects, and natural objects he picked up. A harbor-seal skull, the severed head discovered by the fascinated boy of eight at a local fish monger's, held a preeminent position among the specimens of the ad hoc natural-history museum he founded in his bedroom. He collected species of insects unknown to many field guides, pinning and labeling them with Linnaean exactness. His taste in reading ran, to the verge of obsession, to the stories of pioneers, adventurers, and explorers, like Dr. David Livingstone's *Missionary Travels in South Africa* and the woody tales of Fenimore Cooper.

Some come into the world with hunting grown in the grain. For others it is a conscious decision that lights in a moment of inspiration. In 1872, it was the gift of a gun, to accompany the eyeglasses he'd received the year before, that set the young man on the road to becoming the hunter he did. The family sailed that fall for Egypt and the Nile; and the young man unwrapped his birthday present onboard ship, finding a shotgun, conceivably a pinfire by Lefaucheaux. Docking in Liverpool, he dashed around the waterfront in search of arsenic for preserving the skins of the birds he meant to mount, drawing the unwanted attention of the local guttersnipes who mocked his still-scrawny frame and spectacles.

By the time the young man found a chemist, he was red-faced with indignation and demanding a pure pound of poison. Apparently, an unnamed adult intervened and vouched for the furious boy, assuring the shoppe owner that the purchase of the arsenic was without homicidal intent. Thus provisioned, the boy reboarded the ship for the voyage to Egypt, where he shot his first birds–probably his first game animals of any kind–and along with others he purchased in a Paris marché au gibier, skinned them and treated and preserved the pelts. At the time he thought his future lay in one day becoming a professional naturalist.

Before the gun and the hunting in Egypt, he suffered a life-altering insult, unlike the emotional ones delivered in Liverpudlian accents. In the late summer of the year of the trip to the Nile, following a violent asthma attack, he was sent by his parents to Maine's Moosehead Lake in the hope that the clean mountain air would benefit his lungs. From the railhead to the lake he shared a stagecoach with two other boys his age, who immediately set upon the weedy fourteen-year-old the way young Lion plagued the runt of the pride. Instead of allowing the incident to mortify him, the future Harvard man used it as a spur to ensure that he never suffered such ill treatment again. He meant, in the words of his biographer, Edmund Morris, to punish muscle and bone till both grew strong, and began at once an intense manly regime of weightlifting and pugilism.

His younger brother was born, sixteen months his junior, in Oyster Bay, just before the Civil War; and it was the second son who seemed to have all the advantages you might be born with. He was strong, sweet, and lovable–which would later translate into a reckless duende–gifts that came as unaffectedly as footspeed to a running wild animal, yet would not save him from a swift plummet. Academically gifted, for a time he was even thought to have a mind superior to his exceptional brother's, though there was finally no examination to determine that. Their younger sister thought the second son was more of the social leader who gave his elder brother the necessary prodding to engage with others, and set the course for his future career. The two boys were never less than close; yet they shared a keen rivalry, with the older brother's feeling it perhaps more acutely.

In his mid-teens, the younger brother began to experience seizures that eluded diagnosis, so were ascribed to neurasthenia. For nervous exhaustion in women at the time, the prescription was lengthy bedrest, a diet of rich creamy foods, and almost no taxing mental activity such as writing or painting. For male neurasthenics, the therapy was diametric. Men, especially Easterners, suffering from what we would today probably call depression or bipolar disorder, were urged to get away and rough it, particularly Out West. They were even encouraged to set down their emprises on paper, which led author Owen Wister to pen sketches, stories, and novels, *The Virginian* the most famous, out of his cure in Wyoming in the 1880s.

When the younger son, Elliot, began suffering those seizures, his parents removed him from boarding school; and following medical advice, they sent him to Texas in the company of his doctor and the doctor's wife for an extended sporting tour. It has to be said, Elliot enjoyed himself immensely, though almost certainly not in a fashion of which his parents or chaperones would necessarily have approved. On Sundays in frontier Houston, he attended services in the morning, then made for the faro tables in the afternoon and the Mexican fandangos at night. He seemed to make it his studied object to encounter as much of the Texas demimonde as he could, witnessing such a profusion of knifings and shootings that they came barely to warrant notation in his diary. And every chance he got he went hunting.

On his return home, he seemed to have benefitted enough, in the estimation of his parents, to be allowed to return to Texas at sixteen in less than a year, joined by a twenty-three-year-old cousin, John, planning to hunt Bison south of Houston. In Dallas, though, they met an heir to the Jameson Irish whiskey fortune who with a party of other hunters was heading west to the South Plains where Buffalo lingered; and the two cousins accepted without hesitation an invitation to accompany them. Three hundred miles of travel brought them to a camp at the bottom of a canyon by a good waterhole, forty miles east of Lubbock. As quoted in a 2019 article in the *Lubbock Avalanche-Journal*, Elliot recorded having Buffalo, Antelope, deer, wild hog, turkey, duck, [prairie] chicken, quail, 2 kind[s of] rabbit, dove, & [wild] cat in the camp–with wolves and panthers not only howling and crying in the darkness but being drawn in by the aroma of cooking food, and battling the dogs.

Elliot found that he had come under-gunned for Buffalo, a wounded bull charging him and dropping only feet away after Elliot desperately reloaded his single-shot and got off a fortuitous second round. He acquired a heavier caliber, and the hunt went on. Worse than Buffalo or Panthers, though, were horse thieves, either Comanches or renegade Buffalo hunters, who came in the night and left the hunting party to trek afoot off the prairie, a hundred forty miles over frozen trails with no water and only mud to strain along the way, reduced to pilfering from empty camps they passed. Once more back in Dallas, Elliot and John resumed their original hunting plans, finally making it back to New York in May, 1877.

Elliot's being the first to light out for the territories may have roused in his brother no small jealously. Instead of going West in patent imitation, though, Theodore Roosevelt made his way to the North Maine Woods, at the time mostly untouched. On an early September evening in 1878 a young man stood on the front porch of an Island Falls, Maine, farmhouse. The house's owner was William Wingate Sewall, thirty-three, a six-foot-four hale and hearty woodsman and nineteenth-century trailblazer in the enduring wilderness of the deep forests of the Pine Tree State. And Sewall's initial impression of the young man in front of him was not an all-together enthusiastic one.

The caller, a boyish-looking junior from Harvard College, stood a respectable five-foot-ten, but weighed no more than a hundred thirty five. In spite of the years of physical toughening and exhausting activity, pale and sickly was the description that suited him, accentuated by large thick spectacles, a guffle from asthma, and a hidden weak heart.

Mighty pindlin' was the guide's first thought when he saw what fetched up at his door.

Sewall could not, frankly, understand what someone as manifestly unfit as the young Theodore Roosevelt could possibly want, all the way up here in Maine, hardly crediting his stated wish to go hunting. What the Down Easter could not know was in what genuine need the boy was of both physical and mental invigoration. Only months before, his father, Theodore, Senior, worshipped by his namesake son–who nonetheless found fault in him for having paid a substitute to go in his stead to the Civil War–died of gastrointestinal tumor while Theodore, Junior, rushed home by train from Cambridge.

The remorse at being unable to say farewell clung to Theodore. Added to that was a sense of abandonment he felt when he found himself journeying to Maine alone. Two other Roosevelt cousins discovered Sewall by chance a few years before, and could not recommend him more highly to Theodore. So for two years, he and his best friend at Harvard planned a hunt together, when just before it was to begin, his friend's father withdrew him from the college and out of Theodore's life. Yet as so often was the case, when life struck at Theodore Roosevelt, he struck back only stronger and in his way more effectively. None of that was anything Sewall could know then, and what he could see was far from promising. He would, though, take him hunting.

According to Andrew Vietze in his book *Becoming Teddy Roosevelt*, from almost his first day in Island Falls, Roosevelt showed Sewall that if there was a steeper path, that was the one he traveled by. He hiked ten miles to shoot a lone Pa'tridge. Offer him honest pine boughs or a plush feather bed to sleep on, and there was no question in the matter. A canoe was meant for paddling to the farthest end of the lake, rain to shake off your hat without breaking stride. Sewall was taken with the zeal of the youth for the wilds of Maine. True, he was a greenhorn, but a good-humored, inquisitive one, eager and quick to learn. For the young man, Sewall notched a mark to aspire to.

Sewall did not drink or smoke and read the Bible daily–of his two older brothers, Roosevelt noted, Sam was a deacon; the other, Dave, was not a deacon. William's bushcraft was nonpareil; but he also expressed an interest in, and sought out, news of the wider world, reading much more than Scripture. Likely most remarkable to Roosevelt was the backwoodsman's sharing his uncommon appreciation of literature, both of them able to quote at length swaths of Sir Walter Scott's tale of Flodden Field, *Marmion*. It wouldn't be too difficult to venture what a young man, suddenly bereft of a beloved father, saw in an older, model man like Sewall.

Roosevelt returned to Maine again in February, less than six months after his first outing, jumping a rare Caribou from its bed, though never sighting it. On this hunt, he took his first Deer with the first rifle he ever owned, a 38-caliber Ballard, perhaps, from the old photographs, the Perfection model. For the rifle, he packed fifty cartridges–along with a spare flannel shirt, strong duck trousers, thick under-flannels, wool stockings, one blanket, a heavy jacket, his Bible and diary, and a Green River knife–into his haversack. He was so delighted with taking that first Deer, after chasing it for a mile through deep snow, that he afterward presented his guide with a brand-new Winchester rifle that Sewall passed down to his son.

Once more, the following summer, Roosevelt came back to Maine for a season of rough Arab life in the big woods, as he spoke of it to Sewall, broader, stronger, and even more a man each time he stepped onto the guide's porch. Roosevelt spent most of August in the County, Aroostook, the very top of Maine that encroached an unseemly distance into Canada, so that it almost ignited another British-American conflict–the Pork and Beans War, so called for the standard provisions of the lumbermen on both sides of the border–at the end of the 1830s. Again, the wild game amounted to no more than a sidelight to the trip: a Duck here, a Grouse there, maybe a Rabbit for the pot, and old tracks of Bear, Moose, and Caribou.

Most of the time in Maine was about bushwhacking through the dense woods; portaging around Beaver dams; ascending to the summit of Mount Katahdin and leaving two winded companions from New York in his wake; walking through the soles of his moccasins–trying to ford the Wassataquoik barefoot, he dropped into the current one of the hobnailed boots he carried, leaving him only his moccasins–writing letters and reading the Psalms on Sunday–Keep back thy servant also from presumptuous sins; let them not have dominion over me: then shall I be upright, and I shall be innocent from the great transgression–when he would neither hunt nor fish. Confiding in his diary, he felt that by the end of the trip he'd become tough as a pine knot, and had taken to heart Sewall's backwoods wisdom: Don't get scared of anything until it hurts you, and you won't get scared very often.

At the end of summer Roosevelt and Sewall gave themselves two days to hunt their way back to the train at Kingman Station, ten miles north of Mattawamkeag, a trip that normally took seven hours by buckboard over the corduroy tote road. There, on the wooden platform, the college man shook hands with the Maine guide, and returned to his studies, a far cry from the youth who first appeared at Sewall's door only a year before.

When Theodore graduated from Harvard, those harbingering physicians who had circled his life from as early as he could remember sounded another tocsin, that he must do absolutely nothing to strain his asthenic heart. By then, though, he was having none of it.

I'm going to do all the things you tell me not to do, he advised his medical advisers. If I've got to live the sort of life you have described, I don't care how short it is.

Maine was prelude to that conclusion he would reach upon leaving Harvard. Privately he gave himself till sixty, exceeding that–as he in so many ways exceeded so many other expectations–by seventy-one days.

There was one more North American outdoor pastime for Theodore and Elliot together, shortly after Theodore graduated from Harvard and before marrying Alice Hathaway Lee, and before beginning his great True West self-testing in the Dakota Territory that would confirm him as a legendary hunter. For six weeks in the late summer of 1880 the brothers went out to Illinois, Iowa, and Minnesota, Theodore hoping the trip would remedy some of his chronic ill health that included colic and asthma still so severe that he had to sleep sitting up–physically, Elliot was just about as healthy as the proverbial equine, though Theodore could not help but notice his growing affinity for alcohol. The hunting was somewhat spotty, although Theodore was assiduous in tallying each one of the hundreds of items, large and small, taken by his brother and him.

As in Maine, though, game was secondary to the strenuous life, emblematized for the normally dandyish Roosevelts by cropped heads, unshaven faces, dirty gray shirts, still dirtier yellow trowsers [sic], and cowhide boots, rather than animals taken. Theodore also could not conceal the fact that he relished being in the company of assorted rustic guides and reformed desperadoes. Nor were malfunctioning firearms, snakebite, getting pitched from a wagon, and near freezing under nor'wester gales anything other than inconvenience rightly considered.

Shortly after that trip, Elliot, flush with his share of his late father's substantial estate–thanks to which he could afford, at least financially, to set no firm course in life–set off on an adventure grander than any Theodore seriously contemplated up to that time.

Elliot arrived in India in early 1881 with introductions and set off in March to hunt Tiger with two British colonels. Travel was by palanquin, no less, to the hunting grounds where there were reports of the cats devastating the miserable looking village cattle. It was 96°F in the shade; but the nights were lovely and cool, and the luxury he found on the shikar was in the strongest possible contrast to the Bison range. Camp equipage amounted to twenty Elephants, forty camels and bullocks, thirty horses for the mounted troopers, fifty for baggage, seventeen private servants, twenty-six coolies [sic], fifty-two bearers, an indefinite number of attendants for the livestock, plus camp followers and between a hundred fifty to two hundred natives recruited for beaters, a sum of some three hundred fifty souls. The beats included Elephant and fireworks, while the hunters shot from howdahs. A virtual cascade of game poured out of the forests, and Roosevelt succeeded in taking a number of Mr. [and it must be said, Mrs.] Stripes with his No. 12 smoothbore.

By the time Elliot left the subcontinent in December, he hunted from Kashmir all the way to Ceylon, taking a shipload of big game, from Chital, Barasingha, Sambar–up to four hundred fifty pounds–Musk deer, Wild boar, Goral, Serow, Ibex, Markhor, Urial, rogue Asian elephant, and a rather staggering number of Bear, both Black and Brown. It wasn't all a velvet-cushion hunt, though, especially on the sheer cliffs of the Himalayas where he suffered dangerous bouts of tropical diseases and had to wear spiked grass shoes [sic], which left his feet so sore he soaked them in melted ghee for relief.

Shortly after Elliot's return, Theodore, looking with unconcealed envy upon all his brother's trophies, planned his first Badlands Bison hunt; and the irremediable trajectory of his life as the most renowned American hunter since Boone and Crockett–for whom he would name the nation's first conservation organization–was initiated.

Who knows what makes a hunter? For Elliot Bulloch Roosevelt it was something almost unquestionably innate. Blessed with a robust constitution and a character more than a bit deacon free, a life in the wild was a perfect fit, except for the darkness that was overtaking him from undoubtedly even before his earliest search for a curative in the wilds of Texas.

Theodore could surely be impulsive, but his impulsiveness seemed of a piece with his strengths. Elliot's was otherwise. Despite his shining outward disposition, demons housed in his psyche. Alcohol abuse was symptomatic of them, rather than outright cause. Then sometime while a fairly young man, he was apparently thrown from a horse, suffering a murderous leg fracture, resulting in the prescription of Soldier's Joy. The stage of his addictions advanced from overflow to deluge.

He was sent off to Virginia, out of sight of the family; and Theodore became conservator of his affairs. Facing more than his share of tragedy from early in life–added to the sudden death of his father were those of Alice Lee and his mother of natural causes within eleven hours on the same day in 1884, within two days of the birth of his eldest child, Alice–Theodore seemed to respond by taking action. Elliot, with the death of his wife from diphtheria, and later that of their toddler son from scarlet fever, simply became unmoored. His daughter Eleanor by his first wife would marry her distant cousin, Franklin D. Roosevelt, and become First Lady; but widowed, Elliot fathered a son with a servant. At thirty-four, in 1894, living basically on brandy and Champagne, he threw himself from a window and survived, dying from seizure–perhaps from enforced drug-and-alcohol withdrawal–days later.

Whatever Theodore's emotional response to his brother's death, it seemed not to decelerate Roosevelt's rocket trajectory into higher and higher office, leading to the White House in little more than half a decade. In July of Roosevelt's last year of the Presidency, his personal secretary, William Loeb, Jr., wrote a letter to the Winchester Repeating Arms Company, of New Haven, Connecticut, requesting a catalog. Gentlemen, the letter commenced. The President is going to Africa...

Africa was not Roosevelt's only choice for exploration, but it was the one that appealed most to his vivid...romantic imagination, as was written of him.

From the presidential desk he penned lengthy inquiries to such notable Africa hands as Carl Akeley; Frederick Selous, it goes without saying; Edward North Buxton, author of *Two African Trips*; the Rev. Dr. W. S. Rainsford who wrote *Land of the Lion*; J. H. Patterson of the Tsavo Lion fame and the chief game ranger in East Africa–and participant in the real-life reputed liaison scandaleux upon which Ernest Hemingway based "The Short Happy Life of Francis Macomber"–and the homesteading British East African colonial landowner and ostrich farmer, Sir Alfred Pease, Second Baronet of Hutton Lowcross and Pinchinthorpe and the holder of six thousand acres of wildlife-rich land on the Athi Plains southwest of the newly settled town of Nairobi.

At the beginning of spring, 1909, Roosevelt left by ship from New York for Africa in the company of three naturalists: the fiftyish surgeon Lieutenant Colonel Edgar

A. Mearns, U. S. A., retired, for whom the Mearns, also known as the Montezuma, quail is named; and the two thirtysomething Mr. Edmund Heller from the University of California and J. Alden Loring late of the Denver Zoo, which had dismissed him for holding extravagantly ambitious plans for the institute, certainly an attitude upon which Roosevelt would not have looked with disfavor. It was vital to Roosevelt that he emphasize the scientific motives of his safari, how he was being sent out, as he wrote in the record of the safari, *African Game Trails*, by the Smithsonian Institution to collect birds, mammals, reptiles, and plants, but especially specimens of big game, for the National Museum in Washington–the institution would come to bridle at the repeated newspaper descriptions of the expedition as Roosevelt's, rather than the Smithsonian's.

We believed, wrote Roosevelt, that our best work of a purely scientific character would be done with the mammals, both large and small.

By we he meant himself and his tall and slim, dreamy and interior, mandolin-playing, nineteen-year-old son Kermit, who on hiatus from Harvard accompanied him; while by work of a purely scientific character with mammals, both large and small, was meant by the Colonel the hunting and killing of them.

Roosevelt's initial intent was to hunt in East Africa in the rugged manner in which he had, decades earlier, hunted in Maine and the American West. Then it had been a lone guide and he, sleeping rough under the stars–on a Bison hunt, his guide awoke one night, lying in several inches of water during a driving rain. Beside him, the youngish Roosevelt was sitting up in the darkness with a Cheshire-cat grin, remarking, By Godfrey, but this is fun! The Colonel hoped to undertake something similar with Kermit, whom he thought could do with a taste of the strenuous life that he, the senior Roosevelt, fervently advocated.

They were to have a light, waterproof silk tent with telescoping poles–especially designed by Ezra Fitch, president of the famous sporting-goods firm of Abercrombie & Fitch–and for the day, a relatively restrained list of trophy game; a minimum number of porters; and absolutely no professional hunter–to certify that the only bullets to be found in the animals would be either Kermit's or his. It should have occurred to Roosevelt that for an ex-President of the United States, this was an absurd and thoroughly adolescent proposition–and unfortunately reflective of his propensity for careering headlong into exploits, which would nearly cost him his life five years later on his ill planned and outfitted Brazilian expedition. An English protectorate like Kenya would never allow such a potential diplomatic disaster—as the death or serious injury of anyone with the near-mythic worldwide stature of Roosevelt, not to mention a former head of state—to transpire upon its soil

Roosevelt, finally, acceded to the practical wisdom of his African advisors and let them dictate the equipment and scope of the hunt. In Mombasa, Roosevelt, already costumed in his khaki Willis & Geiger safari-wear and pith helmet, stepped ashore into a torrential downpour. When the skies cleared, he, along with Mearns,

Lieutenant Governor of the Kenya Protectorate Frederick John Jackson, and Selous–who came aboard Roosevelt's ship in Naples and beguiled him with his stories of old Africa all the way to the end of the voyage–climbed onto a bench bolted to the pilot on the prow of a locomotive of the Uganda Railway and rode through the wild heart of Kenya, which he took for a match to the late Pleistocene.

When the train steamed into Kapiti Plains Station two hundred seventy five game-rich miles northwest of Mombasa, Roosevelt and his entourage were greeted by his host Pease and a regiment of porters, trackers, and askaris–whose assigned duties included insuring that the porters did not desert the safari–a three hundred-strong body of men second in size only to that which the Colonel had served with in Cuba during the Spanish-American War. And as with the Rough Riders, Roosevelt was again second in command, having accepted the services of a highly recommended Scots-South African safari manager, R. J. Cuninghame, an expert Elephant hunter. Cuninghame in turn convinced Roosevelt that a second professional was necessary for so large an assembly; and he engaged the crack shot and, more importantly, a man certain to stand his ground in the face of danger, Australian-born Leslie J. Tarlton, later as mentioned before, to found with his brother Henry and fellow Australian Victor Marra Newland, the early safari company of Newland & Tarlton.

Completing the retinue was Philip Percival, who joined them at Bondoni, northwest of Nairobi. In Roosevelt's estimation a fine rider and shot, the sinewy Percival would after years of regular hunting from safari cars bloat up considerably by the time he became Hemingway's professional hunter on both of his safaris. Now, wrote Roosevelt, Percival, wearing merely a helmet, a flannel shirt, short breeches... and puttees and boots, leaving the knee entirely bare, walked beside his twelve-ox team, cracking his long whip, while in the big waggon [sic] sat pretty Mrs. Percival with a puppy and a little cheetah cub, which we had found and presented to her, and which she was taming.

Roosevelt's supreme desire in East Africa was to hunt Lion. Alas, Lion hunting did not always go swimmingly. Never a patient hunter, Roosevelt was visibly frustrated after only a few days of potting Antelope at Kapiti with the sighting of neither hide nor hair of a Lion. At last, hunting with dogs down the thick cover of a donga on the spoor of Lion, they caught a glimpse of tawny hide close by in the brush and fired into it, only to have two badly wounded cubs, the size of mastiffs, come out the other side to be finished off. Luckily for Roosevelt, and his host, later that same afternoon two large maneless male Lion were put up and Roosevelt killed the first one. After fruitless, and disconcerting to Sir Pease, six to eight hundred-yard shots at the second, unwounded one as it ran off, the hunters belatedly remounted their horses and galloped after it, overtaking it two miles later as it loped along behind a herd of Kongoni; and Kermit and Roosevelt combined in some truly hapless shooting to bring this one down.

The real moment of truth for Roosevelt came in June in the Rift Valley as he and Tarlton rode up on a burly and savage old Lion with a yellow-and-black mane. Dismounting, Roosevelt fired at a distance of two hundred yards, lightly wounding the Lion, which then ran off. Giving chase again, they caught up to the big cat; and when Roosevelt once more clipped its hide, the Lion came for them steadily—ears laid back, and uttering terrific coughing grunts. Due to a badly sighted rifle, the usually reliable Tarlton missed with a shot, to Roosevelt's ecstatic guilty delight. Now, as he knelt, the bead of his Winchester's front sight solid on the center of the Lion's chest, it was all up to the Colonel.

The soft-pointed 405 bullet went straight through the chest cavity, smashing the lungs and the big blood-vessels of the heart, the Lion rampant before pitching forward onto its head. It tottered to its feet, but could walk only painfully; and the two hunters put it down. This was the real dream that had brought Roosevelt to Africa, to be able to ride back to camp after dark, as he did that night, with strange stars shining in the brilliant heavens, and the Southern Cross...radiant above the sky-line, bearing the hide of a newly killed Lion.

Soon afterward came more game—Black rhino, including the Keitloa variety whose rear horn is longer than the front, Hippo, Giraffe, Leopard, Waterbuck, Wildebeest, Topi, Antelope, Gazelle, and ultimately Elephant—which they sought for themselves and the Smithsonian. Heller, in charge of preserving the specimens, and his team of native assistants could scarcely keep up with the workload.

Roosevelt read Edgar Allan Poe's demonic African fable "Silence," as they crossed the waters of Victoria Nyanza and sailed down the Bahr el Jebel branch of the White Nile to Uganda and the territory of the now all but fully extinct, and even then extremely vulnerable, Northern white rhinoceros.

After taking Rhino, they reached Gondokoro. With all the professional hunters and scientists suffering from dysentery and fever, Kermit and Roosevelt, who both enjoyed preposterously robust good health while in Africa, climbed onto riding mules and with sixty Ugandan porters struck off alone on an eight days's trip after the largest and handsomest, and one of the least known, of African antelopes, the Giant eland. After long, full days of stalking, Roosevelt ended up crawling after a fine bull, his rifle barrel heated by the broiling sun, too hot to touch. Closing to within a hundred yards, Roosevelt killed the magnificent Eland with a single shot, taking his last major big game animal on the continent.

Roosevelt and Kermit's nearly year-long, iconic safari ended on March fourteenth, 1910, when they landed in Khartoum, meeting Theodore's second wife Edith and daughter Ethel in a hail of kisses, and greeting hordes of raucous reporters, Roosevelt not ceasing from exploration yet arriving almost where he started.

Originally, Roosevelt had envisioned Kermit and his taking perhaps sixty-four head of game. In the end they took five hundred twelve, including large birds,

Crocodiles, Pythons, and a Monitor lizard—the scientists collected thousands more of smaller mammals, birds, reptiles, and fish. Most of these animals were to feed the safari, and all except for a select few went to museums, the two hunters retaining only a handful of trophies for their walls. Roosevelt's book on the hunt ends puzzlingly with his stating that he consumed a mere six ounces of brandy from his personal bottle during the entire safari. This may, though, have been a defensive assertion in light of Elliott's premature, and tragic, death by drink. Somehow, it seemed to him worthy of report.

Roosevelt's bag included six Buffalo, bulls and cows, and Kermit four–Roosevelt's preferences may be made clear by the nine Lion he killed, and a total of eight Elephant, in comparison to Buffalo. One of Roosevelt's was a Nile buffalo from the Lado Enclave, hunted in 102°F temperatures. He took an old bull, as large as an East African buffalo, with worn horns that were different enough that his WaKamba tracker, Kongoni, who came with him from Kenya, was unsure if it was a cow or a bull, until they reached the body and Kongoni pronounced it a duck, his way of saying buck, his catchall for the male of any species.

As always when I...killed [a] buffalo, Roosevelt wrote of that last one along the Nile, I was struck by the massive bulk of the great bull as he lay in death, and by the evident and tremendous muscular power of his big-boned frame. He looked what he was, a formidable beast.

Roosevelt's admiration for the Buffalo extended beyond its being something to shoot, or a head to collect, reaching to the most basic level we as carnivores can have in our attachment to an animal.

We found, by the way, he wrote, that his meat made excellent soup, his kidneys a good stew, while his tongue was delicious.

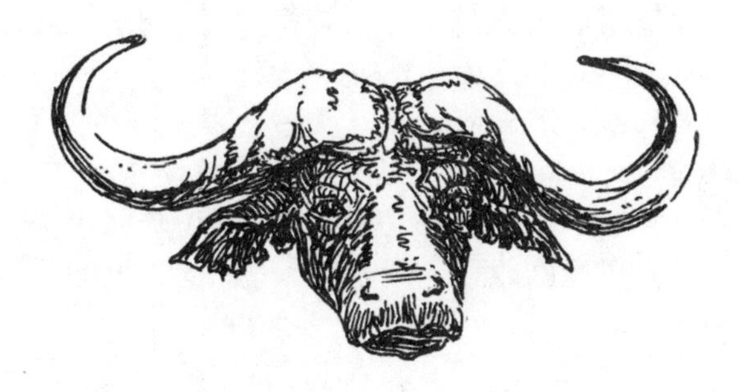

Along the Kamiti, Roosevelt knocked down the advancing wounded Buffalo for good with his heavy Holland double. The two wounded bulls went into the tall rank grass, high as a man's head, that fringed the papyrus swamp. The hunters heard them separate. They put the Boer's three big, powerful dogs in on the bull that went to the left. In a moment the dogs were giving tongue in the reeds, as the Buffalo grunted. Seeing its form, rifles cracked; and the Buffalo went down but was not dead. The dogs bayed louder, and one came out, running straightway back to the farmhouse, where when they returned, they found it dead from the injuries the Buffalo inflicted when it caught the dog with its horn. One of the professional hunters with Roosevelt had his shooting pony, and mounted up to ride in and finish the bull, which he did.

The last Buffalo, that got off to the right, was not found until a week later. Fortunately, the Colonel wrote, the head proved to be in less good condition than any of the others, as one horn was broken off about half-way up; so that if any of the four had to escape, it was well that this should have been the one. From that Buffalo's meat there was made no excellent soup, no good kidney stew, or any delicious tongue.

After the stroke, he grappled for words. He emailed me about a classmate, a Saudi, from college a half-century before, who moved to that house by spain [sic], his way of saying the classmate now lived with his wife in an orange grove in Rabat. His words before could at will be graced with the charm of a mother's favorite blond, blue-eyed boy. Imperially slim and almost tall with high cheekbones, angular nose, engaging smile, wicked eyebrows and glances, he was favored by many others. His first wife he met on a bus in Lima, Peru, just like that. He was introduced to his second–there would be no third–by her childhood friend, he tutoring her in Spanish which even after cerebrovascular accident he went on speaking fluently. The flaws surfaced inevitably. He was not among the many who are strong at the broken places, but only like the Killdeer skilled in feigning injured wings to draw attention to itself, though unlike the bird, not from altruism.

When Father died, I said to him all that had been in me for so long. I said it again with Mother's death, and had occasion to say it once more, for another reason when I considered it deserved, three times at intervals of fifteen years. My words seemed to glide over him like water sliding over the slickness of a fish's scales. I could not know if he really listened to them, only that outwardly they were ineffectual. It may be that they were never for me to say.

I encountered him in dreams filled with frustration and rancor–in others I found Father and vehemence. He was in that twilit metropolis–to which in one form or another I returned, night after night–of high-rises, hallways, potted palms —why?—sidewalks, glass fronts, stairwells, alleys, and an unending search for a way out. Dreaming, I walked its streets with him there, ahead of me, always just beyond the grasp of my incorporeal hand.

In the hours lying in bed before entering second sleep, I entertained infuriated thoughts about him, growing from opaque to stygian, knowing he was far from evil. Nonetheless, he took much and lost more. Then he had nothing, a green-glass bottle in the ocean, bearing a rolled message, indeciphered. No, not nothing. He still had the most unexpected thing: Somehow, he held onto what for him never seemed enough, the love of others.

CHAPTER FOURTEEN

Nyama

TAKING FLIGHT ON camelback from their encampment at our approach, the Sudanese raiders–come into the C. A. R. not for subsistence but for the bushmeat market–left behind a charred round terracotta pot. We found it that morning on the march; and now, halting at midday, one of the trackers sank it into a small waterhole, the precipitate of a dry river without a name. After letting the muck settle, he presented it to the white professional hunter with the grizzled spade beard and mustache. He took a deep draft and pronounced it ice cold. The other hunter, the ghastly one from Chicago whom we could barely tolerate, brandished a rictus of belligerent crowns and drank, too. Then there was Carey, the trackers naming him Patron Sans-souci. He drank. When my turn came, I asked him how it was. If you strained it somewhat through your teeth, the Patron allowed, it was not entirely foul.

Though I abandoned long before any pretense of drinking only chemically purified water on this safari, the thought of schistosomes performing vigorous wee scissors kicks and synchronized backstrokes in my intestines was too much. I tapped the toe of my boot against the plastic jug of warm treated water–our last for the day–set near me, and finding the jug still half full, drank sparingly from it instead.

We were a full ten miles west of the previous bivouac at the source of the Ouandjia. Walter, Jane, Carey, and I at dawn yesterday gathered at the minatory carcass of a camel that died in the night. Walter was in need of medication–to be definite, a stiff physic–and the Whites were hiking cross-country back to the French safari company's thatch-roofed headquarters in Ouanda Djallé. François Bendima, the evangelical missionary, and a few trackers went with them. Out of equal parts fatigue and depression–from Carey and my being left alone with the ugly Chicagoan and the miry hirsute P. H.–I lay down and slept through to supper, arising only long enough to go off into some tall grass and, setting fire to my bung wad afterward to help keep Africa beautiful, inadvertently igniting not more than an acre or two of tall grass, the fire swift and cool, doing no visible harm to any of the surrounding trees.

The white P. H. and the gentleman from Chicago, occupied their day with an unrewarding horseback–poor, sad horse–hunt around the country, failing to slay a thing–though a Duiker wounded with a 375 did, heaven only knows how, manage to escape.

Today, at least, his feet felt sufficiently healed for the gentleman to walk and spare the pony further misapplication. We lay under the trees by this waterhole now until the sun passed its zenith and then, with our trackers, gunbearers, porters, weary horse, and the remaining two camels, moved on to the next water that the Africans indicated was, by the snapping of their fingers in the air to count off increments of distance, another ten miles or more farther on. They showed us, by saluting to the elevation to which the sun would sink in the western sky when we reached our destination, that it would take several hours to reach it.

The afternoon heat was windless and searing. The country, though, was beginning to show green trees and shaded parklands. And when I became lost in the unbroken rhythm of my walking, wild animals spiraled me out of my daze: bounding triplets of Oribi; herds of Hartebeest; dark elk-looking Sing-Sing waterbuck; and Equinoctial, or Nile, buffalo.

Late in the day, I watched the white professional hunter and the gentleman stalk those heavy-muscled animals, that were every color from sleek black to bright red. As I watched from a hunker, dreaming of oxtail soup and sincerely wishing the gentleman all the luck in the world, it was as bracing as a slash of iced bourbon–which we also did not have anymore–to see the wild cattle of Africa once more. None of these creatures met the gentleman's trophy standards, though. When he and the P. H. stood, breaking off the hunt, a Lioness, who from the opposite side of the herd had as well been stalking the now-stampeding Buffalo, ran off. As I stood, I thought how no one, understandably, wanted to eat the camel, dead from suspicious causes. But, by God, here was fresh meat, and as good as it got, on the hoof. Couldn't either of those men see, or feel, the hunger of all the rest of us, watching them with great expectations?

The long day went on till at sunset we crossed the Galénguélé Ridge, the divide between the Oubangui and Chari watersheds. My sore-footed hobbling had come to resemble the pirouetting of a trained Bear with a brass ring though its nose. I was bearing up under hunger like a bundle of sticks on my back as we came to the flowing Poto Poto at the foot of a grassy hillside where we pitched our tents. With Jane gone, I stripped off all my clothes and lay down as the Lord made me in the shallow, chill river. After setting up a spike camp, a delegation of the Africans, subsisting for some days solely on cooked manioc, confronted the white P. H., holding their stomachs for emphasis, implored him to make the gentleman shoot something fleshy first-thing yesterday, by which they meant tomorrow–or maybe they did mean yesterday–never mind bloody horns! Carnivorous lusts are, it seems, planetary.

At dinner, while the gentleman indulged in a philippic of political and racial crudities of the coarsest nature while the rest of us sat in beerless stunned paralysis, we four were served a single, very small tin of cooked chicken–one for all, not one for each–the absolute bottom of our iron rations, with a bowl of unsauced boiled macaroni, making for some kind of antic Looney Tunes Last Supper set before cartoon characters. Above us on the hill campfires went skyward in skirls of flame.

Stretched out on a ground pad in the small tent, I was awakened from my famished sleep at midnight by a high wind, intense light, and crackling. All of the slope, inclining toward the river, was engulfed by a tall lashing yellow levee of flame, pushing downhill toward us. The Sudanese raiders, to stress what were the Central African principles of my-beach-my-wave, fired the dry grass as an invitation for us to shove off. In my slippers and underwear outside my mosquito net, I felt the banked heat on my face. I was unsure in which direction to rabbit, while the Africans lying on blankets near us at the foot of the hill, arose and, yawning, adroitly lighted backfires. Then went back to sleep, leaving the two surviving camels tied down five yards from me to grumble their outrage at this molestation and for the fire to consume itself. Les chiens aboient, la caravane passe, in more than a manner of speaking.

Tomorrow, we hoped for meat.

> Buffalo are among the best-eating of all African game–I think they are *the* best, better than eland–and there's a lot to them.
>
> —David Petzal

At the southern end of the Rift, three and two thirds million years ago, a meter-tall hominin, *Australopithecus afarensis,* made, unlike the splayed stride of a Chimpanzee, cross-footed prints like the gait of a fashion model on a catwalk, or John Wayne in a showdown in Lordsburg. She walked upright, holding, perhaps, on the basis of her track, an infant child, through volcanic nephelinite tuff likely from the eruption of Ol Doinyo Lengai, the Maasai Mountain of God, her prints with time turned to impressions in solid rock, to be excavated in the late 1970s by paleoanthropologist Mary Leakey, wife of Louis Leakey and his superior in discovery. This is the original known evidence of bipedalism within the human ancestry.

As we've seen, there are no immediately visible assets to bipedalism–a Chimpanzee on four limbs runs as fast as, or faster than, a champion human sprinter on two, with less chance of stumbling and falling; and we cannot draw anywhere near to the almost forty-five-mile-per-hour top speed of two-legged Ostrich. Yet it aids us in covering greater distances for longer durations, cradling babies as we walk, carrying tools or weapons on a trek, perhaps helping thermoregulate bodies on baking savannas, and looking over tall grass, and therefore making it easier to sight game.

The human brain trebled in size across six million years of evolution–one noted stage of material growth arriving a little less than two million years ago, coincident with, as one paleoanthropologist writes, the arrival of *Homo ergaster*, considered by some the earliest true human for a number of features not present in the earlier *Homo habilis. Ergaster* was the initial human to commit to terrestrial bipedalism; and the brain that evolved from him to this day was a calorie sump, an organ that at 2 percent of bodyweight now commands 20 percent of our energy. To accommodate our larger, more luxurious brains–in terms of tissue use and food demands–we traded off size in our guts and livers and kidneys: Compared to those of a primate of a body mass similar to ours, our gastrointestinal tract and major organs weigh considerably less than what would be expected. This created the need for quality food that was easy to digest, a requirement met by the nutritionally dense flesh of fellow animals.

Meat has been integral to the hominin diet from the beginning of our genesis. From the fossil record of cut marks on bones, we were eating at least some meat from our pre-human past of more than three million years ago. Even meager scraps were worth consuming for an agglomerate of micronutrients–vitamins and minerals–unobtainable from plants alone. Intuiting the unique value of meat, hominins dedicated themselves to acquiring it in greater and regular quantities. Unlike the Chimpanzee–our diverging from a common ancestor perhaps as much as seven million years ago, while continuing to share all but two-fifths percent of the same D. N. A.–we humans brought routine scavenging, tools, voluntary distribution, and the hunting of large animals to the getting of meat.

Chimp for a variety of reasons–maybe the lack of open landscapes where carrion is more visible and alluring–rarely scavenge; we hominins scavenged intrepidly, and still do. Humans developed a sophisticated kit of fabricated tools; Chimpanzee don't use tools much more complex than sticks, sharpening some with their rather intimidating teeth. Out of seeming altruism, humans sublimate consumption to bring meat back to others in their troop; Chimp eat their kills on the spot. More significantly, while Chimp hunt and eat smaller animals, hominins hunt megafauna the size of Elephant, Giraffe, Rhino, and Buffalo.

For much of hominin existence, we relied on scavenging for obtaining meat. In truth, large wild predators are spendthrift carnivores, leaving substantial portions of flesh on carcasses. And for millions of years, leftovers were the prime source of meat for us. The aerial whorl of vultures drew hominins to the periphery of feeding Lion, where the ancestor of our species squinched down to wait–hominins also proactively climbed trees to rob from the kills of solitary Leopard, its being easier to brazen it out with them than with Lion prides. When the Lion ate their fill and went off, the hominins moved in ahead of other scavengers and took what was edible, not always muscle tissue.

Without knowing it, what hominins wanted in particular from what the Lion left of their Buffalo kills was bovine lard's singular arrangement of lipids–omega fatty-acid molecules, some in existence for a half billion years–working industriously on us on the cellular level, in anti-inflammatory, healing, and nerve- and tissue-growth processes, such as encephalization–brain building. One hypothesis is that bovine fat is composed of some specific triglycerides that are highly suited to fording the blood-brain barrier to accelerate the enlargement of cerebral matter. However much, or little, meat Lion left on a carcass, they consistently left the long limb bones and heads. Even stripped of flesh, these body parts were jewel boxes of fat.

The exorbitantly high-fat marrow of all the tibia, femur, humerus, and radius bones that the predators did not rive, was left for hominins, if they could outcompete Hyena. The Hyena's bite, twice the strength of the Lion's, was made for breaking bones. Our ancestors relied on tools to accomplish the task. Simple rocks, at first, could be lifted and dashed down. What may also have taken place was the fracturing into smaller pieces of the rock when it struck bone, and the hominin perceiving individual flaked tools in the stone rubble.

The head was a total jackpot. Lion left it virtually intact. Based upon similarities of Buffalo to domestic cattle, the head might yield some five pounds of fatty brain tissue, providing a premium of more than eight thousand calories–there could also be the eyeballs, gratifyingly chewy and another source of fat. For the hominin, cracking a Buffalo skull was like opening an oyster for the pearl. The question unresolved is whether meat itself was directly instrumental in making the brain bigger, or if it was the energy it supplied overall that allowed the brain the opportunity to grow: larger brains, better hunters, more meat, greater survival, more robust lineages. Either/or, there seems to be a link that is certain between a carnivorous diet and brain size.

The boost in meat eating that came with a transition from scavenging to hunting–or to be more accurate, the addition of it to scavenging–cannot be overstated. Instead of the scraps left by other predators that we made do with, by capturing and killing prey animals ourselves, we had whole carcasses to consume. In the hunting dawn we likely caught small animals by hand and dismembered them with those same hands and our teeth, as Chimp do today. With tools, we could eviscerate, skin, and butcher large quadrupeds. With spears of sharpened wood, hardened by fire, or with stone points, and after that, arrows, later augmented with poison, we could deliver force at a distance, making animals as forbidding as Buffalo viable to hunt. As for the physiology of taste of what we hunted, ranched beef is a landscape painting of the savanna. Buffalo beef is the savanna. Eating it returns us physically to our origins of growing brains, as we can return in no other way.

Another manmade tool may have been, for a variety of applications, most important of all. From fossil evidence of controlled burning in southern and eastern Africa, the Age of Fire began between one and two million years ago, as *Homo ergaster* developed a smaller, more efficient digestive tract, and larger brain. Cooked meat, easier to chew and digest than raw, provides greater energy and more of some nutrients than does a similar amount of uncooked–and cooking can also detoxify poisonous plants. Cooking preserves meat; it promotes higher rates of hominin reproduction; and as long as three quarters of a million years ago, with the establishment of hearths, it made a place to come home to. It also happens to make food better tasting. Further, setting grass fires let hominins modify landscapes to favor their prey species and the hunting of them.

As for the nutritional worth of Buffalo, should you ever find yourself in the position to milk a Buffalo cow, you will have something with a lactose and protein content similar to domestic cattle and Water buffalo milk, but with five times the fat of a cow's, and twice that of a Water buffalo's. Were it made into a formaggio, it could only put the mozzarella di bufala of Campania, Lazio, Apulia, and Molise to shame.

Buffalo dress out at nearly 60 percent of live weight, about what domestic cattle returns. And that is muscle meat. Hunting, killing, and possessing a carcass, nose to tail, earns a windfall in offal. There is little else quite as nutritious as organ meat: lights, liver, heart, kidneys, tongue, the tripe from the four-chambered ruminant stomach–and often the partially digested contents–intestines, even udders, and testicles. As an endorsement, these are the parts of the prey that the apex wild predators feed on first and with the utmost avidity, leaving little or none for scavengers.

As much as a hundred twenty thousand years ago, when *Lawrence of Arabia*'s hellish Nefud Desert was far more temperate and watered, modern *Homo sapiens*–with their soccer-ball, versus Neanderthal's N. F. L.-regulation football-shaped, skull–started roving out of a parching Horn of Africa, trailing their customary game, including mesomorphic Giant buffalo. As they went, they left traces of their distinctive footprints, cast in the beds of ancient freshwater lakes, long vanished, to be seen again after the eroding of overlying sediments. From then through perhaps fifty thousand years of emigration, this was where all our D. N. A., found beyond Africa–the same sequence of nucleotides carried in Basques, Bedouins, Sherpas, and Crees–originated. In that time, another side of our genome remained in Africa.

Along with those hominin tracks as the human pilgrimage pointed toward the Fertile Crescent, were those of the ancient bovines in whose slipstream we trailed. Our migration, though, cost us population numbers and genetic diversity. Even in Central and Eastern Africa, those who became the Bantu declined. Who ascended were those we now know as the Khoisan.

With the ancestors of the Khoisan in Central Africa was also *Syncerus*. In the first days of *Homo sapiens*, two hundred thousand years ago, the Buffalo species expanded and divided into *S. c. nanus* and *brachyceros,* and *S. c. caffer*, the first dispersing west, the latter east and south. Within a hundred thousand years, our own clade separated into two populations of hunter-gatherers: into forest people who would go on to become the emigrants of the African exodus, their bloodline to inhabit all of Eurasia, Australasia, Polynesia, and the Americas; and into the savanna and desert people, to become the Khoisan. The two branches of humans, then, were apart for a hundred millennia, meeting again only half a millennium ago, both owing their origins and progressions to Buffalo in one biotype or another. Everywhere that *Syncerus* went, we were sure to go–which we did not as manifestly do with other prey animals.

One part of our race–when we became human–seemed never to find a fit place to settle, having ceaselessly to set off, once more, until there was no new land to enter. In East Africa, mega-droughts from about a hundred thirty to seventy five thousand years ago, sent *S. c. caffer* into a decline, to recover within a moister environment some eighty to fifty thousand years before now. Across this span the two living subspecies of Buffalo made successive colonizations of West and Southern Africa, ultimately descending upon the Cape as the *S. c. antiquus* subspecies died away. As they went, they left their trails; and on those trails to the south went the future Khoisan.

In the country of *Syncerus caffer caffer*, the Khoisan recognized an enduring home; and not needing to go on or to backtrack, they let their ancient culture develop. And for much of human time, they were the most numerous of all the world's people. This correlation, our fusion with *S. caffer*, steers us toward a conclusion: More than Wisent or Bison, Aurochs or Banteng, Buffalo are at the heart of our phylogeny, making us near completely creatures of the Buffalo.

When I landed on the grass strip to reach Songo Camp in Zimbabwe, Rory Muil, who came to meet me in the Defender, looked inside the Cessna.

Did they give you any tucker to bring to us? he asked when he saw nothing in the plane. They were running out of tinned food and dry goods in the camp kitchen. What there was to eat was Buffalo.

When a Buffalo was killed, the trackers cut it in two with their Tonga axes and knives and claimed everything from the body cavity–even stabbing handholds in the bulging pearlescent wall of the stomach to roll it out onto the ground and cut it up into tripe. When they were done, all of the Buffalo, except the two hundred-pound bale of grazed grass from the stomach and the contents of the lower intestine–what Lewis and Clark's wrighthand cook Charbonneau described as not good to eat when it came from a Bison, and that he squeezed out before using the intestines in the making of boudin–was loaded into the Land Rover and transported back to camp.

In the shady cool room beside the kitchen hung Buffalo meat taken by previous hunters. Then I killed my first one, here; and we had an abundance. We ate Buffalo as rolled fillet; braised oxtail; charred steaks; biltong; cold tongue in sandwiches; the liver, fried; testicles, likewise; and in traditional muriro stew with onions and rape greens, scooped from the pot with stiff cornmeal sadza–the primary native staple of the country–kneaded into a ball in the hand.

On maize day we went to the village that was nearest.

It was almost noon and shadowless as Rory Muil and I drove the Land Rover onto the dirt street in the middle of the village, a quarter of my Buffalo with the hide on, lying in the back. Thin young men walked together, carrying their axes hooked over their left shoulders, blades-backward. We passed women and small children, the women in long skirts and the children in T-shirts and shorts, carrying fifty-kilogram pillow-looking woven-polypropylene bags of U. S. A. I. D. dried corn, FROM THE AMERICAN PEOPLE, some of the bags bigger than the children underneath them. A line formed outside the community mill where the bags were slumped down on the ground by the women and children who waited. As the line moved, they hoisted the bags and stepped one human space forward, closer to the grinding machine.

In the dark interior of the grinding room, the bags of corn were opened by pulling the running stitch at the top, then lifted by the operator, flecked in maize dust, and loaded into the hopper, the emptied bag placed under the chute, to be refilled with ground meal, then tied off and carried, somehow, back to where the woman or child lived so a family could eat.

We drove to the iron gates of the whitewashed village hospital where the high stake-bed truck with the canvas canopy was parked, the back rolled up and the bags of maize handed down to the people waiting for them. As we stopped, the chief doctor came through the gate. He was tall and wore glasses and a tie, his hair looking even blacker with the dazzling white coat he wore that moved as he walked quickly. He and Rory spoke in Shona as two hospital workers dressed in ordinary clothes came out to lift the Buffalo quarter and carry it into the hospital. From every Buffalo taken from the camp, meat was brought to the hospital.

After Rory and the doctor shook hands, the doctor shook my hand. That was all. He didn't need to say anything, and didn't. There was nothing more for us to do in the village as the children and women under the flat midday sun carried the fat bags of maize to the grinder and took away the bags of ground meal. Rory put on his sunglasses and started the Defender, turning around on the dirt street. We drove the miles back to the Songo camp.

It was early yet to be out hunting. I sat at a folding table under my tent's awning, writing. I was expecting a call for a late lunch; but I looked and saw one of the waiters, sockless in dusty tire sandals, bringing a tray with food on it. He put it down; and there, by some sorcery, was a cheeseburger. The bun was baked in a wood stove in the camp's wattle-and-daub cook hut. The onion slice and the slice of tomato, with a leaf of lettuce, came out of the camp's small kitchen garden, with the sting of mustard mixed from powder from a lidded yellow can. The cheese was the last of the Zimbabwean cheddar that was flown in before I came. And the glistening patty, fried in a skillet on the stovetop, was ground Buffalo, made from the one I killed. For a time I stared at the cheeseburger, unsure of its reality. Then I started to eat.

A drop of meat juice dripped onto the china plate as I chewed contemplatively, Fletcherizing each bite thirty-two times to get all there was out of it. As it cooled, it seemed to become only more amazing. I was in despair over having to finish. Eating yesterday's Buffalo made me want to hunt next day's all the more.

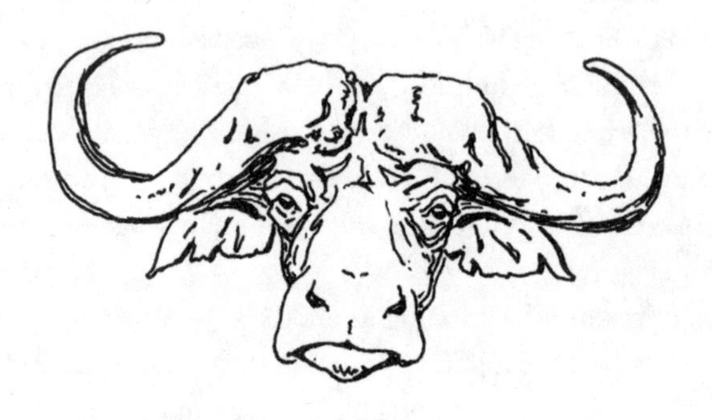

CHAPTER FIFTEEN

Happy

IN THE WEEKS of hunting Buffalo in Kenya, we chased breeding herds in and out of the thick cover, jumping them and driving them ahead of us, unable to sight any large bulls. Finally with one herd, we circled ahead into a clearing of chest-high grass. We hunkered down and watched the Buffalo come out, filing in front of us. The bull appeared but was only a young animal, big-bodied, not good in the horns yet. As it passed, a tremendous cow, herd matriarch, walked out, sixty yards from us, halting. It stared straight at us, into us. Its calf was beside it, and I knew that the cow could come for us because of its being there.

I waited for the fear.

All right, John Fletcher whispered, his 500, two cartridges with 578-grain softs in it and two more in his left palm, held in his curled ring and little finger under the fore-end–carrying the rifle across his body like a gravedigger's spade–we'll stand now, and she'll run off. Or she'll charge.

As binary as that.

We stood, Fletcher, I, the trackers behind us, and my friend Bill; and the Buffalo cow did not move. There was nothing to read in its face, just its nostrils flaring a little as it scented.

Fletcher and I raised our rifles without a word between us. I centered the cross-hairs of my 375 on the chest, just below the lifted chin. Seconds passed. Then more. Until the cow snorted loudly and spun away, now at the back of the herd that was running, pushing itself forward into it with its calf. I took my finger off the trigger and purposefully reset the safety, feeling inside something satisfactory. And all the trackers came up and clapped me on the back, smiling, holding my thumb as they shook my hand.

It felt strange. I was glad, though not relieved, that the Buffalo hadn't charged. There was another hunter, aiming and shooting.

...The bits of horn flying from the boss like chips from a slate roof.

That is the way the character Francis Macomber in the story by Ernest Hemingway faced the charge of the wounded Buffalo, his final act after the crucible of debasing cowardice, sexual humiliation, and the discovery of true courage–true the most Hemingway of adjectives–his life to be ended in an instant, with the white-hot, blinding flash of a bullet fired into his head from his inconstant wife's Mannlicher.

If you remember those words about the bits of horn as being written in "The Short Happy Life of Francis Macomber"–and earlier titles Hemingway flirted with included "The More Dangerous Game," "The Fear of Courage," and, yes, "Through Darkest Marriage"–you are misremembering. In the story–first published in the September, 1936, issue of *Cosmopolitan* magazine–Macomber as he fired, unhearing his shot in the roar of the professional hunter, Robert Wilson's double rifle, saw fragments like slate burst from the huge boss of the horns, and the head jerked. He shot again at the wide nostrils and saw the horns jolt again and fragments fly.

The first description, of his friend Charles Thompson's firing on a charging Buffalo as Hemingway, terribly weakened by amoebic illness, sat on the ground, backing Thompson with his Springfield rifle, is from handwritten notes Hemingway made about his first hunt in Tanganyika in the winter of 1933-34. That was the genuine safari, even if the cost, somewhere between a hundred fifty and two hundred fifty thousand in today's dollars, was covered by stocks given to the Hemingways by Gus Pfeiffer, the uncle of Ernest's second wife Pauline–P. O. M., Poor Old Mama in the book he wrote about it–Uncle Gus, having made his fortune in pharmaceuticals, always fulsome toward his niece. The second safari, two decades later, all expenses paid by *Look* magazine, was an alcohol-deluged tire fire–Hemingway admitted that drinking led him to ignore the birds, a sin to him that was in league with the most grievous. On that safari he reunited with his old professional hunter Philip Percival from their first time together in Africa, Percival observing a travesty of the hunter and man he had known. And those notes may in fact have been written on the second trip, from his memory of the first, or perhaps from the story he wrote based upon the real events, making them a third generation copy of experience.

Not content to let the past rest undisturbed, Hemingway in later life seemed to look to reclaim an idealized former time, and was not above making gestures of trying to recreate it. So *The Old Man and the Sea* was his parodistic exercise in reclaiming the true-simple-declarative sentences of his remorseless but fine Paris apprenticeship; the sojourn in Spain for *The Dangerous Summer*, that reprise underwritten by Henry Luce, was an essay at resurrecting the fiesta of his twenties; his second safari, a calamitous simulacrum of the first, a fourth wife standing in for a second, concluding in planes falling from the sky; finally, there was his formative time in the apartment above the sawmill at 113 Rue Notre-Dame-des-Champs, that came out in his early short stories, which he tried to recapture in *A Moveable Feast.* Like all who end in suicide, he lost faith in a bearable future; and so he orbited the past obsessively, and eccentrically, back and back until there was nothing left to orbit about.

"Macomber," at least the scenes of action, was based on the genuine experience of ten weeks of hunting in Tanganyika–two of those lost to the onset and treatment of life-threatening dysentery which Hemingway believed he contracted on a filthy French ship on the voyage from Marseilles to Mombasa, his medical extraction from the bush by light aircraft an inspiration for "The Snows of Kilimanjaro." The thirty days of hunting following his return from hospitalization became the nonfiction-novel *Green Hills of Africa* before he turned to the material to produce two of his most famous stories–and perhaps the last irrefutably good writing in his lifetime.

Hemingway, like Theodore Roosevelt, was profoundly biased toward Lion.

I am not a butcher, but I would like to kill a few lions, wrote Roosevelt to John Henry Patterson a year before his leaving the Presidency and setting out on his grand East African safari.

Hemingway may have seen the Lion as his totem animal, his admiration for it a band never to be broken–on the other hand, Hyena and Shark, heralds of death and defeat to him, were bêtes noires to be slaughtered indiscriminately, his going so far as to acquire a Thompson submachine gun to carry aboard his fishing boat, *Pilar*, for keeping Galanos, Requiem sharks, from savaging his hooked gamefish, and his killing over thirty Hyena to no good purpose in 1933-34—he said, if he could have spared the ammunition, he would have killed a hundred. In honor of Lion he produced a very short, bibulous child's tale about "The Good Lion" who ate only some tagliatelli and drank a glass of pomodoro while the bad Lion killed and ate Maasai cattle, and Hindu traders. In time the good Lion left Africa and flew home to its father, the winged bronze Lion of Venice perched on a column in the Piazza San Marco. In the *Sea* novella, Santiago no longer dreamed of storms, women, great fish, or his wife, but only of the Lion on the beach in Africa, the Lion playing like young cats in the dusk and he loved them.

In Hemingway's estimation of the jeopardy posed by the African Big Five–Lion, Leopard, Rhino, Elephant, and Buffalo–Buffalo ranked well below either the Lion or the Leopard.

In "Notes on Dangerous Game: The Third Tanganyika Letter" from the July, 1934, issue of *Esquire*, he described watching a Lioness take down a Wildebeest, the cat's speed, that unbelievable smooth rush [she] made to close the gap between herself and the fast galloping...antelope, making him see what a charge from a slightly wounded Lion could be if allowed to get under way.

Admitting in the *Esquire* piece to a deficit of knowledge of the Buffalo, having killed but four, he measured it condescendingly against the gauge he was most familiar with, the arena:

> The buffalo has courage, vindictiveness, and an incredible ability to absorb punishment [I shot all six 220 grain 30-06 into a patch of hide you could cover with the palm of your hand and the bull died with his head in my lap–truly: this from Heminway's handwritten notes about the charge of Thompson's buffalo] but I believe in the bullring he would be more like the big truck that comes charging in during the intermission to water the dusty sand than like the light hoofed, quick whirling, fast charging fighting bull.

To Hemingway, the Buffalo seemed unbelievably slow, compared to a Spanish fighting bull, and he could see no reason why a man who could wait for the Buffalo as it came could not be sure of blowing the front of its head in if he let it get close enough and shot carefully with a heavy enough rifle.

Actually, there are several reasons to see why, starting with misestimating the Buffalo's actual speed, plus the superstructure of its skull and horns that presents no easy target for such a deliberate, ideal shot, but only offers slopes and angles and helmeting capable of deflecting even the largest-caliber bullet. As well, a Lion or Elephant may start, then abandon, a charge. A Buffalo never does. A charge begun is one carried to its finish. And Hemingway had to admit that a tunnel in thick bush, or high reeds, or any dense cover can make the wounded Buffalo dangerous.

You must take him where you find him and follow him where he goes, and he goes into bad places, he wrote. Nonetheless, that is a case of circumstances rather than the animal, and in the open a Lion or Leopard is a hundred times more dangerous, he concluded.

Yo soy yo y mi circunstancia, wrote Ortega y Gasset twenty years earlier. I am myself and my circumstance. Perhaps Hemingway once read that and forgot. Should that apply to humans alone? Isn't the risk the Buffalo represents tied inextricably to its inborn behavior, its instinct to find the most advantageous ground from which to deal with what threatens it, to create the bad places? Once wounded, a Buffalo seems to make it its sworn duty to confront the person who inflicted the wound when that person follows it into its cover–what might in the bullring be identified as its querencia, its sanctuary–but which a Buffalo will treat not as a bunker but as a redoubt from which to attack in ambush.

It has to be said that neither the Lion nor the Buffalo poses any general threat to people, other than in exceptional cases, unless it is faced with human aggression; but if the criterion for danger is how an animal performs in the open, such as in an arena, the Lion as shown in orthostats–standing slabs of rock carved in relief–fared rather badly in Nineveh at the hands of the seventh–century B. C. king, Ashurbanipal, glorified in the act of killing them with bow and arrow from his chariot. How dangerous must those Lion have been if the king, and more importantly his court, considered it safe for him to expose himself to their attacks? How many Lion did venatores kill with their gladii in the Roman amphitheaters?

Granted, there may be no known examples of African buffalo in arenas; but you wonder what the result might be if a Buffalo ever met a torero in a corrida. A fighting bull may be swifter and more agile than the Buffalo, but speed does not always equate to danger. To a man or woman on the ground, under assault from one or the other animals, how quick or nimble that animal is won't matter as much as the ferocity and determination of the attack. Imagining el momento de la verdad, the moment of truth, when the matador goes in for the kill with the sword, it's difficult to believe that there would be less stress in facing a Buffalo rather than a bull. Both animals are about the same weight, and if one is faster in the charge than the other, both are fast enough to defeat the defensive talents of the bullfighter. Going in for the kill, a bullfighter in the ring with a Buffalo would have an animal with a longer neck, meaning a farther, more precarious reach to get the blade over the morrillo, or neck hump, also known in this context by untranslatable Spanish names such as cruz and rubios, and into the vital heart and lungs. There would also be the matter of the horns. The Buffalo's are wider and less expediently eluded. This makes a kill volapié, foot flight–moving toward the animal and lunging over its head to place the sword–menacing at best. The other type of kill, recibiendo, receiving–in which the matador stands in place and lets the bull come to him–would be an act of willful self-destruction.

To be sure, that is all speculative; but if engaging in speculation, how would a fighting bull, if it were hunted in its native environment, compare to a Buffalo: For one, fighting bulls unlike Buffalo do not have their lives ordered by the daily likelihood of encounters with Lion. Why not compare as well the bucking rodeo bull, an arguably better-tutored opponent? Hemingway doesn't say, but I am confident that the Buffalo is smarter than the bull, or certainly more wary, which amounts to the same thing when facing a human. As quarry, the toro bravo's chief demerit is its bravura, its behavior entirely predictable. Once wounded, it will rush forward until it reaches the instigator of its pain; and critically it lowers its head sooner than a Buffalo as it comes. How a Buffalo will react under similar conditions is virtually unknowable. It may charge. It may run. It may go to ground. And wait–while a hunter has to withstand torturous tickings of stillness, trailing the unknown, wanting solely for there to be an end to it.

Add to that, the long lineage of the toro resulting from deliberate breeding by humans to make for the most pictorial performances in the ring. It is God, as the Ndebele say, who breeds Buffalo.

What was not speculation was what the late P. H. John Fletcher told me about taking a Mexican matador on safari. The hunter, actually a rejoneador who fought his bulls from the backs of white stallions caparisoned in Leopard skins, had his body servant along to tend him in the nyika, told Fletcher he had a powerful urge to kill a Buffalo with a sword, and had indeed brought along his estoque to that end. The first Buffalo they faced turned into a charge, both men firing and hitting well. Fletcher emptied both barrels of his William Evans 500 N. E., and was trying to reload his broken-open rifle when the Buffalo was almost on him. Off to the side, his hunter, with the virtue of being an excellent shot, swung his rifle through the running bull till the reticle was on its muzzle, then fired and broke its neck, the dead momentum of the animal knocking Fletcher down, without serious injury.

The hunter, taking stock, asked Fletcher with a flourish, And how is that for a client?

Did he still wish to use a sword on a Buffalo, Fletcher asked, seated flat on the ground, supporting the bull's head. The rejoneador replied in the negative.

Hemingway concedes the danger of the Buffalo in the words he has the P. H., Wilson, say to Macomber as they are going in after a wounded bull:

> "When the buff comes, he comes with his head high and thrust straight out. The boss of the horns cover any sort of brain shot. The only shot is straight into the nose. The only other shot is into his chest or, if you're to one side, into the neck or the shoulders. After they've been hit once they take a hell of a lot of killing."

For Hemingway, for that to be true in the writing it had to be true in fact, however much he wished to assert the superiority of his idolized Spanish bull.

A telling of some of Hemingway's actual Buffalo hunting is in *Green Hills of Africa*, an attempt to write, in his words, an absolutely true book to see whether the shape of a country and the pattern of a month's action can, if truly presented, compete with a work of the imagination.

What he put in the book was seeing Buffalo scrambling up the other bank of a reed bed, the black back, the wide-swept, point-lifted horns and then the quick-moving, climbing rush.

In spite of stating that the ethics of shooting dangerous game is the premise that the trouble you shoot yourself into you must be prepared to shoot yourself out of, he tells of trying to kill a Buffalo bull for the meat with the 470 N. E. he rented from the bunduki–gun dealer–in Nairobi. How its trigger break was frustratingly like the last turn of the key opening a sardine can; and the Buffalo ran off with the first shot, and he clearly missed with the second, yet sure he hit it somewhere with the first, not knowing exactly where. After giving the Buffalo time to stiffen up, they, he and Percival, went in search of it, Hemingway taking his more familiar and reliable 30-06. They skirted around a sudden influx of Rhino, then decided to rest out the heat of midday. Afterward they found blood and followed it into a slough of dead papyri so tall and thick that Hemingway went back to the disreputable 470, carrying it with the safety off and his finger over the trigger guard, even though he no longer had any confidence in it except for its noise.

It was two Buffalo that came out of the reeds, the trackers shouting back to the hunters. Hemingway and Percival ran to where they saw them, far off in the sunlight on a hillside above the rocks. One of the trackers exchanged the Springfield again for the N. E., and Hemingway slipped his arm through the bolt-action's sling, held the bead of the aperture sight on top of the shoulder, and as the Buffalo ran, swung the rifle with it and fired. And hit it at a range later calculated at four hundred yards. The two Buffalo vanished from sight, and Hemingway and the tracker, Droopy–there being a more than fair chance that his name, like that of the other tracker, was not his real one but what he suffered to be called by white men–started running up the ridge and heard from the trees, the clear...long, moaning, unmistakable bellow.

The very sad noise Buffalo make when dying is one that a professional hunter finds musical.

P. O. M. says in the book, It's like hearing a horn in the woods.

One critic of the time recognized this as a lift from the French Romantic poet Alfred de Vigny and his poem "Le Cor": Dieu! que El son du Cor est triste au fond des bois!–God! how sad is the sound of the horn deep in the woods! Hemingway's dead Buffalo lay on its back, throat stretched out to the full, its weight on its horns, wedged against a tree.

It was not the wounded one.

That was the other one that ran with it, and which in the words of Dirty Harry Callahan, was kinda lost track of in all this excitement, and forgotten about after that, in spite of the business about shooting yourself out of the trouble you shot yourself into.

Green Hills landed with a splat as a défaillance critique. Many reviewers during the prolonged Depression questioned Hemingway's writing about matters of such inconsequence as the hunting of Buffalo and Kudos–as they spelled them–when he ought to be applying his talents to the momentous causes of Leftist politics. Edmund Wilson in an eight thousand-word précis of Hemingway's writing career up to the beginning of the 1940s, branded *Green Hills* an unsatisfactory book, at best.

As soon as Hemingway begins speaking in the first person, the disquieted littérateur wrote, he seems to lose his bearings, not merely as a critic of life, but even as a craftsman.

It may be added here, whenever he resorts to the word Gentlemen as a term of address in his writing, that passage may confidently be deled.

Wilson also slighted Hemingway's later alignment in the onset of the Spanish Civil War with Communists, and the turgid prose it generated.

Taken in tow by the Stalinists, wrote Wilson, Hemingway was soon feverishly denouncing as Fascists other writers who criticized the Kremlin.

Wilson was numbered among those writers, which possibly prompted his sharpish observation about Hemingway's losing his bearings. For Wilson, it may have been as much of a riposte as a judgment. As for Hemingway, he may have gone so far as to become a freelance agent of the Soviet N. K. V. D. in 1940, probably more in a self-perceived beau geste than in a full-hearted commitment to the aims of the Comintern.

The two other significant works that came out of Hemingway's African experience were received far more favorably. Of the two, "The Snows of Kilimanjaro" is certainly the more highly regarded. There is, though, no better story, even in the very slim portfolio of such, about or around the hunting of African buffalo than "The Short Happy Life of Francis Macomber."

The armature of "Macomber" was bestowed upon Hemingway before he ever put pencil to paper. You imagine Percival and he seated by the fire ring in canvas camp chairs–perhaps warmed against the night cold by a shovelful of red coals placed on the ground beneath each of them by one of the staff–their feet in mosquito boots, Percival with his pipe, telling Hemingway about Patterson and the Blyths.

"Macomber," as with almost all of Hemingway's writing, was the product of something he had seen or heard, or read, rather than of pure imagination–whatever outright imaginative writing he accomplished, hardly any, was customarily not very good. What he heard, undoubtedly from Percival, and retained, was the story of Colonel John Henry Patterson.

If Hemingway knew anything about that Colonel besides rumors termed as of a sinister character, it was that the Irish-, and perhaps illegitimately, born Patterson, was sent out when he was thirty-one from the army in India, where he met and married his wife, Frances, to the East Africa Protectorate. There, he was to supervise the completion of the railroad being constructed from Mombasa on the coast to Lake Victoria, almost six hundred miles distant. Named the Uganda Railway, it would be known more colloquially as the Lunatic Express.

Track had been laid into the Tsavo country in what is now southeast Kenya. Tsavo is thought to be a Kikamba word for slaughter, for the bloody Maasai battles fought there. Just before Patterson arrived in March of 1898, with experience in engineering military forts and an imperfect knowledge of Hindi, the thousands of predominantly Indian laborers began to be preyed upon by two maneless man-eating Lion, marauding first singly and then, more harrowingly, hunting as a coordinated pair.

The Lion would enter the camp and even the tents at will and carry off workers–sometimes they took their kills into the thick bush, but only a short way, so unconcerned that as they fed they could be heard purring. At the height of the killing all labor on the building of the railroad ceased. The Lion were believed by the workers to embody the angry, immortal spirits of two dead chieftains who wanted the railroad halted. It was clear to Patterson that he had to kill both animals, whatever their supernatural attributes.

Before he could accomplish that, he needed to foil a plot among the work gang to murder him because of the more-stringent job requirements he implemented, stamping out slacking. Bushwhacked one morning, outnumbered one hundred sixty to one by the plotters, he escaped assassination by haranguing them, promising that if he died they would hang.

In Africa, if it wasn't one thing, it was another.

Patterson's strategy for the man-eaters was to wait in trees or on scaffolding at night at the scenes of the Lion's previous attacks, exposing himself, as well, to being leapt upon. It took him nearly nine months of failure and hazardous attempts before he succeeded in killing both Lion, separately, the last one charging him repeatedly before he could keep it down. Because of the man-eaters, along with disease and desertion, Patterson estimated that progress on the line had been set back by a full seven months. The workers, though, many of whom once wanted him dead, honored him with the presentation of a silver bowl, the inscription in Hindi giving him thanks for saving them from the fate of being devoured by these terrible monsters who nightly broke into our tents and took our fellow workers from our side.

Patterson returned to England in time to ship off to South Africa for the Boer War in which as a second lieutenant, later elevated to lieutenant colonel, he was second in command of a company of the Essex Imperial Yeomanry, commandeering a locomotive, unmasking spies, and with two other men facing an enemy force of fifteen Boers, killing one, wounding one, capturing two, and driving off the remainder, earning him the Distinguished Service Order, awarded by the hand of King Edward VII. After the war, along with taking the specimen that would be recognized as the Patterson's subspecies of common Eland, he wrote the bestselling *The Man-Eaters of Tsavo* about his hunting of the two Lion, whose skins he eventually sold to Chicago's Field Museum where they went on display. The book was an international success that made Patterson famous and drew fanboy letters from the likes of Roosevelt, the two remaining friends till the end of the President's life. In 1908 the British Colonial Office appointed him a game warden in East Africa. In that position he combined surveying trips with taking hunters out on safari, one of those hunts becoming perhaps the most notorious in the history of the British protectorate.

Back again in England after serving as game warden, he became a fixture of high society as he read military history. He also went to Sierra Leone to look into a business venture–in the center of where the murdering Leopard Society was at large–returning home after abandoning the scheme. After the outbreak of World War I he led the Zion Mule Corps, a unit of Jewish volunteers drawn from refugees expelled from Palestine by the Ottoman military commander on the grounds of their being pro-British–Turkey one of the Central Empires with Germany, Austria-Hungary, and Bulgaria in the war. At Gallipoli Patterson and his corps transported supplies and matériel under withering Turkish artillery fire. The Mule Corps was disbanded in 1916, partly for refusing an order to go to Ireland to help suppress the Rising against British rule. Patterson then worked to form a Jewish Legion and commanded a battalion in battle against the Turks in Palestine at war's end.

Following the Armistice, Patterson remained with the Legion in Sinai; but soured by the institutional anti-Semitism he encountered in the British government and military, he left the army in 1920, after thirty-five years. Up until his death in Bel Air, California, in 1947, he worked for the founding of a Jewish state and the forming of a Jewish army, both arriving in the establishment of the State of Israel and the Israel Defense Forces the year after his death. He became such good friends with the Zionist Benzion Netanyahu and his wife, that they named their eldest son Yonatan–Jonathan–after Patterson, who attended the baby's bris. Yoni was the only Israeli commando to be killed in the Raid on Entebbe–on the same day as the U. S. bicentennial in 1976–to rescue Jewish hostages held by the Popular Front for the Liberation of Palestine-External Operations and the Ugandan dictator Idi Amin. His brother Benjamin became the longtime prime minister of Israel.

The key incident associated with Patterson that Hemingway would have learned from Percival, was from his game-warden days. In 1908 he was preparing to leave Nairobi to map the northern and eastern territory of the protectorate when an old acquaintance and former officer of the Imperial Yeomanry asked if he and his wife could join his safari. Patterson thought they would make for pleasant company and received official permission for the couple to accompany him.

The son of Baron Blyth, Audley James Blyth was in his early thirties when he asked Patterson if he could come along. His wife Ethel Jane was in her twenties, slender, blond, and blue eyed. The safari was ill-starred from the start. Porters deserted almost at once, meaning the remaining ones had to carry more burdensome loads of equipment and provisions. Worse portents followed within two days when they passed a Somali caravan, and two miles farther came upon a dead Kikuyu. Patterson questioned natives they met about the body, and they told him the Kikuyu had tried to steal goats from the Somalis. Later, seeing a tree to rest under, Patterson discovered beneath it the desiccated corpse of another native who from the contorted state of the body seemed to have died in horrible pain.

Patterson and the husband and wife rode, Audley struggling with his horse. He somehow developed an abscess on his instep which even with the application of a Maasai remedy of warm cow manure become so severe that he was conveyed in a hammock. Soon he was running a high fever and had to be confined to camp, while Patterson and Ethel went out to hunt, the woman proving a fine shot. They resumed safari-ing, and farther along, Patterson urged Blyth and his wife to return to Nairobi; but Blyth refused. The safari went on. Blyth grew more ill.

The shooting of a rogue Elephant went badly wrong, the enraged, single-tusked bull trampling through the bush, goring to death Patterson's prized Arabian horse, Aladdin, before it, the bull, died. They made a camp in a miserable spot known as Laisamis, a short march from Patterson's goal at Mount Marsabit–where the Johnsons later discovered Paradise–hoping the more hospitable country would bring relief to Blyth. Patterson told the Blyths to remain in the camp while he explored the area. When he returned, he learned that Blyth had left the tent to kill a Giraffe, and now had sunstroke. In Patterson's telling, he sent Ethel to his tent to sleep and sat up all night with Audley, applying wet compresses and having him drink lime juice mixed with cool water from the canvas water bags.

As usual, Lion lurked; and Patterson, according to his later report, instructed the native askaris to keep the fire aflame and checked regularly with them to make sure the Lion were staying away. Before dawn, when Audley seemed to be sleeping well, Patterson woke the cook to prepare breakfast, then went back to sitting in a chair outside Blyth's tent, dozing until he heard him moving around inside. He spoke to him, then searched out the headman to discuss the route of march for the day, with Audley to be transported again in the hammock. As they spoke, there was a gunshot. Patterson ran to Blyth's tent and found him with a revolver in his hand, a bullet through his head.

Patterson contrived a fantastic theory about how Blyth killed himself accidentally with the pistol he kept under his pillow for protection, suicide still a posthumous crime under British law. Things became even more bizarre when Patterson, claiming to want to complete his surveying assignment, decided to continue the safari rather than return to Nairobi immediately. While he was off burying Blyth, the porters–shades of Tsavo–mutinied against their not turning around. Again, Patterson regained control; and he and Ethel rode on in silence as the porters shouted at them to hurry because of the peril Lion presented.

Rhino harassed the safari, even driving off the horses and mules at night; and the going became harder as they went from desert to dense thickets and steep ravines. Patterson finally reached the end of his survey area, and they could return. What happened on the way back would raise the deepest suspicion.

Patterson had the blood-spattered Blyth tent burned, and because of the ongoing threat from insubordinates and the ever-present danger of wild animals, he divided his own tent in two and had Ethel sleep in one half. He later stated that he would have given the entire tent over to her, if he had not come down with dysentery and been able to sleep outside. He claimed he lay down fully clothed, with his rifle, when he slept, an askari posted outside as a sentry.

Although there were safer routes, for reasons best understood by Patterson, he chose to take the safari into the Meru country at the foot of Mount Kenya where tribes warred and where he was persuaded to lead the raiding party of one tribe against another. In the end, he succeeded in making peace between the warriors.

It took more than a month from the time of Blyth's death for Patterson to bring the safari back to Nairobi, seeming to betray no urgency in getting there. He took time out of the march to photograph a large herd of Buffalo with Ethel, and she killed a bull that charged them, dropping it at their feet as Patterson held his fire. Then the entire herd charged. Patterson told Ethel they had to kill the lead Buffalo, carrying horns four feet across the spread, and climb onto it so the herd would pass around them. They both fired, lying in the grass, sending the Buffalo down at thirty yards; and the herd halted, approaching no further. It seemed over, when the askaris opened up with wild rifle fire at the Buffalo, thankfully not hitting any, which would have provoked the charge to resume, the sound and smoke of the Martini rifles merely sending the herd stampeding away.

Even before that, Patterson admitted to admiring Ethel's cool courage; and some would suspect more. As they were nearly to the end of their adventure, and ordeal, the last obstacle was the Tana River in spate. Where they forded, the mule Patterson rode, following the death of Aladdin, was swept downstream to be hauled out of the water by its lead rope. In many ways, all of this would prove easier to contend with than what followed.

Patterson reentered Nairobi with a young and attractive widow and her husband's corpse buried in the desolate bush. Patterson was in bad enough health that he was ordered to return to England, submitting before he left a written account of the incident with the colonial governor, continuing to maintain that Blyth's death was the result of misadventure. Shortly into his recuperation at home, he accepted an invitation from the U. S. President to visit him in the White House to discuss things African prior to Roosevelt's historic safari; the invitation extended to his pregnant wife, but she remained in England. On his trip, Patterson also traveled to Alaska, Yellowstone–where he was confronted by a riled bear–and retraced Stonewall Jackson's march through the Shenandoah Valley. In Kenya rumors burgeoned.

The expatriate mores that led to the stories of mischief in Adamite Happy Valley were already much in evidence in British East Africa, creating the assumption that Patterson and Ethel Blyth had of course found a design for living in the wilderness which drove her husband to take his own life. There was enough of a question of impropriety for the district commissioner to investigate. The men who worked for Patterson on the safari were all long scattered when a year after Blyth's death, two witnesses were located and interviewed and seemed to substantiate at least partially what was being gossiped about. Both reported a violent argument between Blyth and Patterson. While Blyth had to keep to his cot like the dying writer Harry in "Kilimanjaro," his wife and Patterson went out hunting together.

In the witnesses's testimony, Blyth seemed to grow well enough to hunt Zebra, taking three of the rare Grevy's. That night at supper, though, he fell backward in his chair and was carried to his tent. His wife, according to one witness, around midnight left the tent where she had been caring for her husband and went to Patterson's. Another witness believed she left her husband because he had begun to rave and she was frightened–this the woman capable of dropping a charging Buffalo at her feet. Both witnesses stated that she left Patterson's tent early in the morning and when she went into her husband's he shot himself in the mouth. Most telling, though, was Patterson's decision to carry on with the safari and not to return immediately to Nairobi after the death of Blyth. Finally, it was all Rashomon.

Patterson, continuing to protest his innocence, could only wait in England for a verdict, while his wife gave birth to their son Bryan. His concern about what would become of his reputation was such that he had the baby boy registered under another name, Lionel–the Lion, if it needs to be noted–Brown, so he would not have to bear the burden of Patterson's if the colonel ended up disgraced–the false name inspiring another legend that Lionel was his and Ethel Blyth's love child, though Patterson never seems to have met with her after their safari. Ethel would move to New Zealand in 1920 to be the mistress of a married man, dying of cerebral thrombosis, though there was a medical reference to a cut on her hand, perhaps hinting at another Blyth suicide, this from a slashed wrist.

After much tsuris for the Colonial Office, it was determined that Patterson, in light of the possibility of mutiny among the porters, had to continue on with the safari to maintain discipline, and that he was in no way connected to the death of Audley Blyth–Ethel's name seems not to have been brought up, apparently intentionally. The mitigating factor may have been that Patterson's health was so wrecked, he could not return to British East Africa in any case.

It was conceded that Patterson may have had, as they say, an eye for the ladies, but he was hardly a villain or criminal. One who disagreed was Winston Churchill. In a private conversation, the President of the Board of Trade, analogous to the U. S. Secretary of Commerce, called the colonel an adulterer and murderer. When Patterson learned of this, he threatened to bring suit for slander. Churchill was concerned enough to consult an attorney friend who told him that to fight the charge would be appallingly risky. As it happened, nothing ever reached a court of law, and Churchill's biographers have seen fit to overlook for the most part, the incident.

Some of that would have been heard by Hemingway from Percival, and remembered. The part that stuck was the alleged cuckoldry–Edmund Wilson wrote that the emotion which principally comes through in "Francis Macomber" and "The Snows of Kilimanjaro," is a growing antagonism to women.

Francis Macomber was very wealthy, and would be much wealthier. With an American face that would stay adolescent until it became middle-aged, crew-cropped hair...good nose, thin lips and handsome jaw, his fine eyes were only faintly shifty. He knew about motorcycles and cars, duck shooting, fishing, court games, dogs, and sex in books, many books, too many books. Margot Macomber had been a great beauty, enough so that she had once commanded five thousand dollars as the price of endorsing, with photographs, a beauty product she never used. Cuttingly, she was still a great beauty in Africa. She missed her chance to leave her husband but was confident he would not leave her. And the nicest thing about him, wrote Hemingway, was a great tolerance, if it were not the most sinister. Known according to the columnists as a comparatively happily wedded couple in spite of rumors of disruption, they were adding more than a spice of adventure to their much envied and ever-enduring Romance by a Safari in what was known as Darkest Africa.

If the Blyths would seem to be the prototypical sporting couple, even with the nasty business, they were not the first, though. It would take some research to determine whom that might have been; but the most sporting couple was conceivably the peripatetic nineteenth-century global explorer, eventual anti-slaver, and big-game hunter Sir Samual Baker and his ex-slave second wife Florence who never parted from him on his expeditions. The Macombers would have represented the more usual sort.

Novelist Thomas McGuane paralleled Hemingway's description of the Macombers in his caricature of a latter-day sporting couple, the Rudleighs, of Rumson, Connecticut, in *Ninety-Two in the Shade.*

> "Darling," [Mr. Rudleigh] would have said to Mrs. Rudleigh, "it is time we had sport." Then the Rudleighs go to the city of New York. They go to the great brown store where pictures of Theodore Roosevelt and stuffed heads of tigers adorn the walls. A well-mannered lesbian shows them "tropical outfits" which include mosquito netting, a bonefish rod, a pith helmet, and a prophylactic; all stapled to a large piece of cardboard upon which has been printed a tropical scene, the entire outfit protected by cellophane and displayed under disinfected ultraviolet light.
>
> Rudleigh's motto is, "I pay, I take."

Although labored and dated, it says something, however unspeakable, about such couples.

One may assume that the usual imbalance existed in the Rudleighs as much as in the Macombers: The husband did all the shooting and fishing, while the wife sat in the dress circle. When the situation became fraught, as it did with Hemingway and Percival trailing the wounded Buffalo in *Green Hills*, P. O. M. was to stay behind, kept apart from the best parts. She didn't and wasn't.

At least Pauline seemed to enjoy being in the field with Ernest, while his other wives were less enthusiastic. On Safari 2.0, Mary Hemingway probably did not truly want to kill a Lion, but would do so for her husband–while Mary's reluctance to join wholeheartedly in the fun may have grown, Hemingway became infatuated with a young WaKamba woman, Debba, who appreciated all the scars on his body, like the scarification and tattooing on the warriors of her tribe. This may have been another of his misguided efforts at recapturing the past, an homage to the savage–in his vision–Native American girls he loved, or at last avouched to, up in Michigan.

I guess that was the way it was with my old, late friends Walter and Jane White. Jane had joined Walter in his hunting, at first; but the killing of large animals was never pleasurable. So she stopped, though she remained happy to travel with him–possibly enjoying the adventure and to make certain of his whereabouts–and I believe Walter felt better to have her there. Call them Ma and Pa Macomber.

If there are sporting couples anymore, there must be less imbalance. They hunt or fish together–or more likely trek or climb or ski–now by choice, I like to think, with neither obligated to attend passively to the indulgent feats of the other. They participate together or go off on their own private excursions. Or sometimes safaris.

Hemingway takes several pages to bring us to his description of the Macombers, beginning the story in medias res with the dramatis personae sitting under the double green fly of the dining tent pretending that nothing had happened.

The thing that happened was Francis Macomber's showing himself, very publicly, to be a coward.

The story in synopsis is well known. Macomber, an American boy-man, on safari with his wife Margaret, Margot, runs in terror from a charging Lion he wounded, leaving his professional hunter to finish it off. Margot pounces on her husband's display of cowardice, using it as a rationalization to sleep with Wilson. Not the first instance of his wife's infidelity, Macomber was already long unmanned by her. This was different, though.

The real relationship was not between Macomber and his wife, Margot, but between Macomber and Wilson, his professional hunter. Wilson was of a far-different class from Macomber, experienced–flat, blue, machine-gunner's eyes–and living in ways and with values not merely foreign to Macomber, but quite alien, yet that he admired and wished he could have had and adopt. Worse than cowardice in front of his wife, was cowardice in front of Wilson. Macomber's feelings for Wilson are what made this adultery truly difficult to endure.

Wilson was also more than a Greek chorus. He begins in toleration of the Macombers, tries to sympathize with Macomber's shame, comes to deplore his character and to hate the wanton cruelty he perceives in the wife, then witnesses Macomber's rite of initiation in the course of a headlong hunt for Buffalo across the East African plains, gaining–in the jargon of these times–the agency at last to leave his wife. With that awful knowledge, Margot, either by mischance or in a calculation, shoots her husband about two inches up and a little to one side of the base of the skull. While alive, Macomber compounded his funking it with the Lion by asking Wilson if word of it will get around.

> "It doesn't have to go any further, does it? I mean no one will hear about it, will they?" "You mean will I talk about it at the Mathaiga [sic] Club?" Wilson looked at him now coldly. He had not expected this. So he's a bloody four-letter man as well as a bloody coward.

It was not, though, for Wilson, about Macomber's being a coward, but about his verging on a friend.

Hemingway drew both Margot and Macomber from people he knew, the she from a great beauty and the worst bitch I knew (then), he wrote, whom he nonetheless slept with and who challenged him in fishing and hunting facility. The he was her husband, a nice jerk. Macomber's acting like a shit for asking Wilson if the reporting of his cowardliness needed to go any farther–that what happened in the bush, he implored, might stay in the bush–may have been based on another person Hemingway knew in what we often refer to as real life. In the winter of 1936, Wallace Stevens, he of concupiscent curds and the Hartford Accident and Indemnity

Company, vacationed in Key West. At a cocktail party one night, he brought to tears Hemingway's younger sister, Ursula–who would, like Ernest, their father, Clarence, their brother, Leicester, and Hemingway's granddaughter, Margaux, become a suicide–by insulting her brother's talent as a writer. Hemingway went over to the party at once and called out Stevens, who was in his late fifties, overweight, and deskbound by his day job. He was also drunk. Hemingway, in his thirties and still fit, knocked Stevens down into a puddle three times, Stevens to his credit getting up each time and landing finally a punch on Hemingway's jaw, the only effect the breaking of his own hand, concluding one of the screwier skirmishes in the annals of literary history.

When he sobered up, the bard of the Connecticut state capital was thoroughly abashed by the affray and asked Hemingway if they could keep the events a secret between them, worried about what the insurance company might think of their vice-president's inept and intoxicated brawling. They mutually agreed that the older man fell down a flight of stairs, and Stevens put back on his dark glasses to disguise the bruises and when he healed returned to Hartford.

Of greater interest may be Hemingway's reaction when the party hostess announced she would call the sheriff. He and Ursula, both in a panic that he might go to jail, rushed to the house of Charles Thompson–whom as the character Karl, Hemingway belittled in *Green Hills*. Thompson recollected in the book *Remembering Ernest Hemingway*, Ernest always had a perfect horror of getting involved with the law. Throughout his life revenue people, game wardens, all authorities, held abject terror for him–Alfred Hitchcock shared the same phobia after being locked in a cell for a short time when he was a very small boy, his father having asked the local police to do so as punishment for misbehavior by the young auteur. At the end of his life, Hemingway was certain the F. B. I. was building a case against him–they in fact kept a file on him for many years, but early on dismissed his being any threat to the republic, classifying him as a relatively harmless drunk. On April 19, 1936, two months after the fight, he completed the story of Macomber in which the protagonist wants to make certain his shame does not become known among his set, Hemingway selling it for $5,000 to *Cosmopolitan* when the annual wage in the U. S. averaged about $1,700.

"Macomber" is an inkblot for contemporary agenda-driven critics. "Actually, I Felt Sorry for the Lion" by the late literary historian Nina Baym offers a feminist perspective of the story by seeing the Lion as the real subject, noting the centrality of it to the telling, including all the times Hemingway writes from its point of view. Nearly ten pages into Hemingway's story, within a frame narrative, we come to where the story really begins.

It started the night before when he [Macomber] had wakened and heard the lion roaring somewhere up along the river, wrote Hemingway.

So it is the Lion's voice that starts the story from within the story, and is present all the way up to the line, That was the story of the lion.

Our knowledge of the story is repeatedly transmitted through the Lion: no man smell carried toward him and he watched the object, moving his great head a little from side to side; he heard a cracking crash and felt the slam of a 30-06 220-grain solid bullet that bit his flank and ripped in sudden hot scalding nausea through his stomach; his flanks were wet and hot and flies were on the little openings the solid bullets had made in his tawny hide; he could hear the men talking and he waited, gathering all of himself into this preparation for a charge as soon as the men would come into the grass.

Baym's insistence, that if the attentive reader does not hear the voice of the Lion, and the woman Margot, the reading of the story becomes an episode of forced indoctrination into the dominant male ethos whose hypocrisies and inconsistencies the story presents, is actually more sensible than the perfect agitprop analysis of a Virgil Hutton in "The Short Happy Life of Francis Macomber"–his title–that in Wilson's red face lies the red coloring once used on maps to designate areas of the world under British rule–the color was pink, a compromise for Imperial red so the printed names could be read through the tint–and that he represents an unwitting hypocrite who harshly judges others on the basis of various strict and false codes that he himself does not follow. Wilson disobeys laws, promising to flog rather than fine the safari staff for infractions, which the Africans prefer to losing wages, though they appreciate neither; chasing Buffalo from the doorless, box-bodied motor car, which Hemingway did with Percival and Thompson–from his handwritten notes: three big bulls we found in the open and galloped with the car–after the chase, Wilson's disdainfully rebuffing Margot when she disingenuously remarks to the professional hunter that she did not know that pursuing animals with a motor vehicle was permitted.

It's illegal, he says, if that's what you mean.

With his clients their standards were his standards as long they were hiring him, which is how he makes his living and seems simple pragmatism rather than hypocrisy. There are limits, though.

[He has] his own standards about the killing and they [his clients] could live up to them or get some one else to hunt them.

No one shot from cars, said Wilson stonily when a disheartened and vindictive Margot, apprehensive that Wilson has ignited in Macomber what it will take for him, really, to abandon her, has accused him of it in her honeyed way.

They traveled a wild forty-five miles an hour across the open in pursuit of the Buffalo, the car liable to wreck at any moment.

When they caught up to the bulls and Macomber raised his rifle, Wilson shouted at him, Not from the car, you fool! making Macomber leap out as the vehicle skidded, plowing sideways to an almost stop, Macomber stumbling as his feet hit the still speeding-by earth, firing at the running Buffalo, remembering to get his shots forward into the shoulder.

Seeing the bulls go down, he was not thinking at all, as a lifetime of torments were scorched from him. For Wilson, it seemed sporting enough while they were doing it–trumping blackletter law.

As for the double size cot he brought on safari to accommodate any windfalls he might receive, Wilson worked for a clientele where the women did not feel they were getting their money's worth unless they slept with the white hunter. And he was free to despise them afterward, though he liked some of them well enough at the time.

Besides, he was no bloody plaster saint; and a husband, such as Macomber, should keep his wife where she belongs, he rationalized. What he had that he never gave up was what he lived by, that the worst that could happen was to be killed, and in the words of Feeble, a conscript in the army at Agincourt in the second part of *Henry IV*, that we owe God a death and he that dies this year is quit for the next–Hemingway probably found the lines in the epigraph of the first chapter of Frederic Manning's World War I novel, in Hemingway's estimate the best written about the war, *Her Privates We*, centering on the Battles of the Somme and Ancre. Manning, an Australian Catholic by birth, was an exceedingly strange man. The first version of the novel, under the title *The Middle Parts of Fortune*, was published in an edition of slightly more than five hundred copies and contained such Anglo-Saxon words as fuck and cunt; the revised edition, *Her Privates We*, underwent expurgation before publication.

We owe God a death is, of course, a *Boy's Own* sentiment.

The short story and memoir author, Frank O'Connor in his 1962 study of the short story, *The Lonely Voice*, wrote that Hemingway's obsession with physical courage was certainly some inner turmoil.

If you think this is merely the conclusion of another bookish Irishman, who for all that, never-the-less thought Hemingway's work capable of being read thirty years before and read again today with the same admiration, O'Connor was fighting in Ireland's War of Independence when he was fifteen and joined the I. R. A. in the civil war in opposition to the Anglo-Irish Treaty creating the Irish Free State, and was jailed between 1922 and 1923 by the new government of Ireland, examples of courage perhaps beyond the foremost of Hemingway's, particularly for having been carried out against the dreaded authorities.

To say that the psychology of this story is childish would be to waste good words, was O'Connor's estimation of the work.

As farce it ranks with...any...Victorian morality you can think of. Clearly, it is the working out of a personal problem that for the vast majority of men and women has no validity whatever.

Cowardice, and the thirst for courage, are more universal than O'Connor credits. When Macomber wakened and heard the Lion, he had to lie there with his wife breathing quietly, asleep. There was no one to tell that he was afraid, no one to share his fear; and, lying alone, he did not know the Somali proverb that a brave man is always frightened three times by a Lion–when he first sees its track, when he first hears it roar, and when he first confronts it. Knowing fear and wanting courage would seem valid enough for anyone.

After all, he said to himself, it is probably only insomnia. Many must have it, thinks the older waiter in the clean, well-lighted café.

Hemingway was an insomniac from childhood. The isolation of waking in a darkened room, or tent, where another person is sleeping placidly can be the deepest there is, comparable to dying as a man who, as Hemingway wrote in his bull-fighting book, lived many years with a good wife and then outlived her. There is, ex Hemingway, no lonelier man in death except the suicide.

It is an ultimate isolation, and expulsion, believing you are excluded from the cosmopolis of sleep, everyone else insensible to whatever torments you are tenanting. Oblivion is the most exclusive of clubs–sleeping, along with being the nearest thing to death we know, is, wrote Jorge Luis Borges, the most secret thing we do–and being deported from its citizenry is a crushing banishment. As an adult, Hemingway sought relief through getting up and swallowing a drink or two–and sometimes drank in bed, as during a night in his tent in Kenya on his second safari when his wife Mary commented on it–then trying to go back to sleep, desperate to rejoin the muted choir of the inconscient.

You can imagine waking to the sound of a Lion's roaring–an animal your ego says you must hunt, though toward which all you have is foreboding–and feeling you are utterly alone among the sleeping. With the Whites in the C. A. R., my friend Carey and I–in the Koubo camp to which we traveled north, when we had vehicles–shared a grass-walled boukarou.

Hyena came through the camp at night, and I pointed a weak penlight out of the boukarou and caught yellow eyeshine. I was fond of their whooping calls, something cheering about hearing their manic sound coming out of the darkness, though they were known to attack with face-crushing force, people asleep out on the ground. Before going to bed, we stacked chairs in front of the open doorway in a pretense of erecting a barrier; but I never worried about the Hyena.

Carey came in one night, having enjoyed some of the red wine from the foil pouches, and was soon snoring. I lay down and went to sleep, too, until the Lion started roaring on the other side of the small creek that passed by the camp.

A Lion roar by measurement is louder than an ambulance siren, the decibel level sufficiently high to cause hearing damage if listened to close and long enough. You cannot gauge how far or close a Lion may be as its roar fissures the night, the sound echoing for miles. With the first roar I sat up on my cot and reached for my 375, leaning close by. Carey slept.

That was the worst thing, being afraid alone. I called to Carey, but he wouldn't wake. So I went on sitting in the dark, the hardest times being the silences between the roars when I couldn't tell where the Lion moved to. When it roared, as if into an oaken barrel, ending in those coughing grunts, it seemed it was claiming all that surrounded it. It went on for over an hour while I was by myself in my awakeness, the Lion never fording the creek. Even after it stopped, I could not fall asleep again for a long time, waiting for another roar that didn't come. Almost to morning, I finally slept. When the camp worker came to the tent to waken us, Carey sprung up, fully refreshed, a person who probably never experienced insomnia.

Dramatically speaking, wrote the Princeton professor, and future Hemingway biographer, Carlos Baker in his 1952 study of Hemingway's work, *Hemingway: The Artist as Writer*, physical courage is often a convenient and economical way of symbolizing moral courage.

Still, it is true, Baker wrote, that Hemingway's satirical steam, never far below the surface, tends to erupt whenever he deals with leisure-class wastrels–and even though, I might add, that nothing bears out the proposition that dying is easy, comedy is hard, quite as persuasively as Papa's forays into attempted funny, his portrait of the Macombers may in fact be more deadpan and sharply executed than McGuane's of the Rudleighs. Yet Baker accepts the reinvention of Macomber, describing it in a sentence: But where the lion was an instrument for the establishment and build-up of emotional tension, the oncoming horns of the buffalo are the pronged forceps of Macomber's moral birth.

Yikes.

What is learned, or experienced, is that the pillars of fear are anticipation and reflection. At the apex of the arch is a vanished keystone. In the precipitating event is nothing. In the instant–when the vehicle at speed leaves the highway on a patch of black ice, the realization that a bullet has struck, that a stumble has accumulated into a fall from height, that the animal charge will arrive, there is only ultimate clarity and serenity. The fear is in expectation, to overcome, and in aftermath, to endure. In the moment itself, is a void. If you know that, the pillars are undermined.

Edmund Wilson, in his chapter on Hemingway in 1941's *The Wound and the Bow*, wrote that "Macomber" perfectly realizes its purpose.

The male, he writes, saves his soul at the last minute, and then is…shot down by his woman, who does not want him to have a soul.

It's been noted how often Hemingway's heroes end in physical defeat.

In the story, Hemingway, according to the critic Wilson, at last got what Thurber calls the war between men and women right out into the open and has written a terrific fable of the impossible civilized woman who despises the civilized man for his failure in initiative and nerve and then jealously tries to break him down as soon as he begins to exhibit any.

Certainly "Macomber" is all that, and the proof of its excellence is in all the interpretations it will sustain. You can argue about red faces, or seating positions in the safari car, or the faintly rosy khaki of Margot's safari clothing, or whether her killing of her husband was intentional or her panicked failure to save his life when she perceived the Buffalo about to strike him with its horns–a matter far from settled in the story. But Edmund Wilson, while downgrading in general the depictions in *Green Hills*, found the landscape and animals of "Francis Macomber" alive and unfalteringly proportioned.

It was in *Green Hills* that Hemingway impeached Melville for being a writer of rhetoric. Yet O'Connor identified Hemingway as one of the first of James Joyce's acolytes by his use of such techniques as the repetition of key words to slow the movement of his prose, calling it a rhetorician's dream.

It was only through good fortune, opined Hemingway, that Melville found a little…of how things can be, whales for instance, and this knowledge is wrapped in rhetoric like plums in pudding.

Occasionally, he allowed, it is there, alone, unwrapped in a pudding, and it is good. This is Melville.

In "Macomber," beyond the human dynamic, and free of Hemingway's anthropomorphic presumptions, the country and the animals, the Lion and especially the Buffalo, are good.

> … the buffalo got bigger and bigger until [Macomber] could see the gray, hairless, scabby look of one huge bull and how his neck was part of his shoulders and the shiny black of his horns as he galloped a little behind the others that were strung out in that steady plunging gait… they drew up close and he could see the plunging hugeness of the bull, and the dust in his sparsely haired hide, the wide boss of horn and his out-stretched wide nostrilled muzzle…

After this for the remainder of his career, Hemingway began more and more to wrap up his own writing like plums. "Macomber" was, though, still among his best. It was at the king tide of his artistry; and even if you know of another story of the African buffalo, it could not be better. The people are there; but if they are there only in the service of the Lion, the Buffalo, and the African landscape, that is good.

What could Hemingway have truly thought about the Buffalo? Nothing more than what he said, perhaps. Let it be stated, though, that the Lion was not the contributory cause of the death of Macomber. By running from the Lion's charge, he gave his wife no cause for shooting him, premeditatedly or not. It was facing the Buffalo that cost Macomber his short happy life. So in which, Lion or Buffalo, did the greater danger, one of Hemingway's key measures of value, lie?

In working-class San Francisco de Paula is Outlook Farm, its name in English. The sloping lawn is Bermuda grass, royal palms and ceiba trees growing around and over it. The house on the highest part of the property is reached by wide concrete steps to an arched entryway set on columns, a bronze bell hanging outside. It was over fifty years old when he first rented it in 1939, one of his future wives finding it for him so he would move out of Room 511 of the Hotel Ambos Mundos, and its libidinous temptations. When he later bought it with royalties from *For Whom the Bell Tolls,* he restored it, clearing the grounds of the overgrown poinciana. A tower was built. He put up book cases throughout the house and filled them, and on the walls of the high-ceilinged airy rooms he hung paintings of the corrida and art by his changeable friends, such as Picasso–who often mocked what the painter saw as the writer's pretensions–and trophies from his hunts in the Yellowstone High Country and Africa. He lived there until he left Cuba for the last time after the Castro revolution. From the back veranda was a view of downtown Havana, nine miles to the northwest.

Visitors may not enter the house, only compass it, looking in through windows and open doors, passing the graves where four of Hemingways's dogs are buried and where the black Wheeler Playmate *Pilar,* modified for big-game fishing, sits, dry docked in a pavilion. Through a window were, on the white wall behind the doctor's scale in the bathroom, his daily weights inscribed in pencil, always hoping to see them be less. Another window looks in on a walk-in closet where his military uniform, upon which its war-correspondent patch is stitched, hangs. In the Ritz after the liberation of Paris, his rival, at least to him, André Malraux paid a visit, Malraux outfitted in Saumur pants, a magnificent tunic, jacket laddered with gold galons down the sleeves, and exquisite cavalry boots, in keeping with his official rank of a

French colonel. Hemingway, meanwhile, was in dirty irregular battle dress. Over seventy-five years later, on a closet shelf beside the uniform stands a pair of tall polished oxblood cavalry boots, barely broken in. I thought of the picture of my father, dressed in his military-school uniform.

On the wall in a spare bedroom is the head of an impala above a low bookcase filled with, among many other volumes, the anonymous spines of French livres, his mentor Ezra Pound's *XXX Cantos*, Arthur Koestler's *Darkness at Noon*, A. J. Libeling's book on boxing, *The Sweet Science*, and a copy of Ruark's *Horn of the Hunter*, the dust jacket tattered from repeated readings, a fact that would have meant more to the author of that book than he might have cared to acknowledge. A manual typewriter is set on the top of the case. There is where, because of the pain in his legs from the shrapnel wounds received at Fossalta di Piave–the scars Debba admired so–and internal injuries from the two plane crashes in two days on the second safari, he wrote standing up, beneath his feet the back skin of the Kudu from the first safari, which he believed transferred to him creative power.

There is a small side library where he also worked, seated at a desk, facing a wall of more books. When he sat there he let the cats climb on him. The tall cases step down to a low one on which sit paintings and drawings and a large apothecary jar filled with amber fluid and a wet specimen of unrevealed nature. As he worked, he faced the wall with the head of a Buffalo on it–This is a real bull, Percival told him–that he killed at four hundred yards with his Springfield as it ran. It is mounted in a sneak pose, the head lowered, the way it would move through thick cover when it would be at its most dangerous. Whenever he raised his eyes from his writing, the Buffalo was before him, no Lion in sight.

CHAPTER SIXTEEN

Hona

BEFORE DAYBREAK, THROUGH the wind wing of the Nomad doing sixty, the cooling air off the rows of fresh-cut alfalfa in the fields on the sides of the long straight road smelled of the grassy heat of the previous day. Out the moth-spattered windshield, the headlights rushed forward to the point of convergence on the two-lane blacktop, Burrowing owls sculling through the high beams. At the light's fringe, white bloomed bolls stood on the withered stalks and leaves of the defoliated cotton plants, waiting harvest, flashing by along the edge of the eighth of a section of once-chicken ranch my grandfather bequeathed my father.

Turning north on the crossroad, my father, Roy, and their friend Charlie drove beside an earthen canal to another crossroad and turned again to come to Elmer and Mary's house. Going up the drive, they stopped at the backdoor under the yard lamp hung on a telephone pole, crane flies and night moths circling in its halo. Elmer, who rented my father's inherited land, came out. He was short, a face like, of all people, J. Carroll Naish, his fingers thick, blunted, roughened by a lifetime of farming, his belly rounded above the belt of his worn riveted jeans, feet stockinged, still-dark Portuguese hair combed back, with a rolling limp from a leg atrophied by infantile paralysis. He held open the screen door.

The door banged shut and it was cool inside the house's wide white-plastered adobe walls and on the terracotta floor after the men removed their boots in the anteroom. Under the ceiling lamp at the long oak dining-room table, the four men drank coffee and ate coffeeshop doughnuts, talking the best of all talking, not only natural but actually fitting that it should have begun with whiskey, the night before; and tonight would go on with whiskey. Later this day, they came back to pluck the morning's birds and to the breakfast made by Elmer's second wife, Mary–cooked eggs, iron-skillet-fried potatoes, linquiça, squeezed orange juice, toast. After sleeping some hours in the afternoon back at the curtained motel rooms, the three men stood under oaks and sycamores waiting for the Mourning dove to return to the roost; and in the evening they ate at the oak table the roast beef Mary cooked, the ripe, wet beefsteak tomatoes from her garden on the sunside of the barn beside the beehive in the siding of a farm shack, sliced with red onions and dressed with oil, vinegar, salt, and pepper.

Now they were done with the doughnuts. They carried their plates and cups and saucers and placed them in the sink. Elmer drove his farm truck with the old cracked vinyl seat coverings; and the three men followed in the Buick, crosshatching the farmland as they turned from road to road.

After several miles, Elmer pulled over onto the dusty shoulder of the field of volunteer Turkey millet, where he had scouted for birds, and shut off the truck. The men parked behind, my father turning off the headlights, and took out their shotguns: Roy's a well-used ribless Model 12 and my father's a Model 50 semi-auto, its barrel cut down with an added Cutts Compensator for interchangeable chokes. Elmer had a long-barreled farmhouse pump looking longer than he was tall; but he carried it more as a formality, in any case. What Charlie carried, no one noted.

They waited for their night vision to return and pushed down the squalling top strand of barbed wire, crossing the fence into the field, walking over the hard ground to spread fifty or sixty yards apart along the east side where there was dead brush and Russian thistle for camouflage and the Dove would fly in and across. Loading the shells, they set the safeties and rested their guns on the butts, before the Dove started to fly.

In the hot September valley, the morning was just cool enough to keep off the insects; but my father wanted to be back asleep in the warm motel bed. Waiting for the sun, he had his back to the blackness of the eastern horizon, when his shadow flashed in instant daylight across the ground in front of him. He turned and saw the toothed line of the Sierra crest lighted in an instant, silhouetted on the far side of the valley. As he watched, the big light brightened. For less than a minute it showed there, doming, before dimming and going down again. He felt neither awe nor dread as he watched the actual sun beginning to rise. The sun was only the light of a star, not a flaring of the apocalypse. Somewhere within himself, he might have wished to absorb the atomic explosion's rays.

He heard a shot from Roy's gun, and turned to see the falling black teardrop of a folded Dove. The birds started to fly; and if he were not deaf, he would have heard their whistling wingbeats, or perhaps he did and wouldn't say. He began to shoot. Two hundred miles away, radioactive dust settled around the tortuous charred steel of the skeleton of a five hundred-foot-tower.

The Maasai have a proverb. He who has a father is still not circumcised–Memurata olayioni oota menye. In 1982, I still had a father–a man of smoke and lead, wafting or holding rigid in mute obstinacy, for reasons known only to himself–a story I wrote about Buffalo was awarded a prize from a national sports magazine as the best outdoor story of the year. Shortly I received a call from an editor at a New York publishing house–its authors included Borges, Peter Matthiessen, Joyce Carol Oates, Gore Vidal, as well as Cleveland Amory and Mickey Spillane–asking me if I, perhaps, had enough stories to collect into a book. I thought I was being ushered in.

In New York–it was summer–I wore a sport coat and tie and rode in the elevator in the publisher's building up to the office of the editor. He had a mustache, red veins webbing old-man cheeks, and a hunch. We went to lunch.

In the white tablecloth and silverware restaurant, he ordered an Old Fashioned. We talked. It seemed that most of the books he edited were on the topic of dog training. Looking at him, I noticed the patch on his chin he'd missed with his razor that morning. The cocktails came, and the basket of bread. He put the butter on his bread plate, where he had also lain the stem from the Old Fashioned's maraschino cherry. Removing a slice of baguette from the basket, he picked up the butter with the butter knife and started spreading it on the bread, a mild tremor of intent showing in his hand. The too-red cherry stem stuck to the knife and he buttered it onto the bread. He took a bite, and picked the stem out of his teeth

The galleys came the day before I left for the C. A. R. They had to be edited by me in two weeks, when I would be gone in Africa for more than a month. It was five a.m. the next morning when I finished, in time to get to the Air France flight to Paris.

Carey and I flew together. In Charles De Gaulle my rifle came off on the carousal. It should be declared in some way, I thought. Looking around, I saw a gendarme in the old-style kepi. Pointing to the rifle case, I tried to mime what was in it and ask what the ordinance might be. He flourished his hand and pointed me out of the terminal, dismissing me as only the French police dismiss.

We met the Whites for the first time that night in the restaurant of the hotel where we arranged to take rooms together. Jane laughed the way a well-bred college girl laughed, though she was in her fifties. Walter wore a blazer with some sort of sigil made of gold threads and had a cowlick in front that made him look small-boyish, especially with the faint freckles he still showed. We shook hands; and as we sat down at the table, Walter produced a small flag of the Explorers Club from his inside jacket pocket, flourishing it and planting it in the sugar bowl.

In the morning the Sarajevo Winter Olympics were on the television in the hotel room, and we switched them off and went out into Paris. Carey and I walked to Avenue Franklin Delano Roosevelt and the Gastinne-Rennette store, half a mile from the Arc de Triomphe, to overdose on best guns and rifles. I had changed a traveler's check into francs, and as I left the shop, a loose five hundred-franc note with the portrait of Blaise Pascal, fell from my pocket to the sidewalk; and I walked on without noticing. After some blocks, we came to a man selling oysters on the Boulevard Haussmann and stopped. We stood, eating them raw in their brine with a squeeze of lemon as he opened the shells on the gray winter day. He asked in broken English where we were from. We told him California, and that we were going to Africa that night. And he? He tilted his head and raised an eyebrow a little. Paris, he said. Only Paris, making the city of lights sound sunless. As I took out my French money to pay him for the raw oysters, I counted the bills, and counted them again, and knew I lost the five hundred-franc note. A small piece of the cost of safari-ing in the C. A. R.

I returned from Africa; and when the book appeared that summer, I soon saw that the publisher had done nothing to promote it, to the point where I took to sending books to reviewers from out of the author's copies I had on hand. One wrote back, that if he had seen it before publication, he would have reviewed it on the front of the book section of the city paper's Sunday edition. Now, of course, it was too late.

Later in that summer a woman in Santa Cruz contacted me. Somehow she read a story about a bear in my book, and it evoked the poem of Galway Kinnell's–enduring odor of bear–for her. She and her friend would like to arrange a book signing for me near her home.

I drove the six hours north and reached her house in the late dry afternoon. She was divorced with a young son. I ate dinner with her friend and her, and then went to the bookstore. I could tell that I was not as she had foreseen. Nor were the three hours at the signing table, when exactly two people, a couple who appeared somewhat baked, came up and made the single purchase of one signed book. I left in the morning without saying goodbye.

Much later I was with Elaine at the second wedding of my widowed friend's. The night of the wedding dinner, the friend's fiancée welcomed her friends from Canada. One of the women was young. The best man, there with his wife and baby, started calling her a "Titian-haired beauty" in front of everyone, and the groom-to-be spent the rest of the weekend watching her like a lynx chained just out of reach of live food. From that, I could see how it would all be. I remember the wedding party, then awakening the next morning. Bad Bob Jones threatened to fistfight everyone the night before, and the groom was carried bodily back to his nuptial bed.

While we were there, the editor from the publishing company called my answering service and left a message. It was in the matter of my new book. He was distressed when I reached him because the entire sales staff during a meeting demanded to know why they were carrying this title about the killing of endangered species. It was a book about a broad range of hunting, including the ethics and philosophy, without a single endangered, threatened, or vulnerable species in it. The editor knew nothing, nothing whatsoever, about wild animals or the chase.

This time, the book was reviewed on the front page of the book section of the city paper's Sunday edition. The reviewer remarked on how it was filled with superfluous commas like scattered kisses, and would have benefitted from a decent editor, and then came the trashing of the subject, telling the musty story of how a phantasmic little girl leaped out of a duck blind with her father, and screamed at him righteously about what did those birds ever do to him? The late painter and fishing writer Russell Chatham wrote me a note, telling me that Tom McGuane told him that a literary attack was always an inside job.

There were other books. None ever appeared again on the front page of the book section of the city paper's Sunday edition, to good or bad reviews. I continued writing. My father died.

I could never know how life would have gone, into the marches of old age, had my father persisted into his seventies or eighties–his spirit long defunct before the end he settled upon. I can't know if I would have found, unalloyed, the courage necessary to stand for myself. But he died, and I could stand, and did. Love came to me, beyond my father's surveillance, so many years already into life. The impress of skin to skin; lidded eyes and shining, bursting lips; the warm scent of hair and scalp; fingers twined like the reeds of a handwoven basket; hearts beating in those parts outside the body. Nights in the mercury light from the lamps in the street beyond the bedroom window; behind the bungalow, horses whickering in the darkness from the stables of the mounted-police patrol, along the concrete river; at the end of the afternoon, sunlight in motey crossbars floating off the wall behind the headboard as the eddy moved onshore and hastened toward the mountains, rippling the blinds in passing; shudder joined to shudder; the silent lying; and laughter. And to know that it's not having been there before was of much less consequence than its being there, then.

A wife, a home, the birth of a child. The will with my family to move to a rational place of mountains and prairies where not a day passed when there was not some token of the wild, running, grazing, bedded, in flight, circulating through the sage like some cardiopulmonary system on the earth, or in the scudding clouds in the sky. Against that sky, hazel ridges and white summits instead of roofs. When I could have died as deplorable as my father.

We walked, still watching for Elephant, sighting Blue rollier on the branches and Hornbills in the trees. There were Mongoose, Hare, and Squirrel. Flushed flocks of Guinea fowl flew over the heads of

Roan, starting the antelope running. The Desert crocodile lingered on the edge of a pool in the daylight.

My safari was drawing to its last days and nights, without a Buffalo. In the sky hung a supermoon. Two days were left to hunt, and I wondered how I would find a way to return to this camp in Burkina Faso, wanting to return even if I did take a Buffalo this time, having found something here categorically African. We went out early to the place called Malaga, the far part of the concession where the Lion hunted. After day after day of hunting on foot, it was from the truck that we spotted the Buffalo.

Djanjoua saw them first. Two bulls alone, one dark, the other rust red, coming out of the brush toward the road. Djanjoua let us drive a hundred yards past before drumming his thumb on the cab roof.

We climbed down silently, quietly chambered rounds, then stepped off the road and into the dry grass and brush. Djanjoua carried the shooting sticks and jogged in front, me following, with Kamiri behind, holding the 375 for Djanjoua. We moved at a pace, but softly, then saw the Buffalo coming out from behind cover. The dark one was first, nose up. The second rust-red one was less wary, depending on the senses of the other. The second was the larger, horn tips curling above its head. They were only sixty yards away. Djanjoua set up the tripod sticks, not taking his eyes off the Buffalo. I placed the fore-end of the Blaser in the inner-tube-wrapped crotch of the sticks, the magnification on the crystalline Zeiss V6 dialed down to three.

A moment later, Djanjoua, barely containing his urgency, hissed in English, Shoot.

With the crosshairs holding a third of the way up on the chest of the rust-red bull, a finger-width behind the left shoulder, I let off the backward safety on the Blaser and, trying not to think of all the ways there were to miss a shot, even at this range, drew back the trigger.

The break was clean, the 350-grain bullet going where the scope's crosshairs rested. Both Buffalo ran with the shot, the second hard hit, bolting for the road, tails ribbony. Djanjoua reached back for the 375 from Kamiri and ran after them, looking to make a followup shot. Reloading and setting the safety, I tried to keep up with the thirty-two-year-old hunter; but he was well ahead of me as the two Buffalo reached the road, black ash swept across it in mares's tails. Djanjoua fired once.

He ran back, and now he and Kamiri were pushing and pulling to get me across the road faster. I could see the bigger bull, moving slower as the smaller one went away; then I stumbled in the rush across the road and went down, keeping the rifle pointed ahead of us. I got up, and Djanjoua handed his rifle to Kamiri and set up the sticks again just off the road, telling me to shoot now. At once.

The Buffalo, slowed to a walk, was circling behind a tree. I needed Djanjoua to stay calm.

Tranquil, mon chéri, I said to him, pretending I was about to stroke his shaved cheek with the back of my hand. Djanjoua stared at me in fathomless alarm.

I moved to my left, circling around the tree as the bull sank, front knees first, to the bare ground at its base. I shouldn't have been coming toward it head on, but there was something about approaching from behind to finish it that smacked of assassination. Facing it, I could see its left shoulder clear of the tree. I fired at the front of it, the copper bullet angling through, the buffalo's muzzle falling and the rest of its body, like a tent being struck, collapsing.

Djanjoua and Kamiri were calling at me as I now circled around the bull to come up from behind, my rifle reloaded, and touched the Buffalo on the rump with the toe of my boot, then nudged it harder, and again. I stepped back and ejected the loaded cartridge from the chamber, closing the bolt over the unused solid.

Black heart blood came from the bull's nostrils. It was hardly smaller than the Cape buffalo I had taken, its hide crosshatched with white lines of closed wounds and insignia of pearl scar tissue from fighting other Buffalo bulls. With bases that almost touched, its horns were long, worn, wide, shaped like the lunate crest on a samurai helmet. It was a first-day bull on the second-to-last one.

On his cell phone, Alassane the driver called another hunting truck not far away; and they soon drove up. It was Lance's truck, Carey hunting with him that day. They got out, and the usual congratulations were exchanged; but the real one came as Carey relit his half-smoked Cohiba, then folded his arms and nodded to himself at the Buffalo.

After six or seven of us loaded the bull whole into the back of our truck with the help of a pulley, we turned back toward camp. It was just midmorning. Hartebeest ran again among the scattered trees on either side of the sand road. We turned onto the road between the buttes; and when we reached the campfire and the feathers in the shade, I thought of how this Africa of now was yet the Africa of then, more than forty years before, wondering how it stayed as it was, my knowing that hunting was much of it, but wondering if hunting could keep it that way.

Tropical storms in the Gulf of California made the night air in August heavy and warm, though a freshening from somewhere, off the ocean, was coming onto the land. I parked on the circular concrete driveway among the police cruisers, lights flashing blue-red, and walked to the avocado painted, paired barn-door gate. Unlatching the left half, I pushed the gate open and walked through, closing it behind. I walked through the lighted breezeway, toward the bluish shafts of flashlights of the police on the dark lawn. As can still be said, no way has yet been invented to say goodbye to them.

Earlier in the year he had the stapedectomy. You wondered what he heard, all the unknown sounds and voices. Did he welcome them or regret losing the consolation of a lacking: I am deaf, you must care for me for that, because you will not care for me in any other way. In midsummer, prone to hernia, he had another inguinal repaired. He lay in bed in his room at home, recuperating, the drapes drawn, dressed in pale-blue pinstriped pajamas, considering how everything was dissolving. He had to hear, to listen; he convinced himself he would never drive a car again, attaching untold consequence to that; mother and father, a brother who died too easy, a wife, sons, all arcana from which he experienced exclusion. Unloved because he never got it–how to love. None of that mattered, or mattered more than anyone else would know.

It was night. He moved his legs and sat on the edge of his bed, feeling the pull of the sutures, bracing himself to standing. Walking to his closet, he took down the dented, small, wrinkled powder-coated tool box from a shelf. Placing it on the vanity in his closet, he got the key to open the lock.

He held a pillow in front of him in his left hand, his right hand behind it, as he walked out of the bedroom in slippers, and down the hall. In the living room, my mother was on the phone with Roy's wife, and my six-year-old nephew–spending time in the summer with his grandparents–watched television.

He paused beside the boy and shifted things around to bring out his right hand, empty, from behind the pillow and touch the boy's cheek. Then, drawing his right hand back behind the pillow in his left, he opened the sliding-glass doors and walked out, then through the back porch room and its double doors.

I had an apartment–hideous green-shag carpeting and popcorn ceiling–for almost a decade across town in Downey. I was thirty-three, the age of crucifixion, and I could not resolve how to break free from him or her. Mostly him. I was on the phone to a friend when the operator broke in. I sensed crisis from the first sound of the operator's voice. She connected me with a Detective Compton. He told me what had happened, and I asked if he were still alive. I was there in ten minutes and saw for myself.

Roy was already there, my mother telling his wife when she heard the report from outside and Roy's leaving his house at once. It was his tortured soul that brought my father out here, where he lay down on the grass beside my mother's beloved rose bushes, putting the pillow under his head and pressing the muzzle of the Colt Official Police 38 Special against the right side of that head.

The pistol lay by the body on the lawn, juddered from his hand. His knees were drawn up on the dew, posed as a fetus. A stippled wound bled pitch into his gray hair. The temple of his eyeglasses was at an obscure angle across the side of his head, below his ear. He had convulsed. He left no note.

Did he cock the hammer and fire the gun single action, or was it double action? Was he tensed in every muscle, ready to scream out? Or did he simply lie down and pull the trigger, hollow inside, succeeding in making everything worse for those he quit? If he hesitated, there was no a sign.

Dying is the unsuspected foreordained. We feel it coming without knowing how it will be, we meant never to know. Suicide is cheating by the fearful, far more performance art than we give it credit. And it may be handed on like misery, deepening like that coastal shelf. Hardly ever sui generis, we must learn it, or learn from it. With unmerited favor, the latter. And with grace, we do not become our fathers.

We scattered his cremated remains at sea off the Marina del Rey breakwater, three miles from shore as the ordinances insist. The mortuary cabin cruiser had top-flight fishing tackle–Penn reels and Sabre rods–stacked discretely on the lower bunks for jolly pleasure-trip excursions, burial trips making for a handy write-off of nautical expenses. Under the overcast summer-morning Catalina eddy, gray ashes bubbled a little, like porridge cooking, when poured onto the black water, then swirled and settled from sight. The pistol with dried-blood scales on the bluing and the insignia of a rearing young horse, came back in a manila envelope from the coroner's.

It was my father's tortured soul that brought all this nothing.

My father's tortured soul.

Tortured soul.

The question, never fully ceasing: Did I do this?

Fuck tortured souls.

Ad te clamanus exules filii Hevæ.

It was almost a year beyond the safari before what happened to Burkina Faso, happened.

Only a fool or someone irrationally optimistic could have believed that terrorism–or just call it the twenty-first century–would not reach out farther than Ouaga or the northeast of the country bordering the perpetually murderous Sahel. In the late fall after the previous winter's safari, terrorists, some antic outgrowth of al-Qaeda or Islamic State, or a local-grown variety, came through Arly, burning the camp–all the painted walls–to the ground.

Suddenly, the part of Burkina Faso with its wildlife and wild land, once thought immune to what happened in Ouaga, was in the Africa of not then, but now. The southeast of the country became at once a no-go zone where the military and the official government abandoned control. And the hunting stopped and the invested guardians of the wildlife, the safari operators, left.

I spent a year, seeing if attention would be paid outside Burkina Faso–where even the Burkinabé took scant notice of their own Southeast–to what was happening in and around Arly. Whether that game or that wilderness meant anything to anyone besides a hunter who knew it.

I inspired no one to action.

The forest rangers in the region finally, understandably quit their posts–facing impressment, kidnapping, or beheading–leaving no one to track the game or monitor the toll of anarchy on the tens of thousands of suddenly unprotected hectares that were once Arly Safari's hunting concession, or in the hundreds of thousands of hectares of national parks and reserves that adjoined it. The game might have moved to the west, into reserves not yet under assault. That couldn't be known, though, no one left who could or would report. All that was left for certain was hope.

Thousands, to paraphrase W. H. Auden, have lived without hope, not one without water. The wildlife of Burkina Faso could not survive on hope, but no one seemed willing to offer anything more substantial. Worse, Burkina Faso might have been the stone cast into the middle of the pond of the W.A.P., the ripples spreading to the shared game and habitat of Niger and Benin–Benin, where the hunting camps, rivaling Burkina Faso's, may be winking out one by one, like lights switched off in windows at night.

Riding between the chimney buttes, the rust-red buffalo tied down in the back of the truck, Djanjoua and Kamiri perched upon it like lookouts, I could feel as if I were in the Africa of then. I knew I was not; but I wished just to know that in an Africa of now, a Burkina Faso, as I once saw it, can exist. And that there may be an Africa of next, where all wildlife and wild land are honored and conserved, with places where a hunter can still walk with a worn rifle on his shoulder, years away from now, following traditions he has not through counterfeit bequeathment made his own, but has found to be ones in which he may be permitted, with diffidence, to share.

Mother died in 2001. Or maybe it was 2000, I don't know. I kissed her brow in the coffin. By the time of her death, attached to a ventilator two decades before it was all the rage, she was another woman, in no account chastened but softened and smoothened by fifteen years as her husband's widow–manumitted from what being his wife entailed–and by the eventual presence of four grandchildren, all of whom she doted upon and who in turn adored her–until coming with juvenile eyes to evaluate her as just a little silly–maternal madcap legends abound–loving her not, as it may be, as devotedly, but not less. All of it was an emollient for her laments, even her lifetime of febrile Eastern European anti-Semitism blanketed. She drew her friends from her hairdressers, cruiseship stewards, and departmentstore floorwalkers.

I mark the date of her death by its being before the Buffalo hunting in the Binga lands with Rory Muill. That memory is certain.

Two decades on, four years after the hunt for Buffalo in Arly, the days of my years reaching threescore and ten, I take stock. Equilibrium teeters. An Achille's tendon, once avulsed; the other chronically enflamed. A persistent decubitus ulcer on my naked left buttock. Shins permanently tattooed by thorns–the ones that catch and tear–from the opposite side of the planet. Negligible cicatrices over hands, fingers, face, scalp. One knee should have a brace, the other not far off. A surgical scar tracing the flex of the knee; along the inner thigh a river-delta-birdsfoot where slough from gunshot was debrided, the scent, not of madeleine, but of decomposition remembered. Baby toe, pelvis, rib–cracked. Orbital rim shattered. An incision from sternum nearly to navel, healed dusky with melanin–the surgeon told my wife during the days I was intubated and comatose after the procedure that it was possible I could die; and I remember seeing not a white light but a pattern like the game Tetris, then what looked like the *The Deep* by Pollock; I at last shuddered violently into aghast consciousness when my son, who drove up from Colorado and sat beside my hospital bed, tried to read to me aloud a review from *The New Yorker* of the Tom Hanks movie, *A Beautiful Day in the Neighborhood*. An ensemble of handcuffs and tuxedo. A back that has lain on the azure P. V. C. covers of jailhouse cots under thin cheap blankets while awaiting arraignment. Too much shooting, even after an auditory specialist said it must be discontinued, the thief of the hearing of my left ear; now, even recoil problematic. A cannula feeds oxygen when the pulse oximeter sputters down to 79 percent. There is a continuous-positive-airway-pressure machine for sleep, which comes in only partial payments anyway. Prescriptions for eyewear grow more inordinate with succeeding exams. A cocktail of pharmaceuticals dispensed for a spectrum of conditions. Little appetite for food, but too much alcohol too often. Hair, white; vitiligo creeping over the forehead. Memory, befogged: incidents of gazing at watch hands, palpably flummoxed by how they are read. Leakage–a given. A staunch erection a curio, while there are no words for the satisfaction imparted by agreeable bowel movements. By the grim reckoning of years squandered upon forlorn essays at friendship, not anybody's boon companion. The lifelong murkiness of the spirit may no longer be as exquisite, but its monotomy promises scant relief. Work has not brought what was wanted, but it could be that what is

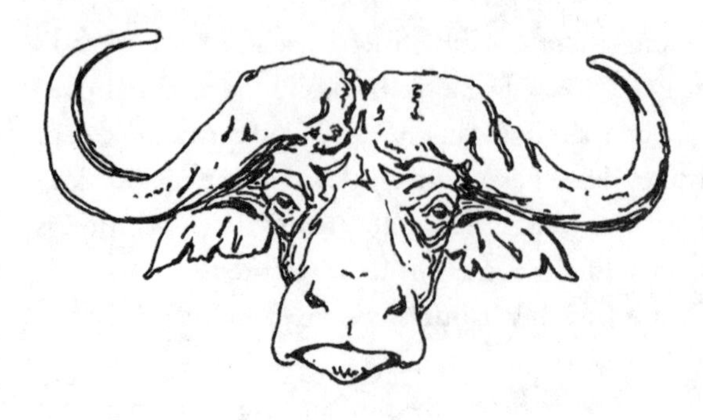

wanted is not for work to supply. If by reason of strength the days of our years be fourscore, yet is their strength labor and sorrow; for it is soon cut off, and we fly away.

But then I return in memory to what balances it all out.

My father, dead five months, inside, seeming longer: A greater time passed on that internal clock, that secret timepiece, of my own, hours sometimes the length of days.

The entirely uncalled-for heat of December hunkered on the northwest horn of Zimbabwe, refusing to leave until the wet season's rains broke; but despite the temperature, there were Elephant to see again. Tar black from the mud of the river, they glided together across the harsh green flats beside the Zambezi west of Victoria Falls, retiring to the relative coolness of gusu woods above, moving smoothly and steadily as large wheeled carriages drawn in stately procession down imperial viæ.

This Zambezi River–whose upper reaches Glasgow-born Dr. Livingstone first saw very near here at the Zambian town of Sesheke in 1851; and seen some years before that by the Portuguese trader-explorer António Francisco Ferreira da Silva Porto, wrongly accused of being a slaver and dismissed by Livingstone as a vulgar negrito, who in despair at seventy-two, lay on top of barrels for gunpowder and lit a fuse; and Africans had known about all along–came out of a bog near Kalene Hill in the far north of Zambia. It passed through Angola before re-entering Zambia, then constituted a portion of the border between Zambia and Namibia, flowing next past the unique point where the borders of Zambia, Namibia, Botswana, and Zimbabwe touched. Establishing then the boundary between Zambia and Zimbabwe, it ran east to where the falls threw up a ten-story, nineteen hundred-yard curtaining barricade across its bed. In late 1855 Livingstone, exploring the river entirely alone except for the presence of one hundred fourteen African porters, came onto these falls and named them in honor of Victoria Regina, seated upon the Sovereign's Throne five thousand miles away. Farther east, now, were hydroelectric dams, impoundments, Mozambique, and the Indian Ocean. Which paled in comparison to Elephant, black and glistening in their coats of river mud.

With its fertile Kalahari-sand-structure soil, this land once, decades earlier, encouraged improbable schemes of killing all the game and not looking back, putting hands to the plow. Naturally, the animals and land tolerated such presumptious folly only so long and in the end reclaimed it all. What remained today were indeterminate dikes and ditch banks subdividing the river flats, and in the hills overgrown tobacco patches and the ruins of drying barns and abandoned whitewashed farmhouses. In place of cash crops, the giant Elephant-gray baobab grew. In the dense brush of once-cultivated fields, Impala bucks issued startlingly loud warning snorts. Atop the old agricultural earthworks on the flats stood Waterbuck, with horns lyre-curving and the bodies of Elk, any plows gone long ago to rust.

Even with Elephant, Cape buffalo, Sable antelope, Greater kudu, Lion, Leopard, Southern impala, Warthog, Bushbuck, and more, here in this Matetsi, December's kiln-hot days during which the tropic daylight seemed to cover everything in an encrusting metallic dazzle, were an appalling time to hunt, because of, first, that shimmering mad-dog sun; second, because all the bush as far as the eye could see was leafing out into a verdant drapery impossible to spot animals through; and third, once those rains–already long overdue–broke, they would fill every pan and depression, allowing the wildlife to spread out over the land in a thin, nearly transparent film, instead of forming huntable congregations around a few permanent waterholes. It was a chance, though, to see Elephant again, and to hunt Buffalo. I had no intention of shooting Elephant, having gotten such a maggot out of my head long before. Which did not preclude my messing about with them.

During my third night in Matetsi, a new-moon night, Lion roared not far off outside my green tent; and on the dirt road that we followed from the camp the next morning we found the tracks of a large pride, giving the day a certain piquancy, in just knowing Lion were there. Sandy, the bearded, Canadian-born professional hunter and I, bracing ourselves in the back of the worn-out pumpkin-colored Land Rover–resolutely branded Solihull, Warwickshire, England–stitched our way across the country. In a long valley of wheaten grass we saw two Giraffe galloping, their necks and ossiconed heads in rhythmic oscillation like superstructures in high winds. Then a dark-as-gun-bluing Elephant, Zhou or Nzou in Shona, wrinkled, myopic, and drowsy, its short tusks clean white, stood alone on a hill. Sandy and I chambered rounds into our 375s, mine scoped and his with iron sights and a grip wrapped in black electrician's tape, the previous owner's having cracked it, literally, over the head of a charging Warthog. We set the safeties, and with Sandy's tracker Enoch went to see how close we could come to an Elephant.

The bull threw up its trunk to shower itself in dust as we got to within two dozen yards. The Elephant grew alert, its ears fanning, and stared toward us, seeing no doubt, approximations. We froze. The bull raised the great pyramidal slab of its forehead, evoking the prow of a steam locomotive about to chug out of the gare. It came, splintering a rotten stump in its path, scattering us screaming, and laughing, too. Some distance downslope, I threw a glance over my shoulder and saw it turned back and running straight-legged over the hill.

Another day and there was a fine big boar Warthog, Njiri; and we set out after it on foot. It moved off, tail high, Enoch tracking it across the volcanic tuff, up a small draw, and over the crest of a rise where in the pale papery grass I saw its verrucous, ivory-tusked profile. I took a rest on my shooting stick and put a 270-grain soft-nosed through the grass and just behind the heavy left shoulder. It bolted a dozen yards before collapsing, and that night in camp we dined by lantern light on Warthog chops.

Sweltering game-less days followed, no reliable pattern to any day in Africa. The sixth morning we came out onto the dirt road above camp again, heading for the tar road from Vic Falls to Botswana, slicing across the upper rim of the safari concession. Below the road, Cape buffalo were in the tangled cover, returning from the river and their nocturnal waterings. Sandy, Enoch, and I went in to look at them, paralleling them as they moved in a black wall through the thicket, trampling trees and bushes. They went slowly, nervously, at first, knowing we were there and uncertain yet which course to follow. Then they stampeded.

Sandy, Enoch, and I ran with them, no more than twenty yards from the column. I could hear bovine grunts, horn bosses cracking against limbs, hooves splitting deadfalls. Dust rose. There was the continuous hollow thump of big running meat colliding with other big running meat, and above it all the beating of my heart.

The stream of a hundred or more low, squat, round-bellied herbivores, the Cattle of God, ribbon tails, square muzzles thrust out, with great grumbling hearts, broke uphill, drawing away and heading for home ground in the broad sweep of trees and savanna that spread to the south, passing almost near enough for us to put hand to hide. Among them all was none shootable; or perhaps it was simply, by the concealed clock within me, not the instance to shoot.

We ceased to run. Panting, I watched the Buffalo going off into the timber, vanishing first into more ascending dust, going farther in distance and time. Yet never so far, not passing from some faculty of sight, outer or inward, as to arrest my pursuit deeper into connectedness. Reaching forth.

The Maasai conception of themselves is iltunǵana loo ngishu, people of cattle. It may be that we in heart are all people of the cattle of God.

When you hear thunder without rain—
it is the buffalo approaching.
—Yorùbá Ìjálá

The End
–Sheridan, Wyoming, 2017-22

Endnotes

Epigraph

... A quatre ans...

At four, he wrote novels, about life
From the great desert, where delighted Liberty shines,
Forests, suns, shores, savannas!–

Rimbaud's words are "A sept ans"–at seven. For me, the thoughts, if not the writings, began at four, as told in the text.

Prologue

... in every...*Hottentot* Country...

Hottentot for the name of the non-Bantu-speaking indigenous peoples of the Cape is a purely nonsense epithet invented by Dutch settlers. To themselves the peoples were the Khoikhoi, approximately men of men or the human beings of human beings. Because of patented European incuriosity about what correct forms of foreign names might be–the Romans called the peoples who called themselves Rasenna the Etruscans; Inuit were called Eskimo by the *qallunaaq*, the bushy eyebrows; Spaniards used another peoples's, the Yavapai's, name for enemy to derive Apache, the Apache calling themselves Inde, people–Khoikhoi was extruded as Hottentot. While the Khoikhoi were cattle-owning pastoralists at the time of their first encounters with Europeans, the more northerly, co-linguistic–the Khoisan language–San were, and are to the extent still viable today, hunter-gatherers. San is another exonym, like Hottentot, this one from the Khoikhoi word *saa*, meaning those who pick up from the ground, doubtless from the San practice of gathering. The combined groups of native non-Bantu of Southern Africa are referred to in this book as Khoisan.

Before Kolben observed them, before the Dutch came, the Khoisan had dealings with Europeans, and perhaps even Chinese. They of course met the other aforementioned Africans, the Bantu, extending out of West-Central Africa into East and Southern for some five thousand years, one way or another displacing earlier peoples. The original inhabitants depicted the arrivistes on rock art as shield-bearing warriors, signaling that those meetings, less memorialized than later ones with Europeans, were perchance no less catastrophic.

Among the first encounters between the Khoisan and Europeans–predominantly Portuguese–one of the earliest was with Dom Francisco de Almeida. Counsellor to King John II of Portugal, pillager of Arab ports along the coast of East Africa, viceroy of Portuguese India, and securer of Portugal's century-long trading monopoly in Indian waters, he put in for potable water at what is now Table Bay on the Cape in 1510 on his return voyage to Portugal. Allowing his crew to raid the Khoisan's cattle, he drew an attack which killed sixty-four of his men, himself included.

Being borne back ceaselessly, we come to the Castilian-Portuguese navigator António de Saldanha, dropping the anchors of his caravels off the Cape in 1503 and scaling table-topped Hoerikwaggo, the transliteration of the click-tongued Khoisan name Mountain in the Sea. In his case, he was said to be only slightly wounded in what seems the obligatory violent engagement with the native peoples, before returning to his command.

In 1497 the Khoisan had their first true contact with the Portuguese when the small fleet of Vasco da Gama's naus–the nau a type of large merchant carrack–and caravels hove into sight of the bay now called St. Helena, three hundred miles northwest of the Cape. Da Gama's having been thirteen weeks out of sight of land, while hoping to be already past the stormy landfall the earlier explorer Bartolomeu Dias labeled Cabo Tormentoso, had to beach his ships expertly so they could have their hulls scraped of barnacles and the collected seaweed torched off.

Initially cordial, the Khoisan on the shore turned belligerent when some of the crew walked into their village unbidden, da Gama suffering a spear thrust to the leg. Making hastened repairs to their vessels, the Portuguese set sail again, rounding the Cape in the heavy weather that mariners had come to expect, and sailing on to land in Mossel Bay. There he and his men spent more time, trading brass bells for ivory bracelets, until the Khoisan accused them of stealing their precious freshwater. Da Gama disabused them with volleys of gunfire over their heads, giving him time to break his storage ship, redistribute its cargo, and burn the hull. As they sailed away in the remaining three ships, the dismayed crews watched as the Khoisan demolished the padrão, a sacred stone cross and pillar the sailors erected on an islet in the bay.

Coming to what is now Malindi on the coast of Kenya in 1498, Da Gama was greeted enthusiastically by the town's sultan. There, da Gama entered into a trade agreement—within two years, the Portuguese ruled Malindi—hired a pilot for the voyage to India, and as a landmark for ships, left behind another padrão, topped with a cross of Lisbon stone, that did better than the one destroyed in Mossel Bay. The pilot brought a kamal, a simple piece of wood attached to a knotted cord, a device invented by Arab sailors in the A. D. ninth century. With it, the latitude of the ship could be calibrated, and since Marinus of Tyre in the A. D. second century, ports had coordinates in degrees of latitude and longitude. A known latitude could be sailed along and a port reached. The accurate measurement of longitude at sea, though, remained an obstacle for many centuries to come.

Europeans may have sailed to the lands of the Khoisan far earlier, however. The perplexing evidence for this is the report of the Greek navigator, Eudoxus of Cyzicus, in the service of King Ptolemy VIII, the Fat, of Egypt, who learned to ride the monsoon winds to India around 118 B. C. On the return from his second voyage to the subcontinent, he was blown down the east coast of

Africa where he found the wreckage of a ship which he identified as having sailed around the Cape from Gades, present-day Cádiz, Spain. Inspired, Eudoxus journeyed to Gades and outfitted his own voyage to circumnavigate Africa. Turned back on his first essay, he launched a second and was never heard from again, although the likes of Pliny the Elder believed he succeeded in his quest, though just not in returning. For as long as Europeans have been seeking the Cape, though, the Khoisan had been moving toward it for the previous a hundred thousand years.

...Kolben tasked with studying...

Kolben–or variously Kolb or Kolbe–was far from the first foreign observer to gaze into the South African night. In the sky in December 1652, the recently arrived First Commander of the Cape, Jan van Riebeeck, made the unaided observation of a "strange star with a tail," later known as comet C/1652 Y1. After van Riebeeck, the French Jesuit missionary, Père Guy Tachard, en route to a post in Siam, made telescopic observations of the occultations, egresses, and eclipses of satellites of Jupiter and by them approximated the latitude and longitude of the Cape.

Kolben began his professional celestial observations when at loose ends after the death of his father at the close of the seventeenth century, he apprenticed himself to an astronomer before completing a thesis on the nature of comets and taking an advanced degree in astronomy. He became secretary to a Freiherr nobleman of the Holy Roman Empire and tutor to the baron's son. The noble, with an interest in the science of the skies, sent Kolben to South Africa with those letters of reference from the thirteen-time mayor of Amsterdam, Nicolaas Witsen. Kolben was greeted warmly upon his arrival at the Cape and set up his telescopes among the cannon in the stone fort, the Castle of Good Hope, built by the Dutch East India Company to defend against envisaged British attack.

Kolben, teetering on a small plank perch on a parapet, made desultory observations of the lunar parallax, which went unpublished by him, his having passed, it was said, "more time in the Company's gardens with his newly made friends than he did with his telescope." A "fireside traveler," as one French naturalist discounted him, Kolben appeared all too predisposed, in the most egregious example, to report as fact what he had been told by the white farmers about the Hottentot's Pissing Ceremony in which an individual was placed within a circle of men who proceeded to urinate upon him as an invocation of supernatural powers, the rite judged a high honor, Kolben tells us.

In George McCall Theal's 1888 history of South Africa, the Holy Roman astronomer is taken to task: "But Kolbe did not prove worthy of the confidence that was placed in him. Too indolent or too conceited for patient research, too credulous in believing idle tales, too unscrupulous to abstain from writing conceits and terming them facts, he forfeited the esteem of his patrons, and after a time found himself in South Africa without employment and without a means of living."

Kolben also sided with the colonists in their grievances against the governor and was facing deportation unless he began paying taxes and accepting the duties of a burgher. He became, then, secretary to the Court of the Landrost–think of the sheriff–at Stellenbosch until dismissed due to failing eyesight. Returning to his home in Germany for treatment and to write his lengthy and fanciful book about the Cape, he later turned into a high-school principal. Never married, he died in his sister's house at age fifty from bad lungs.

... enrag'd at the Sight of red Cloth...

As late as the 1840s the conviction that the color red wrought sure infuriation in the Buffalo was expressed by the African explorer-hunter, Captain W. Cornwallis Harris:

> We were splicing the rotten *trek touw* for the third time, when a stately herd of Buffaloes
>
> Crook knee'd and dewlap'd, like Thessalian bulls,
>
> were perceived at a little distance in the open plain. They were throwing out signs of defiance, in consequence, it was conjectured by a wag, of the warlike appearance of poor Coeur de Lion [*one of Harris's Khoisan retinue*], whose *caput* was as usual decorated with a woollen night cap of that crimson hue, to which the bovine class are proverbially averse!

...some municipality-destroying Japanese kaiju...

In Japanese, a strange beast or giant monster. Also, the genre of film in which those like Godzilla appear.

Chapter One: Praenomen

...Herodotus, called it Libya...

Beyond the Egyptians whose land seemed never entirely of Africa, the Libu were the first people on the continent with whom the Greeks of the Periclean Age came into contact. For Greeks of Herodotus's time, Libya meant the entire landmass from the Isthmus of Suez west–excluding Egypt from east of Catabathmus Magnus–Halfaya Pass. With, as noted by one Elizabethan writer, "this parte of Africa being utterly unknowne" to Ptolemy the scholar, as well as "all the ancient writers"–id est, Western–the continent for the Greeks bled into a speculatively borderless Terra Incognita below Ethiopia's interior, ending somewhere above the equator on the shores of the Austral–Southern–Sea. The Nile was surmised to flow out of the Atlas Mountains, with the complete outline of Africa awaiting "later times" to be "thoroughly discovered by the Portugales." In the A. D. eleventh century, before Portuguese exploration, Al-Biruni, a Persian geographer, challenged Ptolemy's truncated notion of the continent, stating that Africa extended far into the ocean of the South.

...which were believed to be Rhinoceros...

From prehistoric rock art, African Rhinoceros are thought once-native as far as the thirtieth parallel north–the latitude of Houston–across what is modern Libya, retreating south with growing desertification of the Sahara. If Herodotus, called as we know by some The Father of Lies for including a plethora of folk tales in *The Histories*, ever saw one with his own eyes, it might have been during his travels to Egypt when he was in his thirties, but that would be a longshot. A hundred fifty years later in 300 B. C., Rhinoceros were in fact exhibited in Ptolemaic–for Ptolemy the pharaoh–Alexandria. They appeared frequently in ancient Roman coliseums, slain in venationes. Around A. D. 90, two-horned Rhino were stamped onto coins of Domitian's after the emperor saw one in the Colosseum. This would mean that the Rhino was African, either the Black, *Diceros bicornis*, or White, *Ceratotherium simum*, both of those common names misnomers, though for causes inconvenient to disentangle here. For reasons of the remoteness from Rome and its African colonies, and its problematic disposition, the Black rhinoceros seems never to have been brought to Latin Italia. The Rhino that were brought would have been the now-virtually extinct Northern white from Nilotic Sudan on the west bank of the Nile.

...Only the Buffalo was absent...

Here matters grow bleary, or blearier. Although the other dangerous game–Elephant, Lion, Leopard, and earlier Rhinoceros–were present in the ancient Libya of Herodotus, the modern African buffalo never seems to have crossed the Sahara. In its place, a giant species of African buffalo was present in the Maghreb until extinguished twenty five hundred years before *The Histories.*

Yet there are some translations of Herodotus that list Buffalo as among the animals in "Wild beast territory" while others read this as the Bubal hartebeest.

...from the Greeke worde φείκη...

Other fancies about the name allude to aprica–Latin for sunny–or efer–dust or ashes in Hebrew. A Greek lexicon identifies Afer, a son of Saturn–whose offspring as we know fared but poorly, as the British colonial professional hunter, J. A. Hunter, put it in a different context–as the source of the name; or from another source, a son or companion of Heracles who in Libya defeated that land's giant, Antaeus, by hoisting him off his mother, the earth, sapping him of all his strength and crushing him. To the Judeo-Roman historian Titus Flavius Josephus, the name derived from Epher the grandson of Abraham who invaded Libya. Leo Africanus, in translation, gave naming rights to the "Arabian toong" in the word Iphrichia–or Ifriqiya–meaning either to divide in recognition of Africa's being cut off from Europe by the Mediterranean and from Asia by the Nile, or after King Ifricus of Arabia Fœlix, who routed from his kingdom by invading Assyrians, fell back to what became Carthage.

...according to John Pory...

Pory says of the Africa unknown to Ptolemy–

> ...beginneth to the Northwest about the great river of Zaire, not far from the Equinoctial: from whence stretching southward to thirtie five degrees, and then Northward along the sea-coast on the backside of Africa, as far as the very mouth or enterance of the Arabian gulfe, it limiteth the south and east frontiers of the Abassin

> Empire...In this part also are many particulars very memorable, as namely besides sundry great empires and kingdomes. The famous mountaines of the moon, the mightie rivers of Magnice, Cuama [*Zambezi*], and Coauo [*perhaps the Rufiji*], springing out of the lake Zembre [*maybe Lake Tanganyika, though its outlet is ultimately westward into the Congo*], the renowned cape of good hope, and other matters...
>
> This portion of Africa is divided into sixe principall partes, namely: The land of Aian, the land of Zanguebar, the empire of Mohenemugi, the empire of Monomotapa, the region of Cafraria, & the kingdome of Congo.

Knowing nothing of the continent beyond that named Libya, Aristotle wrote that its animals were nonetheless the "most varied in form; and it has passed into a proverb that Libya is always producing something new." His explanation for why this should be is a rather novel pre-Darwinian take on the evolutionary process:

> For the want of water brings many heterogeneous animals together at the drinking places, where they copulate and produce young, if their periods of gestation happen to be the same, and their size not very different. The desire of drinking makes them gentle to each other, for they differ from the animals of other countries, in wanting to drink more in winter than in summer; for on account of the great want of water during the summer they are habituated to do without water; and if the mice drink they die.

An Andalusian-Berber raised in Fez, Morocco, whose travels carried him as far as Timbuktu, Joannes Leo Africanus, seemed, maybe due to his middle name, inordinately fixated on the Lion. "The Lyon is a most fierce and cruell beast," he wrote, "being hurtfull unto all other beasts, and excelling them both in strength, courage, and crueltie, neither is he onely a devourer of beasts, but of men also." His references to the Lion throughout his *descrittione dell'Africa* all appear of a piece, sometimes drawing in other predators–"continually molested and haunted with lions and woolves," "full of terrible lions and leopards," "the furie of lions," "the fury of the lions," "making supplication to be delivered from the danger of lions," "most cruell and devouring lions," "thicke woods haunted by fierce and cruell lions," "certaine wilde deserts frequented with lions and leopard," "solitaire woods haunted by lions and other wilde beasts," a "montaine" "full of woods and lions," shepherds "daily vexed with multitudes of fierce lions." At least, unlike other writers of the time, Leo Africanus physically encountered Lion in Africa, along with other dangerous animals.

The Crocodile was another "cruell and noisome beast." It "commonly frequenteth the rivers of Niger and Nilus, and containeth in length twelve cubites and above"–not hyperbole for the outsized length of an exceptional Nile crocodile–"the taile thereof being as long as the whole bodie besides, albeit there are but fewe of so huge a bignes." One night, Africanus claimed witnessing a traveling companion swept into a river by the swipe of the tail of a Crocodile and lost in the darkness. It was never a one-sided contest, though, as he wrote:

> Of these beasts I sawe above three hundred heads placed upon the wals of Cana [*a formerly major city in what is now Benin–though Africanus may have seen little more of it than Kolben saw of Khoisan country, relying on other travelers tales*], with their jawes wide open, being of so monstrous and incredible a bignes, that they were sufficient to have swallowed up a whole cowe at once, and their teeth were great and sharpe. [*Africanus does not indicate how many years or decades of Crocodile hunting were represented in that collection of heads; so, the slaughter may have been not as outrageous as the raw data suggest.*]

He wrote of the Wild ox that it "resembleth the tame oxe, save that it is lesse in stature, being of a gray or ashe-colour, and of great swiftnes. It haunteth either the deserts, or the confines of the deserts. And the flesh thereof (they say) is very savory." The African buffalo is not a true desert animal; so unlike with the Lion and the Crocodile, Leo Africanus probably never saw a Buffalo, alive or dead, a supposition reinforced by that "(they say)."

He wrote of another animal like an "oxe, saving that he hath smaller legs and comelier horns...[h]is haire is white, and his hoofs are as blacke as jet, and he is so exceeding swift, that no beast can overtake him, but onely the Barbary horse..." From the hide of this beast "were made shields and targets of great defence, which will not be pierced but onely with the forcible shot of a bullet." Leo Africanus called this animal a Lant or Dant, which from the description above sounds like an Eland, more or less, or possibly an Oryx.

Leo Africanus's translator, Pory, added "A DESCRIPTION OF PLACES UNDESCRIBED BY JOHN LEO," including wildlife he almost assuredly never saw. In "the kingdome of Congo" was the "Zebra or Zabra," "being about the bignes of a mule...a beast of incomparable swiftnes, straked about the body, legges, eares, and other parts, with blacke, white and browne circles of three fingers broad; which do make a pleasant shew [*shoe*]." He went on to mention, over a century before Kolben, the African buffalo, and other wildlife:

> Buffles [Bubalis brachyceros–*according to Victorian taxonomy, the West African savanna buffalo*], wilde asses, called by the Greekes Onagri, and Dantes (of whose hard skins they make all their targets) [*Leo Africanus's Dant, almost certainly*] range in heards up and downe the woods. Also here are infinite store of elephants of such monstrous bignes, that by the report of sundrie credible persons, some of their teeth do weigh two hundred pounds, at sixteene ounces the pound...[*At the base of Kilimanjaro in 1898, the armed slaves of an ivory raider killed a bull Elephant. Not a large Elephant in body, its el Hadam, the servant, tusk–the one more worn due to greater use because of dominance–weighed two hundred twenty-eight pounds, while the other came to two hundred thirty-two. Each was twelve-feet long. No bigger Elephant ivory has ever been found, and none conceivably is ever to be.*]

Pory went on to describe the Elephant in terms more theoretical than empirical, but in spite of that, wonderfully, and tragically, lyric:

> ...upon the plaines this beast is swifter than any horse, by reason of his long steps; onely he cannot turne with such celeritie. Trees he overturneth with the strength of his backe, or breaketh them between his teeth; or standeth upright upon his hinder feete, to browse upon the leaves and tender sprigs. The she elephants beare their brood in their wombes two yeeres before they bring foorth yoong ones: neither are they great with yoong, but onely from seven yeeres to seven yeeres. This creature is saide to live 150 yeeres; hee is of a gentle disposition; and relying upon his great strength, he hurteth none but such as do him injurie; only he will in a sporting maner gently heave up with his snowte such persons as he meeteth. He loveth the water beyond measure, and will stande up to the mid-body therein, bathing the ridge of his backe, and other parts with his long promuscis or trunke. His skin is fower fingers thicke; and it is reported, that an elephant of this countrey being stricken with a little gunne called Petrera, was not wounded therewith, but so sore brused inwardly, that within three daies after he died.

Pory also tells us what he knows, and Leo Africanus did not, about the southern extreme of Africa where Kolben would voyage:

> *Cafraria the fift generall part of the lower Ethiopia.*
>
> Cafraria, or the land of the Cafri, we esteeme to be both the coasts and in lands of the extreame southerly point of Africa, beginning from the river Magnice [*Limpopo*], and thence extending by Cabo da pescaria, Terra do Natal, Bahia da lagoa, Bahia fermosa, about the cape of Buena esperança, by the bay called Agoada Saldariha, and thence Northward along the western coast of Africa, as far as Cabo Negro, or the blacke cape, which is situate verie neere unto eighteene degrees of Southerly latitude. The saide Cape of Buena esperança is devided into three smaller headlands or capes; The westermost, being called Cabo de buena esperança, or The cape of good hope after the name of the whole promontorie, and being cut from the rest of the firme land: The middlemost is named Cabo falso, because the Portugales in their voiage homewards from the east Indies, have sometimes mistaken this for the true cape before mentioned...The third and eastermost cape stretching farthest into the sea, is called Cabo das Agulhas, or the cape of Needles, because there the needles of dialles touched with the loadstone, stand directly North, without any variation either to the east or to the west...This [entire] cape at the first discoverie thereof was called by Navigators, The Lyon of the sea; & Cabo tormentoso, or The tépestuous cape; not so much, as I take it, for the dangerous and stormie seas more about this cape than any other...

Pory speculates that the baleful names and reports of these waters served a purpose aside from the geographical:

> And as the Spaniards for a long time (that they might discourage all other nations from attempting navigation upon The south sea beyond America) blinded all Christendome with a report, that the streights of Magellan were unrepasable: so perhaps the Portugals, to terrifie all others from sailing to the east Indies, and to keepe the gaine and secrets of that rich trade entire unto themselves, have in their writings and relations made the doubling of the cape of Buena Esperança, and the crossing over those seas, a matter of farre greater difficultie and danger, then it is of late manifestly found to be.

Think of it as the antithesis of naming a housing development, constructed over a Native American graveyard, something like Pleasant Grove.

Pory also described the Cape's inhabitants:

> The people of this place called in the Arabian toong Cafri, Cafres, or Cafates, that is to say, lawlesse or outlawes, are for the most part exceeding blacke of colour, which very thing may be a sufficient argument, that the sunne is not the sole or chiefe cause of their blacknes; for in divers other countries where the heate thereof is farre more scorching and intolerable, there are tawnie, browne, yellowish, ash-coloured, and white people; so that the cause thereof seemeth rather to be of an hereditarie qualitie transfused from the parents…The Hollanders in the yeere 1595, entering the harbour of Saint Bras, somewhat to the east of Cabo das Agulhas, had conversation and truck with some of these Cafres, whom they found to be a stoute and valiant people, but very base and contemptible in their behavior and apparell, being clad in oxe and sheeps skins, wrapped about their shoulders with the hairie sides inward, in forme of a mantle. Their weapons are a kinde of small slender dartes or pikes, some whereof are headed with some kinde of mettall, the residue being unheaded, and hardened onely at the points with fire. They cover their privie parts with a sheepes tayle, which is bound up before and behinde with a girdle. Their horne-beasts are, like those of Spaine, verie well limmed and proportioned. Their sheepe are great and faire, not having any wooll on their backes, but a kinde of harsh haire like goates. Other particulars by them observed, for brevities sake, I omit.

…thoroughly discovered by the Portugales…

By the end of the fifteenth and start of the sixteenth centuries, the Portuguese had explored the coastline of Africa extensively. Yet in the A. D. first century, Arabs, Greeks, and Romans traded with market ports perhaps as far south as the delta of the Rufiji River. The delta is found in the *Periplus of the Erythraean Sea*–technically the Red Sea, but taking in the Indian Ocean as well as western parts of the Pacific–a manuscript for navigators of Roman Egypt, which covers as far as could be reached in the non-Christian part of the known world, limited only in scope by seas too distant to explore and winters too fierce and ice formations too great to transit.

By A. D. 400 it is believed the Waqwaqs of Indonesia, named for their ocean-going outrigger, the waka, had sailed to the African coast, to be driven off by native Africans, before settling on Madagascar with Elephant birds and Lemurs. In time the Waqwaqs were joined by migrations of Indonesians, as well as Khmer driven from Cambodia by the Chinese.

Greeks called the East African coast Azania; and in the A. D. eighth century, it became Zanj, Land of the Blacks. Arab and other Middle Eastern voyagers by the start of the first millennium were probing progressively farther down it in sewn dhows. Iron was a scarce commodity in Arabia and Persia, earmarked for saif and shamshir swords rather than nails; so ship's timbers were corded together with spun coconut fiber rather than nailed. Sewn boats had the signal advantage that along the African coast, they could be put in and re-corded almost everywhere. With no need of nails, entire new ships could be built from natural materials at hand.

Sailing in such craft as far as the now-vanished port of Rhapta, possibly on the coast of what is today Mozambique, traders in tortoiseshell, ambergris–a substance Sperm whales secrete from their bile ducts; it is thought to help in the passage of hard, sharp objects, such as Giant-squid beaks, through the Whale's intestines; excreted in lumps that can weigh over a hundred pounds, it washes up on beaches around the world and is used as an ingredient of perfumes–Leopard skins, ivory, and slaves. Black slaves were highly valued because they were kafir, unbelievers and purported blood drinkers, a practice ḥarām according to the Qu'rān. Coming from beyond the boundaries of Islamic rule, they were open to bondage under Sharia; and if you could bring a Black slave alive and healthy to market in the Mediterranean, he or she fetched a price over five times that of a white slave or a horse of any color.

The one barrier to travel below the Tropic of Capricorn was, according to Richard Hall in *Empires of the Monsoon*, sailing beyond the winds, making the return voyage a laborious one against the Arghulas Current. One solution for Arab voyagers was simply to live in Africa; and by 750 they were building outposts out of local wood and thatch in the style of African villages, rather than in the stonework of their native land.

Before that in the A. D. third century, the Chinese were already engaging in trade with Africa, sometimes through third parties, Ptolemy–geographer among his many aptitudes–knowing of routes overland and by water to the Han Empire even before then. Ninth-century Chinese writer Tuan Ch'eng-shih recorded trade in ivory, ambergris, and slaves with what was likely present-day Somalia. The Ming Emperors possessed a passion for exotic African wildlife and were accepting gifts of Zebra and Giraffe from Somalia by the thirteenth century. The first map of southern Africa was drawn by a Chinese cartographer in the 1300s. A Lancaster was on the throne of England, a Valois on the throne of France, and a Trastámara on the throne of Castile when the great armada of China set sail from Nanjing on the Yangtze River in 1405 with sixty-two massive wooden vessels, bǎochuáns, four hundred feet long with a hundred seventy feet of beam, one-and-a-half acres of deck under fifty thousand square feet of sail, accompanied by clippers, frigates, supply ships, and troop transports, a total crew of thirty thousand sailors supported by physicians, court officials, eunuchs, carpenters, tailors, cooks, astrologers, and more. Three hundred ships, commanded by the admiral Zheng He.

A Mongol Muslim, Zheng was spoils of the reconquest of Chinese territory by the Han from the Mongols. Captured as a boy in 1382, he was made an imperial eunuch by ritual castration. He is described as a monumental seven-foot man with a sixty-inch waistline and a voice that rang like a great bronze-metal bell.

Zheng and his fleets, loaded with treasure for trade, undertook seven voyages on the Indian Ocean in twenty-eight years, sailing more than one hundred thousand li, twenty seven thousand nautical miles–mileage and speed were calculated by a sailor pacing the length of the deck, timing a float passing by in the water against the steps taken. The fleets touched shore in Vietnam, India, Ceylon, Arabia, and east Africa from Somalia to Mozambique. Fifteenth-century Chinese porcelain is found throughout Africa. Africans with apparently Chinese features are said to live on an island off Lamu, Kenya, descendants of survivors of shipwrecks from Zheng's fleets, marrying into the island's people. Even earlier, other Chinese may have been castaways in Africa.

North of Cape Town lived a tribe whose appearance was reported to resemble Mongols, and their language to carry sounds like Mandarin. They called themselves–it's reported–Awatwa, the abandoned people, believed to originate from the crew of a lost Song dynasty ship. They are now gone; and so all this, like the best mysteries, lies beyond proof or refutation.

By the time Zheng and his fleet were headed homeward in 1433 on their seventh voyage, Confucian isolationists in the Ming court had already put an end to the age of Chinese exploration. Zheng He might never have known that, dying on his flagship bǎochuán at the age of sixty-two and buried at sea.

...and the Lion, Elephant, Bear...

The mention of Bear seems curious, because there are none in Africa. Not any longer. There was once, however, the Atlas bear, *Ursus arctos crowtheri*. Of unknown origin, the Bear was thought by some to be imported into Africa by the Romans for hunting; games of *venatio*–hunting contests–staged in the arenas; and *damnatio ad bestias*, the condemnation to beasts in which convicted criminals, fugitive slaves, and Christians were fed to Barbary lion, Caspian tiger, Barbary leopard, and Atlas bear. While patricides usually suffered *poena cullei*–being drowned inside a leather bag of serpents–they could die *ad bestias* if there were no suitable body of water in the vicinity.

Based on remnant mitochondrial D. N. A., the Atlas bear's only relatively near relation may be the Polar bear, which lived as far south as Paleolithic Andalusia, less than nine miles from Africa across the Strait of Gibraltar–weakening the case for the Roman origin of the African brown-bear species. Once found broadly in ancient Libya, what was considered the last of the Bear in the wild was killed in Morocco in 1870. Another factor, though, was the reported demand for specimens of the Bear for zoos, frequently separating potential mating pairs kept in captivity.

...limiting Africa then to the Punic colonies...

Periphrasis, a circumlocutory way of speaking–I am going to, versus I will...–is found in Celtic and English, as well as Basque. It is uncommon in other languages, except for those of Egyptian Copts, Ethiopians, Somalis, and North Africans, which tempts some to speculate that manners of speaking may have traveled on the sea-lanes from out of the Mediterranean, to be carried farther north by fishermen from Euskal Herria.

...The Greek was based on βοῦς, ox or cattle...

βοῦς relates tangentially to the translation of the Rosetta Stone, as related by Joan Acocella in "What the Stone Said," in the November 29, 2021, issue of *The New Yorker*:

> But wasn't there the Rosetta Stone? Yes, but it was frustratingly incomplete. Pieces had broken off, not just from its hieroglyphic text but from the Demotic and Greek texts as well. What had the missing lines said? Then, too, no one was sure, early on, which way hieroglyphic writing ran: from left to right, as in European languages, or, like Hebrew, from right to left, or even going back and forth between those two, like ribbon candy. (The last pattern is called boustrophedon, from the ancient Greek *bous*, or "ox," and *strophe*, or "turn"–hence, "as the ox turns" while plowing–and was sometimes used in Ancient Greek, Etruscan–Rasennan–and a few other writing systems.)

The name of the Bosporous, dividing Asian Turkey from European, comes from the Ancient Greek Βόσπορος—*Bósporos*—"cattle strait," where Io, the daughter of Inachus who is said to have introduced the cult of Hera, the sister-wife of Zeus, into ancient Argos. Zeus upon seeing Io, lusted after her, and in various tellings she was, on various grounds, transformed into a heifer and left to wander the world. When she crossed the Bosporous, she found the Titan Prometheus who consoled her by saying that Zeus would return her to her human form, and among her ancestors would be the hero Heracles. There is a tradition that Oxford in England, is equated with Bosporous.

...the word is *g^{w}ṓws, cattle...

It also derives from the morpheme stā-, place or thing that is standing, leading in its basal form to steed, stud, staunch, and in secondary full-grade form–with a vowel–steer, as well as in a zero-grade form–without a vowel–in stalwart and obstinate.

...more than ninety separate species names...

In *African Game Trails*, Theodore Roosevelt reports reading a pamphlet by a "German specialist," dividing African buffalo into fifteen or twenty different species, based on differences in the shapes of their horns. Considering the three dagga boys, taken together out of the papyrus by the Kamiti River, he concludes:

The worth of such fine distinctions, when made on insufficient data, can be gathered from the fact that on the principles of specific division adopted in the pamphlet in question, the three bulls we had shot would have represented certainly two and possibly three different species.

...we crossed the Gambia bridge...

In 1957, Prince Philip, the Duke of Edinburgh, much farther downstream in Gambia, took a crocodile, saying of it, "It's not a very big one, but at least it's dead and it took an awful lot of killing!"

...game birds of the area...

Latin names, in order: *Francolinus bicalcaratus, Pterocles quadricintus, Streptopelia decipiens, Streptopelia roseogrisea, Treron waalia.*

Chapter Two: Pursuit

...old Cleveland money...

The Whites's wealth that paid for all the safaris and Tiger shikars, came first from the crank sewing machines of the White Sewing Machine Company founded by Thomas White just prior to the outbreak of the Civil War, aiding the Union cause, and building his fortune, by facilitating the more efficient production of dark-blue military shell jackets with their brass buttons. Thomas's eldest son Rollin redesigned a Locomobile steam engine and convinced his father to go into the automobile business. A White steam racer set a record of seventy-three-and-three-quarters miles per hour in 1905, and a White was one of the first automobile's purchased by the White House in 1907. Theodore Roosevelt let his Secret Service agents follow his horse-drawn carriage in it and is reported to have taken the wheel of a White in Puerto Rico on his return trip from the Ditch in Panama.

Thomas's third son, himself Walter, was around fifty when his son, Walter, again, was born. A few years later, Walter père died in a speeding accident. White cars disappeared after World War I, and the company went into the truck business–they also built small touring buses for the national parks of the West. Through ups and downs, the company boomed again during World War II with scout cars, halftracks, and other vehicles. Final decline followed through the 1960s and '70s, the company becoming insolvent in 1980 and then absorbed by Sweden's Volvo. Today the only products carrying the original White name are White Planters for agriculture.

...Even the sky was made sepia by the January harmattan...

From the end of November to March, the harmattan blows down from the Sahara to the Gulf of Guinea, yellowing the sky and tarting up sunsets to the shade of goldfish given out in water-filled plastic bags at carnival ring tosses. Some call the dry breeze the Doctor for remedying the summer's dampness. The word, though, derived from *haramata* in the southern Ghanaian language, Akan, has roots in the Arabic *ḥarām*, evil thing, which derives from *ḥarama*, to prohibit. The wind comes, advancing in Africa colds, asthma, meningitis, and increased cardiovascular disease.

...of twisted strands of copper, brass, and iron...

Had I never put on the bracelet, I might have called it, in the language of the native Gourmantché, *bulicaabu*, spirit-destiny bracelet. If a sand-writing diviner instructed me to, I could place the unworn bracelet as a sacrifice on the semi-circular ancestress's altar, *jingili*.

Our destiny is bound to what our mothers requested of God before our births; and if we neglect to honor our mothers in *sala*, sacrifice, we risk the loss of good fortune.

Refer to Swanson, Richard Alan. *Gourmantché Ethnoanthropology: A Theory of Human Being*. Lanham, MD: University Press of America, 1985.

...driving off the spleen...

From where Melville drew the title of his novel has been at least a minor riddle. Literary scholars amuse themselves by conjecturing about it, as geographical ones do about the name of Africa. The most accepted version is that Melville found it, before he had ever been to his Yale College and his Harvard on the deck of a whaleship, in a May 1839 article in the New York *Knickerbocker Magazine* about the taking in the Pacific of a white sperm whale infamous for stoving in ships's hulls–Melville also drew from, among other stories, Richard Dana's *Two Years Before the Mast* and narratives by the survivors of the ship *Essex*, struck and sunk by a whale. Notorious cetaceans, as well known to whalers "as Marius or Sylla to the classic scholar," earned names. The white whale that swam around Mocha Island off Chile, the subject of the *Knickerboker* article, was called Mocha-Dick, Dick, a sobriquet for Richard used to set it apart from other whales in the same sea. Less certain is the source of Moby. It may have been in homage to Melville's shipmate, Richard Tobias Greene, with whom he jumped ship on his first whaling voyage aboard the carvel-built *Acushnet*, in the Marquesas. "A Story of Toby," telling of what became of his friend, was appended to later editions of his first novel, *Typee*, a book of travel and eroticism among the savages. So Tobias-Toby could have been transmuted into Moby.

...mad affection for the Mbogo...

Native names for the African buffalo include:

Boo, *Mboho*, and *Mbowo*–Kichagga

Buffel–Afrikaans

Ɓauna–Hausa

Efon–Yorùbá

Ekosobwan–Ateso

Gardas–Kiliangulu

Gessi–Somali

Güâgüâ and *Ngbä*–Sango
/Gaobsib–Nama, perhaps imitative of the lowing of Buffalo
/Gaub–Hukwe
/Hao–Hie
Hona–Gourmanché
Imboo–Bemba
Imboogo–Luhya
Inyathi–Ndebele
Inyatsi and *Nare*–Sotho
Jowi and *Jubi*–Luo
/Kau–!Kung
Làò–Ju
Lâo–Khoe
Leu–Sandawe
Losowan–Samburu
Lqhâi–!Xóõ
Mbogo–Kiswahili
M*boko*–Baka
Nák'óma–Hadza
Nali–Lozi
Nari–Shangaan
Njari–Kuamba
Nyahi–Kirabai
Nyathi–Xhosa, possibly from the transitive verb *nyathela*, to trample
Nyati–Shona
Odru–Lugbara and Madi
Olosowaan and *Olarro*–Maasai
Ongelenge–Umbundu
Soet–Kalenjin
Soyet–Kipsigis
Unyati–Yei
!Xudi–Khoikhoi

...Harry Selby...

Hardly twenty-five when he took Ruark into Africa, Selby began his career with the doyen of African professional hunters, Philip Percival–Roosevelt, Hemingway–in 1945 when he was twenty. He hunted professionally in Tanganyika, Kenya, Botswana, and more, spending a full fifty-five years in the field, 416 rifle in hand. From some things he wrote in his eighties, you may suspect that he was never entirely certain that Ruark was not a fool. Though if Ruark did not ensure Selby's lifelong profession for him, he did make his fame.

...with his 470 Westley Richards...

"For my personal purposes, on anything that can kick me, bite me, claw me, or trample me, I use a Westley-Richards .470 double-barreled express rifle. I notice that most pros use too much gun, and what's good enough for pros is good enough for amateurs."

–Robert Ruark, *Use Enough Gun*

...You'll hunt more Mbogo, all right...

Often considered the last from the great days of African professional hunters, Bunny Allen began hunting Buffalo in 1927; and in old age over sixty-years later said he still had "a great admiration for the buffalo, a magnificently strong, brave, and pretty formidable opponent."

"They're quite the most dangerous animal in Africa," he said. "I'm sure they take more human life than any other. Though I grew quite tired of killing, I'd shoot a buffalo today if I had the chance."

...Burkina Faso, the name at any rate...

As the former Great Powers of Europe grow increasingly impotent, and the erstwhile United States of America has been to Africa no better than a drowsy chaperone, the Chinese advance in their march of colonizing and determining the fate of the continent and its people. For the chore of finding names for the countries they draw increasingly into their orbit, they turn to pinyin, the Romanization of Chinese syllables. Burkina Faso becomes, then, Bùjīnàfǎsuǒ.

...the country was once known as the Republic of Upper Volta...

As late as early 2022, pundit Peggy Noonan, writing in *The Wall Street Journal*, seemed to believe still that the country's name was yet Upper Volta.

...horns like steel girders and a disposition to curdle milk...

Hunters, especially those who write, can wax mythomaniacal about Buffalo. It does not improve Ruark's literary repute when he carries on, thus–

> His body is bulky, short-legged, and too long for symmetry. He smells of mud and dung and old milk. His patchy hide is scabby and full of flat ticks. Bits of his own excrement cling to him. Dirty moss grows on his horns, which are massive enough to bust everything inside you if he even hits you a slight swipe with the flat, and sharp enough to put a hole in you big enough to hide a baseball bat in, and dirty enough to infect an army. He has a big bull's cloven hoofs, for he is a true unaltered ox and the progenitor of the Spanish fighting bull, and he delights to dance on your carcass until there is nothing much around but spatters of blood and tatters of flesh. Even his tongue is a weapon. It is as rough and harsh as a wood rasp. If you climb a tree or an anthill on the *mbogo* he will crane his ugly neck and lick the meat off you as far up as he

> can reach. His tongue erodes your flesh as easily as a child licks the point off an ice-cream cone.

Ruark also tells of "animals weighing from eighteen to twenty-five hundred pounds," and offers his Mickey Spillane *Kiss Me, Deadly* verdict on Buffalo that has remained operative, prized, and echoed for some seventy years: "He looks like he hates you personally. He looks like you owe him money."

Ruark on the physical description of Buffalo is lively and evocative. He can make you see and smell them–there is that sour feedlot smell when you trail a herd to where it tarried to graze or mob. His eye for detail and turn of phrase are keen–"too long for symmetry," "point off an ice-cream cone." In the above, though, he does not tell us how their tails ribbon almost bonelessly as they run, and how they sound, barnyard lowing transforming into a lumbering grunt like a large unfit man exhaling after climbing a tall staircase with heavy suitcases, or the music of their death bellow as they lie up in cover, announcing it is safe to look for them. And the bodhrán beat of butter-plate hooves drumming the earth in flight. Then comes the rest.

From "eighteen-hundred to twenty-five hundred" pounds? The African buffalo is not even the largest member of the Tribe Bovini, surpassed by at least four other tribal members. If you ever got these wild cattle on accurate scales in a rigorous scientific study, they would average out considerably lighter.

As far as the African buffalo's being the "true unaltered ox and the progenitor of the Spanish fighting bull," the Buffalo's Latin nomenclature, *Syncerus caffer*, and for the *toro de lidia*, *Bos taurus*, speaks for itself, the two sharing nothing more than the same subfamily, Bovinae. Some consider the fighting bull a subspecies of the now-extinct Aurochs, *Bos primigenius*, while the African buffalo's line of descent is much separate. The most implausible urban legend–savanna legend?–swirling about the African buffalo is that even "his tongue is a weapon," a box grater that shaves away skin. Who knows where that fable began?

John F. Burger, an Afrikander professional hunter born, it's said, in 1888, wrote the 1947 Buffalo book, *Horned Death*. Burger's family trekked across the Kalahari to Southern Rhodesia after the Second Boer War. His father died shortly after the end of the trek, and Burger had to work. In a few years he was leading safaris; after decades in the bush, he recorded his more adventurous experiences. In time he began corresponding with Ol' Elmer Keith, proponent of magnum calibers and one of the developers of the 44 Remington Magnum handgun cartridge. Keith read Burger's collected Buffalo stories and got them into the hands of a publisher.

The lurid story of the tongue, in Burger's testimony, comes from his sending a runner back from the site of a Buffalo kill to return with porters to pack out the meat, while he and a client continued to hunt–

> When we returned [*to the kill*] about an hour later we could hear cries in the distance, and on following up we were astonished to find our runner sitting in a very small tree, whilst below a buffalo bull menaced him. We disposed of the

> buffalo and on examining the native, who had been crying and groaning during the proceeding, we found his right leg badly lacerated and bleeding profusely; much of the flesh had been scraped to the bone. The native explained that he had not been able to get entirely out of the reach of the buffalo, the tree would not support his weight higher up, and whereas he had got beyond the reach of the horns, the buffalo had promptly started to *lick* his leg.

Burger's report achieved great popularity, and perhaps reached Ruark before his first safari, but it is scarcely the initial such assertion. Almost ninety years earlier, in his *Narratives and Adventures of Travellers in Africa–With a Map and Numberous Illustrations,* Charles Montague Williams writes of a British officer who in one hunt–

> ...was pursued by a wounded buffalo [and] took refuge amidst the branches of a low, stunted tree. The infuriated animal, though unable to reach him with its horns, effectually used its tongue as a weapon of offence, with whose rough, grating surface–by licking the legs and the thighs of the unfortunate sufferer–it so completely denuded them of flesh, that although at last rescued from so dreadful a situation by some Hottentot that *word* attendants, who shot his tormentor, the colonel only lingered on for a few days, when he died in the most excruciating agonies.

And ahead of that, Cornwallis Harris when not telling us about the effect of the color red on Buffalo, supposedly learned about the Buffalo's tongue's extraordinary gift as far back as his 1836-37 safari in South Africa. According to Harris, it is the Buffalo's custom–

> ...to stand over the inanimate corpse for a considerable time, goring and tossing it in vindictive fury with his formidable horns, trampling it under his feet, crushing and mangling it with his knees, and stripping off the skin with his rough and prickly tongue; desisting occasionally, but to return again with renewed appetite, as though his revenge might never be glutted!

No one can say where or when the story was told for the very first time, but it should always have rung hollow. A Lion's tongue is covered in tiny rear-pointing papillae, keratinized on the tips, and is indeed sharp and raspy. It is ideal for grooming, scooping up water when a Lion drinks, and rough enough to unhair the hide of a kill before the big cat cuts into it with its carnassials. A Buffalo's tongue, on the other hand–as it were–is long and flexible and smooth, made for cropping grass, not flensing human limbs. And it all begs one simple question: Why, if a Buffalo is licking your shanks to the bone, do you not tuck them up? Why would they be lower than your buttocks when you are seated in the tree? It is amazing, nonetheless, how much purchase this figment retains.

He looks like you owe him money. The line is imperishable, and even more estimable when you consider that it came out of a book that Ruark took fully one month to write. A Buffalo charge, aimed at a person, is always in earnest, and frequently to the death, unlike at least the initial charges of almost every other one of the Big Five, the alleged dangerous game of Africa. Yet at no more than three to six millimeters in length, weighing about five milligrams unengorged, while able to ingest up to three times that weight in blood, and traveling at a speed of perhaps a mile per hour, the undisputed champion of death in Africa, and the world, is and for all time will be, the *Anopheles* mosquito. The female of the species is indeed more deadly than the male, which isn't deadly in the least, taking more than a third of a million African lives a year–bruited about is how many of us, throughout human history, have been killed by mosquito-borne disease, and that number is given as fifty-two billion, half of all of us who ever lived.

"The last Buffalo I killed did not look at me like I owed him money."

It was David Petzal, one of the best reasons for reading the now-vanishing *Field & Stream* magazine over the last forty-plus years, who said that to me, though we ultimately argued about whether he actually did. I can only insist that it is something he alone could have said; I can hear in it his inimitable lugubriously acerbic tone, and from whom else could I have possibly gathered such wisdom? What we do know that he has said about Buffalo, taking off from Ruark, is that, maybe they did look at you that way in the early 1950s when Ruark made his first safari, but now they look at you in fear and loathing, and with good reason.

David, who has hunted Buffalo into his seventy-fifth year, so far, said of them, "...in a contest with a hunter who has a big rifle and can shoot, and who is backed up by a P. H. with an even bigger rifle, the Buffalo has practically no chance. The Buffalo know this. They don't yearn to pound you into jelly..."

Yet Dave does not hesitate to say that while this is how Buffalo feel in general about humans, you only have to shoot one to have that all change. A wounded Buffalo, he goes on, is a vengeful Buffalo, and the last thing many an African sees is old Nyati boiling out of the bush at him, ready to kill for some real or imagined insult. And, Dave is quick to note, his favorite Buffalo are the dagga boys, who have come to be the preferred trophies for enlightened hunters.

"It's healthier for a herd to have its prime breeding bulls left in peace and have the old-timers taken off to trophy rooms," he says

So right on so many points, Dave must be questioned withal on his, and Ruark's, implication that it is possible to read in an animal's visage–unlike its posture–what its intent may be. It's a prejudice of ours, loving the domesticated dog because, unlike the wild wolf, it can raise it eyebrows fetchingly. We fancy an ability of ours to read animals's facial expressions, when all we are doing is reading into them.

I also wonder about the notion, another of Dave's, of the Buffalo's nature having changed significantly since the 1950s due to big-game hunting. Evolution does not strike me as much of a forced march as that. Unquestionably, the more brash Buffalo were bound to find their portion quicker than retiring ones who would have been left to breed. Does this mean today's Buffalo are more circumspect than earlier ones? It seems to me that the largest Buffalo bulls, most sought after as trophies–and having been hunted far longer as preferred prey of Lion, the big-cats's depredation infinitely more instrumental in shaping the body and mind of *Syncerus* than association with humans–have forever inhabited the densest cover and behaved the most crepuscularly, and with sometimes the greatest treachery, although treachery is an all-too partisan and fallibly human evaluation.

...the common denominator of *Syncerus caffer*

How does the African buffalo figure in the imaginings of other hunters? Here without comment is the way it is for these American hunters and writers, still living, for now, who have gone to the range of the Buffalo.

Silvio Calabi: The older I get, the variety of animals I'm willing to kill gets steadily smaller.

I'm now down to birds and ungulates. As my ex-wife used to say, "Birds don't have eyelashes, so they're OK." And we eat ungulates...

I used to fly-fish. Anglers say that God designed the tarpon for them—there's no shortage of tarpon, they're seriously big and flashy, and hang out in the shallows where we can marvel at them; they're usually challenging to stalk and hook up, and the battle that follows is spectacular. Finally, if we win, which is not certain, we release them.

Cape buffalo are much the same thing except heightened by mortal danger and we can't release them afterward—it's a fight to the finish and at least one of you is going to die. If we win, which is not certain, we feel super-alive—and a touch regretful. Nyati is a worthy opponent; if deer-hunting is "the most ethical form of shopping for meat," hunting buffalo is something much, much more.

When you wear down a tarpon enough to bring it to the boat, it's easy prey for sharks when it's released. When we kill an old buffalo bull, we've spared it a nasty death in the jaws of lions.

Is it acceptable these days to say that Cape buffalo were made to be hunted?

Craig Boddington: The African buffalo is a lot like a whitetail that can turn the tables on you. All his senses are keen, and he's usually on alert. After all, buffaloes spend their lives evading lions...and, often, they defend themselves successfully.

Terry Wieland: Hunting buffalo you come face to face with yourself, at your worst or at your best. The same is not true of any other animal. Certainly not whitetails, where there is no real danger involved, unless you count spraining your ankle or getting lost in the woods...

My own experience on Mount Longido in 1993 was the closest I will ever come to the watershed moment where I see what I am capable of being, and which I would want to be always (but, of course, can never be, as Hemingway ruefully realized). There was just me, and the buffalo, and Duff Gifford [*the P. H.*]. No trackers. Just us. I spotted the buffalo. No one else did. I stalked him, I decided when to shoot. The next ten minutes became a confrontation between the buffalo and me. He became the most admirable creature I'd ever encountered, and when he came out after us, it was just me he was seeking. And when I put the final bullet in his forehead at four feet off the muzzle of the rifle, I had reached the pinnacle of my existence as a man.

Hunting whitetails, now, is something different. I hunted whitetails in Ontario, off and on (mostly on) for 27 years before I shot one. I remember every detail of that, but I really don't remember every other deer.

Buffalo, on the other hand, I can tell you every single detail about every single one (I've killed seven, and the Mt. Longido bull was number three). In the four since then, I've felt that I could revisit myself of that day, and maybe reach that height once again. Never have, but I've been within sight of it.

Another way to put it, less baldly, is that when you hunt buffalo, you have a chance of confronting God.

David Petzal: My last buffalo was the biggest-bodied one I ever took. I killed him in Zimbabwe in 2017 [*David's first was in 1981, with many in between*]. He was a dugga [*sic*] boy with two younger friends (who deserted him) who ran from us for the better part of a week. He dodged and he danced, and he was very good at it, but eventually his luck ran out and I shot him, in the shoulder, with my .416 Remington, and he took off. After a long minute or so we heard the characteristic *mmmmmmmmbawwww* of a Cape buffalo saying his goodbyes.

Ambush and retribution were not on his mind in his last moments on earth. In his terror and desperation he had run between two trees, and was caught at the loins. He died there, stuck in place, and that is how we found him.

The poor son of a bitch only wanted to live a little longer. Just like the rest of us.

Diana Rupp: The experience of hunting Cape buffalo encompasses all the reasons I love to hunt: the excitement inherent in the stalk, the intimate contact with nature, the fascination of exploring new lands, and the solemn responsibility and satisfaction of making a good shot. With buffalo, all of it is amplified to the nth degree by the very thing that puts the "wild" in wilderness: the presence of danger. There is no room on a buffalo hunt for the slightest miscalculation; a single screw-up risks the lives of everyone on your hunting team.

Maybe that's why I remember everything about my Tanzania buffalo hunt with razor-sharp clarity. I can still taste the chalky dust that hung in the air as we walked up to my bull after it had fallen, the PH and I approaching very cautiously, touching its unresponsive eye with the muzzles of our rifles. And then everyone crowded around, repeating, *Kubwa sana nyati!* But the bull on the ground before us was more than a *very big buffalo*. It was a testament to the skills of the trackers and PH, and to the shared success of a challenging stalk. It was an embodiment of the beauty and magnificence of savannas and sunsets, an inseparable part of wild Africa.

John Barsness: Some American hunters have no curiosity about Africa, or indeed much of Planet Earth beyond their own locale. This seems odd to me, because I'm one of those human beings blessed (or cursed) with curiosity about many things. I also feel somewhat sorry for them, because every American hunter I've known who's ventured to Africa has been astonished by its natural variety and abundance. For some, it's as if their life began all over again, decades after taking their first deer, back when their world was still filled with wonder. Maybe there is a fountain of youth, located in the heart of wild Africa, and from the spring at its source flows a herd of Cape buffalo.

...turning past the tall baobab...

There is a tale that because the baobab is three-quarters water, people can drink from it. They cannot. They can wear it, make usable objects from it, eat it, fight illness and disease with it, use it for insect repellent, sell it as a commodity, and have it feed the wild animals on which they may depend for meat. For African bees, within the bark of the baobab is ideal for hive building; and hominins scaled baobabs to rob the bees of their honey and larvae, gaining for the risk and pain, concentrated energy, fat, and protein, and perhaps larger brains.

The people, the Gourmantché, who live around Arly Park, believe that trees like the baobab growing beyond the woven-branch fence around the compound, possess a guiding spirit, a *ciciliga*, that may be good or evil. It may also be ancient. Baobabs are estimated to have a maximum age of as much as fifteen hundred years–on many can be found signs of where humans were once shackled as caravans called a halt, before going through to the Slave Coast. Even with those branches that look malevolently like inverted roots, though, the baobab possesses so many beneficial applications, its spirit must be aligned with the good.

For ten thousand years, beginning some fifteen thousand years ago, before breaking the ground to sow it, the hunter-gatherers of the land of Burkina Faso lived on wild plants and wild animals, ancient scrapers and arrowheads documenting their time on the savanna. The historical origin of the Gourmantché is not well known. People may have migrated north out of what is now Ghana in the A. D. twelfth century. Tradition holds that Na-Yalaŋa, warrior daughter of the northern Ghanaian king of Gambaga, Nedega Dagomba, never married but was impregnated by a wild animal. Learning of it, her infuriated father sentenced her to death, sending her fleeing with her retainers to the region of Pama where Arly is now, Na-Yalaŋa miscarrying her wildling as they went.

One day on the route, Na-Yalaŋa's warhorse broke away and carried her to an isolated hut. The others caught up to her, and soon the great Elephant hunter Dyaale–son of a prince of Malinké, the people of Mali, Gambia, and eastern Guinea, who went into exile after disputing with his brother over succession to their father's throne–returned; and Na-Yalaŋa, attracted to him, bore him a son out of wedlock. The three returned to her father's kingdom, Dyaale soon leaving to go back to the hunting grounds he loved.

When grown, the son marched north with his mounted troops and straightaway conquered the inhabitants who did not have horses. This man's eldest son, the legendary Jaba Lompo, then founded the Gourmantché kingdom–although some believe him to have been the son of Elephant-hunting Dyaale, who despite his conflicts with his brother, left the boy to be raised by him in Mali, from where Jaba Lompo advanced southward onto Burkina Faso. There was also talk of Jaba Lompo's having come down from heaven on a white charger.

In another tradition, the Gourmantché were driven in the tenth century by the Berbers from the shores of the terminal Lake Chad, going west on horseback and prevailing over the unmounted peoples they encountered. Or they may have come out of the Bornou Empire, found in what is today Nigeria and Chad. In all cases, it was the tactical advantage of their horses that let them conquer. What they created were strong, relatively caste-free kingdoms that stood for nine hundred years, before starting to crumble and attracting French-colonial occupation in the nineteenth century. And what the French found for their troubles was a store of manual labor.

Where I sat at dinner in the southeast of Burkina Faso, the night air free of insects and feeling like warm moquette draped around me, was in an underpopulated region of the country. The reasons? Though a major African producer of gold, Burkina Faso's chief export has for centuries been human lives. Cavalcades came through the country, starting in the eighteenth century, carrying off slaves to the infamous market at Salaga in Ghana. Today, the Burkinabé diaspora is nominally voluntary, émigré workers found throughout Africa and Europe–my translator on the hunt, Thomas, told me he had an uncle working as a yardsman in Italy. Being taken away from your land in coffles or abandoning generations of village life for euros that can be found only in exile, is a distinction without a difference. Both leave behind a creatural emptiness in the country, and for the expatriate and expatriated, even the stars they find in the lands they reach are, in a lovely saying Nabokov quotes, tinny.

Behind every great fortune there is a crime. Behind almost all the wild lands that we now have is a calamity, whether the killing off of Indians, the enslavement of tribespeople, the wilderness created by radioactive contamination, the collapse of an empire, a great cattle plague like rinderpest that struck Africa a century ago, or economic exodus. The results are the same, making it hard to know where your loyalties ought to lie, whether with man or nature.

This hunting concession rested within the, for West Central Africa, nearly anomalous, and stately named, W-Arly-Pendjari Transboundary Biosphere Reserve–W. A. P.–overlying contiguous tracts of the three nations of Niger, Benin, and Burkina Faso. With core protected areas–the trinational W Regional Park, the enigmatic W affixed because of the location of the park in a bend of the River Niger which meanders through in the form of a *dubleve*; Arly Total Faunal Reserve; and Pendjari National Park, these last two shared by Burkina Faso and Benin–W. A. P. also includes at least sixteen additional reserves, partial reserves, and hunting zones. Taken all together, this represents–or represented–more than one point seven million hectares–four and a quarter million acres, about twelve thousand five hundred square miles, three-and-a-half times the size of Yellowstone–of a representative suite of dry-land savanna known as Sudano-Sahelian, of annual grasses and spiky trees, the ecosystem that in various states of preservation and deterioration spans forty five hundred miles, the breadth of the continent at its widest, from Puntland to Dakar. For perhaps otherworldly reasons, while so much of that broad band of Africa misspent its wildlife, the W. A. P. biome successfully kept intact a major proportion of its. Put simply, it was home to the final significant population of large wild animals in savanna West Central Africa.

...a skeletal bicycle for transport...

In "The Snows of Kilimanjaro," the dying writer Harry compiles an inventory of death:

> Because just then, death had come and rested its head on the foot of the cot and he could smell its breath.
>
> "Never believe any of that about a scythe and a skull," he told [his wife]. "It can be two bicycle policemen as easily, or be a bird. Or it can have a wide snout like a hyena."

...The rifle I carried...

The long-grained hardwood stock of my Blaser R93, black tipped at the fore-end, gave it the look of a rifle that could have been carried on safari since the 1950s, when the bulk of my character was formed and before what the late photographer-rogue, Peter Beard, labeled the end of the game for Africa. On the rifle's straight-pull bolt handle was a wooden knob, with case-hardened Selous plates on either side of the action, and on the silver grip cap a cartouche with my three initials engraved inside. The scope was a Zeiss Conquest V6, 1-6×24 mm, meant for dangerous game. And because it was a Blaser, the mount was a detachable Blaser *sattelmontage*, a piece of fine miniature craftsmanship an engineer or an artist could appreciate.

Two small studs on the barrel fit into shallow holes, drilled partially into the underside of the mount, and wonderfully machined levers in the mount locked into paired crescents on the opposite side of the barrel. Looking with pleasure at the precision work of the small object, I thought of my father's setting up Cincinnati lathes from the time he was fifteen, remembering how when as an adult he came home with silvery steel shavings from the concrete shop floor in the soles of his oil-resistant work shoes, smelling of sweet cutting fluid and sweat. It was one of my memories of him I did not want to give up–though I also remembered being taken to the Knapp store for my yearly pair of ugly factory safety shoes he made me wear to school, as if he did not know what could be wrong with that.

Four sixteen Remington is ballistically equivalent to a 416 Rigby, the caliber Harry Selby carried for the bulk of his long career, backing up hunting clients on Lion, Leopard, Buffalo, Elephant, and Rhino. Selby originally used a 470 N. E. until laying it in the grass one day in 1949 to attend to the skinning and quartering of a downed Buffalo. He was hunting with his boss, Donald Ker, of the famed safari outfitters, Ker & Downey–later to become Ker, Downey & Selby, with whom I made my first safari in Kenya in 1974. And Ker, driving over to assist Selby, ran the double rifle under his wheels, deeply bending the barrels.

Needing a rifle for the remainder of the safari season, Selby went to Nairobi where he found a bolt-action Rigby in the proprietary 416 caliber at the dealers May & Company. The rifle, ordered from Rigby in Pall Mall, London, by a game ranger who found it a bad fit for him, was listed as a Model No. 5, serial number 5XX3, built from a military Mauser '98. Modifications to the original action included lowering the bolt handle and milling a clearance notch into the receiver ring to accommodate the long cartridges. It had three shallow-V iron blade sights, regulated to fifty, two hundred, and three hundred yards, the fifty fixed and the other two folding–the wide Vs made for fast pickup of an animal in a moment of urgency. The rifle had a righthand action, while Selby was left-handed. Years of adapting to righthand actions, though, made him feel uncomfortable with sinistral designs. Selby was quoted as saying, "If someone gave me a left-handed rifle I would fumble, I wouldn't know what to do."

After half a century, Selby sent the rifle back to Rigby to be reworked, "Burning all that cordite," in the words of firearms writer Layne Simpson, "had washed the riflings from the barrel." While his Rigby was being smithed, Selby acquired a 458 Winchester Magnum that he went on using.

For my 416 Remington cartridges, I had them loaded with 350-grain Barnes copper polymer-tipped TSXs, along with Barnes four hundred grain Banded Solids for finishing shots. When I hunted I pressed two solids into the bottom of the magazine, to be brought up as following rounds if the tipped bullet, fired first, did not bring a heavy animal down.

Adequate calibers for Buffalo are a source of constant debate and no little amusement–Pam's father Roy took that impossible forty-eight-and-a-half inch bull from Tanganyika with a 30 caliber. Calibers from 30, even 257, and unquestionably 303s, ubiquitous military arms in British colonies, up to 375 which in many countries represents the minimum legal round for Buffalo, have all accounted for bulls with single shots–frankly, Buffalo have been killed with whatever caliber was at hand, one time or another. Whatever the regulations, the 375 seems the measure of where Buffalo calibers should begin. At the 40 calibers and above, though, something superior seems to take place, especially with Buffalo at closer ranges.

The 375 with a good scope is without peer for shots of a hundred fifty to two hundred yards, but you want to hunt Buffalo much closer. A 416 with 350-grain soft-nosed bullets, backed up by 400-grain solids, is a choice for Buffalo at a hundred yards and less, which is where hunting them becomes what it ought to be.

Chapter Three: Taurolatry

...the viridarium of a Mefloquine dream...

According to the Centers for Disease Control and Prevention, possible side effects of Mefloquine include "dizziness, difficulty sleeping, anxiety, vivid dreams, and visual disturbances," which is not all downside. "In rare instances," though, "mefloquine can cause seizures, depression, and psychosis." Previous mandatory administration to U. S. military deployed in malarial regions has been associated with post traumatic stress disorder, brain damage, acts of violence, and suicide. It is a drug now of only last resort for strains of malaria resistant to other remedies; yet it is experiencing a general comeback in zones where piperaquine, formulated by the Chinese as a substitute for the infamous chloroquine–which has its own side effects, including not necessarily being a remedy for Covid–is failing.

As for the name, cuspidor was claimed by James Joyce to be the most beautiful word in English. He died, though, two decades before the development of mefloquine, meh·fluh·kwain.

...Echolocating Bats swooped past...

> The weather has been very hot for the last three days–too hot. I have a little fever towards evening and rather bad nights. I am disturbed by the bats that come into my room, in spite of the mats I put in front of my window, and the newspapers I put over the doors.
>
> –André Gide, Fort Archambault,
> French Equatorial Africa,
> January, 1926, Retour du Tchad

...the Belt of Orion rising...

Orion's Belt is viewed by cultures through their various lore. Arab astronomers knew it as Al Alkāt, The Golden Grains. To the Seri the three stars of the belt are the Mule deer, Pronghorn, and Desert bighorn, the Deer the blue-giant middle star wounded by a hunter and dropping blood onto Tahejöc, Tiburón Island, in the Gulf of California. While others see a hunter in the constellation as a whole, the Lakota see the portions of a Bovini, the American bison–the belt the spine, the great rectangle the ribs, Sirius and Canis Major the tail. The Tswana of Southern Africa identify the belt as three Warthogs, the animals having their litters when the constellation is most prominent in the sky. For the Nama of the Khoisan, the belt is three Zebra.

...Aldebaran had other names...

Eighteenth- and nineteenth-century astronomers tried to employ Aldebaran to extend the origin of Persian astronomy to Three Thousand B. C. In 1771, the French Orientalist Abraham Hyacinthe Anquetil-Duperron produced the first European translation of the Zoroastrian sacred text the Avesta, by tradition considered to be from the Second Millennium B. C., containing the names of stars and constellations. Four years later, as another student of astronomy put it, "the exceedingly interesting, if not always accurate, writer on astronomy," Jean Sylvain Baily, "whose throat became too intimately connected with the blade of the guillotine" in the welter of the Revolution, attempted to prove from the Avesta that Persian astronomy began in 3209 B. C. and that Aldebaran, Antares, Regulus, and Fomalhaut marked the equinoxes and the solstices and were therefore the royal stars of Persia, the four guardians of the heavens. Historians of astronomy subsequent to Baily repeated the assertion. It was in 1945 that that other student of astronomy, George A. Davis, countered, in an article in *Popular Astronomy*, that there could be no Persian cosmogony from the Fourth Millennium B. C. because everything prior to Two Thousand B. C. was believed by the Persians to be emptiness and darkness, vanity and vexation, without a single ray of light. Davis also used translations from the Bundahishn, an encyclopedia of Zororastrian cosmology, to dismiss the notion of royal stars in the ancient Persian universe–they were at best four chieftains meant to lead the stars and constellations in battle against evil planets, a conception of the heavens coming from the Magi priests of the Medes–and in any case, he said, Aldebaran cannot be found among the four chieftains.

As detailed by the Society for American Baseball Research, Davis, a graduate of Harvard Law and a major-league pitcher, did his undergraduate work at Williams, his strength confined, according to Ring Lardner, "to his brains," leaving him with "the physique of an Oliver Twist." His freshman year, though, he virtually vanished from the Class of 1913 as he became, shades of an earlier Harvard man, Theodore Roosevelt, a gym rat. Upon his reemergence in his sophomore year, he was unrecognizable, having metamorphosed into Iron Davis. It was then he took up baseball, where he earned a reputation as the finest collegiate pitcher in the country and caught the eye of scouts for the New York Highlanders, soon to be the Yankees. While still at Williams, Davis signed a five thousand-dollar contract with New York, the biggest money ever paid for a pitcher out of college up to that time. He had control issues, though, and soured his manager by wedding a pre-World War I flapper and suffragette who had the nerve to reveal her ankles. By August of 1914 he was with the Boston Braves, to become recognized as the best spitballer in the National League. That season, Boston became the Miracle Braves, the team that rose from the cellar to take the World Series from the Philadelphia Athletics. During the regular season, Davis threw a pre-moistened no-hitter. It was an imperfect win with Braves errors and walks from Davis, though he contributed three hits himself. The game, part of a doubleheader against the Phillies, was played in Fenway Park on September 9–fifty-one years to the day of when Sandy Koufax pitched his perfect game against the Cubs: If you sat that evening in Aisle 33, Row R, Seat 6 in Dodger Stadium, all you heard was, aside from near-hysterical uproar for every Koufax strike crossing the plate and every out gotten, the spectral echo of Vin Scully around the otherwise memorially hushed park, coming from thousands of Japanese pocket transistor radios tuned to KFI. It was Koufax's greatest game and maybe the premier pitching contest in history with the Cubs Matt Cain matching Koufax's fourteen strikeouts and giving up no earned runs with only a single, meaningless hit, spoiling what might have been a double no hitter. Final score: 1-0.

By 1917 Davis was in the Army where his skills as an intercollegiate fencer made him a bayonet instructor, and out of baseball, on his way to his father's law firm with a compiled seven career victories in the majors, the second-lowest number ever to include a no-hitter. The law seems to have been secondary to Davis's other interests, though. He was soon doing graduate-level work in philosophy, comparative religion, and astronomy, founding the Buffalo Astronomical Society in that New York city, and teaching classes in the subject at the museum there for thirty years. He read and wrote Greek, Hebrew, Latin, and Arabic, read Sanskrit, and was not unfamiliar with Chinese hànzì and Egyptian hieroglyphs–it was said that in his ball-playing days, to earn extra money, he worked on translations from the Latin while in the dugout.

As his attitude toward the astronomers who propounded the theory of royal stars suggests, he did not suffer fools gladly, his personality steeped in arrogance. Though when his irrepressible wife Kiddo–who on social occasions added Ex-Lax to the cookies she served to guests who displeasured her–died suddenly in 1951, Iron Davis was desolated. He soldiered on, remarrying, retiring from the law when turning seventy in 1960. He reported that he would focus his remaining years on the completion of a work on the origins and history of the constellations, in a mere two volumes. Most of the family money was lost in 1929, however; and impending insolvency, on top of the lingering pain of the death of Kiddo, further impacted Davis's pride and mental health. In one year more after leaving the law, his sole asset of any consequence his private library, he chose to hang himself.

Even if the Persians of five thousand-years ago did not have an established science for the study of the stars, astronomy was in full effect six thousand years ago in central Portugal.

Sheep and goat herders there built both tumuli, burial mounds, and megalithic dolmens, tombs constructed of large rock walls and flat stone roofs. The dolmens were erected at the elevations where livestock was pastured in the winter; and from the tombs's orientation, a window was created through which the rising of Aldebaran in the spring, about a month after the vernal equinox, was observable. This rising was the sign to the transhumant herders that it was time to move their animals to higher ground without fear of killing snows. Aldebaran no longer rises in these windows, having drifted with Betelgeuse too far north in our sky due to axial precession–the wobble of the Earth's rotational axis. And in the precession of the solstices, it is summer that now begins against the backdrop of the constellation abbreviated as Tau in which Aldebaran resides, where it will remain for more than twenty five hundred years before shifting to Aries.

If you can last another twenty thousand years, Aldebaran will return–or rather the angle of the earth's view of it will–to where it was when the dolmens were built. Though not quite. There is also proper motion, the movement of stars through space itself, irrespective of precession. At some time, before without any fuss all the stars go out, the constellations will disassemble and reassemble as ones never before seen from our planet. For today, though, Aldebaran continues on, under yet another name. In the Middle Ages it was Cor Tauri, cor meaning heart. We know it now as Alpha Tauri, the maddened red right eye of Taurus the Bull, glaring across the galaxy at Orion the Hunter.

... the constellation, abbreviated as Tau...

As much as it may be pretty to think so, that tau, τ, the nineteenth letter of the Greek alphabet may be connected to the bull, Taurus, tau actually comes from tāw, the last letter of the Phoenician alphabet, from the Egyptian for a tally mark. Alpha, ά, the first letter of the Greek alphabet comes from the first letter of the Phoenician, alf representing the head of the ox, going back to an Egyptian hieroglyph.

The earliest alphabet from which most modern alphabets, including Greek, Arabic, Latin, Hebrew, Cyrillic, and others, derive was the Proto-Sinaitic inscribed almost four thousand years ago on the stone stelae erected by Canaanite workers at the turquoise mines at Serabit el-Khadim in the Sinai, in honor of Hathor, successor to the earlier Egyptian cattle goddesses. The first letter of that alphabet, and the first of all others that descend from it, was 'alp, the head of the bull. Anytime we see the letter a, we are looking at an image of Taurus.

...maddened red right eye of Taurus...

The left eye of Taurus, Epsilon Tauri, was once known as Ain, not surprisingly, the eye.

The L. A. band Spirit released an instrumental song entitled "Taurus" in 1968. Robert Plant heard Spirit playing the song in a club in Birmingham, England, in 1970. The opening chord progression of Led Zeppelin's 1971, later oppressively ubiquitous, "Stairway to Heaven" sounds nearly identical to what late Spirit guitarist Randy California [*né Wolfe*] wrote and played for "Taurus." The lawsuit between, Spirit, on behalf of California's estate, and Zeppelin dragged on for years, becoming something of a rock 'n' roll Jarndyce and Jarndyce, before California's estate's appeals were denied, the bustle in your hedgerow then all Zep's.

...Orion the Hunter...

Orion's birth and death have many tellings. In one, his relationship to the bull is prenatal. Hyrieus, a figure of undetermined ranking in Greek mythology, is visited by Zeus, Hermes, and Poseidon and roasts a whole bull for them. Grateful for his generosity, they ask him his desire. Childless, Hyrieus asks for a son; and the three gods urinate–other sources say ejaculate–into the bull's hide and bury it in the ground to gestate. When it comes to term, Hyrieus exhumes it and finds the infant Orion.

Orion was said to be too intimate with the "wine faced" king Oenopion–other tales have him drunkenly assaulting the king's daughter and Oenopion blinding him for it, Orion's sight restored by Helios–and boasted while hunting with Artemis that he could kill every animal on Earth, enraging Gaia. Gaia created what Orion had not anticipated, the scorpion, to kill him. Elsewhere he is killed by friendly fire when Artemis is challenged to strike with an arrow a distant form swimming in the ocean, which turns out to have been Orion. As consolation, he is placed by Zeus in the sky as a constellation, giving chase to another, Lepus the Hare. Some find such small game unworthy of Orion, so see him chasing Taurus instead.

...naturally identifying shapes of the bull in the sky...

For more than ten thousand years, throughout the traditions of the ancient Near and Middle East, the Mediterranean and Aegean, as well as Gaul, Albion, and Ierne, along with the Americas, Taurus has been pictured as a bull.

Western astrological ages–*It is the dawning of the Age of Aquarius*–are believed to be influenced by the twelve zodiacal signs. Built around the precession of the equinoxes, each age lasts approximately two thousand one hundred six years. The Age of Taurus was of the Earth, agriculture, and of course, the bull, running from about Four Thousand Three Hundred B. C. to around Two Thousand One Hundred Fifty B. C., give or take, when the vernal equinox appeared in it. This coincides with the building of not only those dolmens in Portugal but the Pyramids, and of a time when Egypt, Assyria, and Crete all had bull cults. Though there is no conclusive evidence, one theory is that the ankh, the Egyptian life symbol, represents a bull's vertebral segment. The Egyptians of Memphis also worshipped the bull Apis, son of the goddess of fertility, Hathor. Beyond Egypt, sacred bulls appeared in ancient cultures across Asia, the Middle East, and Europe.

Tauros in Greek and Taurus in Latin, the names share a root with the Proto-Indo European stā-. The force within a wild bull is most visibly displayed when it is still. Pliny the Elder held that there "is a Majesty in the Aspect of a Bull; their Countenance stern, their Ears covered with stiff Hairs, and their Horns standing as if they were ever demanding to fight." It is a bovine energy collector, a Leyden jar with split hooves. A bull harbors its power in its poise and pose, in the symmetry of raised head, fixed gaze, front hooves squared. The tensing, the accumulating of strength, is the mounting of load voltage approaching discharge. Like a time-delay electrical fuse, a Buffalo gathers an overload of energy before blowing. Motion, even in a charge, is that strength's dissipation from its peak, most spent in blastoff.

The speculative genesis of language moves progressively back to earlier and earlier iterations of *Homo*, some suggesting all the way back to *H. habilis* more than two million years ago. But a wager might be made that however the wild bull may have been spoken of, in whatever tones hushed or otherwise, it would not have been as eloquently portrayed as it was in the most ancient figurative human art at whose unmistakable heart it, literally, stands.

Perhaps humans took what they saw in the night sky to be the art of some stellar hand and were inspired by it. Material testament to the creation of art may extend down from at least the Lower Paleolithic, seven hundred thousand years ago. That was long after the first tool making, once thought to have occurred around two million years before the present; but now older artifacts recognized as stone cutting flakes, hammers, and anvils have been discovered, dating tool making to possibly three point three million years ago and therefore crafted by hominins not yet *Homo*. Where along such a line might implement have transfigured into objet?

Besides recognizing a bull in a constellation, it seems that beyond plastic art, almost every society's culture and mythos also has a bull of some species as a symbol of wealth, strength, and potency, even satori.

In the oldest-known written work of literature, the thirty eight hundred-year-old epic of the historic Sumerian hunter-warrior-king and hero, Gilgamesh–identified with both the Greek tradition of Orion and with Nimrod, the hunter-king great-grandson of Noah in the Hebrew Bible–the bull appears for the first known time. In the story of Gilgamesh is the man of the wild, Enkidu, formed by the goddess of creation from clay and water to humble the king for his harsh treatment of his subjects. Enkidu, who may also be a bull man, Kusarikku–one who aids the gods and humans in keeping chaos at bay–lives among the animals, freeing them from hunters's traps; and when Gilgamesh learns of him, he slyly sends the temple harlot to domesticate Enkidu by copulating with him for seven days and nights, after which, having been sapped of his speed and strength but gaining very particular wisdom and enlightenment, he is no longer recognized by the wild animals as one of them. With the harlot he returns to the temple and begins protecting the shepherds's flocks from the Lion and Wolf with which he once ran.

Gilgamesh has already dreamed of Enkidu's coming as a rock and an ax falling from the heavens; and when Enkidu hears that Gilgamesh, powerful as a Wild bull–his mother, shades of Hathor, the Great Wild Cow Goddess–is going to a wedding to exercise the *jus primae noctis*, Enkidu proposes to oppose him. The two grapple, and Gilgamesh wins; but they become as brothers afterward. When Gilgamesh rejects seduction by the goddess Ishtar with a litany of despicable imprecations, she implores her father Anu, Lord of the Gods, to send her the Bull of

Heaven–Taurus–to gorge itself upon Gilgamesh: Elsewhere in the Sumerian religion, the Bull is viewed as Gugalanna, first husband of Ereshkigal, Queen of the Netherworld.

In Genesis, Pharaoh tells Joseph of his dream of seven fat-fleshed and well-favored kine coming up out of the Nile–Aurochs?–followed by seven lean-fleshed eating the first seven, yet remaining ill-favored. Joseph interprets this as God's promise of seven years of plenty, succeeded by seven of famine. Away from Egypt in the land of Uruk, the Bull of Heaven brings drought and earthquakes for seven years as well. When Enkidu tries to take by its horns the Bull Anu sent, it covers him in spittle and shit–which along with urine and semen are perhaps the principal bodily products of a live bull. Enkidu tells Gilgamesh that they must slay the Bull of Heaven together, with his seizing it by the thick of the tail and Gilgamesh's driving his sword into the nape of its neck in back of the horns. When Ishtar bewails, bemoans, and ululates over the defeat of the Bull, Enkidu tears a hindquarter from it and flings it into her face–to our time, Taurus the constellation still lacks a rear half. The horns of the Bull are fashioned from thirty pounds of lapis lazuli each and will hold six measures–approximately six liters–of oil apiece. The god Anu, resolving to punish Enkidu for killing the Bull of Heaven, taunting Ishtar, and earlier defeating Humbaba the Terrible, guardian of the Cedar Forest, home of the gods, strikes him with a fever rife with anguished dreams–Mefloquine?–until after immense suffering he dies, at which point the epic fairly well stops making sense, even as fable–possible blame may be laid upon missing clay tablets.

Gilgamesh is sent into an existential crisis by the death of his best friend–though perhaps that should be written fiend–making him wander in the wilderness, clothing himself in Lion skins and feeding on the flesh of Lion he hunted, and driven by fear of his own mortality. Enkidu returns from the Netherworld to speak with Gilgamesh, telling him what he has seen there; and Gilgamesh returns to Uruk. He is reconciled that his life cannot be eternal, but the kingdom he rules will continue on after him, as will the stars.

To the Greeks Taurus is Zeus in the form of the white bull, the shape he assumes to abduct and rape Europa, siring Minos, King of Crete–Robert Graves in *The White Goddess* inventories the other names for the Thundergod that took the form of a bull: Tantalus, Jupiter, Telamon, Heracles. In turn, Poseidon presents Minos with a white bull to sacrifice; but Minos admires the bull too much to do so. So Poseidon makes the king's wife fall passionately in love with the bull; and she in turn has the craftsman Daedalus, father of Icarus, build a wooden cow she can hide within so the bull mates with her, procreating the Minotaur, which Minos places in the Labyrinth–also built by Daedalus, and so cunningly he almost loses himself permanently within his own creation–feeding it seven Athenian girls and seven boys as part of an annual sacrifice. Poseidon leaves his bull to rampage across the island, until Heracles, as one of his twelve labors, comes to Crete to wrestle it and ship it to the Argive king Eurystheus, the bull escaping to Marathon where the King of Athens, Theseus, captures it and drags it to the city-state to slaughter and offer to Apollo. Theseus then goes to Crete to rescue that year's crop of seven boys and seven girls, unwinding the Labyrinth with the aid of Ariadne's thread to find the Minotaur asleep in its heart and to decapitate it after a terrible struggle.

On the Pillar of the Boatman from Gaulish Paris appears the divine Tarvos Trigaranus with three perched cranes on its back. The Gospel of Luke is identified with the bull from the four faces–Man, Lion, Eagle, Ox–of the tetramorphic creatures the prophet Ezekiel sees emerging from a burning whirlwind when he is captive in Babylon. The Celts have the Donn Cúailnge, the Brown Bull of Cooley, the grand stud at the heart of the legendary Irish cattle raid, later to be pitted against the rival stud Finnbhennach, Donn Cúailnge's killing it but suffering a mortal wound in the fight, going on to travel around the island, lending place names as it went, before dying itself. And it, too, is identified with Taurus. The Lakota see in both Orion and Taurus parts of, as might be expected, the Bison.

...eroded rocks often mistaken...

Seeing art in unworked rocks is the result of pareidolia, the visualizing of shapes, like mares's tails or sailing ships, in clouds; or they could be mimetoliths or geofacts, rocks that just happen to look like representative stuff while never having been in human hands. Venuses that might be more than half a million years old have been found in both Morocco and the Golan Heights, making them potentially the artwork of *Homo ergaster*. They may perhaps be fertility icons or apotropaic–designed to avert evil, *Merriam-Webster.com Dictionary*–talismans that could be held in the hand and carried around; and many more could have been made and lost; or if fashioned from wood or bone, they might have disappeared into the stratigraphic profile, dust to dust. Finding two of such age, no-more-than-inches-high, are extraordinary discoveries, if correct. They could very well be, though, nothing more than intriguing pebbles.

There is a suspiciously wide time gap between these and the next oldest-known, verifiably human-fabricated mobiliary figurine. The forty thousand-year-old Aurignacean-carved Mammoth-ivory, remarkably preserved Löwenmensch–Lion human–discovered in the Hohlenstein-Stadel Cave in southern Germany, is a towering foot-tall product of an estimated four hundred hours of handicraft and bears signs of lengthy, reverent, human handling.

Among the oldest forms of parietal art was that painted on rocks by Neanderthals an estimated sixty five thousand years ago. Discovered in separate cave sites in Spain, the works are made up of symbolic dots, handprints, and other shapes. In the cave of La Pasiega near Bilbao, an image like a ladder contains in one of the squares a red-line taurine sketch. There is the thought that it may have been added later by *Homo sapiens*, or it may be the oldest discovered human figurative image of a Wild bull, Neanderthal in origin.

Wherever there were blank cave walls that human hands could reach, Wild-bull depictions migrated. With the diffusion of modern humans along the coastline of Southern Asia out of Africa, reaching to Oceania, hunter-artists found the Banteng bovine on the Wallacean island of Sulewesi; and in a cave at Lubang Jeriji Saléh on Borneo they painted it, its large reddish-orange image enduring forty thousand years of deterioration in the environment, yet still recognizable.

In Europe with the extinguishing of Neanderthal and the ascendance of gracile and cursorial *Homo sapiens* hunter-gatherers–occupying, or taking over, new territories and cave complexes, surrounded by herds of astonishing megabovines such as Steppe bison and Aurochs–parietal art experienced a grand flourishing, largely settling upon bovines as its subject. One assumption, a fair one, is that bovines became central to art, elevated to totems related to clans and tribes, because they were at bottom good to eat. Certainly, a preference for the taste of beef, wild or ranched, is close to universal, profound, and dateless. Whatever the arguments may be for the superiority of other meats–fowl, rodent, caprid, cervid, or fish, not to say *quel dommage*, a diet exclusively of vegetables and plants–beef where obtainable is the spontaneous preference for what's for dinner in the majority of cultures–why else should there be such frenetic industry behind transmorgrifying vegan food into facsimile beef?

Appetite wasn't all that lay at the heart of the impulse to recreate in masterworks–exhibiting chiascuro and imaginative use of rock features to raise muscle and bone out of the second dimension–bovines in charcoal, ochre, ferric oxide, and blood–symbolic of the warm waters of fertility [*see* **...ochre of wild bulls on cave walls...** *in Endnotes, Chapter Four*]. Anthropologist-ethnologist Claude Lévi-Strauss believed that the choice by humans of which natural species to select for totems was foremost not about how they tasted but about how they could be thought about and meditated upon. ...*[M]ais comme bonnes à penser*. Because, he wrote, they are good to think. Soul, not belly, inspired their application to walls.

(You "had to go there to know there" was how Zora Neale Thurston indirectly expressed her teachers's, Franz Boas, approach to modern anthropology. Lévi-Strauss, however, famously claimed to hate traveling and explorers–*Je hais les voyages et les explorateurs*–and you may suspect the humans in their grottos felt something of the same. The paintings of ancient bovines do not appear to be milestones or road markers, celebrating an exodus, that anyway must have come out of existential necessity. The art seems more like the fashioning of signs of residence and habitation, No Vacancy, petroglyphic samplers, bonds to the place in lines of pigment, meant for serial, ritual contemplation and not as legends left by parvenus, in brief recess from moving on. They demonstrate gratitude for finding such a place to come to, not pass through. Nor are they grocery lists.)

The progress of taurine art leads to the Cantabrian Cave of Altamira thirty six thousand years ago. The Sistine chapel of Pleistocene painting, its Polychrome Ceiling is being grazed by a herd of Steppe bison. Early skeptics pointed to the lack of soot on the walls and ceilings as proof that is was not prehistoric humans who produced the art by the illumination of smoking torches, but modern ones with lanterns. The amateur Spanish archaeologist, Marcelino Sanz de Sautola, who in 1879 was led to the cave by his eight-year-old daughter, was roundly accused of fakery. Fourteen years after Sanz's death, the professional French archaeologist Émile Cartalhac, the one-time severest critic of the cave's authenticity, published his paper "*Mea culpa d'un sceptique,*" acknowledging that more than thirty five millennia earlier, the artists could have used far-less smokey marrow-fat-burning lamps to light their work.

Four millennia after Altamira, humans painted Aurochs, the enormous Wild bull *Bos primigenius* fully twice as big as the Spanish fighting bull, on the walls of Chauvet Pont-'Arc Cave on the cliffs of the Gorges de l'Ardèche in southern France. And to the Wild cattle they added not only the usual Mammoth, Horse, and Bison but Cave bear, Panther, Cave lion, Cave hyena, Deer, perhaps even a Minotaur, and jaunty Rhinoceros. Undiscovered until 1994, the cave also revealed a horned

Oryx skull and the tracks of a child and a Dog or Wolf, walking side by side, possibly among the earliest evidence of domestication, the question of whether of child or canine unsettled.

Lascaux in the Dordogne, dated to some seventeen thousand years ago, owing its discovery to a dog named Robot's falling into it in 1940, is a gallery for over six hundred petroglyphic paintings, the sixty-two-foot-long Great Hall of Bulls its most spectacular feature.

Lascaux may reign as the vertex of prehistoric parietal taurine art.

Not all bovine art was parietal, though. In a Bison kill site at the far western edge of Oklahoma, up against the Panhandle, a ten thousand five hundred-year-old skull was found, streaked with a lightning bolt painted in hematite–blood stone–the oldest known painted artifact in North America. In the almost six thousand-year-old kurgan, a tumulus burial mound, excavated at Maykop in far southwestern Russia, were found golden figurines of long-horned cattle, their satin surfaces smooth as apple skin.

One of the most exquisite objects of mobiliary taurine art is the foot-high Bull's Head Rhyton from thirty four hundred fifty years ago, unearthed in A. D. 1900 at the Little Palace at Knossos. It is only appropriate that such a tour de force–veined blue-gray soapstone, rock-crystal eyes set in jasper and painted on the back sides in black with red irises, the muzzle delimited by white inlaid shell, the tall, lyred wooden horns leafed in gold–should come out of the Minoan culture of the island of Crete, home of the Cretan bull and the Minotaur. It was a vessel for drinking ritual libations of wine, milk, or honey, and sometimes, it is believed, the blood of a sacrificial bull. A portion of the liquid was ceremonially poured onto the ground, after which the rhyton should be destroyed as a twin sacrifice. The Bull Head Rhyton of the Little Palace of Knossos happily avoided this dissolution.

Bucrania are carved bull skulls and were common decorative elements of the spaces between the triglyphs of Doric friezes in Greece and Rome, the carvings known as metopes. Nine thousand years ago, though, the ur-Neolithic Anatolian settlement of Çatalhöyük with as many as eight thousand inhabitants was transitioning from hunting and gathering to cultivation and expressing the plastic arts. Along with innumerable chiseled and painted bulls and bull heads, the residents formed bucrania by coating the skulls and horns of bulls in plaster, often staining them with red ochre and setting them into the walls, primarily the eastern and western ones, or on platforms, the horns pointing into the living spaces and communal areas. Five thousand years ago the Assyrians flanked palace doors with the high-relief lamassu, protective deities in the form of bull-bodied men with wings.

Other appearances of the bull in ancient art were on the back of a large pylon in the mortuary temple, Medinet Habu, of Usermaatre Ramesses III, at Luxor, facing into the private ritual palace and unseen from the outside, a three thousand-year-old relief, covering almost nine hundred square feet, of the pharaoh spearing from his chariot an Aurochs bull which, tongue lolling, is collapsing into the reeds of the Nile.

Yet, go back twenty centuries more to the low-relief siltstone palette commemorating the unifying of Upper and Lower Egypt under King Narmer. And at the top of the shield-shaped object, front and rear in two earlike projections, appear a pair of anthropomorphic bovine heads thought to represent the cow goddess, Bat, though it does not take much deep looking to see in the acutely curled, flat-planed, joined horns, the Buffalo of Africa.

The legend of bugonia from the ancient Mediterranean gave instructions on how to perform the ritual of spontaneously generating bees from the carcass of a bull beaten to death with clubs. Minoan culture was nothing but bulls. In the Old Testament there was that representation of Moloch by a bronze idol with a bull's head to whom the Canaanites sacrificed children; and there are repeated references to the Re'em, Aurochs, in the Hebrew Bible.

In pre-Islamic southern Arabia, gods were often iconified as bulls in stone, bronze, and gold. The bull was considered one of the earliest similes for Zen meditation, the "Ten Bulls" a series of Chinese and Japanese poems and drawings, from numerous authors and artists, outlining the steps to enlightenment. Cattle also provided the vellum for Medieval books. If you wanted snowy vellum, you used the skins of white cattle. The finest quality parchment was labeled uterine vellum and was said to be harvested from slunks, unborn calves. It derived mostly, though, from the hides of veal calves–in thirteenth–century Paris, over three hundred such calves were slaughtered per week, more than enough to supply the city's *fabricants de livres*; the word vellum comes from the French, *veel*, calf. The British Parliament has repeatedly debated replacing vellum with archival paper for the writing of Acts; but there's no consensus that paper would last for centuries, as parchment does.

Albrecht Dürer drew bulls passably, but no one drew the muzzles of bulls better. Rembrandt's finest painting of an Ox is of its flayed carcass, hanging. George Stubbs stepped away from thoroughbreds for the moment–he also did an admirable Kangaroo and a Nilgai–to paint two impossibly ideal bulls fighting, this when the taste in cattle portraiture in the United Kingdom ran to rectilinear cattle, like ruminant signboards. In the Northern Cheyenne Sun Dance the skull of a Buffalo is painted in black lines and the life color of red, a black sun under the right orbit of the skull and a black crescent moon under the left, tied bundles of buck brush, the earth's vegetation, inserted into the nasal cavities and eye sockets in prayer for plentiful trees, plants, and grasses.

It's hard to say what Blake was envisioning when he drew Behemoth. The Book of Job is hardly clear on the subject. Some see a Hippopotamus, which is close to Blake's depiction. Or an Elephant. But if it "eateth grass as the ox," takes food from the mountains which neither Hippo nor Elephant would be likely to frequent, "lieth under the shady trees"–and not in the rivers as a Hippo would–and "can draw up Jordan into his mouth"–rather than with its trunk as would an Elephant–Behemoth may have been the Re'em, that "moveth his tail like a cedar," has "his strength in his loins," whose "bones are as strong pieces of brass" and "like bars of iron," the "sinews of his stones are wrapped together." If you seek a symbol of Enkidu in the Testament, Behemoth's "nose pierceth through snares," conceivably destroying them as the wild man did.

In the time of Blake, Francisco Goya was his almost exact contemporary, as he was as well, with the great Spanish matador Pedro Romero, credited with turning bullfighting into an art; and out of this period Goya made art of the corrida and toros. In between work on *The Disasters of War*, he produced La Tauromaquia, thirty-three prints that trace the bullfight from ancient Spaniards hunting Wild bulls from horseback and afoot; through the Moors, seduced by Spain, "prescinding the superstitions of their Quran" and adopting art and the hunt, as evinced by depictions of them spearing and caping bulls; to the inchoate esthetic in the plaza before Romero, marked by *locura* and *desgracia;* to the formalized, elevated art of the ring. And there was yet another, later Spaniard, who identified perhaps too closely with the Minotaur in his carnal life, but created a most excellent bucrania out of handlebars and a bicycle saddle and called it "Tête de taureau."

Not to be outdone, the hispanophile Francis Bacon brought the fighting bull into his art, too, one of his final characteristic triptychs, completed in 1987, focusing on the death by gangrene, brought on by a goring, of the matador Ignacio Sánchez Mejías in 1934, whom Frederico Garcia Lorca memorialized in his eponymous lament–*A las cinco de la tarde/Eran las cinco en punto de la tarde*, of which the title of Hemingway's *Death in the Afternoon* is more than a little evocative. Bacon's three panels show the open *cornada* in the naked thigh, the decomposing flesh, and the weary bull with its head canted downward, one horn blooded, above it some vacant-eyed being looking like nothing so much as a stricken pterodactyl, rectangles of sky blue against burnt-orange backdrops and above blood-stained sand. Bacon ultimately abandoned his lifelong attendance at the corrida not out of remorse or regret or an upwelling of humanitarian sentiment–Bacon, never!–but because he found the arena steps too precipitous to negotiate in his advanced years.

The other side of bull art is its destruction, which is perpetual, brought on by sectarianism. Israel's King Josiah "defiled" that sacred Canaanite sacrificial site of Topheth and the enormous bull-headed bronze idol of Moloch on which children were made burnt offerings. Before Josiah, Moses "took the calf which they had made, and burnt it in the fire, and ground it to powder, and strawed it upon the water, and made the children of Israel drink of it"–some astrologers point to this as the ending of the Age of Taurus and the beginning of Aries. And the image of the bull is dreaded even today.

In 2015, the Islamic State of Iraq and the Levant–I. S.–occupying Mosul in Iraq, crossed the Tigris and went to the gates of the ancient city of Nineveh, guarded by a twenty seven hundred-year-old lamassu carved from a single slab of limestone with a beard in Assyrian ringlets. That statue was seemingly enough of an imminence to I. S. that its future martyrs found it indispensable to obliterate the human face with a pneumatic hammer.

Bulls still persist in art, though, even to a sixteen-foot-long, three-and-a-half ton bronze bull that appeared unannounced one night in December of 1989 on Broad Street in front of the New York Stock Exchange. In Tultepec, Mexico, Thanksgiving-float-sized papier-mâché bulls are annually paraded by squads through town, whose major industry is fireworks, and exploded in a shower of white sparks and orange embers, bulls turned back to stars, retrieved by the sky.

...produced through percussion...

The earliest parietal art is, it is believed, cupules. Cupules, resulting from humans's tapping one rock against the surface of another, whether a slab, wall, floor, or ceiling, appear as no more than hemispherical hollows. Natural geological features can appear to be cupules, as can man-made indentations and cups used for storage, as mortars for grinding, or as holes for ancient stone games of strategy such as *mancala*. A genuine cupule must be authenticated as not only manufactured but made not for a merely utilitarian function, instead representing abstract expression. The earliest cupules and graven meanders are found in the Bhimbetka rock shelters in the Madhya Pradesh, the Central Province, of India and are gauged by some to be at least contemporaneous with the presumed age of the presumed first Venuses.

...his bocio grinning maniacally...

https://www.metmuseum.org/art/collection/search/318416]

Chapter Four: Fatherland

... no, that is dishonest...

Liquid chlorine bleach was in fact a necessity of war. It was needed for numerous cleaning and sanitizing tasks on and off the battlefield and as a water purifier. And chlorine was, of course, the first large-scale gas weapon deployed in combat, in World War I. The Nazis developed sarin nerve gas during World War II, but Hitler never ordered its use. There is a legend that his experience of being invalided in a chlorine-gas attack at the end of Great War made him loathe to let his military employ the agent. Considering, though, the Reich's use of tens of thousands of pounds of Zyklon B–developed by the German Nobel laureate in chemistry who invented the method of synthesizing ammonia from nitrogen and hydrogen gases to make artificial fertilizer, sparing billions from starvation–to kill over a million internees by itself during the Holocaust, empathy or sympathy were unlikely to have exercised much suasion. It's speculated that Hitler really didn't want to use it because with Blitzkrieg, troops had to occupy a territory as soon as possible after it was bombed or shelled into submission, and sarin contamination was too long-lasting for that strategy. He also realized that Churchill–who within British bounds possessed a degree of mercilessness comparable to the Führer's–was ready to unloose gas himself if Hitler did. When it looked for a time that Hitler might use gas against the Red Army, Churchill told his Chiefs of Staff that if *der Füher* did so, "We shall retaliate by drenching the German cities with gas on the largest possible scale."

... Firestone Boulevard and Old River School Road...

More than half-a-century ago Tom Wolfe tried to make something of Downey by identifying it with the Hair Boys with their razor cuts. The cruisers beneath the lights of Harvey's were overseen by the Kustom Kulture adept Ed Big Daddy Roth. Roth is most closely allied with his cartoon creation Rat Fink. Gray or green with hugely bulging bloodshot eyeballs, fang-like teeth, crocodilian jaws, red overalls, it was a deranged mainstay of Roth's weirdo T-shirts. From the official Ed Roth website:

> Ahhh, the anti-Mickey we all know and love. The name Ed Roth is associated with many things, from pin striping and drag racing to custom car building and more. However, it is the Rat Fink cartoon character for which Ed is best known.

> The Rat Fink cartoon started life, like so many great ideas, as a doodle on a napkin. Ed said that when he drew it, he knew that would be his life, that the world of his parents wasn't for him. The Rat Fink cartoon came to represent Ed's life and legacy.

Wolfe saw in the cruisers trendsetters as comparable as arbiters of the style of their day as the Merry Monarch was of his:

> –the men's fashion trumpet of the Sixties is sounded and out of the dewy air of Harvey's...there amid the Dubble-Bubba-Burgers, the French fries, Shrimp Splits, Mexicali Chili-Barbs, and tough little bun carhops, comes, arising, the fashion vision, the *silhouette*, the Downey, Calif., doublets, fluffy, puffy, the breeches and stockings, stove pipe, blat pipe, the new *role* for Everyman, dropped out, blatted out...rank! blown out of the tub. Happy mass fop.

And then, nothing more came of it.

...in the shape of a car key...

In the early 1980s, I hunted Alligator–the hide for boots, the meat for sauce piquante–in Lac des Allemands in Louisiana during one of the first years the animal came off the Endangered Species List–they are today practically unceasing–and somehow my father came with me, the two of us driving out together, often following Route 66–the old Okie Mother Road from California, when I found the state still hallowed land. But let us leave that for now.

When we met up with the white-rubber-booted Cajuns in straw hats, with whom we would be hunting, we learned we would be staying in a fishing shack built on stilts out in the lake; and I could see my father's accelerating panic. Before we left in the boat to go across to the shack, I asked my father for the keys to the Cadillac de Ville. Remarkably, he handed them over and had, I estimated, a good time over the next few days on the water and with the Coonasses, eating soft-shell crab–which he tried to peel until told that was not needed–and étouffée for the first time in his life.

... pinned insects...

The oldest pinned insect, still on the original pin, is a Bath white butterfly, two inches wide. The uppersides of the wings of both sexes are cream with black spots and "irrorated with black scales" with patches of a beautiful lime green on the undersides. Perhaps only a few hundred reach southern Britain every year. The specimen in the Hope Entomological Collection in the Oxford Museum of Natural History is from 1702, viewed by appointment. There could be no photograph of it alive from that time; but if only illustrated, without the actual pinned specimen, vital features of the three hundred-year old lepidopteran could not be examined, or experienced.

...there is no smiling photo...

In the black photo album is an early twentieth–century photo of my grandfather, Alfred Samuel, and my grandmother, Emma Maude, presumably at the time of their wedding in Goldfield, Nevada, standing on the wooden porch of a desert clapboard house with my grandmother's parents. The couple stand apart. The three Vaughans, her maiden name, father, mother, daughter, are together, looking into the camera with flinty late-day hardscrabble-pioneer visages. Alfred is beaming broadly, near to bursting. The fifth person in the picture is the last Vaughan, Emma's brother Bill. He is seated, relaxed and content in a plain front-porch rocker, in front of the others. He wears a simple band on his left little finger, is stroking a cat in his lap, and smiling in a sly way that a cat appreciates. Bill and his grin vanished in a short time. It seems none of his family ever knew what became of him, another desert rat gone missing. All that can be said is, if you look at the picture with some care, Bill is not in the least displeased by his being gay.

...while the city still burned after the quake...

In the May 5, 1906 issue of *Collier's Magazine*, Jack London wrote "The Story of an Eyewitness" about the quake and subsequent fire, with photos by him and his second wife, Charmian.

> Within an hour after the earthquake shocks the smoke of San Francisco's burning was a lurid tower visible a hundred miles away. And for three days and nights this lurid tower swayed in the sky, reddening the sun, darkening the day, and filling the land with smoke.

Forgotten is how much dynamite was used to demolish buildings in the path of the flames to halt the fire, without significant success.

...describing in gruesome detail the chronic ravages of venereal disease...

What the hospital corpsman told my father might have included the likelihood of sharp, burning pain and discharge, and the risk of becoming blind, deformed, or hopelessly insane, a brain ravaged by social disease worse than death. There could be genital chancres; sterility; destruction of heart, spine, and bones; and a suite of gonorrheal ailments such as arthritis or tenosynovitis. And the shame.

...ochre of wild bulls on cave walls...

There's this mouthful:

> The translation from an original Khoi-San *≠gā !xudi*, as "red ox," or "red buffalo-like beast," alternatively, derived directly from *gumi* for "ox," specifically "trek ox" in Kung...that was adapted with loss of clicks to *jamludi/janludi* (note: with retaining the nasalization of the component *≠gā*), to the Afrikanerized ("*verAfrikaantse*") form of it as Jambloed (with folk-etymological adaptation from *≠gā! judi* or *jalu-di* >

janludi > Janbloed). This was a natural process of derivation and translation as any of the myriad of other such folk-etymological and idiomatic adaptations. The word for "red" in Bushman is *!gã* from Auen, *!gã:* and *≠gã* from Kung...as indicated by Bleek [*a name not made up*]...This reference to the color "red," realized in a metaphoric sense as "blood," (as Bleek indicates elsewhere, under *atama* for blood ..."it is red like blood"), could well be interpreted as deriving from *!gã:* or *≠gã* + *!ludi*, thus the "blood-red colored ox." *However* [italics mine], *the concept and root words are more ancient than any other folk etymological derivation of these names. The explanation of the name as discussed by Raper* [also not made up]...*that the name of a "red ox" was actually a reference to a "blood cow," derived from the !O!kuŋ...word for "blood"* jalu + *feminine ending* -di, *could indicate another underlying etymology and may be traced back to ancient beliefs and token symbols. It recalls the original designations of the "blood cow" in ancient mythologies, and seen and revered as symbolic of divine warm waters... the incarnation of the fertile potency in certain "waters"*...[i.a. such as "blood"–author *Möller's* comment]. *This quote, as discussed by Van Vuuren...referring also to the symbolism in the ancient Veda texts and how it was used as metaphor in the poem* Vurbees *by D. J. Opperman, providing a complex context to the rock art and symbolism of the San. Where this color was used to depict the aurochs, it was also applied as a mixture of blood and red ochre in rock paintings of the "first artists" in cave shelters of Africa as well.*

– Lucie A. Möller, *Of the Same Breath*

One further note from Graves:

Bull's blood was most potent magic and was used, diluted with enormous quantities of water, to fertilize fruit-trees in Crete and Greece. Taken neat it was regarded as a poison deadly to anyone but a Sibyl or a priest of Mother Earth; Jason's father and mother died from a draught of it. So did ass-eared King Midas of Gordium.

...seeming to do no harm to that animal...

Wildlife photo tourists can actually habituate wild predators to the presence of humans, causing them to loose their natural fear and caution. This, as with tigers in India, may nurture man eaters.

...restrict contact with wildlife to that through a lens...

Photographic hunting is a mannerism and not a refinement; it is an ethical mannerism no less deplorable than the intellectual pose of the other mandarins...In the preoccupation with doing things as they should be done–which is morality–there is a line past which we begin to think that what is purely our whim or mania is necessary. We fall, therefore, into a new immorality, into the worst of all, which is a matter of not knowing those very conditions without which things cannot

> be. This is man's supreme and devastating pride, which tends not to accept limits on his desires and supposes that reality lacks any structure of its own which may be opposed to his will. This sin is the worst of all, so much so that the question of whether the content of that will is good or bad completely loses importance in the face of it. If you believe that you can do whatever you like–even, for example, the supreme good, then you are, irretrievably, a villain. The preoccupation with what should be is estimable only when the respect for what is has been exhausted.
>
> –José Ortega y Gasset,
> *Meditations on Hunting*

A letter from a reader, to the *The Wall Street Journal*, June 6, 2022, on retirement strategies:

> If you have pets, don't replace them. My wife and I travel a lot more in retirement, and the bills for kennel care were over $1,000. Get out the pictures of them and enjoy hair-free furniture. You won't miss the constant picking up and cleaning up after them.

...a thin Nairobi phonebook...

About a year ago, my friend Bill who went to Africa with me the first time, found the directory in his house. Curious, he flipped to the "O's." And it was there—Barack Hussein Obama Sr.

...Roy hunted in Tanganyika...

Not long ago, Pam emailed me a newspaper photo of her impossibly young father and Bob, a diastemic grin under his Open Road Stetson. Roy had always asked my father to go with him and Bob on hunts for Elk, Deer, Bear; and my father, in spite of the enigma of the polar hunts, accepted every invitation unfailingly, revealing always at the last second an excusatory logic for not going, not able simply to decline cleanly, gracefully, honestly from the beginning. In the photo from 1962 from Scandinavian Airlines, Roy and Bob grin out of a waist shot on the tarmac in front of their plane, about to board, in the words of the caption, to "visit Copenhagen, London, and other Continental cities." What they can hardly wait to do, though, the cutting continues, "is to get to Nairobi where they'll join a safari and hunt lions." My father, of course, never went near Lion. Or Buffalo.

...You know your father's fundamentally a coward...

Hemingway excised this passage from *Green Hills of Africa* before publication:

> A brave man had a certain pride. A coward said this pride was of no importance. Perhaps it wasn't but it was of great importance to whoever had it...A man without inner dignity is an embarrassment. The cowards had the charm though. Not

> all of the charming ones were cowards. Look at [*Gene*] Tunney. There was a very brave man and he had great charm…My father was a coward. He shot himself without necessity. At least I thought so. [*This surpasses irony.*] I had gone through it myself until I figured it in my head. I knew what it was to be a coward and what it was to cease being a coward. Now, truly, in actual danger I felt a clean feeling as in a shower. Of course it was easy now. That was because I no longer cared what happened. I knew it was better to live it so that if you died you had done everything that you could do about your work and your enjoyment of life up to that minute, reconciling the two, which is very difficult.

Charming was a favorite word of heavyweight Gene Tunney, who seems to have had an improbably tasteful manner of speaking. After some charming martinis with Hemingway in Cuba, Ernest wanted to spar; and almost immediately started fouling the former champion. When enough was enough, Tunney timed a charming little liver punch that sagged Hemingway, draining all the color from novelist's face. For the next several hours, Ernest was impeccably charming around the boxer.

Chapter Five: Bovinigenesis

…the last hunters not Aboriginal…

By the abstruse logic of correct names for peoples, the names to be used by those who are not among or from the people of the name, those names subject to change without notice, or not infrequently logic, Aborigines should be named First Nations peoples, except when they prefer being known as Aborigines.

In a certain light, people itself is objectionable. An Italic cognate and derivative, *populari*, speaks, according to the *Online Etymology Dictionary*, to laying waste, ravage, plunder, pillage.

…new uranium-mine town of Jabiru…

From Wikipedia, two items:

> In May 2010, it was reported that a tailings dam may have released millions of litres of radioactive water into world heritage-listed wetlands in Kakadu National Park, home to about 500 Aboriginal people.

> On 7 December 2013 there was an incident at a mine site inside Kakadu National Park, with about a million litres of slurry, comprising crushed ore and acid, believed spilled, workers evacuated and production shut down. A leaching tank containing the slurry burst at about 1 a. m. The spilled material

was entirely contained within the safety bunds and no material leaked into the wider ecosystem.

... nothing more than cull...

From the *Online Etymology Dictionary*:

> cull (n.1)
>
> 1610s, "a selection, something picked out," from *cull* (v.). From 1791 as "flock animal selected as inferior"; 1958 as "a killing of animals deemed inferior."

...descent grow perhaps apart...

Living things belong to three domains–sometimes referred to as super-kingdoms–one of them being Eukarya, organisms whose cells contain nuclei, the other two Bacteria and Archaea, whose cells do not. Kingdom is the taxonomic rank below domain and the Bovini's, Animalia, includes mammals, reptiles, insects, microscopic organisms, and other forms of life capable of spontaneous movement. Phylum contains groups with similar bodily characteristics; the phylum Chordata to which all cattle belong, possess some manner of spine. Class, a division a step after phylum, is based on the organization of organ systems. The Tribe Bovini are of the Class Mammalia, giving birth to live young, unlike egg-laying monotremes, today, the prototherian–"first beasts"–mammalian Platypus and four species of Echidna, harkening back to the Cretaceous period. Mammals have mammary glands, which the monotremes possess, as well. From class we come to order. The Order Artiodactyla, even-toed ungulates–hooved mammals–has been expanded to Cetartiodactyla to take in cetaceans such as Whale and Dolphin which evolved from even-toed ungulates–only we primates belong to a more diverse order of large mammals, suggesting we are too variable not to outlast every other–which might not spark joy in Probscidae, Pholidota, and of course Cetartiodactyla.

...horned cattle, wild and domestic...

From *Merriam-Webster.com Dictionary*:

> Horn: Middle English, going back to Old English, going back to Germanic *hurna- (whence also Old Frisian, Old High German & Old Norse horn "horn," Gothic haurn), going back to Indo-European *ḱr̥-n-o, perhaps originally "object made of bony material from the head" (whence also Latin cornum, cornū "horn," Welsh carn "hoof, hilt, handle," Breton karn "hoof," and, with an additional velar suffix, Sanskrit śŕ̥ṅgam "horn"), derivative of a base *ḱer-, elsewhere with laryngeal element *ḱer-h_2- "bony material constituting the skull or horns."

...stomachs digest vegetation continuously...

Many hunting peoples do not shy away from stomach contents as a source of Vitamin C and trace elements, not otherwise available to them in their environment. Inuit on the tundra will today, as they always have, kill a caribou and eat parts of its raw liver wrapped in a piece of the reticulo-rumen wall and dipped into the chewed lichen from within the stomach compartment while the animal still lies on the ground or snow. Some writers claim that the Inuit consider it "a special delicacy with a consistency and a flavour that is not unlike cream cheese." It isn't like that at all; but in its own way, it is not bad.

... hoofed hornless Chevrotains...

Though lacking horns or antlers, Chevrotains, incorrectly called Mouse deer, grow long, visible canines, found in both males and females.

... The horn represents...

Edward Byrd Davis, et al., in *Ecology, Evolution, and Behaviour of Wild Cattle*, edited by Mario Melletti and James Burton.

...to paleontological finds in Pakistan...

Melletti, Mario and Burton, James (Eds.), *Ecology, Evolution and Behaviour of Wild Cattle. Passim.*

...Aegodonts and Boödonts...

From Werdelin, Lars and Sanders, William Joseph, *Cenozoic Mammals of Africa*:

> Boödont features are large occlusal area, strong ribs, large basal pillars, and a complicated outline of the central fossettes [*small pits or depressions*]. Aegodont features are flatter or straighter labial walls of upper molars and lingual walls of lower molars, absence of basal pillars, and straighter or more simple central fossettes. Goat folds can occur in either type.

...Pronghorn antelope sheds its horn sheaths annually...

A Pronghorn grows a new sheath annually beneath the old, splitting it open to fall off. Because they never see the exposed horn core, some folks, even in Pronghorn country, don't believe in horn shedding by Antelope—Antelope being what they are really not, being the sole member of the Antilocapridae family and not of the Antilopinae or related groups.

...What [horns] are for, exactly, remains unresolved...

The Bovini are classified among the pecorans as hollow-horned ruminants. In *Horns, Pronghorns, and Antlers*, Alan W. Gentry offers this evolutionary arc of the horn, sounding like a report on the development of the épée:

> Horns evolved in the Miocene ancestors of these pecorans [*giraffids and bovids, inhabitants mainly of Africa and Asia*]. Early horns were simply lunging or piercing weapons, used for infraspecific dominance-testing encounters. Later came the more elaborate horns, which can be used for guarding and parrying, for ramming, for interlocking, and for display. [*The appearance of horns has been linked*] more specifically with territorial behavior. As species with a body weight of about 18 kg or more moved into more open habitats, horns would evolve to be of use to territorial males patrolling their boundaries.

… probably the greatest despoilers…

Born in Zimbabwe–then Southern Rhodesia–the ecologist and cattle rancher Allan Savory controversially believes that the use of "livestock, bunched and moving, as a proxy for former herds and predators" to mimic nature is the "one option left to climatologists and scientists" to counteract desertification and climate change, admitting his theory is conventionally "unthinkable." Savory's ideas can be found in *Holistic Management, Third Edition: A Commonsense Revolution to Restore Our Environment*, co-authored with his wife, Jody Butterfield. Not all other ecologists, to be charitable, agree.

…arts material, utensils, totems, and trophies…

Julius Caesar, the future dictator in perpetuity of Rome, until the Ides of March in the Theater of Pompey in 44 B. C., writing in the third-person singular his chronicle of the Gallic Wars, tells of the trophies from Bovini, in this case the Aurochs: "These the Germans take with much pains in pits and kill them. The young men harden themselves with this exercise, and practice themselves in this kind of hunting, and those who have slain the greatest number of them, having produced the horns in public, to serve as evidence, receive great praise."

…large herbivores shaped the environment by browsing, grazing, trampling…

For four generations, the Cottar family, originally from the United States, has been professional hunters and safari operators in East Africa. Today, the business, sans hunting, is carried on in Kenya by Calvin Cottar, the great-grandson of the founder, Bwana–his name choice–Charles Cottar.

In August 2010, in his eponymous blog davidlansing.com, the travel writer describes game viewing with Calvin, who provides a lesson in the role Buffalo's feeding and movements play in the existences of other wild animals:

> Calvin stopped the car and studied the grass around us, pointing at it and saying, "There." I couldn't see what he was pointing at. It just looked like more dry grass and a couple of smallish termite mounds to me. Calvin got his field glasses and studied the slope in front of us.
>
> I asked him what he was seeing. He put down the field glasses and looked at the grass again. "You see how it's shorter?" he said. And now that he'd pointed it out,

I could. The grass we'd driven through was at least three feet high and the area he was pointing at was a foot high at most. But I didn't know what that meant.

"There's a relationship all of these animals have with one another," he said. "Buffalos graze on tall, coarse grass—like what we've been driving through. But they don't eat it down to the ground. They leave a foot or so of the grass for the grazers who come behind them—dik-dik, oryx, impala. So look *here*," he said, pointing at the clipped grass, "and follow the path with your eyes." Then he nodded towards a green patch of acacia trees down a sloping hill maybe a hundred yards away. "The buffs are in there."

And they were.

By cropping down the long grass, Buffalo improve security for smaller game, making the landscape more difficult for large predators to conceal themselves in.

...ecological value of bullshit...

Several hallucinogenic fungi grow on Buffalo dung in Africa. The late ethnobotanist and proponent of 2012 eschatology, Terence McKenna, hypothesized–often from the clothing-optional hot tub at Esalen–a tripping ape in the form of *Homo ergaster* whose consumption of manure-loving psilocybin helped evolve his descendant, *Homo sapiens*, McKenna contending that the mushroom made the earlier humans into better hunters by improving their edge detection–the ability, for example, to recognize one zebra standing in front of another by the heightened distinction in the stripes of the nearer one, vital to judging range for spear throws or arrow shots. Better living through alkaloids led to hunting success, which led to reproductive prowess, especially with the psychedelic enhancement of erectile energy. McKenna also suggested that visions triggered language formation in the brain, as well as opening the pathway to religion.

How we came upon the psilocybin, according to McKenna, was with our alighting from the trees with the spreading of savanna, and the shifting from an almost exclusively plant diet to one rich in animal protein, specifically beetles and grubs from beneath the Buffalo gâteaux in which also grew the fungi, which *H. ergaster* ingested in small quantities with the insects.

Undaunted by overstatement, McKenna's claim was that the mushrooms, spread by the spores picked up by Cattle egrets who also fed on the insects in a symbiosis that ultimately involved fungi, insects, birds, bovines, and humans, created an intricate matrix across space and time, "a divinely spun cobweb of planetary information that has been the catalyst for everything about us that distinguishes us from other higher primates, for all the mental functions that we associate with humanness."

McKenna's notion has continued support among some mycologists, but drew criticism from psychopharmacologists, and worse, disregard by most scientists.

...Gaius Julius Caesar admiringly described the Aurochs...

Writing of the continental Hercynia Silva, the vast woods that ran north along the Danube for nine days travel and to the east, sixty days, Caesar marveled at the exotic wild animals he encountered:

Alces, the European elk that we call Moose in North America, said by Caesar to have no leg joints and so having to sleep leaning against trees lest it topple over and be unable to rise, which trait huntsmen exploited by undermining trees or sawing part through them, so when the Alces slumped against one for sleep, the tree fell to the ground with the floundering Moose atop it; a stag-shaped ox with a single horn growing from the middle of the forehead, the tops branching like palms, similarly in the females, which probably describes the Reindeer seen in profile; and the Uri–Aurochs–admired by Caesar for their "strength and speed" that were "extraordinary"; untameable even when taken as calves, as adults they spared "neither man nor wild beast which they espied."

Within two centuries of the extinction of the species in the 1600s, a Polish zoologist, Feliks Paweł Jarocki, was proposing breeding back the Aurochs from domestic cattle, an idea that has traction to this day.

The term *Ökölogie*, ecology, was coined in 1866 by the German zoologist, naturalist, philosopher, physician, professor, marine biologist, artist, eugenicist—Africans were "four-handed" apes because of their wonderfully flexible toes—Ernest Haeckel who synthesized Goethe, Darwin, and Lamarck into his own school of *Naturphilosophie*. What in the way of an ecological background one twentieth–century figure–with, like Caesar, imperial aspirations–may have had when he was made *Reichsjägermeister*, Reich Master of the Hunt, and later *Reichsforstmeister*, Reich Master of the Forest, in the early 1930s, is hard to say. Regrettably, Hermann Göring's name remains linked in some circles to the concept of rewilding nature, even though his championing the protection of nature and wildlife was at best lip service, the true purpose of his offices to expand his power base in the National Socialist ring. He created parks, reserves, and monuments, as well as siphoning off funds from the German Nature Protection Law of 1935, to amass his own hunting estates where he kept pet Lion and indulged in fantasies of being a huntsman out of German mythology by playing dress-up as the heroic Dragon-slayer Siegfried and tiptoeing through the woods like a Macy's balloon on 34th Street, dressed in leather skirt and armed with a Teuton spear, presumably a stand-in for the Lance of Longinus. His friend, the zoologist Lutz Heck, director of the Berlin Zoo, convinced Göring to finance his experiments in employing back-breeding to reproduce extinct species of the wild Aurochs bull and Wild horses, and other harebrained biological schemes that went pretty much nowhere, or grotesquely the wrong way, as Nazi science was wont to do.

...which he called the Uri...

Uri comes from the Latin Urus for Wild ox, which became Uro in Spanish. In French and English, the German word Aurochs was borrowed as the name for the giant *Bos*, until the bovine started slipping into extinction, which is when the name began to be applied to the European bison, or Wisent.

...a little below the elephant in size...

If Caesar's reference is to the Elephant of Hannibal in the Second Punic War, which was fought more than a century before his birth, his size comparison might not be that much magnified.

Some speculate that Hannibal drew his three dozen or so battle animals from a subspecies of small Elephant which disappeared not much later, from the Atlas Mountains of Morocco or Algeria. These reached about eight feet at the withers, versus the eleven feet or more of sub-Saharan African elephant, while the Aurochs stood as much as six and a half feet.

In the mid-1950s, the Director of the British Museum of Natural History wrote that Hannibal's Elephant's "appearance, their smell, and the noise of their trumpeting" not only alarmed "both men and horses opposed to them, but they were highly dangerous when charged, fighting with their tusks and their trunks and trampling down their opponents." In light of this a British geologist, one in a long line of scientists to speculate on the still-unknown origin of Hannibal's Elephant, concluded in the 1990s that he found the idea of the Carthaginian's employing less than large-format pachyderms "unsatisfying."

...they largely favored lowland fens...

Anglo-Saxon rune verse, quoted in *Ecology, Evoltion, and Behavior of Wild Cattle*, described the Aurochs–

"***Ur*** byþ anmod and oferhyrned;
–felafrecne deor–feohteþ mid hornum–
mœre morstapa; þæt is modig wuht

The ***aurochs*** is fearless and large-horned;
–a fierce animal–it fights with its horns–
the ***famous marsh walker***; it is a brave animal"

... *Bison bonasus,* Wisent in German...

Wisent: The name may have come from a Baltic or Slavic language, meaning "the stinking animal," for its smell when rutting. The word shares a base sense with Weasel, both animals bearing a foul stench.

A hundred centuries ago, Steppe bison vanished from the British Isles. They were more similar to American Plains bison than Wisent, and functioned in the environment in much the same way as the Aurochs, which still inhabited Briton.

Today, funded by lottery money, European wisent have been introduced in the Blean Woods, Kent, northwest of Canterbury. Their presence, it is hoped, will help the species's survival, while the animals will benefit the woods by eating bark and dust wallowing, opening the dense canopy to let sunlight reach the ground.

...Tatanka to the Lakota and Cuhtz to the Comanche...

The phrase, to buffalo someone, has been for a century or more an homage to the accepted disposition of the American bison, meaning to intimidate or overawe someone. Despite that–or maybe because there has also been attached to the verb a certain undertone of vacant bluster and bluff–the risk of hunting the American bison has been depreciated, when it was always proportional to the method of the hunt.

"Indeed," wrote Francis Parkman, the "running" of Buffalo on horseback, rather than stalking on foot, was "of all American wild sports" the "wildest."

After graduating from Harvard Law School at twenty-three, Parkman, at almost the same time Baker came to Ceylon, went out to the California and Oregon Trail to see the Plains Indians, and found mounted white Americans hunting Buffalo with rifles–Indians still preferred the bow or lance for Bison, judging them, rightly, more dependable. As long as a Buffalo remained strong and unwinded, Parkman observed, there wasn't much danger for the hunter chasing it. When the Buffalo tired, and the "tongue lolls out and foam flies" from its jaws, "then the hunter had better keep at a more respectful distance; [because] the distressed brute may turn upon him at any instant; and especially at the moment when he fires his gun."

Parkman watches; and the "wounded buffalo springs at his enemy; the horse leaps violently aside; and then the hunter has need of a tenacious seat in the saddle, for if he is thrown to the ground there is no hope for him."

Buffalo runners carried spare rifle balls in their mouths for finishing shots. Charging their rifles on the fly from their powder horns, they spat in a ball and tried to ram it down by pounding the rifle butt on the pommel. Dropping the hammer often resulted only in burst barrels, shattered hands, and blinded eyes.

A true master, eventually, of running Buffalo over open ground was George Armstrong Custer. In his memoir, *My Life on the Plains*–Custer's subordinate at the Little Bighorn, Captain Frederick Benteen, called it "My Lie on the Plains"–he describes his hunting when he campaigned with Major-General Winfield Scott Hancock in Kansas in 1867. Although "an ardent sportsman," and "exceedingly desirous of tasting of its excitement," Custer "had never hunted the buffalo" prior to galloping out ahead of the column into "Indian country" one morning at daylight. Mounted on a large thoroughbred and with a pack of fine greyhounds, accompanied by his chief bugler, he began to chase a band of Pronghorn antelope, which effortlessly outpaced his dogs. By the time he broke off the dubious pursuit, his bugler had turned back on his played-out horse, leaving Custer to turn back, himself.

It was then he saw "a large, dark-looking animal grazing nearly a mile distant," the first of what would be hundreds of thousands of American buffalo, or Bison, he would see over the following years; yet no other bull, he was sure, ever "corresponded with [it] in size and lofty grandeur." Using the cover of a ravine, he and his dogs moved to within several hundred yards of the Buffalo. As they emerged, the Buffalo saw them and set off at once. Custer's horse was still too tired from the previous race to catch the Buffalo in a short sprint; but eventually after a long chase on the "springy turf," it pulled up beside "the shaggy body of the huge beast" that towered over the thoroughbred. Custer might at any time have pressed his Colt 44 Army revolver into the flank of the Buffalo; but his blood was up as he "yelled with wild excitement and delight," wanted to prolong the "race for life or death."

After some miles, the Buffalo showed signs of wearying–recall Parkman's aperçu about a worn-out Buffalo–and Custer made to kill it. As he rode by it, extending his 44, it "suddenly determined to fight, and at once wheeled, as only a buffalo can," to gore his horse. As the horse leapt away from the Buffalo's horns, Custer brought up his pistol hand to control the reins, and deftly misfired the revolver between the horse's nervous ears and into its brain, the horse dead as a Sage chicken folding in midflight.

Kicking instinctively out of the stirrups–he had eleven horses shot out from under him during the Civil War, so was practiced at it–Custer launched beyond the falling animal. He had ridden it in battle during the "late war," which the horse obviously survived; and Custer was "strongly attached" to it. Yet his "first thought on reaching *terra firma*, was, 'What will the buffalo do with me?'" The Buffalo, apparently astonished by the utter spectacle of it, did nothing other than wander off, leaving Custer alone to his "own bitter reflections."

With whining dogs and no clue in which direction his column lay, Custer struck off on what seemed a likely course, without the least landmark to guide him across the featureless prairie, a pistol in either hand in case he met with hostiles. In time he saw dust, then the heads of riders. Unable to identify them, he dropped into another ravine with his hounds "to await developments." After what seemed a very long time, to Custer's relief he sighted the cavalry guidon waving over the approaching riders. Reaching him, they were surprised to discover him unhorsed. He explained his circumstances and sent a detachment out to retrieve his saddle. Then with a fresh mount, "Richard was himself again."

Notably, Theodore Roosevelt, according to Elizabeth Custer, a professional widow until her death at the age of ninety and a far from trustworthy hagiographer, claimed that the President had sent her a treasured letter in which he declared her late Brevet General husband to be "a shining light to all the youth of America," embodying, one imagines, the credo since become a standard, that Roosevelt lay down at the Sorbonne on his way home from Africa in the spring of 1910:

> It is not the critic who counts; not the man who points out how the strong man stumbles, or where the doer of deeds could have done them better. The credit belongs to the man who is actually in the arena, whose face is marred by dust and sweat and blood; who strives valiantly; who errs, who comes short again and again, because there is no effort without error and shortcoming; but who does actually strive to do the deeds; who knows great enthusiasms, the great devotions; who spends himself in a worthy cause; who at the best knows in the end the triumph of high achievement, and who at the worst, if he fails, at least fails while daring greatly, so that his place shall never be with those cold and timid souls who neither know victory nor defeat.

This no doubt captured the buoyant sentiments of the 210 men Custer led to their deaths at the Battle of Greasy Grass.

For their parts, genuine military men, like Ulysses S. Grant, while still in the White House, and General Fightin' Phil Sheridan were less enamored of Custer. The statement of

Sheridan, Custer's superior as head of the Department of the Missouri, damned with faint praise.

The defeat at Little Bighorn was, he said, "an unnecessary sacrifice, due to misapprehension and a superabundance of courage."

Grant took no official notice of the destruction of Custer and the men under his command, including two of Custer's own brothers, a nephew, and a brother-in-law, perhaps because it was only half the day's Union dead from Grant's assaults at Vicksburg on May 22nd, 1863, and hardly comparable to far bloodier other battles he knew in the Civil War. Two months later he did give a newspaper a statement.

"I regard," he said, "Custer's massacre as a sacrifice of troops, brought on by Custer himself, that was wholly unnecessary–wholly unnecessary." Custer, then, was no shining light to all the old soldiers of America.

Two random notes on firearms in film.

In the famous closeup in the 1903 Edison Manufacturing Company film *The Great Train Robbery*, the gloriously mustachioed lead outlaw, played by Justus D. Barnes–later to find work as a milkman–holds his revolver pointing heavenward, then lowers it crisply 90 degrees to snap off six shots without sighting down the barrel. This and similar scenes throughout a century of cinema Westerns have amused knowledgeable handgun marksmen to no end because of their supposed absurdity. Then a friend of mine was reading the great pistolero and cowboy throwback, Elmer Keith, who described this exact manner of firing a six-shooter as the only one that could be performed under real-life circumstances from a galloping horse.

In a single shot from the chase scene across the dry lakebed in John Ford's *Stagecoach*, one of the Navajo extras, in the role of a full-tilt mounted Apache, is armed with a Springfield 45-70-405 trapdoor carbine, which at a gallop he fires from the shoulder, clears the empty from the hinged breechblock, reloads a new cartridge, locks the action, and fires again without dropping the reins, all done in seconds uncut in the camera. This could not be taught by any amount of rehearsal but only accomplished by the most ingrained muscle memory.

...Bison are represented today by two closely related species of shaggy beasts...

Paleontologists will say that the "taxonomic history of extant Bovina is quite complicated and highly confusing"; no more so than when it comes to *Bison* and *Eobison*. There were large, small, Early Pleistocene, Middle-Late Pleistocene, Azov Sea, Siwaliks, Mygdonia, *B. tamanensis*, *B. suchovi*, *B. (E.) georgicus*, and species inquirenda. Not to mention "horncores of oval basal cross section set closely to the orbits and not widely apart from each other, implanted laterally-postero-laterally and on short pedicles that bent weakly down..." etc.

...three subspecies of European Wisent...

Other species of Old World bison exist in fossil beds, including *B. palaeosinensis* discovered by the paleontologist, geologist, philosopher, Jesuit priest Pierre Teilhard de Chardin in 1930 in China before he began his study of the Peking Man fossils, which are unexplainably vanished now for eighty years. His posthumously published Le phénomène humain concerning evolution and theology hit the Exacta by not only earning a place on the Roman Church's *Index Librorum Prohibitorum*, but howls of execration and outcries of charlatanry from British and American public scientists cum implacable chittering atheists.

"... surpasses all others in dogged ferocity..."

In Annette Susannah Beveridge's tranlation of the *Bābur-Nāma* (*Memoirs of Bābur*), Zahiru'd-din Muhammad Babur Padshah Ghazi, founder of the Mughal Empire and great, highly literate hunter, in the A. D. fifteen hundreds anticipated Baker's estimation of the wild Water buffalo, this the one Babur found in Hindustan: "It is much larger than the (domestic) buffalo and its horns do not turn back in the same way. It is a mightily destructive and ferocious animal."

...military officer...

Commissioned in 1869 a pasha and major-general in the army of the Khedive of Egypt, Isma'il Pasha, Baker, with his wife following the drum, led a command of seventeen hundred men, many released convicts, to the province of Equatoria in what is now the south of South Sudan to suppress the slave trade, as well as to bestow the blessings of commerce and civilization. In Equatoria he was appointed Governor-General for four years at an annual salary of ten thousand pounds–one-point five million dollars today; in 1880, Leopold II was paying Henry Morton Stanley that amount, three hundred thousand Belgian francs, per month to look after the Congo Free State for him. When Baker left to return to Cairo, he was replaced by Colonel Charles George Gordon who made such reforms as outlawing punishment by lashing with the Buffalo-hide whip, the kourbash, yet resigned in exhaustion seven years later to retreat to Europe, only to return to Khartoum in 1884 to do the "work of God" in opposing the Mahdi, and to fulfill a patent death wish.

...The Rifle and Hound in Ceylon...

Baker considered the Water buffalo more dangerous on the open plains than in the forests. In the woods, Buffalo "could be easily stalked"; and hunters had trees to nip up into. A bull in the open had to be "killed when once brought to bay, or he will soon exhibit his qualifications for mischief." On the plains the Buffalo was apt to "face the guns...[and] receive any number of balls from a small gun in the throat and chest without evincing the least symptom of distress."

"For buffalo-shooting," Baker wrote, "the conical ball is preferable, as, with the heavy charge of powder that I use, it will pass completely through him from end to end." To which he added, the "shoulder is the acknowledged point to aim," but "a difficult shot to obtain."

Baker said he could best explain the Buffalo's character by describing his first encounter with it when he came to Ceylon in the late 1840s "for the sake of its wild sports." Eighty miles from the city of Kandy in the center of the island, Baker and his brother emerged from the jungle within sight of Minneria Lake, finding a herd of a hundred Buffalo lying in a swampy hollow a quarter mile away, with several bulls on the green plains.

As Baker and his brother approached the animals, the Buffalo "ranged up in a compact body, presenting a very regular line in front." Seven large bulls stepped out from the line, appearing "disposed to show fight." When the hunters ran up to within thirty yards, one of the bulls charged. Almost to the hunters, it turned to the side; and Baker and his brother fired simultaneously.

Leaving his brother to finish the fatally wounded Buffalo, Baker ran across the plain, chasing another. For a mile the bull ran, halting to make short charges, before returning to its retreat, until it came to a creek and went in, Baker circling around to intercept the Buffalo where it would climb out, wading into the shallow water to meet it.

"Poor stupid fellow!" Baker thought of the Buffalo. He admitted to knowing nothing, then, about them and thought he had this one dead already. Taking a quick but steady shot "at the point of connection with the throat," Baker fully expected when the blackpowder smoke cleared, to find the bull down. Instead it "literally had not moved a muscle." The only effect of the shot seemed to have been a change in the bull's eye from sullen to furious. Blood ran from a wound in the chest; and "annoyed," Baker aimed at the same spot and fired his second barrel. More blood marked the chest, but the bull did not move. Baker noted the added "lustre" in the Buffalo's eye; and finding he was out of rifle balls, he dropped his hand onto his hunting knife on his belt, realizing at once how futile that would be.

Virtually unarmed and the bull coming forward with short grunts, into Baker's head it now entered that "buffalo-shooting" could be "somewhat dangerous."

"Suddenly a bright thought flashed through my mind," Baker wrote. He poured a double charge of powder down his rifle's right barrel. Tearing a strip off his shirt tail, he took a handful of small change from his money pouch and rolling it up in the fabric, rammed it down the barrel. The bull then put its concentrated rage into a charge; and when its horns bracketed him, Baker thrust his rifle muzzle against the Buffalo's forehead and pressed the trigger. The "three shillings' worth" of coins sent the bull down; but knowing it was only stunned, Baker was away "as fast as [his] heels could carry [him]," taking with him a newfound respect for the Water buffalo.

Contemporary African hunter supérieur Craig Boddington sums up the wild-cattle temperament by declaring, "I do know this: The closer you have to be to any of the wild bovines, the more likely you are to get into trouble."

...largest herd of Banteng...

The Banteng of the Top End are the result of a failed eleven-year scheme by the British crown and the East India Company to establish on the Cobourg Peninsula, a hundred fifty nautical miles northeast of where the harbor city of Darwin would be built, a re-victualing station and military settlement–and ultimately a new Singapore–for ships sailing the Arafura Sea to and from the Torres Strait. In spite of aid from accommodating Aborigines, it was impossible heat and humidity, diseases, cyclones, no doubt the oppression of isolation, and not to be ignored, thick wool uniforms, that led to the abandonment of the settlement in 1849. Left behind were "domestic" Banteng–which were genetically very close to wild–originally imported as livestock capable of withstanding the climate. Instead of dying out, these Banteng went back to the wild, growing their numbers while managing to keep their existence almost entirely occulted for more than a century.

After the Gaur, Banteng are the second species listed as endangered to be cloned successfully, and the first clone to live beyond infancy. That Banteng lived to age seven in a zoo until suffering a leg fracture and having to be euthanized.

...a shadowy Whitetail that can and will kill you...

Solitary Banteng bulls lie up on knolls during the day, able to hear the slightest noise, making them particularly difficult to stalk when they are bedded. Major Evans usually took Banteng after miles of following the track of one on the move through the Burmese forest; but he could take them when they lay up, as well.

Evans found Gaur and Tsaing in the hilly country of the Chindwin River. At about eight a. m. one morning, he and his trackers, and his terrier, Dot, cut the trail of what looked to be a good lone bull–one of his trackers thought the hoofprints were large enough to be a Gaur's–in a bamboo forest with monkeys and jungle fowl. One of those birds flushed; and Dot scented the Banteng just ahead, alerting Evans.

Moving forward, Evan's saw the color of the bull's hide, thirty yards away in the bamboo. It had gotten up from a nest of leaves and was broadside. Evans quickly fired a solid-nickel bullet into it, near, he thought, the shoulder. The Banteng took a few steps and halted. Evans fired his second barrel, just as the bull moved again. When that bullet hit, the Banteng wheeled and charged straight down on him. Without time to reload, Evans waited for the bull to be on him, then jumped aside, the Banteng "thundering on."

Little Dot wanted to engage the bull in a fight, but Evans called her off. Giving the Banteng twenty minutes to stiffen up, Evans and one tracker began following the bloodless trail. In three hundred yards, they found the bull standing, head down, by a clump of bamboo. Evans fired another nickel solid; and the Banteng ran off, this time leaving good blood.

When they found it once more, the bull was still standing. Another shot, this time a soft nose, and the Banteng ran off again. They heard it staggering around on the dry-leaf litter; then there was silence. After ten minutes, they followed. Evans spotted the bull lying down, head raised, looking at him. He quickly snapped off one more shot, but the bull showed no reaction. It was already dead, its horns held up in the bamboo. The bull was ancient, the eyes sunken and clouded by cataracts, the teeth blackened and worn, and the horns "very heavily corrugated" and "massive."

...propelled by sixty grains of cordite...

Cordite is a smokeless explosive–though one of low brisance–rather than producing the shattering power of high explosives, it deflagrates–burns rapidly–generating gases that propel a projectile down a barrel. It is formulated from nitrocellulose, nitroglycerine, and petroleum jelly and extruded in filaments, supplying its original name, cord powder, later shortened to Cordite. Velocity at the muzzle for the load Evans shot would be around two thousand one hundred fifty feet per second, developing four thousand foot pounds of energy.

...The Gaur, though, is also capable of killing the Tiger...

Charles Elphinstone Gouldsbury, who served in the Indian Imperial Police, recorded the forty years of Indian hunting reminiscences of a friend, also with the police, who wished to remain anonymous, publishing them in the book, *Tigerland*, in 1913. In the book, Gouldsbury's friend first hunted Gaur in the Travancore Hills in the southernmost part of India, where he went on his first leave of duty. Gouldsbury's friend was forthcoming enough to admit that "tiger, leopard, and bear in the order named were the only animals" that he really cared to hunt because of the inherent excitement, and the satisfaction of the kill of what were often man-eaters. Then he saw the Gaur.

The hunter Gouldsbury wrote about, returning at dawn from a fruitless night of tree-perching, waiting for an elusive Leopard, was met by the old house servant who came with the bungalow he rented. The servant seemed to possess "some sporting instincts"; but that was the only bond between them, "for in other respects," the hunter said, "we held some differences of opinion, more especially in the matter of my whisky and cheroots, regarding which his views were decidedly socialistic." In this case, however, he trusted the servant when he said he'd seen a bull Gaur with cows on a distant hill.

Traveling as quickly as possible, the hunter used a relay of ponies first to reach the base of the hill, then to climb the steep slope. After an hour of ascending, having been as silent as he thought he could be, he reached the plateaued summit to see the Gaur disappear into the jungle. Unable to follow them through the noisy cover, the hunter waited for the animals to come out into the valley below and began a hard stalk on foot through lighter jungle, until he come to a grassy clearing.

In the waving grass, the hunter saw what he thought were termite hills–to his amazement, moving. These were the tall withers of Gaur.

Crawling on hands and knees, the hunter got to thirty yards of the animals, all grazing except the bull, which was bedded between him and the cows. Lying prone, the hunter started to get his rifle against his shoulder, when loose cartridges in his pocket rattled together. The bull was immediately on its feet, "glaring savagely around," sniffing the air, searching for the source of the sound.

The Gaur was now broadside. The hunter held his "breath, and raising the rifle carefully, pulled for [the bull's] head, just behind the ear." As the powder-smoke drifted away, the Gaur "lay kicking on his side."

Nothing was finished. At the sound of the shot, the rest of the Gaur charged down on the hunter, who sprang up, "yelling with all the energy of despair." The Gaur came close enough for the hunter to touch them with his rifle, before they wheeled sharply left and headed up the valley. Another yard nearer, and the hunter "must have been trampled under foot, killed outright perhaps, or at least probably maimed for life." He accounted it "a marvellous escape, and all due to a powerful pair of lungs!" Bending down to pick up a cartridge he dropped in the commotion, he heard a sound behind him.

There, standing "with glaring eyeballs, and the blood pouring from both nostrils," was the bull, "not a pleasing sight at such unpleasantly close quarters!" Before the hunter could finish studying the Gaur, "down went his head, and with a bellow that shook the very ground, he came thundering down upon me."

"I had barely time to bring my rifle to the shoulder," he said, "and when I fired he had almost reached me."

He "aimed roughly" at the Gaur's head, and "fortune favouring" the hunter, the bullet "struck exactly where it should," the bull rolling over at his feet.

...might conceivably today be sustainably hunted within their home ranges...

The usual alternative to sustainable hunting is largely so-called poaching by native peoples denied any stake in the conservation of the species. An adult Gaur was captured by a camera trap in in Huay Thapthanh-Huay Samrarn Wildlife Sanctuary in eastern Thailand in 2019. This was the first of the species to be recorded in the area in fifteen years. In 2004 a twenty-year-old bull wandered into a village, to die of stress when wildlife officials tried to capture and relocate it. A necropsy revealed a reported twenty-seven bullets lodged in its body, assumed to be from years of attempts to kill it for its meat and horns, the only things of value it possessed for the local people

... renowned for its butter...

Domestic yak milk–yak milk is a misnomer because yak is the masculine name for the animal, 'bri the name for the female. When the 'bri first lets down, the colostrum will be pink from the presence of blood in it. It whitens after that but remains higher in fat, protein, calcium, and iron than cow's milk. Along with pure butter, Tibetans may produce butter tea, cheese, fuel for lamps, dressing for tanning hides, and fermented kumis from the milk of the domestic yak. Buddhist monks also make huge ceremonial sculptures out of yak butter.

...Russian Imperial geographer and explorer, Nikolay Mikhaylovich Przhevalsky...

Stalin, who was around ten when Przhevalsky died in 1888 and bore an uncanny likeness to the explorer, went to no remarkable pains to contradict the rumor that arose that the general secretary was actually the Tsarist-era scientist's biological son, the Georgian Stalin relishing the confusion about whether he could claim aristocratic Russian heritage or not.

...largest endemic mammal in the Philippines...

The Philippines's next largest native mammal is the islands's also endangered Sambar, *Rusa mariana*. Adult males average a little over a hundred pounds on the hoof, about a fifth the size of the Tamaraw and nothing like the Indian stag, which grows as large as the North American Wapiti. The small deer's antlers are generally three-tined–though often growing more points–and can reach perhaps twenty inches in length along the main beams, tilting back to allow easier passage through dense cover. While its numbers continue to decline in the Philippines, on the U. S.

territorial island of Guam, where it was introduced for hunting in the late eighteenth century by the Spanish colonial governor, Don Mariano Tobias, the Sambar, free from natural predation, continually threatens to overpopulate the habitat.

...nearly inconceivable thirteen million years ago...

The ancient animal that the Saola may most closely resemble is a grander version of the runtish but dogged–passing along its genes, now, for some eighteen million years–Eotragus of the Miocene.

...white stockings and white patches on its face, neck, and rump...

A most striking feature of the Saola may be maxillary-preorbital glands nine centimeters in length, covered by thick muscular flaps. Presumably, the Saola scent-marks by lifting the flaps, or lids, and applying a "thick paste-like grayish-green secretion with a very pungent foul odor, reminiscent of the musk of mustelids," from the glands. The flaps are considered unique, while the glands themselves may be the largest "of any extant animal species."

Chapter Six: Syncerus

...the ancient Eotragus...

Today, the Dawn goat's nearest descendants are the Boselaphines, represented in their entirety by the Nilgai, or Blue bull, and the Four-horned chousingha antelope, both of India.

...hypothesis, and downright conjecture...

If you are counting on the shatterproof rationality of science to make the questions of evolution comprehendible, consider this sentence from a peer-reviewed journal on cladistics:

> The term phylogenesis was introduced into biology by Ernest Haeckel (1866) [*the same year he coined* Ökölogie] with a precise meaning, but is mostly used today in a peculiarly vague manner

...were separating ten million years back...

The *Selenoportax*, a large Boselaphine identified from fossils in the Siwalik Hills from the Outer Himalayas in the northern Indian subcontinent, is thought to be the last common ancestor of all the Bovini

...named attestation of hominins: Sahel Man, *Sahelanthropus tchadensis*...

The species is founded upon a cranium, discovered in northern Chad. It was christened Toumaï, hope of life in Goran, the language of the area's nomadic Toubou people. Even though closer to *Pan*, the chimpazee, than *Homo*, it might, nonetheless, be our first regard of ourselves. By November 2020, though, based upon a somewhat mysterious, fossilized partial left femur found near the skull of *Sahelanthropus*, it was suggested that Sahel Man may not be our oldest direct-line relative at all but is an ancient non-bipedal protogorilla. If the ahumanity is proven, other candidates for earliest-known ancestor could be the six-million-year-old *Orrorin turgensis*; and with the most extensive earliest evidence, the almost four and a half million years of age *Ardipithecus ramidus*, one million three hundred thousand years older than Lucy, *Australopithecus afarensis*, long considered the earliest upright walking hominin.

...came the evolution of C_4 grasses...

"The Path from C_3 to C_4 Photosynthesis," Udo Gowik, Peter Westhoff, *Plant Physiology*, January 2011.

...with greater occlusal–chewing surface–complexity...

These are Boödont teeth, the word meaning "ox-toothed." Aegodont means "goat-toothed."

...Yet with *Syncerus*...

The name of the genus comes from the two Greek words, σύν, *sun*, together, and κέρας, *keras*, horn: the abutting of the horns to form the helmet-like covering of the boss.

...the Urial sheep...

Other names are Arkars and Shapo.

...the North American *Bison latifrons*...

Almost unimaginably, the Giant bison, before going extinct during the mid to latter millennia of the Wisconsin glaciation, stood over eight-feet tall at the withers, more than fifteen feet in length, weighing as much as the Giant African buffalo, with horns seven foot from tip to tip.

...carried by *Homo ergaster*...

Whether *H. ergaster* is a different species from *H. erectus* remains to be seen, but not here. Because *H. ergaster* is more related to Africa, while *H. erectus* was prominent in Asia, the former is the one chosen in this work.

...the African buffalo, *Syncerus caffer*...

Some years ago, a science blogger, no doubt of the highest rectitude, picked out the African buffalo's binomial for disapprobation because of the word *caffer*. "Only the most cynical taxonomists would support the use of the term," he wrote. And he simply didn't "know why."

Kaffir was originally an Arab word for a pagan or a Christian; in the eyes of Islam, an infidel. More usually spelled kaffer, it became in apartheid South Africa the Afrikaans equivalent of the toxic English nigger. Now, the public utterance of the name in that country is a punishable *crimen injuria*, the unlawful, intentional, and serious harming of another's dignity.

As far as changing the Buffalo's name, an Australian taxonomist, whether the most cynical or not, replied to the blogger in a comment, noting that the International Zoological Code of Nomenclature places priority as the standard for a species canonical name, offensive or not; and there is no rule in the code about objectionable words, only the recommendation to avoid them if possible. The entire purpose of rules in nomenclature is to maintain the integrity of species names, limit muddle, and restrict capricious self-aggrandizement. As well, as it may sometimes happen, to inhibit authoritarian aspiration.

In 2005 the Turkish Environment and Forestry Ministry changed the nomenclature of indigenous subspecies of animals such as the red fox, *Vulpes vulpes kurdistanica*, and roe deer, *Capreolus capreolus armenius*, removing or altering the trinomials to erase reference to Kurds and Armenians, claiming the taxa were deliberately labeled in bad faith to insinuate that those ethnic groups had actually lived in the areas where the animals were found, which the Turks apparently preferred to deny.

According to the typically tone-deaf ministry functionary, "Unfortunately there are many other species in Turkey which were named this way with ill intentions. This ill intent is so obvious that even species only found in our country were given names against Turkey's unity."

The I. Z. C. N. curtly brushed aside any recognition of the Turkish government's double-speak changes. Of late, the government in Ankara is insisting that the nation now be known internationally as Turquia.

...so that it is classed as *S. caffer antiquus*...

Antiquus's gigantism is thought to represent an example of Bergmann's Rule. That rule states that in climates both farther north and south from the equator, which experience lower regular temperatures–and global temperatures overall were particularly low during the period between eighteen and ten thousand years ago before rising naturally–there is a trend toward larger size in warm-blooded-mammal species: Canadian whitetails are appreciably larger than ones in Texas, though conspecific–size helping to conserve body heart. Though not all mammals have, surprisingly, been homiothermic, warm blooded.

Once found on barren, predatorless Majorca and Menorca in the Mediterranean, the extinct Balearian mouse goat, *Myotragus balearicus*, descended from ovines from almost six million years ago and were present until about One Thousand B. C. when humans first reached the islands, was one of the most weirdly anomalous creatures. Based on skeletal evidence it was an ectothermic mammal with bone growth regulated, like a crocodilians's, by the availability of feed; it was also slow, could not run or jump, and for its body weight had a brain about a third of expected size. The Mouse goat exhibited classic island dwarfism, all to help it survive on a blasted heath; it was a fleecy Iguana with hooves, taken to basking on rocks.

Another reason for *antiquus*'s enormity was an evolutionary bias toward agonistic behavior–intraspecific displays of aggressive interaction usually between males in pursuit of dominance, including head-on-head clashes, in the name of sex. This favored selection for traits like conspicuous horns and big bodies. So, the broad, potentially encumbering span of the Giant buffalo's horns led a batch of Frankish paleontologist to go out on a limb and suggest that the species preferred–wait for it–"very open habitats," in turn leading to larger herds, therefore increased agonistic activity. Outsized horns and bulk, though, especially with habitat change, can be disadvantageous and may have prompted extinction by ultimately advantaging more streamlined Savanna buffalo that carry shorter, but more durably bossed, horns.

There is a question about whether *S. c. antiquus* vanished fully or was overtaken by *S. caffer*'s becoming what paleontologists call a phyletic replacement. If it did go extinct, though, it was not likely the fault of *Homo sapiens*, with whom *Syncerus* evolved. In Australia and the New World, megafauna-extinction events were coupled to the arrival of novel humans among naïve wildlife, giving us not only tactical but strategic ascendancy. In Africa the animals, rather than suddenly confronting unforeseen intelligent bipeds bearing arms, saw their coming gradually enough to increase avoidance, as humans developed more sophisticated hunting weapons and techniques.

While the Savanna buffalo became the alternate species, or lineage, in East and South Africa, the Giant buffalo with a higher tolerance for aridity, and benefitting from a Green Sahara brought on by a mid-Holocene wet interval, could survive until the time of King David in semi-desert barred to Savanna buffalo. Isolating further and further into mountain redoubts that were increasingly contracting, *antiquus* was finally gone forever.

...through relatively similar *brachyceros* and *aequinoctialis*...

The two species are comparatively alike: For bulls, up to four and three quarters feet tall at the withers; eight feet in length; thirteen hundred pounds; horns proportionately smaller than *S. c. caffer*, with *brachyceros*'s smaller than *aequinoctialis*'s. A span of thirty-seven to thirty-eight inches would be a minimum record *aequinoctialis*, while the horn of a *brachyceros* of twenty inches, measured along the outside curve, would make the book.

...record horn length...

According to *Rowland Ward's Records of Big Game, Thirtieth Edition, Africa*, published in 2020, the world's record horns for each subspecies of African buffalo–for records-keeping purposes rather than taxonomic ones–are as follows, based on the year they were entered:

Dwarf forest buffalo, *Syncerus caffer nanus*, found in far-northern Angola, rainforest Democratic Republic of Congo, Congo-Brazzaville, Gabon, Dzanga-Sangha National Park in Central African Republic, southern Cameroon, sparsely in coastal Nigeria, along the shore of the Gulf of Guinea, through southern Ghana, Ivory Coast, Liberia, Sierra Leone, and in southern Guinea. Method of measurement 12-b[1], minimum score 40. Total score for world's record, in inches: **75 4/8**–left horn: **28**; right horn: **27⅞**; left boss: **9⅞**; right boss: **9 6/8. 1921. Congo.**

1 **12-b. Rank on the Sum of the Length of the Horns and the Width of the Bosses.**

Length. Measure the length of each horn on the outside curve. Start in the front and measure along the front edge, keeping to the outside surface and continuing to the tip. To find the starting point, lay the long leg of a carpenter's square against the bottommost part of the boss and place the shorter leg of the square

West African buffalo, *Syncerus caffer brachyceros planiceros*–flat horned. *Planiceros* seems to be a designation for Rowland Ward's records's keeping purposes, more probable than specific. It is scored in the same fashion, and with the same minimum, as the Central African buffalo. Found in northern Cameroon, Nigeria through Benin, Togo, Ghana, Burkina Faso, Ivory Coast, and from Guinea into Senegal. Method of measurement 12-b, minimum score 48. World's record score: **78**–left horn: **27 4/8**; right horn: **27 2/8**; left boss: **11 4/8**; right boss: **11 6/8. 1921. Nigeria.**

Central African buffalo, *Syncerus caffer brachyceros,* found in Chad, Central African Republic, Democratic Republic of Congo. Method of measurement 12-a[1], minimum score 48.

---

against the inner part of the boss between the horns. Make sure the short leg is exactly parallel to the axis of the skull. Now divide the 90-degree angle into half (45 degrees) and mark this spot on the edge of the boss. This is the starting point for the length measurement; keep to the outside surface and continue to the tip. **Width of Boss.** Using a tape, measure each boss at its greatest width, at a 90-degree angle to the centerline (axis) of the horn, not the skull. (This is different from the method for the three larger buffaloes under Method 12-a.) Do not measure "green" or "soft" boss material. Depending on the horn configuration, it can be possible to take a "circumference" measurement for the width. Only measure the top 50 percent of the horn for the width; as soon as the horn starts curving inward (downward), stop the width measurement. Do not press the tape into any depressions; span it over uneven points. Do not measure the skull under the boss; measure the horn only. Boss measurements may not be taken outside the outer edge of the eye sockets because the horns here begin to form an oval around the bone core of the horn, and if taken in extreme, it would lead to a circumference measurement.

1 **12-a. Ranked on the Sum of the Measurements of the Widest Spread and the Width of Bosses.** **Greatest Spread.** Establish the outer limits of the horns using two right-angle forms. Measure the greatest spread in a straight line and at a right angle to the axis of the horns.

The easiest way to measure the spread is to lay the buffalo horns and skull on a smooth, flat surface such as a clean, smooth concrete floor and then place two large carpenter's triangles (an L-shaped device made of hard plastic or metal that can stand up straight) on both ends of the horns. Make sure that both triangles are at a 90-degree angle to the axis of the skull. It is now easy to get a measurement. Mark with a pencil where the carpenter's square reaches the concrete floor (both sides), push the horns and triangles away and measure the distance between the two marks. Do not measure from a wall above the horns and skull to a single carpenter's triangle because an air measurement may lead to a tape measure sagging, and this will increase the score. In extraordinary cases, a buffalo may have genital injury (or is a hermaphrodite), and in such cases malformed horns may occur and the spread measurement can be very large. Such animals must be noted in the comment section on the entry form. Such animals normally have very undeveloped bosses

Width of Boss. Using a tape measure, measure the boss of each horn at its greatest width; this must be taken parallel to the axis of the horn. DO NOT measure "green" or "soft" boss material.

Take the tape and start at the back of the boss and curve the tape over the boss to the front at its widest point. Do not press the tape into any depressions; span it over uneven points. Do not measure green horn or

Total score of world's record: **66⅛**–spread: **43**; left boss: **11 4/8**; right boss: **11⅝**. **1973. Ndele, Central African Republic.**

Nile buffalo, *Syncerus caffer aequinoctialis*, found in Sudan, South Sudan, Ethiopia. Method of measurement 12-a, minimum score 50. Total record score: **67 4/8**–spread: **44 2/8**; left boss: **11 4/8**; right boss: **11 6/8. 1977. Gemmeiza, Sudan.**

Cape buffalo, *Syncerus caffer caffer*, found in South Africa, Namibia, Angola, Botswana, Zimbabwe, Zambia, Malawi, Mozambique, Tanzania, Rwanda, Burundi, Kenya, and Uganda. Method of measurement 12-a, minimum score 64. World's record total score: **91⅝**–spread: **62 6/8**; left boss: **14 4/8**; right boss: **14⅜. 2000. Picked up in Manyara National Park, Tanzania.**

...a bull capable of reaching a short ton...

African buffalo seldom make it to a scale alive. But several bulls were weighed in South Africa and in the Serengeti in Tanzania, averaging around sixteen hundred fifty pounds, considerably lighter in Kenya and Botswana, while the upper limit can be two thousand.

...strength in numbers...

Old Buffalo may be solitary or part of small bachelor herds. Stuart Marks, the independent scholar of wildlife and hunting peoples and author of *Life as a Hunt: Thresholds of Identities and Illusions on an African Landscape*, says that the Bisa of Zambia call such herds *kakuli*. Other names for mixed-sex groups of Buffalo, of up to about sixty, *kasakoambe*, while herds in the hundreds are called *ibumba*. In areas such as the Serengeti that receive a mean thirty inches of rain per year, herd size can go as high as two thousand. Home ranges for herds can vary between four miles square to one hundred seventy five; over twenty four hours, Buffalo can graze across six to nineteen miles of ground.

...fusing into a casque over the top of a Buffalo's head...

Seen from the side with that boss, a Buffalo bears an uncanny resemblance to the profile of Il Duce, Benito Mussolini. In 1934, in place of the First World War helmet, evoking, as it did, in the translated words of the writer Italo Calvino, "the poor infantry in the trenches," Mussolini introduced to the Italian army the drooping German-style, dome-shaped helmet, which belonged to a new age of industrial design, like the aerodynamic line in cars from the same era. From then

skull bone. The angle for this measurement must be parallel to the centerline of the skull. Some bosses have a very thin edge and others have a very pronounced "overhang," so you will have to start the tape quite low near the back of the skull of the animal. Measure the boss to the front at its widest point. Do not press the tape into any depressions; span it over uneven points. Do not measure green horn or skull bone. The angle for this measurement must be parallel to the centerline of the skull. Some bosses have a very thin edge and others have a very pronounced "overhang," so you will have to start the tape quite low near the back of the skull of the animal.

on the classic image of Il Duce became the one with the helmet, which looked like a metallic extension of the smooth surface of his head.

Calvino died in 1985. In the January 6, 2003, issue of *The New Yorker* was published his posthumous essay, "Il Duce's Portraits." This one of Mussolini in his helmet could be considered canonical. As Calvino described him:

> Beneath the helmet, his jaw stands out more, acquiring a decisive importance, thanks to the disappearance of the upper part of his head (including his eyes). Because his lips protruded (an unnatural position but one denoting the power of his will), his jaw stuck out in front as well as to the side. From that moment on, then, Il Duce's head seems to be made up essentially of helmet and jawbones, which counterbalance each other in volume and also counterbalance the curve of his stomach, which was just beginning to stick out.

For Calvino, this was a huge shift in Mussolini's iconography, his character changed thus: Il Duce as thinker was replaced by Il Duce as *condottiero*. The resemblance as described above, to any head of state in the latter half of the 2010s, would be coincidental.

...Lion try to get a Buffalo down...

An example of evolution parallel to *Syncerus caffer* is the Muskox, the African buffalo of the Arctic. A *Caprinae* instead of a *Bovini*, it resembles something like a reproduction of a reproduction of the Buffalo, most similarly in the shape of horns–though growing more downward than laterally–and the boss on males, and there for the same reason: a helmet for agonistic encounters, leading the animal's being called by some, bonnet horned.

Muskox also evolved with Lion; or more correctly, Lion with them, both in Central Asia, though the Muskox was there far longer than *Panthera spelaea*, or the Eurasian cave lion. These Steppe lion–another name for the species–who learned to hunt Muskox before they ever hunted African buffalo, used similar techniques on the smaller northern animal–whose bulls could still weigh as much as seven hundred pounds. And the Muskox learned ways of defense that developed into ones similar to the Buffalo's. With no brush on the tundra, Muskox bunch like the spokes of a wheel, rumps inward, when threatened by Lion and Wolf–including the exquisitely named Dire wolf, *Canis dirus*, Fearsome dog, which Muskox, some of which lived south of the period's glacial boundary, would have known. Fight or flight seems to be based on body size. If a herbivore outweighs a predator by a ratio of at least three to one, it is feasible to stand one's ground and fight with all your available weapons, in the case of the Muskox its pointed horns and sharp hooves. If Lion captured a Muskox, having first escaped the stabs and blows of an animal that could charge unexpectedly out of the mob, the Lion's way of killing was the same as their African descendants's: suffocation, by closing their jaws on the prey's trachea. More likely, though, because of the awkward bulk of the bale of *quiviut*–the world's finest wool–around a Muskox's throat, buffering choking pressure, the predator would clamp onto the muzzle and jaw, hindering airflow.

...Numbers today range from four hundred to nine hundred thousand...
Buffalo are made not of genes alone, but the terroir of the region in which they originate. A "sporting" demand for Buffalo, though, has led to the troubling development of a ranching-breeding industry, predominantly in South Africa, that threatens to upend natural heredity. The object is the blending of different strains, to raise disease-free bulls with exceptional trophy size. In such an operation, the program calls for the Buffalo calf to be weaned at six months, at which time it is darted with a tranquilizer and moved to a boma where it is tagged, microchipped, and tested for ailments, such as brucellosis. It also has its D. N. A. analyzed and parentage recorded. Males are then placed in a bull camp, and females in one for heifers.

At four, twelve, and between sixteen to eighteen months, the bulls's horns are measured and scored according to the Rowland Ward system. Bulls are expected to have a horn spread corresponding to one inch for each month of growth. Bulls are judged on strong hooves, scrotum development, and a tractable temperament. The desired traits in cows are good horns and hooves, fertility, and an "intercalving period" of less than four hundred days. The goal for some breeders is a minimum spread of forty-two inches for bulls. Ones that do not reach that standard are sold to fenced-hunting outfitters—of course, those that do reach it and are not reserved for breeding, are almost certainly going to be "hunted" as well, at no doubt substantially higher fees than those commanded by scrubby ones. Ranchers are not all wealthy, but it helps. In 2016, a fifty-six-inch-wide bull known as Horizon, was valued at twelve point two million dollars and owned by a syndicate of investors. There are reports of funds, ironically from illicit hunting, being laundered through some breeding facilities, though whether washed in Buffalo semen is not substantiated.

...layering chill of the matope...
Kiswahili word for mud.

Chapter Seven: Arly

... shea, Roan-fruit, and Isoberlinia trees...
The Latin name of the shea tree, *Vitellaria paradoxa*, comes from vitellus, the word for egg yolk for the ivory color of the seed, and for paradox–why, I cannot say; perhaps someone else can. A tall, large, slow-growing, long-fruit-bearing tree, its earlier name was *Butyrospermum parkii*: the genus butter seed and the species named in honor of Mungo Park, who found the tree in Senegal and Mali during his expeditions and noted its significance to the people. The tree nut is, of course, from what shea butter is extracted; and gathering them is an important source of income for rural Africans, especially women. It also provides vital nourishment during the hungry season when agriculturalists are most busy working the fields and crops have not yet come in. Rich in fats and oils, and containing protein, it has been semi-domesticated–consciously selected for yield, sweetness of flavor, health of the trees, and freedom from competition with annual crops. Roan,

the name in Arly for the firm yellow plum-like fruit I took to be *Ximenia americana*, its generic name from an eighteenth–century Spanish priest, Francisco Ximénez, and peculiar for a plant native to Africa, the specific name American. A shrubby tree, its seeds are dispersed by animals by the usual mechanics.

Isoberlinia doka, a vuba hardwood purplish red beneath the bark, can reach seventy-five feet in height. As the tree grows, the Central African giant eland, large as a draft horse, a dozen vertical white stripes around its ruddy body, musky scented, curly black maned with a long dewlap, with black V-formed horns that can grow in heteronymous spirals to nearly five feet of length, ghosts through its woodlands, feeding on the green leaves and shoots it can reach.

In the C. A. R. those years before, I rode in the back of a Land Cruiser pickup through tall stands of teak. We'd walked for five days across gameless country, shot out by the raiders coming in from Sudan on camelback, who were still lurking, our hearing as we traveled their random gunfire as they swept up whatever was left, and feeling their lighted fires at night when they tried to burn us out. We came to a camp of thatched boukarous and an undependable safari vehicle, in the cooler box souring Lion meat to eat. I stood in the pickup bed, now, holding onto the rollbar as we bounced over the rough trail.

A quarter mile away through the timber, I saw a flash of reddish-gold. I leaned over the side of the cab and whispered to the driver to stop. I found the reddish-gold in the binocular, the heavy, folded skin on the rump of a big animal, walking in the late-afternoon light. Taking my Remington 375, I climbed down from the pickup as the professional hunter, a bearded British colonial, came out beside me. The tracker, the one-armed, reformed poacher Djouma, was behind him.

What is it? asked the P. H., as if it were an accusation.

Giant eland.

From the ground I lost sight of the bull. I went forward in the trees with the P. H., Djouma in back of us. When I saw the bull again, it was walking easily beyond an open flow of black lava rock. Djouma came to my side and looked for the animal. I took him by the shoulder of his amputated arm and pointed him across the black rocks.

Yes, he said, excited, yes. Thank you, Tom, pronouncing it Tome as François Bendima did. The P. H. could see the eland, too. It was more than three hundred yards away.

You must shoot him from here.

Out of the question.

Djouma, listening but not knowing the words yet understanding the exchange all the same, said softly, Yes, taking me by the cuff of my camouflaged shirt. Leaving the P. H. behind, Djouma and I went off together in a Chuck Berry duck walk, going from tree to tree until the woods ended at the edge of the volcanic rubble, the Eland on the other side of the wide black apron where the trees grew up again. It was sideways to us, walking slowly. Before Djouma and I started, I chambered a 300-grain soft-nosed round and set the safety. It was under two hundred yards, and Djouma wanted me to shoot. I trusted Djouma.

I rested the rifle stock against the trunk of a teak tree and let off the safety. I put the crosshairs below the Eland's humped withers on the midline of its torso, just behind the left shoulder, intentionally not seeing the marvelously long horns. My finger touched the trigger, and the Eland turned to go off into the other teaks with thickets of *Isoberlinia* growing within it.

No, Djouma whispered. I reset the safety. Djouma took my sleeve again; and bent low, we crossed the open basalt as one, lone, rare specimen of trotting bovid.

Within the timber, Djouma led me in wide downwind arcs around the patches of green-leafed young trees. In there, the Eland was feeding as it moved, unseen, its eating sounds probably louder by degrees than its walking, even at two thousand pounds or better. On horned feet in plastic sandals, Djouma half ran, never touching a twig. Jogging lumberingly behind, I snapped down on a dry leaf, Djouma wheeling, tsk-ing. For many minutes this is the way we moved, Djouma biting his lower lip, searching in the trees for one glimpse of the Eland.

Then he halted. Taking my arm, he whispered rapidly at me in the French language. Releasing me with his one hand, he pointed to the solid wall of *Isoberlinia*, ten foot high, then holding his thumb and forefinger a small distance apart. Too small? Wait a moment? What?

As I started raising my rifle, Djouma directed the barrel down.

No. No. No, he said, under his breath.

The Central African giant eland glided from the cover, eighty yards away. Quartering toward us, it held its ears up and head high, sunlight falling through the trees behind it. It tried to place a definition upon us; and Djouma said, Yes.

I brought the 375 to my shoulder, slowly, placing the scope's reticle on the point of the bull's left shoulder at the base of its neck. I let off the safety.

At the shot dust lifted from the hide over the shoulder, like beating a trail Stetson against your leg, the bullet angling through the chest cavity. Bucking, the Eland turned, disappearing into the cover. We ran full out through the trees after the wounded bull, not worrying about noise. Then Djouma clutched my arm, and the enormous animal staggered ahead of us.

Working the action, I was going to fire again with the Eland still moving on its hooves, when it stopped. It dropped its heavy-horned head as if it had become too serious a burden, and swayed. The period of each swing grew longer, and lurching it lay down, head lifted, looking straight ahead, silent. Walking up to fifteen yards, breathing away the panting, I fired into its heart.

On its side, Percheron big, so much meat when we were truthfully so hungry coming out of the empty country, the Eland was now, in the shadows of the trees, sandy golden. The clean stripes, black neck ruff, and large hump were all there, with a bull's powerful perfumed unerasable scent. The black horns, pointing now along the ground, wound more than forty-eight inches around the keels of the spirals.

The light fading, one-armed Djouma tossed off the billed cap I gave him at the start of the hunt, then stripped away his shirt. Bouncing into the air, he proclaimed himself *un tracker fantastique*, over and over. He daubed his finger in the blood in the wound in the Eland's shoulder and blooded himself. Coming to me where I sat on an old termite hill, staring at this perfect and perfectly hunted creature, my opened rifle across my knees, he reached to mark my forehead, too.

In the distance, a Lion began to roar.

...Djanjoua set fire to a large patch of tall dead grass...
For at least five thousand years, Native Americans, intentionally and regularly burned the grass prairies of North America to replicate the benefits that resulted from natural fires ignited by lightning strikes. Fire actually supported and reinvigorated the natural vegetation and made for greener pastures to support herds of grazers, such as Bison. Until the coming of Europeans, Native Americans called and, more importantly, thought of prairie fires as the Red Buffalo.

Chapter Eight: Toxin

...we seemed to suit ourselves to with fluency...
The late environmentalist, Paul Shepard, in his book *The Tender Carnivore and the Sacred Game*, made the case for the human as the supremely adaptable species:

> It is time to bury the nonsense of the "incomplete animal." As Julian Huxley, the eminent British biologist, once observed concerning human toughness, man is the only creature that can walk twenty miles, run two miles, swim a river, and then climb a tree [*and it might be added, open a book and read it, or compose a song, while perched there*]. Physiologically, he has one of the toughest bodies known; no other species could survive weeks of exposure on the open sea, or in deserts, or the Arctic. Man's superior exploits are not evidence of cultural inventions: clothing on a giraffe will not allow it to survive in Antarctica, and neither shade nor shoes will help a salamander in the Sahara. I am not speaking of living in those places permanently, but simply as a measure of the durability of men under stress. Several evolutionary developments have made this possible: highly specialized skin, central nervous system, and self-regulatory physiological systems. Man's ancestors were neither helpless nor incomplete.

...And that's one possibility...
Since Charles Darwin proposed the rise of human bipedalism as a means of freeing the hands to carry–*stuff*, at least forty different explanations for it have been published in the scientific literature, encompassing it all from phallic display to iodine deficiency–treetop life carried hominins into mountain environments where a lack of iodine led to mutations of the legs and arms conducive to upright walking–to the Aquatic Ape Hypothesis–having to wade across seasonally flooded gallery forest floors–as reasons for the posture's adoption.

...their progressively plantigrade feet...

While the digitigrade and unguligrade stance of canines and the likes of Deer make for greater economy in running, the heel-down posture we share not only with the Great apes but with for that matter, Bear and Wolverine, has been thought to have evolved from the tree-walking behavior of Chimp and Gorilla, which is a bipedal movement with a shifting balance along limbs, rather than on all fours. As noted, though, our two-legged mobility on the ground hasn't made us all that fast. So another theory is that by being able to stand flat footed makes us more formidable fighters, as it could also make us in the hunt stronger swingers of clubs, thrusters and throwers of spears, and drawers of bows.

...calling meat-eaters down onto them...

The late, transgressive–the term much overused, but actually fitting him–British writer Bruce Chatwin postulated a specialist *Dinofelis*, a jaguar-sized Terrible feline, that preyed remorselessly on hominins who per force were cave-huddling primates, awash in fear and trembling–rather than the killer-ape etiologies of the human contagion, as put forward by Dart and the screenwriter-anthropologist Robert Ardrey, author of the series of books on human evolution beginning with *African Genesis*. More recent analysis of carbon isotopes in dental enamel, however, demonstrate that *Dinofelis* was a hunter of grazing, herbivorous Antelope. The Evil One for our *Australopithecus* relatives was another Felid, again in a large jaguar-like format, the machairodontine, knife tooth, *Megantereon*, Giant beast, the carbon-isotope ratio in its scimitar canines indicative of a steady diet of hominin. *Megantereon* was also the better of *Dinofelis* in size, though Dart's Taung Child was small enough to show signs of having met its end by being snatched up by an Eagle–and the refuse midden in which its fossils were found may not have been from a protohuman kitchen, but from beneath a raptor's nest.

...the location of the foramen magnum...

Two-legged mammals in the main hop or waddle–the, perhaps, extinct Thylacine was said to have a curious hopping gait like other marsupials, such as the Kangaroo, though on four legs instead of two. The biomechanics involved in human walking and running are displacement of the center of mass within the pelvis, from which with only slight oscillation the impact is transferred through thighs and legs to be absorbed in robust heels, the arches and balls of the feet, and ten toes. Our stride, though it came out of arboreal-primate branch locomotion, driven by dominate hind limbs and sitting upright at rest, is something unique: According to one neuroscientist, two legs being inherently unstable, each step for Plato's featherless biped is a fall forward and sideways toward the lifted foot, turning even the simplest stroll into one of the most daring balancing acts in the animal kingdom.

At least since the time of the emergence of *Homo ergaster–erectus* to some, see above–almost two million years ago, the modern, long-lower-limbed, erect human blueprint was already established by a bending of the spine back in the lumbar region and particularly in modifications to the pelvis: a fine tuning of its inward-curving ilia–the wide, butterfly-wing-shaped, matching bones–short ischia–the twin processes upon which we seat ourselves–and the wedged sacrum–the fused vertebrae just above the coccyx. The real secret, considered by some to be an unrecognized sixth sense, was balance.

Standing still, thanks to the hominin ground plan, requires minimal muscular energy, though more important is the way the vestibular apparatus, as Jackie Higgins writes in *Sentient: How Animals Illuminate the Wonder of Our Human Senses*, performs like a series of spirit levels. The sheer size of the semicircular canals in our inner ear, as a percentage of our relative body mass, surpass other primates's. The equilibrioception we experience without thinking–never noticing it unless we lose it–in our vision as well as upright posture, would not be possible without our brain. We don't receive the sensations of the five outward wits, as listed in *Cursor Mundi*, of touch, sight, hearing, smell, and taste–with balance added–through the stimulation of the faculties but through that and the transduction to the brain, where they are processed. In our minds, or in what lies within them, is where we feel.

...Valerius Geist, an ethologist...

Val's preferred description of himself was a wildlife biologist who studied animal and human behavior in depth, and included among his published works were two books on human evolution. He remembered Lorenz–the nominal conceiver of ethology and winner of the Nobel Prize for making the behavior of animals in their natural surroundings, rather than in the laboratory, a subject of biological inquiry–as a bear of a man who greeted him with hugs when they would meet in Germany. They remained friends, even though coming to disagree on how aggression was selected for among species.

...used as cudgels for bludgeoning...

Dart, 1893 to 1988, arrived at the view–certainly informed by the bootless carnage he witnessed on the battlefields of France at the end of the Great War, and adopted from him and Ardrey by director Stanley Kubrick in the killer-ape prelude in *2001: A Space Odyssey*–that we were the man-beast, the cruelest foe to other animals and ourselves.

On film, as approximate stand-ins for the multi-toed early-horse, *Hipparion*, that *Australopithecina* hunted, Kubrick cleverly employed live Lowland tapir–perissodactyls in their own right, though native to Amazonia far from the savanna of Southern Africa. Kubrick cuts between shots of prehumans's wielding femur bones, and those of inert Tapir dropped onto the ground in detailed slow motion to simulate the animals's falling, bludgeoned to death. The Pliocene battery was not limited to bones and digging sticks, though, but would have included broken bone ends and sharp horn tips for thrusting and mandibles as natural kukris. The downfall for these ancient hominids, as for their rivals in the film when they were overwhelmed at the waterhole by blunt-force trauma delivered by hand weapons, arrived with the next troop or species who showed up with spears with stone projectile points and an even more-extended range of lethality. For millions of years, we have been part of a perpetual arms race, the term arms as literal as you wish to make it–the Gourmantché have a story of how Tienu, God, gave the human bows, arrows, and spears for hunting, the human gaining *ya n'un nua*, the arm that sees, becoming *onubiman-daano*, the owner of skillful fingers, making him an expert shot with arrows or spear.

...foregoing putting our own bodies in contact...

The earliest sharp, flaked-pointed stones are half a million years old, found in the Kathu Pan Archeological Complex in South Africa's Northern Cape province, the handiwork, possibly, of *Homo heidelbergensis.* Studies of cross sections of Eurasian Neanderthals's fossilized humeri suggest strength asymmetries that could be linked to one limb's–generally the trailing–regularly providing greater driving force to hand spears, whatever the means of delivery: handheld or through flight. It is in V-shaped fracture wings in stone points from nearly three hundred thousand-year-old discoveries in Ethiopia, predating *H. sapiens* by tens of thousands of years–and not coincidentally, given *Homo*'s attraction to water, from a site that at one time overlooked a Pleistocene megalake–that spear throwing is demonstrated, far earlier than previously assumed. Examinations showed impact cracks speeding through stone points at greater than twenty six hundred feet per second, considered the maximum that could result from thrusting. In some of these spear artifacts, however, are displayed fractures that traveled at almost five thousand feet per second, considered the highest speed that can be developed by throwing.

...a spear, thrust or thrown by hand...

The study of ethnographic reviews gives the heavy hand-thrown spears of the aboriginal Tiwi, inhabitants of Austrailia's Bathurst and Melville Islands, ranges of up to fifty meters, the same ranges achieved by native Tasmanians with lighter spears. Experimental efforts to determine the maximum lethal range of hand-thrown spears–with trained javelin throwers hurling replicas of three hundred thousand-year-old untipped spruce spears–demonstrated consistent ranges of twenty meters, which with the simplest of our distance-hunting weapons, not counting rocks, put us at a significant advantage over our prey.

...we could pour onto an animal in a horde...

To the degree to which we are disposed to countenance a report of Peter Kolben's, Africans hunting en masse then, and no doubt even now in some parts of the continent, resembled this:

> When all the Men of a *Kraal* are out upon the Chace, and discover a Wild Beast of any considerable Size, Strength, and Fierceness, they divide themselves into several Parties, and endeavour to surround the Beast; which, through their Nimbleness of Foot, they generally do very quickly, tho' upon the Sight of such Danger, the Beast, of whatsoever Kind, always betakes himself to all his Shifts and to all his Heels. If 'tis an Elephant, a Rhinoceros, an Elk [*a Buffalo or Eland?*], or a Wild Ass they thus encompass, they attack him with *Hassagayes.* The hard thick Hides of those Creatures fortified 'em against

a Shower of Arrows. If they lay him not dead upon the Spot, they so loaden him with *Hassagayes* that he runs not long before he tumbles. But It would be diverting to Sportsmen to see one of those Creatures, who escapes Demolition at the first Onset, return the Attack upon the *Hottentots*. They now stand about him in a Ring, as large a one as they can make, so as to reach him with their *Hassagayes*. One or two or more *Hassagayes* are, perhaps, already stuck in his Body. The Creature runs, with fierce Eyes and a great Deal of Noise and Fury, at the *Hottentots* who threw 'em. Then others attack him in the Rear. He turns about to run at the last Assailants, and is again attack'd at the Rear. Again he turns about, and is again attack'd. The *Hassagayes* multiply upon his Body; many are fix'd upon his Back and Sides; and being violently shook, by his violent Motion, tear and enrage the Wounds. He runs, roars, tears up the Ground, and is stark mad with Pain. The *Hassagayes* still pour in upon him; and he is sometimes stuck quite round with 'em, and has, as it were, a Forest upon his Back before he falls.

...so it may be brought to hand...

In the principles of modern game laws it is labeled reduction into possession of the *res nullius*, the wild animal which until dead belongs to no one.

... and may still be, arrow poison...

Poison's etymology is from the Old French for drink. The word toxic, poisonous, comes from the French *toxique*, from Late Latin *toxicus*, poisoned, in turn from the Latin *toxicum*, poison. Etymologically, toxin derives from the Scythian *toxon*, the word for bow–the art of archery known as toxophily. The Greek *toxikón* is the neuter of the male-gender *toxikós*, translated as for use on arrows, meaning poison, with the earliest source for the word being the Persian prefix *taxša-*, bow. *Taxus* is Latin for yew. While bows were made from yew, its more important contribution to the hunt, and warfare, was the toxic juice extracted from the tree, *Taxus baccata*. Long known to, and used by, the ancient Celts and Germani, yew arrow poison, and poison in general, is intrinsically related to the bows and arrows of hunters. Something Africans have been proving for hundreds of centuries.

...Linnaeus's formal name for whites...

The Swedish botanist divided humans into four subcategories. These were, white: European–red: Native American–yellow: Asian–and black: African, based on skin color. The only one with entirely positive traits, according to Linnaeus, was white people.

...On his fourth voyage to West Africa, Tristão

Already on three previous coastings along the West African littoral–his third extending to the sub-Saharan Terra dos Guineus, Land of the Blacks, where skin pigmentation reportedly transitioned from tawny to sable–Tristão initiated in a modest yet repugnant fashion, a slave trade between Africa and Europe. The first small African canoes that came into his view on one of those voyages had innocent natives astride them, propelling them with their feet, the Portuguese thinking–in a time in Europe when Renaissance men believed that Africa was home to one-legged shade-foot monsters and other grotesques–he was seeing an exotic breed of bird skimming low over the water, those the kind of *rarae aves* he would bring back to Lisbon, against their wills. On his last sailing, reaching what is thought to have been the mouth of the Gambia, he set out upriver in a launch with twenty-two of his crewmen, when a party of some eighty armed Blacks who knew what the intruders were about, assailed them with showers of arrows, almost every sailor being struck. By the time they struggled back to the ship, all the wounded, even those hit merely superficially, were dying from toxin, Tristão himself living only long enough to report what had befallen them, leaving just his vessel's clerk and four *grumetes*, ship's boys, to sail the lateen-rigged caravel back to Portugal.

...time-consuming rituals and sacrifices, oath-taking, commandments, taboos and secret ceremonies...

H. D. Neuwinger compounded the theory: The more primitive the society, the more complicated the poison. So-called primitive peoples, without access to dubitable conveniences such as modern firearms, electric lights, motor vehicles, or iPhones, had more time to invest in the formulation of poisons, and would undoubtedly have freer hours for perfecting and refining them.

...the Big Three poisons...

Acokanthera, one of the family of dogbane, was isolated in the 1880s. Its lethal component, ouabain, from the French *ouabaïo*, from the Somali *waabaayo*, arrow poison, is also the name of the woody liana–in Kenya it is called the national poison plant–from which the toxin is derived.

A twining vine, *Parquetina* is cut into pieces and its wrung-out juices collected in a leaf bowl and with a leaf spoon applied fresh to hunting arrows.

Growing throughout Africa from 15 degrees North to the Cape, *Strophanthus* can be in relation to environmental conditions, a liana, small tree, spreading shrub, or a ground creeper. Its role as a hunting poison was first recognized by Europeans in the early 1860s by a member of David Livingstone's expedition to then-Nyassaland, where it was called *kombe*. In the past, in more arid regions it was cultivated for the poison, strophanthin, chemically similar to ouabain. In the markets of Burkina Faso in the early 1960s, *Strophanthus* seeds were priced at one chicken per handful; for enough to cover the back of a hand, a hundred fifty cowrie shells.

The Lobi of that part of Burkina Faso bordering the northeast Cote d'Ivoire are perhaps the most ardent, and dread, enthusiasts of strophanthin. It is said that the bush is their true home and that they live by hunting and warfare, preferring the former in the rains and the latter in all seasons, truly observing no truces with man or animal at any time. And arrow poison is the sovereign specific of their culture. If it is needed by a hunter, a market one or otherwise–or even by those who hunt no longer, but want it for fending off malevolent persons and beasts–he must present himself and state his case to the lompo poison fetish, a piece of wood laid before a clay pot of white earth and water, and minded by the female head of each family, activating it with powdered bone.

While glycoside poisons in general, kill very briskly, not all others do. Sir Samuel White Baker in his *The Albert N'Yanza, Great Basin of the Nile and Explorations of the Nile Sources* relates a tale of horror regarding a human poisoned with a non-glycoside. Persecuted by pillaging and murdering Khartoumers, the people of the Bari tribe around Gondokoro chose to make any stranger a target of revenge:

> The effect of the poison used for the arrow-heads is very extraordinary. A man came to me for medical aid; five months ago he had been wounded by a poisoned arrow in the leg, below the calf, and the entire foot had been eaten away by the action of the poison. The bone rotted through just above the ankle, and the foot dropped off. The most violent poison is the produce of the root of a tree, whose milky juice yields a resin that is smeared upon the arrow. It is brought from a great distance, from some country far west of Gondorkoro. The juice of the species of euphorbia, common in these countries, is also used for poisoning arrows. Boiled to the consistency of tar, it is then smeared upon the blade. The action of the poison is to corrode the flesh, which loses its fiber, and drops away like jelly, after severe inflammation and swelling. The arrows are barbed with diabolical ingenuity, some are arranged with poison heads that fit into sockets; these detach from the arrow on an attempt to withdraw them; thus the barbed blade, thickly smeared with poison, remains in the wound, and before it can be cut out the poison is absorbed by the system.

The ineffectiveness of this as a hunting poison should be evident: No hunter wants his prey to go off somewhere, to be lost and not recovered.

...lengthy clandestine boiling...

The isolation surrounding poison making has practical reasons. According to Neuwinger, producing ouabain requires a large amount of water which may be some distance from a village; secondly, out of caution, the poison should be made away from children; and third, the maker, often an older man, does not want his valuable trade secrets stolen.

...the rubber of the Congo...

The Congolese were essentially impressed by Leopold II to perform the drudgery of collecting latex from the relatively rare vines–sometimes found no more than one to the acre. A pot that might take a full day to fill often brought no more than a cheap five-inch knife in compensation. Failure to meet quotas was punishable by death.

The native paramilitary Force Publique was tasked with presenting severed hands as evidence of having carried out the executions. The colonial government wanted assurances that the paramilitary was not hoarding ammunition for potential mutiny or, just as subversively, hunting. The paramilitary, then, reckoned on conserving live cartridges by amputating hands from the living without wasting a round. In his pre-World War I, and now dishonored, song-poem, "The Congo," Vachel Lindsay condemned the King of the Belgians for this albeit officially unsanctioned policy:

> Listen to the yell of Leopold's ghost
> Burning in Hell for his hand-maimed host.
> Hear how the demons chuckle and yell
> Cutting his hands off, down in Hell.
> Listen to the creepy proclamation,
> Blown through the lairs of the forest-nation,
> Blown past the white-ants' hill of clay,
> Blown past the marsh where the butterflies play:—
> "Be careful what you do,
>   **All the o sounds very golden. Heavy accents very heavy.**
>   **Light accents very light. Last line whispered.**
> Or Mumbo-Jumbo, God of the Congo,
> And all of the other
> Gods of the Congo,
> Mumbo-Jumbo will hoo-doo you,
> Mumbo-Jumbo will hoo-doo you,
> Mumbo-Jumbo will hoo-doo you."

According to Edgar Lee Masters, Lindsay's last words at fifty-two, after intentionally drinking a bottle of lye, were, "They tried to get me; I got them first." They are now trying to get his words, of course.

...the liberty that hunting conferred...

In *Shadows on the Grass*, Isak Dinesen wrote:

> The businessmen, under the motto of "Teach the Native to Want," encouraged the African to evaluate himself by his possessions and to keep up respectably with his neighbours.

...that Africans must not be permitted to hunt...

There was a view among Europeans in the nineteenth century that hunting and warfare were intimately related, the skills learned in one, germane to the other. Opinions about firearms in the hands of natives were not, though, uniform among whites. No less a light than Dr. Livingstone took the stance that because firearms made battle more terrible, and was an equalizer between weaker and stronger tribes, warfare would be reduced. Another explorer, of southern Africa in the 1860s, James Chapman, pronounced the gun a "potent peacemaker."

... John Pondoro Taylor...

Taylor's given middle name was Howard. Pondoro is a Mozambican Bantu name for Lion–shortened from Chimpondoro, said to mean The Roaring of a Lion. Born in 1904 the son of an Irish surgeon, Taylor under threat from Sinn Féin, left the isle for Africa. He hunted primarily for himself, not caring to guide sport hunters on a regular basis, criminality more opportune to carry on without a client to witness it. He wrote a number of successful books in the 1940s and '50s related to safari hunting. In the early 1950s, the officials in Lourenço Marques were preparing to arrest him for his lawless shooting, when he crossed the frontier into the British colony of Nyasaland, where his wanton outlawry there quickly made him persona non grata as well. Emigrating to England after some thirty years in Africa, Taylor, it was believed, based on his expertise, could have found another career with one of the bespoke London gunmakers. He was, though, an indifferently closeted homosexual during the time in England when being a "party" to "any act of gross indecency with another male person," could be punishable by imprisonment "not exceeding two years, with or without hard labour"–the act responsible for the law's being called The Blackmailer's Charter. This made Taylor's finding work as a High Street firearms sales representative problematic and led to his final years spent in pretty-much abject poverty when his last job was as a nightwatchman at a dog kennel.

There was one African, Aly Ndemanga, the "tracker and gunbearer, steadfast friend and companion of the African bush," to whom Taylor dedicated *Pondoro*. They also shared an enduring relationship, beginning when Ndemanga was a teenager–Taylor called him his adopted son–lasting, even when they were on separate continents, till the death of Pondoro in 1969. They now lie together in a grave in Mwambwajila, Malawi, formerly Nyasaland.

...quite prepared to hunt rhino and buffalo...

Taylor told of the WaKamba of Kenya who often hunted Rhino with bow and arrow and poison. They knew of a certain euphorbia tree whose leaves and shoots were appetizing to Rhino when they withered and dried. A hunter would chop this tree down, and within a few days he would return at night to sit up over it. A Rhino came to feed, and the hunter shot it with a poison arrow. The animal ran some distance and died. And because the area directly around the fallen euphorbia was undisturbed, the hunter might take two or more shots in a night. Taylor noted, though, "Let me hasten to say that the African hunter does not kill more than he and his mates can conveniently handle–which is more than can be said in most cases of the rifle-armed whites"–a somewhat novel sentiment, especially one voiced by an incorrigible Irish poacher, in the comparing of Blacks and Europeans.

...driven into cultural extinction in the 1950s...

According to Gareth Roriston, writing on the Watha on the Sheldrick Wildlife Trust website in 2020, based upon Watha oral history told to him, these Cushitic people came down possibly from Yemen, crossing the Red Sea. Thought initially to have been pastoralists, they abandoned livestock herding after droughts and battling stronger tribes over the possession of their animals. Their name is considered a contraction of "to go with the will of god," in honor of their philosophy of living by their wits and knowledge of nature, freeing them from the assaults, natural and municipal, suffered over and again by cattle keepers. As hunters, they entered Tsavo East on the trail of Elephant, and found a near perfect domain. It was only after generations that the balance was tipped.

From Roriston:

> With the arrival of capitalism and the free market during the 20th century, the resolve of members of the tribe was challenged regarding honouring the elephant in life and death, as some began to embark on a more commercial tack, motivated by selling ivory over meat consumption. Wastage became more common. Ironically, they say this increased when Tsavo East was gazetted as a national park in 1948. From their perspective, with the founding of the national park, their entire way of life was outlawed with an abrupt and confusing suddenness by external forces. They were eventually all informed about the government policy that there would no longer be any hunting permitted on their ancestral hunting grounds, but knowing no other livelihood and with the site of each kill now effectively being a crime scene, commercial ivory hunting yielded a safer and more rewarding option than camping by the carcass and utilising every morsel as had been the practice of the past, however "elatcha" (elephant fat) remained/remains a highly prized food source to those Watha willing to risk poaching. For some who did take the risk, pressure to make a living resulted in an inclination toward a volume approach to elephant hunting, slaying as many as possible and removing the tusks and a little "elatcha" as quickly as possible before being discovered by the authorities. This led to the entire community being complicit with the illegal ivory trade during the 50's, 60's and 70's as their customary trade networks were driven underground. It was during this period that marginalisation and stigmatism of the tribe rose.

...he touched the toxin...

The Pogoro test their poison in a similar way, slicing open the skin under their right knees and letting a trail of blood descend to their ankles. Using a knife blade to create a barrier below the cut, the hunter has another one apply a pinch of the poison to the bottom of the trail. If the toxin is effective, the blood is reported to flow backward, "as if by magic."

...Muzzleloaders are probably the most traditional hunting weapons used by Africans...

A well-known firearm was the Dane gun, the name a holdover from Dano-Norwegian muskets imported as West African trade goods. Today, the name is synonymous with a native gun, produced by blacksmiths for use in hunting.

...larger return on their hunting effort...

In the U. S., consumption of animal flesh–beef, pork, poultry, and fish–tallies up to about a hundred forty-five pounds per capita per annum. Among the most successful subsistence African hunters of at least the recent past, over two hundred pounds of wild meat–mostly Buffalo, Elephant, Warthog, and Impala–were eaten every year. Naturally less fatty than domestic meat, the amount of calories from that much high-protein venison may not have exceeded that from the smaller quantity of farm-raised livestock.

...the percussion cap is affixed to the trigger guard with wax...

Percussion-lock firearms most probably had, and have, rifled barrels, as opposed to the smooth bores of flintlock muskets, both the "weapon with the lightning," the term, originally in Portuguese, used by Alexandre Alberto da Rocha de Serpa Pinto in his 1881 Como eu atravessei a África. For centuries to come from the day of Tristão before either firearm–musket or rifle–arrived in numbers, many more poison arrows flew onto white people; and though the white people responded with sword and, if at hand, powder and ball–and finally the storied Maxim–they were for long periods staved off by resistance from natives with traditional weapons. Then even Africans became musketeers: With the European trade in slaves, hundreds of thousands of firearms, largely British, from the eighteenth century on, poured into the continent annually through ports along the western Slave and Gold Coasts alone, human beings coming to be priced in multiples of firearms and other goods.

Sheer force of arms, even as expressed in the machine gun, was not the sole means of taking over land, the process also involving economic, cultural, and class suasions to name just a few, so seductively multifarious that it was not so much that colonialism succeeded, but the duration for which Africans restrained it. Yet through it all, colonizing powers were Argus-eyed about maintaining their edge.

During the 1952 to 1960 Mau Mau Uprising or Kenya Emergency–based upon your political vantage point–ambushing rebels resorted largely to handmade guns manufactured clandestinely, like arrow poisons, in the foothills and forests. Parts came from available materials: native muthiti or thirikwa wood impervious to the weather for the stocks; water pipe for barrels; a smaller pipe or block of iron fitting smoothly within the larger pipe, acting as the striker, propelled by barbed-wire springs and as in a slingshot, bands of tire inner tubes, the firearms lacking sights and liable to rupture. In the face of such armament, the Royal Air Force of the United Kingdom replied with fifty thousand tons of high-explosive bombs and two million machine-gun rounds fired in strafing runs, the toll in human and animal life going unrecorded.

...As our hunting technology progresses...

There has certainly been a great increase in game slaughter in Africa by Africans in the last half century; but the fault does not lie in tradition, subsistence, arrow poison, or muzzleloaders. If a culprit is to be singled out, it is the inventive mind of Russian Lieutenant General Mikhail Timofeyevich Kalashnikov and his most ingenious device scattered like dragon's teeth through the continent by almost constant bush wars.

...from the Gbaya, the foremost hunters in the country...

Related to the Gbaya, the ethnic Mandja of the Bangui region of the Central African Republic still use poison for Buffalo and Elephant, as one assumes the Gbaya do as well.

...We turned back...

When hunting Buffalo, the Gbaya avoid trails marked by the shrubby solé tree, *Annona senegalensis*, wild custard apple, believing that the animals lie in ambush behind it.

Chapter Nine: Gore

...Africans evolved sickle cells...

The stretched shape makes the membranous walls of the cells porous, putting nutrients out into the blood and stimulating the body to eliminate these cells rapidly. *Plasmodium* parasites, such as those that cause malaria, find those leaky cells captivating. Drawn to them, the disease parasites get carried away with those defective cells as the body cleanses itself.

...Sometimes, they merely kill...

Major Sir William Cornwallis Harris, one of the very first safari hunters in Southern Africa between 1836-37, described the "wanton acts of aggression" of the Buffalo as being "the exception, rather than the rule, of the animal's ordinary habits." That if left to itself, it is "the natural instinct" of the Buffalo "to retire from before the presence of the lord of the creation, instead of provoking his hostility." Yet it is "of so irascible a disposition that he will even attack his great enemy, man, without the smallest provocation." A provoked Buffalo will dart "upon the ill-fated object of his vengeance with blind fury, and with a swiftness and activity which could ill be expected from so awkward and lumbering a figure." Though a Buffalo kill may not be what it seems.

When to fly was to die, the early French aviator, Arthur Charles Hubert Latham, set altitude and speed records; but in 1909 he lost his chance to be the first to cross the English Channel due to the crashing of his Levasseur Antoinette plane, and then by the success of Louis Blériot to complete the flight. In 1912 he was reportedly killed by a Buffalo on a safari in Chad. The evidence examined by the colonial commandant of Fort Archambault, though, convinced him that Latham had been murdered by his porters to take his firearms.

...Many woundings are located in the lower body...

Among the Spanish proverbs about the perils to which the lower bodies of matadors might be most susceptible, one that Hemingway enjoyed so truly he repeated it twice in *Death in the Afternoon*, is the one about gonorrhea: "*Mas cornadas dan las mujeres*–the women gore more often than the bulls."

...known as a cornada...

In 1959 Barnaby Conrad, the San Franciscan artist, bestselling author, nightclub proprietor, member of the diplomatic corps, boxer, and bullfighter–one of those enthusiast résumés that seemed only possible in mid-century America–was invited into the ring on a Spanish finca during a *tienta*–a testing of the courage of the heifers before breeding with *toros de lidia*. Into the ring came a "sleek and greenish black" heifer "surrounded by a haze of dust." Almost at once Conrad realized he was facing an animal that had seen a cape before–and knew where the man stood in relation to it–and so was treacherous. He fought it anyway and proceeded to be gored in the upper left thigh. Luckily, Conrad was only an hour away from the most experienced bullfight surgeon in the world, Dr. Luis Giménez Guinea of the Sanatorio de Toreros in Madrid. Giménez Guinea diagnosed a single-trajectory wound that entered the thigh and angled eight inches up toward the groin, rupturing veins and muscles, but fortunately missing the reliably fatal femoral artery. For all that, it was a real *cornada*–"horse-killing," was the doctor's diagnosis.

On the operating table, Giménez Guinea snipped away ragged skin, probed the wound with his gloved finger, then made a five-inch incision to open the field for him to work. He performed with small, extremely sharp scalpels and needles the work of trimming the suturing with catgut the ends of the torn vessels and muscles, administering penicillin and streptomycin, fitting a rubber drain and closing the opening. Conrad left the hospital in fifteen days.

The big question: Did it hurt when the horn entered? Conrad said he didn't remember feeling anything other than a searing in his leg and being lifted off the ground. A goring by a Buffalo would likely not feel much different, at least not the first time a horn entered.

...repairs may be made with endoprostheses...

Such endoprostheses are one of the products of W. L. Gore & Associates, famed for the accidental transformation of polytetrafluoroethylene–P. T. F. E.–when the son of the company founder was trying to stretch the heated material slowly, and instead gave it a sharp, frustrated yank, expanding it by 800 percent to produce a microporous material that would be used in breathable waterproof clothing by hunters. Early, inferior versions of it earned Gore-Tex the reputation that it didn't leak. It sucked.

...replicate being struck by a small car...

A seventeen hundred-pound Buffalo, charging at thirty-plus miles per hour, can generate fifty five thousand foot-pounds of force. The only animal that might be able to inflict a pneumothorax on a Buffalo would be a bull Elephant, which can produce a quarter million foot-pounds in a charge.

The world's biggest African elephant bull, *prétendument* per Phineas Taylor Barnum, was Jumbo. When its mother, when the Elephant was an infant around 1861, was killed in the Sudan by ivory hunters, the calf was bought by an Italian wild-animal dealer and exported to the Jardin des Plantes in Paris, then to the London Zoo where it lived for the next eighteen years, giving Elephant-back rides to children and other zoo visitors, including Queen Victoria. The Elephant developed knee problems from bearing all those loads and was subject to night rages, much later charged to toothaches due to malformed molars brought about by an unnatural diet of soft foods. In 1882 Barnum took Jumbo off the zoo's hands for two thousand pounds sterling, which he recouped in the first few week of exhibiting the animal in Madison Square Garden.

In Ontario, Canada, in 1885 when the Elephant was twenty-four, while being toured by P. T. Barnum's Greatest Show On Earth, And The Great London Circus, Sanger's Royal British Menagerie and The Grand International Allied Shows United, Jumbo was being led back at night to its boxcar in the rail yard after a performance, when it was struck by a freight-train locomotive. It was dead from internal injuries within minutes, the only animal that could kill the world's largest Elephant an Iron horse.

...what would a Buffalo charge be without litigation?...

A Buffalo attack can also beget religious experience, it seems.

Bow hunting in South Africa in 2012, a semi-retired Colorado man stalked a Buffalo that turned to face him as he came into range of it. The unwounded bull charged, and the hunter heard a voice from above telling him to cast aside his bow and beat feet. Wearing a backpack filled with spare clothing and water bottles which cushioned the first impact, he was still sent fifteen feet through the air and down on his knees. The Buffalo hit him again, in the back, hooking the hunter's left arm and flinging him upward all loose limbed, the way a Buffalo does to a Lion when it attacks.

As consciousness ebbed and flowed the hunter felt and heard his bones breaking, the ends grating. Awake again and hearing another voice, he obeyed it by scooting backward on his butt, keeping his head and chest away from the horns and hooves by pushing his boots against the Buffalo's boss. Now the professional hunters with their heavy calibers were shooting, and the hunter saw the bullets hit and the blood spattering, until the bull went down, shot a final time through the brain by a P. H. who reported beholding a pillar of light surrounding the hunter and an angel above his head, protecting him, while all that the hunter saw was a blinding brightness, surely that same as that which overcame Saul of Tarsus on the road to Damascus. The voice, certainly celestial, spoke again, telling the hunter to turn his life to his faith and family, and write a book about his religious reawakening, even if still an Episcopalian. The result in twelve chapters, one for each of the Disciples, was about seeing the light through black death.

You want to believe that there may have been about the Buffalo a light of some kind, lending courage to its attack, even if that light were to be somewhat less empyreal.

...takes on the look of a rugby scrum cap...

In 2021, the London gunmaker John Rigby & Company, founded in 1775, established The Rigby Dagga Boy Award to honor the oldest, post-breeding-age, free-ranging, wild African buffalo bull, drawn from all six subspecies on the continent, and the hunter and professional hunter who took it. Judging was based not on greatest horn spread, but on overall appearance–boss development, horn tips, muscling in neck and shoulder, body color, facial markings, chinlap, size of front hooves–all signs of advanced years, changing the parameters for what may be considered a trophy Buffalo, and making the hunting of one even more a matter of conservation. Final judgment would be determined by the Taylor First Molar Teeth Aging Method–counting the lines of cementum annuli, a new layer added each year, seen in the first molars from both sides of the lower jaw, which will also assist scientific research into the species. The award is planned to be presented biennially.

...Lion the only wild animal that consistently hunts Buffalo with success...

David Petzal offers this scenario of the why and how Lion hunt Buffalo:

> Buffalo do indeed have extraordinary senses of smell, hearing, and sight. This is not so they can better slay humans, but because Nature made them a food item. Buffalo are among the best-eating of all African game–I think they are *the* best, better than eland–and there's a lot to them. A pride of lions–their main predator–that takes down a grown Cape buffalo is going to have good times for a week. All buffalo know this from the time they drop from mama's womb.
>
> Buffalo are also aware at some level that if the lions get to them they are in for a very unpleasant death. About the fewest lions that will take on an adult buffalo is three. More likely it will be ten, and each one is highly qualified. Typically, one cat will sink fangs in the buffalo's anus, which limits its mobility. A second one will leap on the bovine's back and begin gnawing on its spine to sever the spinal cord. A third will grab the buff by the nose, and a fourth will fix its fangs in the throat and chomp down. This last is what produces death, and I swear that lions purr like giant house cats as they do it.

Pondoro Taylor contended, though, from the perspective of his thirty years of African hunting experience, that in good Buffalo country, "[Y]ou will nearly always find a pair of magnificent male lions" trailing the herds; far larger than everyday "hunting lions," they "seldom lower themselves to kill lesser game" than Buffalo. Super athletes, their sport of choice is slaying *Syncerus.*

...a revival of the director's cut of *The Wild Bunch*...

Seeing the on-screen vulgar capering of Edmond O'Brien as the grizzled Sykes at the division of the worthless loot in the early part of the film, my later federal felon, now late, friend George leaned over to me in the darkened theater and declared, "That's what I call growing old gracefully."

Chapter Ten: Plague

... It snapped the wire...

Snaring big game is hardly an occupation for the craven. A trapped animal caught by a hoof or paw, rather than killed outright by a neck snare, is at its most dangerous at the approach of the hunter-trapper, come to finish and reduce it to possession. If the hunter lacks documentation, he probably won't have a firearm–otherwise, why resort to a snare?–or if he can somehow obtain one, won't want to use it because the report of a gun can direct a game ranger to him and the unlawful animal. A caught animal–which very often will have been lying resignedly up to then–can become most desperate at the sight of an approaching human, presumably armed with a spear, and will react violently. So a Buffalo, filled with enough adrenaline, can very handily break free from a heavy-wire snare.

In the West African rainforests where large primates are hunted and trapped, going in for the kill, that *momento de la verdad*, really is the hardest part. A male Chimpanzee can weigh a hundred fifty pounds; and though overstatements are made about its enormous strength, it is nonetheless measurably more powerful than a human. It has also considerably taller canine teeth for inflicting serious wounds–though in terms of bite force, Chimp may be one animal that we may be stronger than. Another significant Chimpanzee feature for both defense and offense is its hand.

Effectively refined for arboreal existence with a shorter thumb and longer fingers, the Chimp's hand is in fact more highly evolved than ours. Unlike almost any kind of foot, a Chimpanzee's hand can be used both for grabbing objects, such as the shaft of a spear thrust at it, or for grappling with a human who comes too close while the primate is snared but has its teeth to unleash. A hunter then can, wrote nature-writer David Quammen, find himself faced with a "tethered, frantic, enraged animal," and a redoubtable one at that, with no other avenue but to kill its way out of the situation, leading to "*beaucoup d'accidents de chasse*" in the words spoken to Quammen, seemingly with a fatalistic *haussement d'épaules*, by a Cameroonian conservator in Boumba Bek National Park in lowland-rainforest Chimpanzee habitat. Or in the words of the poet, James Fenton, "It is a tough world."

...These include the Spanish flu...

More rightly, it might have been labeled the Kansas flu, the initial known worldwide case reported on an army base in that state in March of 1918.

...destroyed entire empires...

A culture, perhaps to some less significant, that was destroyed by smallpox in the 1700s was that of the Khoisan clans–the Damasqua and Gonaqua hunter-pastoralists of the central coastal Cape of South Africa. Among the bounty of game they had to hunt were large herds of Elephant in the forest of Tsitsikamma, place of much water.

...Until the development of a refined vaccine...

The eighteenth-century English scientist Edward Jenner is often named as the father of vaccination. Yet the practice, whether called vaccination or inoculation, was in use for centuries before in China, India, and Africa. African slaves in America, such as an Onesimus owned by New England Puritan Cotton Mather, had received inoculations against smallpox before being taken from their countries and put on the block, and described the operation to their *soi disant* masters.

...from the Danakil tribes...

Before the domestication of cattle, the prehistoric Eritreans depicted Wild buffalo in their rock art.

...in the heart of the Mahdist uprising...

Between 1881 and 1899, Sudanese Moslems, first under the rule of Muhammed Ahmad bin Abd Allah, the Mahdi, the Guided One, were in revolt against the governance of the Ottoman Khedivate of Egypt. In 1883, in the belief that the Mahdi himself was laying siege to the town of El-Obeid, the capital of Kordofan Province in the Sudan, a force of eight thousand Egyptians, made up of one-time rebels released from prison, and a thousand irregular Başibozuk Albanian cavalry, under the reluctant command of a former British colonel, William "Billy" Hicks, which was, according to Winston Churchill, "perhaps the worst army that was ever marched to war," went off to be massacred at the Battle of Shaykan in the woods near El-Obeid. The Egyptians, under the direction of the British, then decided to withdraw from the Sudan; and Charles Chinese Gordon, cleped for his conduct in the Second Opium War, was sent to evacuate Khartoum, entwined by the Blue and White Niles. Instead, he hunkered down and vaingloriously absorbed three hundred thirteen days of siege before the city fell, and he was killed, in January of 1885.

Over the next fourteen years, the Egyptians, British, Italians, and French all played militarist roles in the region. The Mahdists, though, remained under subsequent Mahdis and Khalifas in some form of power until 1898 and the capture of their capital at Omdurman on the west bank of the Nile below Khartoum. The battle was waged by Lord Horatio Herbert Kitchener in no small measure revenging the death of Gordon. It was made notable by the participation of Churchill, then twenty-three, in what many regarded, rightly or wrongly with World War I in the offing, the last true cavalry charge mounted by the British Army–perhaps the last victorious one, at any rate.

Churchill famously described the charge in this manner:

> In one respect a cavalry charge is very like ordinary life. So long as you are all right, firmly in your saddle, your horse in hand, and well armed, lots of enemies will give you a wide berth. But as soon as you have lost a stirrup, have a rein cut, have dropped your weapon, are wounded, or your horse is wounded, then is the moment when from all quarters enemies rush upon you. Such was the fate of not a few of my comrades...

Despite the élan evoked by the galloping of horses, the battle was won primarily by gunboats, cannon, ten-barreled 45-caliber Nordenfeldts, and withering Maxim fire in the face of antique trumpet-butt Kabyle muskets, swords, and spears–some saying this gave rise to Hillaire Belloc's couplet:

> Whatever happens we have got
> The Maxim gun, and they have not.

Churchill, in fact, carried a broomhandled semi-automatic Mauser pistol into battle rather than a saber, owing to a shoulder impaired through playing polo. Perhaps ten thousand Sudanese dervishes and "fuzzy wuzzies" died, to forty-eight, total, dead among the actual British.

The remaining Mahdists fled south, pursued by British forces. At Fashoda, the British met with an expeditionary force from France looking to secure the Sudan for itself. Though virtually nothing occurred in the field, in the English and French capitals were rumors of war. The French withdrew–Thomas Pynchon refers to the incident or crisis in Chapter III of his first novel, *V.* The last stand of the Mahdists came at the Battle of Umm Diwaykarat in the sandy-savanna tribal lands of the Baggara in late 1899, ending in the death of the ultimate Khalifa while seated upon a yearling horsehide with his main commanders and surrounded by his guards who did not desert him.

...crossing...into Kenya and Uganda...

Writing in the 1890s, Sir Frederick John Jackson, big-game hunter, explorer, East African ornithologist, working as well for the Imperial British East Africa Company that administered the territory until the British government took it over, making Jackson Lieutenant Governor of the Kenya Protectorate and later Governor of Uganda, described the landscape of rinderpest, before and after:

> Buffaloes were at one time exceedingly plentiful throughout British East Africa, and in some districts, where the country was best suited to their habits, were to be found in enormous herds. Towards the end of the year 1890, and in the early part of 1891, they unfortunately contracted a kind of anthrax [*sic*] the same disease which carried off nearly all the native cattle, and they were almost destroyed by it. On my way down from Uganda in July 1890, between Lakes Baringo and Naivasha, I saw in one day's march as many as six herds of buffaloes, varying in number from 100 to 600 head in a herd. In this same district in the following March, my friend Mr. Gedge, on his way down to the coast, saw nothing but carcases, and in one day counted as many as fifteen lying rotting in the grass, close to the footpath. In 1892 the officers of the Mombasa and Victoria Nyanza Railway Survey only saw on two different occasions the spoor of a single beast, although they traversed a great part of the country where buffaloes were once so plentiful. Amongst other places where this grand beast was particularly abundant was the Arusha-wa-Chini district, now in

German territory, to the south of Kilimanjaro, and the Njiri plains to the north of the mountain; Turkwel, in the Suk country to the east of Mount Elgon; the extensive undulating plains on the top of the Mau and Elgeyo escarpments; Lykepia, to the west of Mount Kenia; the banks of the river Tana, and the thick bush country on the mainland near Lamu. There can be little doubt that it will take many years for them to recover to any extent, if they ever do so. A sportsman intending to visit this country must therefore not be disappointed at being unable to add one of these beasts to his bag, though of course he may have the luck to meet with an odd one here and there. It is to be hoped, however, that everyone who goes out to shoot will endeavour to give them a fair chance of increasing by scrupulously refraining from shooting at any cow that may be met with.

...unlike desert species such as Gazelle...

Gazelles such as the Sand gazelle in Saudi Arabia have evolved to shrink their livers and hearts, which demand large amounts of oxygen, allowing the animals to breathe less and reduce water loss through respiratory evaporation during droughts. Yet they store greater amounts of fat in their brains to sustain metabolism in times of little food or water. Taking in both water and nutrients from the plant matter they eat, the Gazelle's gut walls maintain their normal size.

...before they fed out into the open...

Arthur Blayney Percival, older brother of Hemingway's professional hunter Philip, collector of wildlife specimens for the British Museum, and the acknowledged first Ranger for Game Preservation in British East Africa, who claimed he could smell a Giraffe at three hundred yards, noted a change in the behavior of another significant species, the Hyena, brought about by rinderpest. With all the dead Buffalo and other herbivores, the Hyena had a windfall; and their numbers soared. As the curve of the dead flattened, though, the Hyena resorted to assembling in packs and hunting down prey, something we now see as natural behavior. They also turned energetically to the eating of human flesh to which they had access because of all the corpses of the starved due to the knock-on effect of cattle plague. In any case, they became a serious threat to Maasai children.

Sixty years later, rinderpest again scathed the Serengeti. Wildebeest and Buffalo were leveled, and Lion and Hyena paid the check. Now it was a case of not so much what rinderpest caused, but what it enabled. Without Lion on the plains, Painted wolf boomed. But then, as rinderpest was brought under control, prey species rebounded and Lion and Hyena returned, driving out the Wild dogs. Today, there is considered to be not one established pack of the canids on the plains.

...could lead to revolt...

Among the Zulu in South Africa in 1906 there was the guerrilla Bambatha Rebellion that may have been partly incited by the lack of cattle for the brideprice. This time, the Maxim guns were matched against asegais, knobkerries, and cowhide shields from before rinderpest. Mohandas Gandhi, then a young lawyer in South Africa, urged the British colonial government to recruit Indians from India and in South Africa as a reserve force, hoping that this would elevate their status. In the rebellion as many as four thousand Zulu died. The British side suffered thirty-six deaths.

...often called simply the thirst...

One who named a drought the thirst was Major Philip Jacobus Pretorius, the hero, so called, in the hunt in the Rufiji Delta for the *S. M. S. Königsberg*, a small cruiser of the Kaiserliche Marine, responsible for the sinking of the Pelorus-class protected cruiser, *H. M. S. Pegasus*, in the harbor in Zanzibar at the start of the First World War. Suffering engine damage in the exchange with the dying *Pegasus*, the *Königsberg* limped south to the river's delta and used high tide to clear the bar and sail into retreat for repair, spare parts borne overland to it. At the end of October, Pretorius aboard the Town-class cruiser *Chatham*, sighted the *Königsberg*'s masts rising out of the mangroves where it tried to camouflage itself.

The Battle of the Rufiji Delta began in early November. The mangroves actually barricaded the *Königsberg* somewhat against British shells; but in the continuing exchange of fire, the German ship retreated farther up the delta–the British scarcely believing there could be sufficient draft for it there. It was not until July, 1915, the *Königsberg* blockaded for months, that two Royal Navy light monitors got into gun range and shelled it. Put out of action, the ship was scuttled by its critically wounded captain, who succeeded in removing all its guns. Those guns were given to Major General Paul von Lettow-Vorbeck of the German East African protection force.

It was a *Schutztruppe*–a German colonial sniper–in von Lettow-Vorbeck's command who killed Frederick Selous near the village of Beho Beho south of the Rufiji in Tanganyika in January 1917. Selous–trinominate hunter, explorer, conservationist–was judged too old for the regular British army at the outset of the war, and joined up through the Legion of Frontiersmen, a paramilitary group of volunteers assembled by a former Canadian Mountie after the Second Boer War. The senior citizen put soldiers forty years his junior to shame on the march and in the fight. Selous, having gone ahead of his men at Beho Beho to glass for snipers, was shot in the side when he lifted up, then in the head as he looked back to his line. Blinded by grief, his long-serving gunbearer Ramizani, with him in the field, grabbed a rifle and charged headlong into the Germans, killing the sniper, other Germans, as well as native askaris.

Von Lettow-Vorbeck wrote to the British commander, the red-bearded South African general, Jan Smuts–later the anti-apartheid prime minister of the Union of South Africa–about the death of Selous. Earlier in the field, von Lettow-Vorbeck had Smuts in the sights of one of his machine-gun posts when the Boer rode in the lead of his troops into a nullah, but considered it "unsportsmanlike"–a curious, antique punctilio in the maw of World War I–to kill an officer of that rank under those circumstances. When Smuts learned from a British askari who escaped German captivity, of the courtesy von Lettow-Vorbeck extended him, Smuts declared him "a fool–but a gentleman." Von Lettow-Vorbeck was not present to prevent the shooting of Selous, and in his letter expressed how well-liked Selous was among the Germans before the war, and his regret over the death of a man of such "charming manner and excellent stories," traits that enchanted Theodore Roosevelt when the two first met some years before.

In 1919 the relict herd of Knysa Elephant, like those once hunted by the Iqua, et al., in the Tsitsikamma Forest, were thought to be imperiling white agriculture in the area now known as Addo at the Cape. They numbered some one hundred thirty when the government, acceding to the complaints of disgruntled farmers, gave Major Pretorius permit to eradicate them. Favoring a lurid full-leather safari suit and a 475 N. E. double, Pretorius in the course of a year prevailed in killing one hundred fourteen animals, taking their ivory and using their hides in the manufacture of, to be sure, whips. Officials then decided enough was enough. Later, in 1920, Pretorius petitioned for permission to kill one of the now-sequestered remaining Elephant, potting five in the process. The fewer than dozen survivors represented the final free-ranging Elephant on the South African cape, a D. N. A. analysis of dung calculating one female descendent of the pure strain lingering on in the open by 2019, possibly the most southerly native living Elephant on earth.

...the story was the same...

As Buffalo vanished and with them the parasites that were their primary source of food, the Oxbirds or Oxpeckers, Tick birds, went from epiphytical to carnivorous, beaking holes in whatever grazing domestic livestock remained, to eat the flesh down to the bone and attacking the femoral areas, killing the animals.

...trypanosomiasis, sleeping sickness...

In horses and cattle, it is called *nagana* and absent a vaccine–there is none–it is, if untreated, lingeringly fatal, in the human form, too. Though treatments exist, they are far from safe, with side effects from drugs for humans including convulsions, fever, coma, rashes, bloody stools, nausea, vomiting, and brain damage. In the day, a horse that survived nagana was considered salted and fit for travel into fly country.

...white conservationists indulged in magical thinking...

The imperious temper of European and American conservationists may have found its culmination in the hallowed martyr, the Cambridge-educated American Dian Fossey, who refused to appreciate or even understand the way of life of the Africans who co-existed with her idolized Gorillas, said to deride the humans as "wogs" and unironically, "apes." Claims were made she bound up "poachers" and smeared them in Ape feces, whipped their testicles with stinging nettles, kidnapped a small child as coercion, and greeted eco-tourists, come to view the Gorillas, and support their sanctuary, with pistol fire over their heads. She, simply put, terrorized the indigenous people living around her research station in the Virunga Mountains, her program there, at its end, one principally of ranting. When the check came due in 1985, it was not enough to murder her but to hack her face with a machete. Conspiracy theories of a government plot against her, of course, teem, though her death seems more an act of pent-up rage than executive action.

One thing Fossey documented about the behavior of Mountain gorilla silverback males was the way they greeted the presence of Cape buffalo with half-second bursts of low-pitched harsh aggressive sounds, along with lunges and bluff charges.

...virtually unobtainable by rural Africans...

In 1890 in the time of rinderpest, the Europeans engaged in the "Scramble" signed a treaty in Brussels prohibiting the sale of breechloading rifles in Africa from twenty degrees north to twenty degrees south on the continent, the treaty renewed in 1899. In 1898, John Rigby & Company developed the 450 N. E. 3¼-inch cartridge. But facing unrest, if not outright insurrection, in India and the Sudan–Sudanese nationalists chafed under the effective colonial rule of Britain in a nominal condominium with Egypt after the end of the Mahdists; and India was, as per usual, India–the English in 1907 banned the importation of all 450-caliber ammunition into either country. The concern was over the bottlenecked 577/450 Martini-Henry cartridge that fit the single-shot military rifles that were universally available. The first chore was accounting for all the known cartridges in that caliber, which amounted to millions. With that task accomplished, it was quickly seen by those on both sides, that even if a N. E. cartridge could not be loaded directly into the Martini-Henry, the 450-caliber bullets could be pulled and with the powder, reloaded into empty military brass. So the solution of His Majesty's government was to outlaw any bullet of 455/1000th-of-an-inch diameter. Meanwhile, the actual bores of the Martini-Henri rifles, produced in many factories by assorted manufacturers between 1871 and 1918, were, as they say, all over the map, bigger or smaller than labeled.

Chapter Eleven: Tracks

...drilling their hook-covered mouthparts into our skin...

With hundreds of species, ticks divide into three families, the argasid soft ticks common in South Asia, ixodid hard ticks found across greater Africa and the rest of the world, and the monotypic nuttalliellid–an enigmatic combination of hard and soft–unique to Southern Africa. Adult hard ticks can draw between half and one-and-a-half milliliters of blood. Climate change has in Maine brought about an explosion of winter ticks infesting Moose calves. These arachnids wait in clusters on foliage for hosts to brush by. Mortality rates among Moose calves of the year may be 85 percent. Drained of blood, the young animals are stripped of all fat in their bone marrow; and their internal organs are bled white. Called Ghost Moose, they may be covered by as many as ninety thousand of the creatures. It would take some seventeen hundred feeding ticks to drain a human body. Neither image fails to trigger my horripilating trypophobia.

Horacio Silvestre Quiroga Forteza was a turn-of-the-previous-century South American poet, novelist, playwright, and especially short-story writer, often referred to as the Uruguayan Edgar Allan Poe and a forerunner of magic realism. Among his more famous stories is "The Feather Pillow." As for its relevance to ixodida–that is best learned by reading "The Feather Pillow."

...Some hate Hyena for their supposed miscreation...

The pioneering wildlife filmmaker, Martin Johnson, was another to embrace the hellspawn repute of the Hyena. They were, he thought, worthy of shooting on sight for their perceived savaging of animals both wild and domestic. He called them "the lowest and meanest of all creation," a beast as "yellow as his ugly [*sic*] striped [*spotted?*] coat," the animal killing solely for the sake of killing. Its nature was "apparent in every line of his body." A pack, he said, "came slinking along on their bellies, tails between their legs, looking at us malevolently out of their green eyes, snarling and showing their yellow teeth, but giving never a sign of fight."

...a ridiculous animal who could be called a dirty joke...

Ruark thought the 220 Swift "varmint" rifle was the solution for hyena. But after nine grisly shots at one of the animals, resulting in no more than ghastly crippling, he reached for his "enough gun" 470 to finish it, swearing that he would never again use the caliber "on any animal I respect."

...shambles...

Where animals are butchered.

...knowing there was none...

> Thinking of Cronshaw, Philip remembered the Persian rug which he had given him, telling him that it offered an answer to his question upon the meaning of life; and suddenly the answer occurred to him: he chuckled: now that he had it, it was like one of the puzzles which you worry over till you are shown the solution and then cannot imagine how it could ever have escaped you. The answer was obvious. Life had no meaning. On the earth, satellite of a star speeding through space, living things had arisen under the influence of conditions which were part of the planet's history; and as there had been a beginning of life upon it so, under the influence of other conditions, there would be an end: man, no more significant than other forms of life, had come not as the climax of creation but as a physical reaction to the environment. Philip remembered the story of the Eastern King who, desiring to know the history of man, was brought by a sage five hundred volumes; busy with affairs of state, he bade him go and condense it; in twenty years the sage returned and his history now was in no more than fifty volumes, but the King, too old then to read so many ponderous tomes, bade him go and shorten it once more; twenty years passed again and the sage, old and gray, brought a single book in which was the knowledge the King had sought; but the King lay on his death-bed, and he had no time to read even that; and then the sage gave him the history of man in a single line; it was this: he was born, he suffered, and he died. There was no meaning in life, and man by living served no end. It was immaterial whether he was born or not born, whether he lived or ceased to

> live. Life was insignificant and death without consequence. Philip exulted, as he had exulted in his boyhood when the weight of a belief in God was lifted from his shoulders: it seemed to him that the last burden of responsibility was taken from him; and for the first time he was utterly free. His insignificance was turned to power, and he felt himself suddenly equal with the cruel fate which had seemed to persecute him; for, if life was meaningless, the world was robbed of its cruelty. What he did or left undone did not matter. Failure was unimportant and success amounted to nothing. He was the most inconsiderate creature in that swarming mass of mankind which for a brief space occupied the surface of the earth; and he was almighty because he had wrenched from chaos the secret of its nothingness. Thoughts came tumbling over one another in Philip's eager fancy, and he took long breaths of joyous satisfaction. He felt inclined to leap and sing. He had not been so happy for months.
>
> –Somerset Maugham,
> *Of Human Bondage*

It is a curiosity that no one I have known or heard of has resolved into the perspective of atheism past adolescence. It is a proposition virtually never arrived at in adulthood.

Chapter Twelve: Mzungu

...a sunken pillowed place for the head...

In season, the ripe marula ferments in the Elephant, intoxicating them, it is said. An old P. H. in Zimbabwe, told of finding a herd blissfully passed out cold on the ground, snoring, around the base of a tree with dropped fruit. One carried exceptional ivory. Despite his client's entreaties, the P. H. could not bring himself to take it as it slept.

...all the trackers halted in silent unison...

As Dave Petzal related to me, "A P. H.—I can't remember who—once told me that when you see the trackers take off their sandals, things are about to get interesting." At least Samuel, John, et al., kept theirs on.

...casts doubt on the predominantly African origins...

According to the U. S. Census Bureau, a white person is defined as one having origins in any of the original peoples of Europe, the Middle East, or North Africa.

...the word safari derives from safar, Arabic for to journey...

The Kiswahili version, and related words are kusafiri, to travel, msafiri, traveler, and usafiri, transport.

...in his vibrant studies of Buffalo...

As well as a fine visual artist, Cornwallis Harris was a decent, if not multiculturally sensitive, writer.

> The following day, after passing the residence of Piet Van-der Merwe, yclept Dickwang, or double chin,–a sobriquet with which a large wen on the throat has saddled him, as a distinction from his neighbors of the same name–we cleared the Sneuwbergen, and arrived at a deserted farm, named Dassies-fontein. Here we were struck with the sight of an old Kafir, smoking dacca, or the narcotic wild hemp, in which natives greatly delight. Seated at the door of a miserable hovel, a squalid picture of poverty, the decrepit wretch was inhaling the pernicious drug through water from a bullock's horn. Volumes of smoke were forced into his stomach by draughts of water, and the result was a violent fit of coughing, attended by raving delirium. We actually saw him throw off his slender apparel, and rush forth into the plain like a wild beast or a maniac from Bedlam.

...deeper and deeper into the Dark Continent...

If you wonder about the role in the mzungu history of the safari of Henry Morton Stanley, né John Rowlands, a bastard out of Denbigh, Denbighshire, Wales, it was relatively minor. In spite of genuinely intrepid exploration–as related in books about his expeditions, *Through the Dark Continent*, which coined the phrase, and sensing a winning formula for a title, his *In Darkest Africa*–it amounted mostly to ripping-yarn self-aggrandizement. Not a game butcher warranting the description, he was a sorry man with courage but slight charm; and his lucrative engagement in the creation and administration of Leopold II, King of the Belgians's Congo Free State of Amputated Hands ought to be abundant grounds for his omission. He's gotten more than his deserved share of press in a century and a half.

In Die Frage der Laienanalyse, Sigmund Freud contended, "We know less about the sexual life of little girls than of boys. But we need not feel ashamed of this distinction; after all, the sexual life of adult females is a *dark continent* for psychology." In the original German, Freud used the English for the phrase. The interpretation of that is yours.

...his scandalous brother Valentine...

Samuel Baker's younger brother Valentine, known in later life as Baker Pasha, was an explorer in his own right in northeastern Persia and a career army man, serving in the Crimea and an eclectic collection of wars of empire. Just after his appointment to the staff at the training camp at Aldershot Garrison, he faced an accusation of indecently assaulting a young woman in a railway carriage, forcing her to escape by hanging to the outside of the moving car. Baker, offering no defense, was sentenced to a year in prison and fined, and was cashiered from the service. He became the commander of the Egyptian gendarmerie under the Khedivate. Unmindful of Hicks Pasha's massacre at Shaykan, in 1884 Baker marched his force of dispirited policemen into another disastrous defeat at the First Battle of El Teb. There, he faced off against the over-matched, on paper, warriors of the celebrated, and perhaps immortal, in the words, again, of no-less-than Winston Churchill, Osman Digna, self-proclaimed Mahdi. Before the battle ended, Baker was required to cut his way out of the apocalypse in which most of his troops were killed, wounded, or taken prisoner. Baker was subsequently wounded in the Second Battle of El Teb, this time a British victory. He died in Tell El Kabir at age sixty. Osman Digna lived well into his eighties, dying *in pace* in Wādī Ḥalfā in 1926.

...a long experience in savage life...

Baker was among the most conversant sportsmen of his day on the subject of hunting weapons, including African hunters's lances and swords–and how to transform pocket change into projectiles–and free with advice. He most emphatically cautioned against the small-bore rifle in the bush, lamenting, he wrote, the use by partially experienced beginners of an inferior weapon, such as any 450 bore, avouching the 577 at twelve pounds, with a solid six hundred fifty grain hard-cast bullet ahead of some hundred sixty grains of blackpowder as the very lightest one to carry.

The compass of his expertise extended to the extreme, as he wrote:

> Among other weapons, I had an extraordinary rifle that carried a half-pound percussion shell [*in essence, a field-artillery piece*]–this instrument of torture to the hunter was not sufficiently heavy for the weight of the projectile; it only weighed twenty pounds: thus, with a charge of ten drachms of powder [*almost two hundred seventy-five grains*], behind a HALF-POUND shell, the recoil was so terrific, that I was spun round like a weathercock in a hurricane, although I had been accustomed to heavy charges of powder and severe recoil for many years. None of my men could fire it, and it was looked upon with a species of awe, and was named "Jenna el Mootfah" (child of a cannon) by the Arabs, which being far too long a name for practice, I christened it the "Baby"; and the scream of this "Baby," loaded with a half-pound shell, was always fatal. It was far too severe, and I very seldom fired it, but it is a curious fact, that I never fired a shot with that rifle without bagging [*I should think so*]: the entire practice, during several years, was confined to about twenty shots. I was afraid to use it; but now and then it was absolutely necessary that it should be cleaned, after lying for months loaded. On such occasions my men had the gratification of firing it, and the explosion was always accompanied by two men falling on their backs (one having buttressed the shooter), and the "Baby" flying some yards behind them. This rifle was made by Holland and Holland, of Bond Street, and I could highly recommend it for Goliath of Gath, but not for men of A.D. 1866.

Frederick Courteney Selous started hunting Elephant and other dangerous game such as Buffalo with a pair of four-bore smooth-barreled duck guns of the very commonest description, he called them. He loaded them with four-ounce round balls and a handful of the cheap trade powder sold in five-pound bags to the native Africans–not the word Selous uses–which he carried in a leather pouch slung at his side: The precise loading measure of a four-bore is to place the ball in the cupped palm of the hand and just cover it with a mound of blackpowder.

Selous averred that he had never used or seen used a rifle which drove better than these common-made old muzzleloaders. They were, however, so light at twelve and half pounds each–it was the practice to wrap the stocks in the green inside skin of an Elephant's ear, left to dry as firmly as iron, to forestall splitting from recoil–that they "kicked most frightfully, and in my case the punishment I received from these guns has affected my nerves to such an extent as to have materially influenced my shooting ever since, and I am heartily sorry I ever had anything to do with them."

My old cowboy friend Leroy, his house above Piney Creek in the ponderosas around Story, let me reload and shoot at his place. His second-story reloading room had press, bench, rests, and a sliding second-story window with a demi-lune hole in the aluminum frame from an injudiciously aimed shot–the shrapnel from an exploded revolver cylinder was also embedded in the ceiling. You aimed through the window at the large plywood target frame set out at a hundred yards. I shot my 375 for what seemed all day, Leroy and I tweaking the powder loads between shots–and waiting on Deer, Merriam's wild turkey, and once a three-hundred-pound Black bear to pass through–tuning the rifle.

For ten seasons we ran a Pronghorn camp together on his land under Pumpkin Buttes near the national grasslands. We put up a big pyramid tent for sleeping and a wall tent for cooking. Hunters who were our friends came out from California and New York, the Dakotas and even Mississippi. Carey came up from Beverly Hills to do the cooking and smoke his cigars. In the summer, Leroy and I camped under the big cottonwoods in Wind River Canyon, hearing the whoosh of Bullbats's diving at the ground. Leroy was up before dawn, scattering Mule deer does from around the tent in the half light, wading into the Wind to cast a line as the sun rose and Trout sipped at the surface.

The best trips were to a back bay in Yellowstone Lake in the summers. The first time, we piled all our gear–nothing but canvas for Leroy; that sound funny to you?–in his little Lund Runabout. By the next season, having been through the winds, he traded up to a larger Alumacraft.

We used fly rods, sinking line, and single-hook streamers, trolling them behind the boat. On the best evening, or morning or afternoon, every few hundred yards, there would be a strike, then a set, a fast run, and reeling in, another run, and another, a leap of gilded fish in the light, and the slow retrieve to the net. Removing the barbless hook, we held up three pounds of gaping fish, a slash of red along the lower jaw, the purest of pure native lacustrine Cutthroat, feeling the power in the slick body down to the truncated caudal fin behind the black spots clustered at the wrist of the tail. Feeding the Trout back into the cold water, we moved them back and forth until the fish slid away, swimming from sight; then we turned around and trolled in the opposite direction. At night we barbecued on the grill on the fire ring, then stared at the impossible stars in the sky, before bedding down on the thick foamies, awakened more than once by the bugling of Elk.

I used to keep Leroy's voice mails on my cell phone, long rambling stream of consciousness monologues that began, "Tom, Tom, Tom," in that Wyoming accent you have to live here to recognize. They were just too perfect, and I thought I would always have them; and if they were erased, that there would be years more of them. Then I lost the messages, and there would be no more new ones.

How do you measure a life, in things of great moment or in cartridges loaded and prairie dogs shot, the number of coyotes called in, lines cast and fish leaping, driving up to Point Barrow just to see it and turning around, stories about flights over the mountain meadows in the rear of a light aircraft, or bringing a watermelon up the trail, hitched to the top of a sawbuck packsaddle? Is it in recollection of children and friends? How do you weigh your life when the memories vanish?

It was a peculiar infectious disorder, named for German doctors, with a one-in-a-million chance of contraction. There was no virus, bacteria, parasite, or even any D. N. A. involved. Just a protein that folded over in a misshapen way and passed on its misfolding to other proteins and destroyed the brain. Born and raised on a sheep ranch, did Leroy eat the downer ewes with scrapie, all the of the ewes including nerve tissue, and then waited more than half-a-century to fall? Maybe the good part is that its course is rapid.

Divorced a long time, Leroy knew a South African woman for almost fifteen years; and they married that last summer, before his mind began to go and he started falling and was unable to walk. Within a few months he was in long-term care–that's how fast the course of the disease runs. It was a good place to be; he seemed comfortable. I visited.

The last time I went, Elaine came with me; and we met his wife there. He was in a wheelchair, and I pushed him around the buildings on a walkway. The air was cold and bright, sun behind the gathering snow clouds like light through a candled egg. We went past a reed pond with muskrats, and he spoke in disjointed phrases that jumped around like a phonograph needle placed down on random lyrics on a vinyl disc. We spent most of an hour with him, with walking and sitting inside; and when we got up to go, he took his wife's hand.

He died while I was away, in Africa, in Tunisia, hunting those wild boar in date groves through which the call to Asr came from unseen muezzins over loudspeakers. I don't suppose it was a unique friendship, but maybe the last good one I will have. Like those common-made duck guns of Selous's, I never had one that drove better.

That day in the care facility, holding his wife's hand, he nodded toward me, his eyes near and far, and said, "I know him."

...lingua venditoris servi...

For the sake of argument, let's say it translates as the language of the slave dealer.

...in reality in good tough condition...

The history is well known. Once brother explorers, Speke and Sir Richard Burton endured terrible hardships and disease in the late 1850s in the quest for the Nile's headwaters, which Speke found–Burton lying too ill in a village to accompany him–when he came upon Nam Lolwe, Endless Lake, to which he gave the name Victoria. Returned to England, Burton launched an acrimonious campaign casting doubt on Speke's having been to the source. A year before the Bakers came back from Africa, the Royal Geographic Society determined to resolve the question with a debate between the two men at a society meeting in Bath in September, 1864.

The day before, Speke, wingshooting at his uncle's house at Neston Park in Wiltshire, crossed a stone fence. He was seen atop the two-foot wall, his double-percussion gun leaning against it. No one was looking when a shot was heard. His companions ran to where he lay on the other side of the wall, his firearm beside him, the right barrel at half-cock, the left having discharged. Conscious, he asked not to be moved, dying in a quarter hour. The death was ruled accidental, and the nature of the wound did make suicide improbable. Yet Burton added the possibility of it to his bill of particulars against Speke, carrying on his vendetta against the man to Speke's grave and beyond.

...his book, the name escaping him...

Big Game and Pygmies: Experiences of a Naturalist in Central African Forests in Quest of the Okapi, was the title of Christy's book. In it he devotes three chapters to a précis on African buffalo in general, and Forest buffalo in particular. A following fourth chapter, by relating his hunting of the little Buffalo, tells us as much about its behavior and habitat as the more methodological pages before.

"Some of the best sport I ever had with any animal was," wrote Christy, "with the little red Ituri buffaloes on the upper reaches of the Ituri river [*sic*] in 1913"–"little" meaning up to seven hundred pounds.

The country overlooking wide stretches of broken water were "most beautiful," but to be avoided as campsites because of their masking the possibly treacherous forest noises with their rumble. Many of the Buffalo Christy shot were taken while he was "standing in a wibbly-wobbly canoe" on the river, which meant staying on the *qui vive* for whatever might be around the next bend. The "*mboga*" meat Christy was able to provide with "snapshots" from his 500 let "contentment [reign] in the evening" in his camps.

Among many tales, Christy told of firing his "second barrel full in [the] chest" of a wounded bull "as he came," the three of them–rifle, Christy, Buffalo–sliding down a steep bank into the river when the bull hit him with a vicious shake of its head, the Buffalo then making three bounding leaps into the forest and falling dead. More notable than the encounter, to Christy the naturalist, was the great number of fly species he collected from the carcass before it was butchered.

In the jungle environment, among the constant discomforts were scads of maddening ticks, as well as all the "months of hard experience" required to be a successful Buffalo hunter, learned only by hunting with Pygmies, "whose friendship and goodwill are by no means easy to obtain."

...the first time upon the sandy shores of Algoa Bay...

Selous's most famous book, published in 1881, was *A Hunter's Wanderings in Africa: Being a Narrative of Nine Years Spent Amongst the Game of the Far Interior of South Africa, Containing*

Accounts of Explorations Beyond the Zambesi, on the River Chobe, and in the Matabele and Mashuna Countries, with Full Notes Upon the Natural History and Present Distribution of All the Large Mammalia–a flawlessly mzungu title.

Selous's landing ground, Algoa Bay, the same as Cornwallis Harris's, was over four hundred miles east of the Cape of Good Hope. The £400 he had in his pocket amounted to around £50 thousand today.

...Lobengula, king of the Ndebele...

As were many African rulers of the time, Lobengula was increasingly tormented by mzungu missionaries, commercial hunters, and concession seekers. By 1882, Commandant-General of the independent South African Republic, Piet Joubert, cautioned the king–thereby implicitly promoting Boer interests–that when an Englishman took anything from you, it was like a monkey with a fistful of pumpkin seeds: It would never let go until beaten to death. Touchingly, Africans such as Lobengula thought Victoria Regina–if she existed, the whites telling him one thing and the other, as served their purposes–would assist them in the troubles they were meeting with.

Seeking proof of life, Lobengula in 1889 sent as his eyes, escorted by a foreign correspondent for *The Times*–who also happened to be an agent for a British exploration concern–two elderly iziNduna–headmen–Mshete and Babayane, to London. In the wake of being suited in Western clothes; motorized travel; a live-fire artillery demonstration on the range at Shoeburyness; a cavalry charge staged for their benefit; high art and houses of wax; and musicals and gaieties, cultural misconstruction of a predictably amusing sort ensued. The audience at Windsor went well, it would seem, her Majesty giving gifts of snuff. She also sent a letter through her colonial minister, Lord Knutsford, stating with nicely poised, matronly, slightly condescending diplomacy:

> The Queen has heard the words of Lobengula...They say that Lobengula is much troubled by the white men who came into his country and ask to dig for gold and that he begs for advice and help...The Queen advises Lobengula not to grant hastily concessions of land, or leave to dig, but to consider all applications very carefully.

Lobengula asked for the Empress to send out a representative to whom he might turn. She sent back her portrait with Mshete and Babayane, who had tales to tell.

From here arises a welter of confusion involving concessions granted and rescinded; cavalier land theft by Cecil Rhodes; escalating ferment; the First Matabele War; crushing defeats for the forces of Lobengula at the muzzles of Maxim guns in their first deployment in battle; the retreat of the no-longer-mighty chief of a savage and barbarous people, but a now-morbidly obese and gout-ridden broken monarch; and shadowy death somewhere north of the Zambezi. Before the end of the 1890s, the Ndebele kingdom was dissolved, any number of walls available in newly constructed colonial offices for the displaying of portraits of the Queen.

...Karamojo Bell of the thousand tusked Elephant...

Africa at the turn of the twentieth century may have been the ideal place for Walter Dalrymple Maitland Bell to take an insatiable rapaciousness for death. In his own mzungu-titled book, *The Wanderings of an Elephant Hunter*, he detailed the way he killed his one thousand eleven Elephant, less than thirty of those cows, the rest bulls. Four-fifths of that score, and his claim to renown, were made with the 7×57 Mauser and the standard military-pattern 1893 172.8-grain full-metal-jacket round-nosed bullet. With that projectile, he perfected an oblique-angle shot from behind the Elephant, through the skull and into the brain, as an especially productive technique of execution–or assassination–this coming to be known as the Bell Shot, the way certain competitive figure-skating elements and gymnastic skills are named after the athletes who debuted them.

In his repertoire were other shots, reflecting an even more fatuous taste in small calibers, as when, hunting for meat in West Africa, he used a 22 Savage Hi-Power to kill a herd of twenty-three Dwarf forest buffalo, lung shooting the lead cow and doing the same for the rest of the animals as they flustered about, the procedure's succeeding in doing nothing to recommend it to anyone else. He became the first and last sobersided advocate of the 220 Swift as a big-game cartridge for animals such as Red stag.

Bell did work for his game, walking through two dozen pairs of boots a year. His affinities were for the lawless vicinities of the continent, where he had the fullest free rein–unsurprisingly he served in the Great War in the most unhampered battlefield, the air, becoming a fighter pilot mentioned in dispatches; he also indiscriminately shot down an aircraft of France, part of the Triple Entente with Britain. What more than a killing floor Bell saw in Africa eludes one.

Bell's childhood hero was that unspeakable butcher, Roualeyn George Gordon-Cumming–please see below.

...There were women as well...

By the turn of the twentieth century, women, married or single, were showing up as explorers and hunters throughout Africa, many behaving on the continent no better than their male counterparts. If the cranky English version of *Vivienne de Watteville: A Writer in Kenya: A History of Women's Colonial Hunting*, is to be relied on–author François Lapeyre, called a linguistics scholar interested in the general question of female independence, reading in translation like someone with a bit too much *temps perdu* spent talking in boulevard cafés, perpetrates in her book such lulus as identifying Beryl Markham's memoir as *West with the Wind;* that Theodore Roosevelt killed five hundred big cats on his East African safari; that the 1977 prohibition on safari hunting in Kenya was the result of the excesses of that group of hunters who were colonists in the 1920s; that the dearest cliché of hunting, according to Lapeyre, is confusing loving and knowing, because obviously, and even necessarily, hunters would know their prey and habits, just as the heinous murderer in a crime novel observes his future victim; that contrary to what one might hope, the love of hunting was not only the preserve of brutes.

Again, behaving in Africa in ways no more enlightened than those of many colonial men of her day, was a Marguerite Roby, traveling under an assumed name in the guise of a nanny for a wealthy English family on its way to Australia. On the sea voyage–her departing at ten a. m. from the Savoy in London, driven to the ship in a motor–she had the privilege of dining with the passengers, rather than servants, and made the acquaintance of a Rhodesian couple who encouraged her to plan on going to the Congo in 1910. From a stop in Cape Town, she wired home for a 303 Enfield sporting rifle, a 22 Winchester, and a 12-bore shotgun, with ammunition, to be sent out to her. Somewhere, she added a 405 Winchester, Roosevelt's favorite rifle for all those big cats.

Lapeyre's account speaks of something of a stylish beauty–as attested to by Roby's frontispiece photo of in her book, *My Adventures in the Congo*, posed for in England when she put herself back together–who was not a crack markswoman–in her first attempts at aiming, she forgot to take into consideration the rifle's front sight–insisted upon riding, and continually falling from, a bicycle on the trail; was at the mercy of her guide, a dodgy white trader with an African inamorata, who robbed her–more grievous was his permitting his woman to be carried in Roby's exclusive *machila*, a hammock slung beneath a pole, rendering it of no further conceivable use to a European such as Roby–taking with him when he abandoned her all but a remnant of porters who refused to leave her, though she commanded with chicotte and pistol, like a Clyde Beatty.

Her ordeal, which it was, in Africa left her emaciated, fever ridden, dysenteric, blind for weeks at a stretch, her hair whited. Yet she managed to dine with colonial officials, played poker, and drank, including a cocktail of cognac, morphine, and chloroform, in sight of two passing Lion going to water. Her book also tendered a lengthy apologia for the Belgian occupation of the Congo.

Roby was raring to kill Elephant; less so, Buffalo. One day, within an hour of her taking an Elephant and leaving the animal to be butchered and the tusks collected; and with her "faithful black boy" Thomas, she went on hunting. After an hour she spotted a Buffalo herd two hundred fifty yards away, crossing the trail. Thomas was "keen as mustard" for Missisi to kill a Boeuf, and Roby within ten minutes got within two hundred yards of a respectable lone bull. Removing her boots, not for greater stealth but for, as has been suggested earlier, faster foot speed in flight, she and Thomas began crawling toward the Buffalo facing them, feeding with its head down. As she crawled into range behind a large bush, she was trembling almost uncontrollably, all the dreadful stories she listened to about the irresistible charge of the Buffalo, resurrecting in her imagination.

It was only for the sake of appearances in front of Thomas that she raised her 405 and resigned herself to pulling the trigger "much as, I imagine, a suicide does," striking the Buffalo in the right nostril. The bull went into a spin as the two people slid over to the left side of the bush Roby shot from. She got in another bullet, broadside, and the Buffalo did, indeed, charge into the bush where they had been hiding before. Another shot smashed the bull's shoulder, putting it down.

Roby was honest enough to admit that she would be happy never again to see a Buffalo within rifle range, calling it "a mighty fine animal–at a distance!" When she reached camp that evening, her "old friend the fever laid hold" of her, her registering a temperature of 106°F, just short of bringing on organ failure. As she recuperated, she was spooned restorative Buffalo broth, lovingly prepared by Thomas.

...she dressed in a stiff black skirt...

Falling fifteen feet onto a bed of sharpened stakes in a plant-covered pitfall on a trail, Kingsley credited her survival, and in fact lack of serious injury other than bruising, to "the blessing of a good thick skirt." Had she followed the advice of many people in England–"who ought to have known better, and did not do it themselves"–and adopted "masculine dress," she "should have been spiked to the bone, and done for." Instead, she found herself "sitting on the fulness [*sic*]" of her skirt tucked between her and "nine ebony spikes some twelve inches long, in comparative comfort, howling lustily to be hauled out."

...with her Fang cannibals...

Kingsley was said to thwart turning into a real-life version of Waugh's Prudence Courteney through the device of presenting herself as a straightforward trader and not a creepy missionary. Facing an onslaught by the Fang at their initial meeting on a riverbank, Kingsley stood her ground, holding out her open hand, quelling the warriors.

For centuries, the Fang were wholesale victims of slavers, who justified the subjugation of the people because of their presumed cannibalism. This claim was based on human skulls and bones found in wooden boxes throughout Fang villages, when the remains were relics for ancestor worship.

...nets handwoven from plant fibers...

Kingsley took down an Igbo–Eboe her name for them–story about the invention of the cloth loom, saying some version of it could be found among all cloth-making peoples in West Africa. It also happens to be a story about the Dwarf forest buffalo, the Bush cow.

> In the old times there was a man who was a great hunter; but he had a bad wife. And when he made medicine to put on his spear, she made medicine against his spear; but he knew nothing of this thing and went out after bush cow.
>
> By-and-by, he found a big bush cow; and threw his spear at it; but the bush cow came on and drove its horns through his thigh; so the man crept home and lay in his house, terribly injured. And the healer found out which of the man's wives witched his spear, and they killed her; and for many days the man could not go out hunting. But he was a great hunter, and his liver grew hot in him for the bush; so he dragged himself to the bush and lay there every day. One day, as he lay, he saw a big spider making a net on a bush; and he watched it. He came to see how the spider caught her game and that the spider was a great hunter, too. And the man said, "If I had hunted as this spider hunts, if I had made a trap like that and put it in the bush and then gone aside and let the game get into it and

wear itself to death quickly, quicker and safer than they do in pitfalls, that bush cow would not have gored me."

So after a time he tried to make a net like the spider's, out of bush rope; and he did this thing and put his net into the forest and caught bush deer–gazelle–and earth-pig–pangolin–and porcupine; and he made more nets, and every net he made was better. He grew well and became a greater hunter than before.

One day he made a very fine net; and his new wife said, "This is a cloth, it is better than our cloth–bark cloth–because when the rain gets to it, it does not shrivel. Make me a cloth like this and then I will beat it with a mallet and wear it."

The man tried to do this thing, but he could not get it a good shape; and he said, "Yet the spider gets a shape in her cloth. I will go and ask her again about this thing."

He went to the spider and took her offerings and said, "Oh, my lady, teach me more things," and sat and watched the spider for many days.

His eyes were opened and he saw more, how the spider made her net on sticks. So he went home and got fine bush rope that he collected and brought there, to make his game nets with; and he took them to the bush near the spider; and fixing the strings onto the bush he made a new net, and he got shape into it. He made more nets this way, and every net he made was better. And his new wife was pleased and gave him sons; and by and by, the man saw that he did not want all the sticks of a bush to make his net on, only some of them.

So he took those sticks home and put them up in his house, and made his nets there; and after a time his wife said, "Why do you make the stuff for me with that brush rope? Why do you not make it with something finer?"

The man went into the bush and took offerings to the spider and said, "Oh, my lady, teach me more things!" And he sat and watched the spider; but the spider, he saw, drew the finer stuff out of her belly.

And the man said, "Oh, my lady, you pass me. I cannot do this thing."

As he went home he thought, and saw that there are trees; and there are bush ropes, thick bush rope and thin bush rope; and then there is grass which is thinner still. And he took the grass and tried to make a net with it, and he did this thing and made more nets; and every net was better.

The man's wife was pleased and said, "This is good cloth." And the man lived to be very old and was a great chief and great hunter. For it is good for a man to be a great hunter, and it is good for a man to please women. This is the origin of the cloth loom.

This is how the black man learned to make cloth from fine grass fiber in the old time. Now, he gets thread on spools from the white man, for the white man is a great spider.

...met in vaudeville...

Of unsettled etymology, vaudeville may have come from Vau de Vire, satirical songs by the fifteenth-century French poet Oliver Basselin. The Vire River Valley, the appellation in English, where Basselin lived, was famous for Rabelaisian drinking songs.

...the writer's forty-five-foot ketch, Snark...

London's intended circumglobal navigation of the *Snark* was something of an homage to the Nova Scotia-born Captain Joshua Slocum's accomplishment of sailing single-handed around the world between 1895 and 1898 on his small boat *Spray*. London spent almost a million dollars in today's money on the bespoke construction of his sailing yacht, and a lousy job it was too. It promised him, though, a dry–alcohol-free–twenty-seven days at sea between San Francisco and Hawai'i.

Returning to Kansas after stowing away on a ship to Europe, a teenaged Martin Johnson read of Jack London's approaching ocean adventure and wheedled his way onto the crew by claiming he was a sea cook. He was soon bent over the rail, feeding chum to the fish, while all the fresh fruit and vegetables in the galley rotted. The *Snark* leaked its way into Honolulu, where five months were called for to make essential repairs, London traveling around the islands, including visiting the leper colony on Moloka'i, committing experience.

On the next leg to the Marquesas–the setting of Herman Melville's *Typee: A Peep at Polynesian Life*–several bottles of fortified dessert wines were discovered onboard and sobriety was jettisoned. In port at the bay of Taiohae, London stocked up on trade rum and absinthe, later in Tahiti, supplying the boat with bourbon and whisky. Happy days, except for malaria, Solomon [Islands] Sores,[1] a double fistula in London's rectum, psoriasis, fast-growing toenails, and hands with such acute inflammation and scaling that they could not grip anything, were here again.

Reaching Australia, London ceased from exploration, sailing for Ecuador on an ocean-liner with Charmian and their Japanese manservant, deserting the *Snark* and her crew at the wharf in Sydney, instructing that a buyer for the ship should be sought.

...their name in bêche de mer, pidgin Bislama, meaning numbers...

Adjacent to the Big Nambas was the tribe unfortunately named the Smol–*smɔ:l*–Nambas.

...portable Akeley Motion Picture Camera...

Carl Akeley was above all a taxidermist who considered it a form of sculpture–it was he who conceived, and made many of the mounts for, the Akeley Hall of Mammals in New York's American Natural History Museum. Called the father of modern taxidermy, his work can also be seen in the Field Museum and Smithsonian.

Akeley's unhappy childhood family was unhappy in its own way. Raised on a farm in western New York in the 1860s and '70s, he had three of his siblings die in early infancy, embittering his mother and poisoning his homelife. Akeley's escape as a boy was to mount

1 Scabies and impetigo.

small dead animals he found. At eighteen with only three years of schooling, he apprenticed to a professional taxidermist. In the 1890s he began leading African expeditions. In Somalia in 1896, in one of those too-good-to-be-true, but true all the same, tales, when shooting at what he took for a Warthog in the grass, desperate for meat, he heard a yowling rather than a squeal. In a blur, a wounded Leopard was on him, biting on his left arm. Akeley managed to get on top and began strangling the cat, ultimately forcing his punctured left arm down its throat–you don't feel pain when a Leopard's biting you; the hell you don't. He then carried the carcass back to his camp, hanging it head-down outside his tent, standing in the photograph, hirsute and with his wounds bound.

Akeley was also an inventor–one of his inventions was the gun for spraying concrete. In 1915, dissatisfied with the performance in the field of the movie cameras of the time, he designed his own, making it easy to transport, focusing and panning smoothly, to shoot in poor light, quickly reloaded, rotatable and maneuverable. Round and flat-sided, it became known as the pancake camera.

By the 1920s, Akeley was disturbed by the overshooting in Africa, especially of Mountain gorilla; and he was influential in Belgium's King Albert I's establishing what is now Virunga National Park, the first national park in Africa, specifically for the protection of Gorilla. In the Congo dry season in 1926, aged sixty-two, he was leading another Gorilla expedition to Mount Mikeno when he died of dysentery, his symptoms suspiciously like those of Ebola or Marburg.

...the Hardy Brothers tackle store...

Hardy held the distinction of being the foremost purveyor of fishing tackle to the era's highest angling echelon, sportsmen such as Zane Grey and Hemingway–Hemingway had a Hardy Fairy flyrod; if not irony, what might it be? A patron of Hardy's tackle, George V dashed off greetings to one of the Hardys, not realizing he had been called upon to commemorate the birthday of the Dorset novelist-poet Thomas Hardy. For decades, the company produced, as evidence of its puckishness, a reel, the Fortuna, for tuna.

...Speak to the Earth...

Hemingway read both this and *Out in the Blue*, as well as Isak Dinesen, and learned.

to eat her écorché carcass...

Da Vinci, along with all his talents, had a marvelous affinity for the drawing of the human body's musculature, divested of its skin.

...wave of thefts and raids...

Rowland Ward lists the world's longest rhino horn as an anterior one from a Southern white rhino cow. Believed taken in the mid-1800s in what is today Namibia, it measured sixty two and a half inches. It is credited to the gun of Roualeyn George Gordon-Cumming–when he was engaging in what one contemporary dispraised as the indiscriminate slaughter of wild animals, which he said, Gordon-Cumming reported in nauseating detail. In 2002, the horn and an almost-as-long other one–possibly the same rhino's posterior horn–were stolen from the trophy collection in the ancestral family home in Scotland. Ian Player, champion golfer Gary Player's late older brother, and the foremost White rhino conservationist in South Africa, was contacted after the theft by the horns's owner, a descendant of Cordon-Cumming's, asking if Player would be able to place a value on the horns for an insurance claim. By the ounce, Player told him, certainly more than gold.

...old friend Uncle Charles Bulpett...

A settler in British East Africa in the early years of the twentieth century, Bulpett was part of an exploration of unknown regions of the Blue Nile. Called a keen amateur hunter, he was once out with only his Somali gun bearer when he shot and wounded a huge Lion that then attacked him. As the Lion and man struggled, the gun bearer launched himself onto the animal, pushing his bare arm down its throat–seems a common tactic with murderous felines. This let Bulpett get back up and retrieve the rifle that had been knocked out of his hands, killing the Lion which still held onto the Somali.

...she blamed the lingering effects of Bror's syphilis...

> In March 1941 [*sic–she married Bror Blixen in 1914*], two months after her wedding, Karen Blixen was diagnosed as having syphilis in the second stage. She was treated initially with mercury and later on in Denmark with salvarsan. Years later she received more treatment with mercury, salvarsan and bismuth, but in fact she was cured already in 1915 and told so by her venerologist Carl Rasch. However, she did not believe him, and several physicians, including well-known specialists in internal medicine and neurology told her many years later that she had to accept the diagnosis *tabes dorsalis*, i.e., syphilis in the third chronic stage. This paper claims, based on her medical records from several hospitals, that her physicians' attitude resulted in the delay of right treatment for her real disease for many years and led to at least one unwarrented surgical procedure (chordotomy). In 1956 she finally received surgical treatment of her stomach ulcer which for many years had caused her attacks of abdominal pain. The procedure was delayed for ten years because of a lumbar sympathectomy, which removes the pain for some years but not the ulcer itself, nor bouts of vomiting. Many doctors (and biographers) have been puzzled by her life-long bowel symptoms. It was often called tropic dysentery, in spite of the fact that this diagnosis was never confirmed by stool analyses. Instead it is suggested that most likely the Baroness caused the symptoms. She misused strong laxatives during her whole adult life. She did not tell her doctors about this until very late in her life and then it was far too late. Many times barium enemas showed a severe chronic condition with dehaustration and dilatation.

> The reason for her misuse was the fact that she was afraid of gaining too much weight. She used amphetamine during her life in Denmark after her return in 1931 in order to reduce her appetite, and probably she used Chat [*sic–khat or qat*] in Africa. She also constantly smoked cigarettes which in combination with minimal food intake facilitated the development of her stomach ulcer. It is concluded that Karen Blixen would have had a much better life, if communication between her and her physicians had been better. She should have told them and they should have been better to listen to that which was unsaid.
>
> –Søgaard I. Karen Blixen og laegerne [*Karen Blixen and her physicians*]. Dan Medicinhist Arbog. 2002:25-50. Danish. PMID: 12561802.

...something about safari life that makes you forget all your sorrows...

"I never knew of a morning in Africa when I woke up that I was not happy."

–Ernest Hemingway

...found their own ways of lodging complaints...

A superannuated colonial at heart, an admirer especially of British colonialism–Beard also expressed less than Progressive views on race and sexuality, even though many of his friends were gay. He installed Blixen's then-aged chief servant and gifted cook, Kamade Wa Gature and his wife and blind son in a house on Hog Ranch, and even co-authored a book, *Longing for Darkness*, with him. Kamande would complain that he never "saw a 50-cent piece from that book"; and that while Beard sent him $50 every month when he was away from the ranch in the 1980s, he would not let him raise any animals or even keep a garden.

...like so many mzungu before him...

A forceful case may be made for Peter Beard as the last mzungu. Yet, in many ways, the most archetypic could have been a perpetually young, intrepid, Belgian boy reporter with a faithful white terrier companion. His assignments for Le Petit Vingtième, the children's supplement to the conservative Roman Catholic Brussels tabloid, Le Vingtième Siècle, were presented in *ligne-claire* cartoon panels, drawn and written, in French, by George Prosper Remi under the name Hergé.

After Tintin au pays des Soviets, the reporter's travelings with his dog Snowy amid the horrors of the Soviet Union–unlike too many Western correspondents in the U. S. S. R., such as *The New York Times*'s Pulitzer Prize-winning Walter Duranty, Tintin at the time at least referenced the beginnings of the murderous dekulakization–his next adventure was Tintin au Congo, serialized between 1930-31. It was a rationale for the colonial rule by the Belgiums of the slothful, simple, violent Congolese, pictured by Hergé like ole Zip Coons. The good Congolese called a white, master; the bad were juju men and/or colluded with criminal non-Belgians–e.g., Chicago gangsters–to control the colony's diamond production.

By the 2000s the *bande dessinée*–comic–albums of the Congo drew by-then standard accusations of racism. American librarians began placing the copies in secure backrooms, to be viewed by appointment only. Sales by bookstores were limited to the adult reader. Complaints of pro-colonial sentiments and insult to the Congolese people were lodged with European commissions and courts. They were, though, rejected by final rulings.

The more lasting attack has been against the depictions of hunting. Pith-helmeted Tintin in puttees shoots fifteen Antelope from a single stand, not realizing he is hitting one and knocking it down, another appearing in its place, like gallery ducks. He kills a Chimpanzee to take its pelt for a disguise. Snowy domesticates a Lion by biting off its tail. Tintin shoots and wounds an Elephant, halting tracking at dark. That night, in an apropos turn of events, a monkey filches his rifle, accidentally killing the Elephant. Tintin takes the tusks. He drives off a Leopard with a soda siphon. For a Rhino whose hide proves too armored for Tintin's bullets to penetrate, he stealthily bores a hole into its back, inserts a stick of dynamite, and blows it to smithereens.

Snowy mistakes a herd of Dwarf buffalo for tranquil domestic cows; then the dog runs, leading the Buffalo to charge Tintin. He leaps into a tree as a bull crashes into the trunk, and the boy reporter falls onto the bull's back. The two rodeo across the savanna until Tintin is bucked off into a river, Snowy coming to his rescue.

With, as he says, his reputation at stake, Tintin devises to manufacture a giant slingshot by tapping two rubber trees and using the latex to form the band. He then hazes the bull into charging and clobbers it by launching a heavy rock into its head.

Remi took most to heart the charges not of bigotry, but of condoning cruelty to animals as exhibited in the hunting. Within only a few years, Tintin was befriending the animals rather than detonating them, and the cartoonist became an implacable opponent of blood sports, if not racial stereotyping.

Chapter Thirteen: "Gentlemen..."

...heir to the Jameson Irish whiskey fortune...

This was Andrew Jameson. There was an atrocious African connection, through Andrew's younger brother, James Sligo.

In 1870 in Southern Sudan, Samuel Baker established the Anglo-Egyptian Condominium's province of Equatoria–containing most of the northern parts of what is today Uganda–as a utopian effort at creating a model state in Africa. Chinese Gordon replaced Baker as governor in 1874, and in 1878 Emin Pasha assumed the office.

Emin Pasha was born Eduard Carl Oscar Theodore Schnitzer in 1840 in Silesia, the child of German Jews. Growing up to become a physician, he was not allowed to practice. Planning to move to Constantinople, he reached Montenegro where he could work as a doctor. Shifting to Albania, Schnitzer added Albanian, Greek, and Turkish to his language skills while traveling throughout the Ottoman Empire.

In 1875 he took his M. D. to Cairo and turned himself into Mehemet Emin. Gordon, hearing of him, invited him to become Equatoria's chief medical officer, utilizing him more on diplomatic missions. Emin came to headquarter himself in the Lado Enclave, being named Gordon's successor as governor and given the title Bey by the Khedive of Egypt. By 1883, the Madhist revolt seemingly cut off Equatoria from outside communication, though provincial mail continued going out through Zanzibar. Emin and his trivial military force decamped farther south. Emin was raised to the level of Pasha. After the capture of Khartoum and murder of Gordon by the army of Muhammad Ahmad, attention toward Emin's situation rose in Europe.

Henry Morton Stanley, doing Leopold II's bidding in the Congo, agreed to lead the Emin Pasha Relief Expedition to rescue the doctor who actually did not need or desire rescuing. Four hundred whites applied to join the expedition, many willing to pay £1,000 to the Relief Committee for the opportunity. Stanley chose nine, plus his personal servant who went virtually unmentioned in *In Darkest Africa*, Stanley's bestselling nine-hundred-page account of the undertaking. The infamous slaver-ivory-trader-and-intrepid-explorer, the Zanzibari Hamad bin Muhammad bin Juma bin Rajab el Murjebi, his cognomen Tippu Tib–said to mean "the gatherer together of wealth," or onomatopoeia for the sound of the cocking of his guns on his raids into native territories–was enlisted to recruit, by whatever his characteristic means, carriers.

Stanley was outfitted with a twenty-eight-foot steel boat cut into sections for overland haul, and one of Hiram Maxim's newly invented machine guns, the sine qua non of late-nineteenth–century colonial advance. Nonetheless, over the course of the nearly two years of the trek from Zanzibar through the Congo and back–living off the land proving infeasible–Stanley had to shed equipment, weapons, and ammunition in exchange for food to feed his hundreds and hundreds of men, hundreds of whom would die or be killed, many others reasonably deserting.

In the Congo, for the sake of more speed, Stanley divided the expedition into an Advanced and a Rear Column, the Rear to wait for additional porters in order to bring up more supplies while the Advanced pressed on through the Ituri Forest toward Emin Pasha.

No new porters found their way to the Rear Column. Of the original five white men left with it, two went down the Congo, one due to illness and the other on a deranged three-month round trip to send a pointless cable to London, requesting further instructions. A third was a casualty to opium. Then commanded by the Second Anglo-Afghan and Anglo-Egyptian Wars veteran Edmund Musgrave Barttelot–on the futile Camel Corps march to Khartoum in 1885 to relieve Gordon, Battelot summarily shot a Yemeni who appeared to be tampering with a waterskin, earning promotion to captain, then a brevetting to major–the contracted column left their river encampment and marched off to seek the long-absent Stanley, and into madness.

Barttelot disintegrated most flamboyantly. He convinced himself he was being plotted against, the victim of surreptitious poisoning, and that Stanley's personal belongings, left in his safekeeping, had to be boated away down the river. He jabbed at Africans with the steel tip of a cane, had porters clapped in irons, saw one lashed to death, and took a bite out of a native woman. When, revolver in hand, he strode out to order a woman with the warlike Manyema porters to stop pounding a drum during a ceremony in the early hours of a morning, he was shot dead by the woman's husband. Many judge him the model for Mistah Kurtz.

The fifth white man of the Rear Column, Andrew Jameson's brother James, already a hunter, explorer, and naturalist in Borneo and Southern Africa, made at least two trips away from his companions to locate Tippu Tib and induce him to keep his word about delivering porters. He at last found the Zanzabari, who had no reinforcements. As they returned empty handed from upriver to Stanley Falls, they came to the village of Riba-Riba which was enjoying a festival. The old reprobate Tippu Tib remarked that the dancing, singing, and drumming would end with a meal of human flesh.

Jameson dismissed Tippu Tib's words as fable. The Zanzabari coolly replied that for the gift of some cloth, the villager's would show him their practice. Jameson, claiming still to be disbelieving, sent a boy to bring six white handkerchieves from his baggage. Receiving the gift, the villagers brought out a ten-year-old girl.

As Jameson looked on in what he purported to be horror, several men fell upon the girl and began stabbing her; he is said to have written in a letter to his wife that the girl "never muttered a sound, nor struggled" until she collapsed. The men then dismembered her for eating, Jameson insufficiently stunned by the scene to prevent his sketching it in some detail.

Stanley finally made his way back to the débâcle of the Rear Column as Jameson lay dying of fever, Stanley feigning infuriation over what had transpired in his absence. He had, after much argument, persuaded Emin Pasha to return with him; and all that could be done was to march back to Zanzibar. As they went deeper into the interior en route to the coast, they met more and more Germans–an unsavory discovery for Stanley, whose interests were no longer with Belgium but firmly with the British Empire, the Kaiser more of a threat to that than to the Belgian King. In early December, 1889, at Bagamoyo north of Dar-es-Salaam, the Kaiser's commissioner held a banquet in honor of Stanley and the Pasha. Having been overserved, Emin mistook a second-story window for the door to a balcony and walked out of it, and had to be left behind, recuperating, as Stanley went on to Zanzibar and then Cairo.

...Roosevelt's last year in the office...

Deciding to honor the "wise custom" established by George Washington–and coming to regret it–Roosevelt declined to run for another term as President of the United States, an office to which he would have been handily reelected. Instead, transferring power peacefully to his handpicked–and later disappointing–successor, William Howard Taft, he had the opportunity, then, to run for the Senate or for mayor of New York or to become the president of his college alma mater. Or to seek adventure.

...Winchester Repeating Arms Company...

While Roosevelt probably had all the rifles he needed, his son, Kermit, who would accompany him, did not; and the President was deciding what to buy for him.

When it came to rifles, Roosevelt was a Winchester publicist's dream, even though he was far from a firearm's expert–he was apparently confused for some time about the difference between the 30-06 cartridge and the older, longer 30-03; though involved in the introduction of the M1903 Springfield rifle which fired the '06 round, his primary input was into the design of the bayonet, which he originally found inadequate, perhaps informed by his experience of bayonet charges in Cuba. Yet it was enough for him–for Winchester, at least–to be on the record as stating that as to his weapon of choice, "I personally prefer the Winchester" when stocked to fit.

Roosevelt had a flair for inadvertent endorsements and product introductions, even when he never actually made them. For many years Maxwell House Coffee claimed the President had proclaimed their product, "Good to the last drop." In reality this was an invention of the company's. Roosevelt's quote, appearing in a newspaper after tasting a cup of coffee on a visit to Andrew Jackson's historical home, the Hermitage, was far better though probably less marketable: "This is the kind of stuff I like to drink, by George, when I hunt bears." Relating to bears, he was, of course, responsible for the creation of the Teddy bear after refusing on a Mississippi hunt to kill a black bear tied to a tree. Leaving office in March of 1909, he made another endorsement, to the effect that, "I do not believe that anyone else has ever enjoyed the White House as much as I."

...Sir Alfred Pease, Second Baronet of Hutton Lowcross and Pinchinthorpe...

Pease is particularly notable because, having visited with Roosevelt in Washington in the final year of his presidency, he offered assurances that he had a hunting lodge awaiting the president—except he did not. After Roosevelt decided his destiny lay in the British colonies of Kenya and Uganda, and the Belgian Congo's Lado Enclave, Pease found himself faced with scrambling to construct an edifice worthy of tenancy by an ex-President, a significant task he did manage to fulfill.

...mandolin-playing, nineteen-year-old son Kermit...

In a letter written on safari in August, 1909, when he was separated from Kermit while hunting Elephant, the Colonel closed with "I miss the mandolin–and the mandolin player even more," hardly the sentiments of the martinet he sometime seemed judged to be.

...only bullets to be found in the animals would be either Kermit's or his...

By firsthand accounts, Kermit was an abysmal shot and even according to Roosevelt, "altogether too reckless." He may also have already been exhibiting the distressing family tendency toward manic-depression, which later joined with alcoholism to lead Kermit to put a pistol to his head in an Army outpost in Alaska during World War II. Though before that, his presence on his father's disordered 1913-14 Brazilian wilderness expedition prevented the suicide the elder Roosevelt deliberated on in the jungle when he feared he could not go on without assistance–in his kit was a lethal vial of morphine, his ultimate catholicon on all his wilderness expeditions since his first time in the West, to abbreviate a drawn out, inevitable death, as a defeated Roman general might fall on his gladius.

As for Roosevelt himself, he was a rather shopworn fifty years of age when he reached Africa. A hushed-up 1902 carriage accident left him with an injured left leg that was chronically prone to abscesses. A boxing match with the cousin of his second wife Edith's, blinded his left eye. The arterial sclerosis, that would contribute to his death, was well underway. And the physical inactivity of his White House years swelled his waist to forty-seven and weight to two fifty, which at his five-foot-ten height classified him today as suffering from "severe obesity," some distance from his once-"mighty pindlin'" self–the Africans labeled him Bwana Tumbo, The Big-Stomach Master, and one commentator noted that his "bulk and conversational powers somewhat precluded" his stalking ability. Never-the-less, he felt his bully approach to life, embracing Churchill's stated attitude of "*de l'audace, encore de l'audace, et toujours de l'audace*"– said to be spoken first by George Danton, ultimately an opponent of the French Committee of Public Safety on which he served–could overcome any and all obstacles.

...let them dictate the equipment...
Permanent camps and lodges are the way of safari today, and canvas tents were not necessarily part of the origin story of the great African hunting adventure. Africans built huts and lean-tos as they travelled. Arab traders had shelters of Bedouin cloth woven from goat and sheep hair, the loose weave allowing the wind to pass through in the heat and smoke to escape, while rain swelled the fibers to make the fabric waterproof.

The earliest British hunter-discoverers, Burchell, Cornwallis Harris, even Selous, used ox-drawn covered Cape wagons rather than tents. Then the exploration of Africa enlarged to where the wagon could not easily go, not least because of the tsetse fly spreading sleeping sickness to the oxen and due to the pace of bovines, which did not rise much above two-miles-per-hour. Porters on foot travelled faster and died less–or were, to cast it brutally, more expedient to replace.

With porters, large tents could be carried, pitched, and struck, and proved ideally suited to safari. Theodore Roosevelt, who initially planned on roughing it in Africa with his son Kermit, as the "early pioneers" had done in the Rockies and Great North Woods–and those pilgrims were nonetheless "as hardy as bears, and lived to a hale old age, if Indians and accidents permitted"–grudgingly acknowledged that one had to care for oneself in Equatorial Africa as he "would scorn to do" in "lands of pine and birch and frosty weather."

Throw a blanket down on the ground in Africa and be prepared to deal with venomous serpents and scorpions, perhaps ticks that could be in the long run even more deadly, exposure to malaria-transmitting mosquitoes, and the odd chance of getting dragged away into the night by something out of *The Ghost and the Darkness*. The first explorers came to realize that the tent was the capsule they returned to after their African space walks during the day. And it could not be just any tent.

In *Into Africa*, Kenneth Cameron's history of the East African safari, he notes that Joseph Thomson, the Scots geologist who began his explorations of Africa leading an expedition in 1878 when he was twenty, made the mistake of having tents too small and too thin, ones you could not only not stand upright in but had to crawl on hands and knees to enter, and which leaked like cheesecloth in a gentle shower. At the end of an arduously long day's trekking in Africa, you needed–at least whites did–a stout canvas tent–rolled, they could weigh sixty pounds and required two porters to carry, along with a third transporting lines, pegs, and poles–that you could walk around in, sit on a chair, sleep in a cot or bed above the ground and which had netting against flying insects, and some sort of extension in which to take a hot, never cold, bath each evening, a ritual as vital as the boiling of drinking water to surviving weeks or even months in the bush.

The tent was never optional equipment on a safari, unlike heated seats in a car, but an essential fixture. For seventy-five years, safari could not have been safari were it not for tents–produced by such British makers as Wilkinson, Edgington, and Low & Bonar–tents that were more than shelter. They were home in a way no room, reduplicated behind each door along the hallway of a safari lodge, however palatial, can ever be. No room radiates the heat of the sun and the smell of paraffin into a dark interior the way a tent's roof does. Or gauges the wind by the stirring of its cloth-duck wall. You cannot feel the surface of the ground in a room the way you can in bare feet on the floor of a tent. In a room you probably couldn't hear a Lion roaring or Leopard coughing. But in a tent, as you are submerging into sleep, those sounds can be heard and leave you open eyed, wondering what, if any, security a sheet of fabric, hanging between you and the outside, provides, until you resolve to let sleep cope with it and pull the blanket over your shoulder. In a lodge, you live at room temperature. In a tent, it is always the temperature of Africa.

Before his advisors were through, the modest shooting party the Colonel contemplated morphed in his words into "a full-blooded picnic," wrapped in the mantel of a scientific-collecting expedition. For the collecting, tons of salt, skinning tools, traps–for large and small animals–shipping crates and barrels, and assorted other items were parceled out in sixty-pound loads per porter. The silk tent was replaced with sixty-four heavy green canvas ones, eight alone for the riding horses, most of which would die from tsetse flies. The food boxes, padlocked to discourage pilfering, contained everything from paté to sardines, chutney, lard and tallow for cooking the lean game meat that would be the staple of the safari, liquor from England–the local spirits deemed "mostly poison"–canned pea soup, and ninety-two pounds of jam.

Among Roosevelt's personal accoutrements were, with much more, nine pairs of eyeglasses; a "very ingenious" beam scale for weighing game, a gift of the nature writer Ernest Thompson Seton; a "Whitman-tree" army saddle; army field-glasses; a telescope given to him on the ship by a Captain of Irish Hussars; rain slicker, army overcoat, and a mackinaw if he needed to stay out overnight, along with compass and waterproof matches; custom-made rope-, rubber-, and hobnail-soled boots for his surprisingly tender feet–apparently a far cry from their condition on the slopes of Katahdin, perhaps further ruination brought about by the Presidency–spine pads to button onto the backs of shirts to negate the effects of the equinoctial sun's lethal actinic rays; complete changes of wardrobe for all possible weather conditions; six different hats, including a white military helmet in a tin case "for ceremonial occasions"; appropriate evening wear for formal dinners; and a lucky gold-mounted rabbit's foot from "one-time ring champion of the world" John L. Sullivan. And yet for all that, recalling the manly rigors of his Western days, he was slightly disdainful of the hovering presence of two tent "boys," two armed gunbearers, and two horse grooms, or saises, and especially of a canvas tub in his tent for regular hot baths.

Roosevelt's most vital equipage was his guns and books. In some reports, he brought fifteen wooden crates of firearms and ammunition with him to Africa. He certainly brought a custom Army Springfield 30-06–for his disinterest in technical matters of firearms, he was instrumental in having the military develop the '06 after he and his Rough Riders–their adopted anthem, *There'll Be a Hot Time in the Old Town Tonight*–faced the high-velocity Spanish Mausers. The U. S. military, in fact, stole the design for the Springfield from Mauser, requiring some $200,000, in 1900s dollars, of royalty payments to the German manufacturer. Roosevelt's 30-06, "stocked and sighted" for himself, shot the most-recent army ammunition with 150-grain Spitzer bullets that he found devastating in comparison to the 220-grain round-nosed bullets in previous military loadings; a Winchester 405 which, loaded with 300-grain round-nosed bullets, he reported "did admirably with...giraffes, elands, and smaller game," but was the "medicine gun" for Lion–a 500/450 Holland & Holland double rifle, throwing a four-hundred-eighty-grain 458-caliber solid projectile, the rifle presented to him–in a clear case of foreign emoluments–by a syndicate of more than fifty English admirers; and a side-by-side 12 gauge compliments of the makers, Ansley H. Fox, Roosevelt's verdict that "no better gun... [was] ever made." Kermit was similarly armed with a Winchester in '06 rather than the Springfield, and a side-by-side rifle, built by Rigby, for heavy game. For the reading he pursued as vigorously as every other passion in his life, Roosevelt assembled fifty volumes and had them trimmed down for size and weight and bound in pigskin for durability. Packed in a "light aluminum and oil-cloth case" to make a load for one porter, the "Pigskin Library" ran from the Bible to *Alice in Wonderland.*

Predictably, the expense of almost eleven months spent on safari in such a style was astronomical. Half of a one-million-dollar advance, at current values, that Scribner's publishing house paid him for a series of safari dispatches and a book, *African Game Trails*, was used by Roosevelt to cover Kermit and his private costs–Roosevelt was hopeless about money; and his finances, especially because there was no pension, yet, for ex-Presidents, were always precarious, to his wife's constant distraction. Besides safari fees, these costs included, today, $7000 worth of licenses, apiece, entitling each hunter to some fifty head of game from Elephant to Rhino, Hippo, Buffalo, Eland, other Antelope, and Cheetah–Kermit shot seven; Roosevelt, none–among others. Additional Elephant were on license for $2500 each–Roosevelt would take a total of eight; Kermit, three–Rhino for something over $680–again, eight and three–and about $280 would buy you another Wildebeest or Waterbuck. It was Roosevelt's good fortune that because they were classed as vermin, Leopard and Lion cost nothing: The most poorly concealed wish of Roosevelt for his safari was to come face to face with a Lion in the African bush.

Despite the book advance from Scribner's, Roosevelt was running out of money by the halfway point of the safari. The Smithsonian was disinclined to provide any further backing, piqued over the safari's being identified as Roosevelt's, and not the institution's. It was Andrew Carnegie who financed the rest of the expedition.

...Hemingway's professional hunter on both of his safaris...

As Roosevelt chased game on the Kenyan plains, in Oak Park, Illinois, the ten-year-old Hemingway, who liked to dress in his version of Roosevelt's khaki safari outfit and travel to Chicago to stand transfixed in the Hall of African Mammals at the Field Museum with his father, Dr. Clarence, was assiduously tracing the President's steps in the press reports and Roosevelt's dispatches.

...and even then extremely vulnerable, Northern white rhinoceros...

Roosevelt's motives for killing these placid creatures–a total of nine, bulls, cows, and calves, between Kermit and him–are problematic, if not possibly inexplicable, though perhaps not to him. He fully recognized the perilous thread by which the White rhino clung, as early as 1910, to survival, stating in *Game Trails* that "it would certainly be well if all killing of it were prohibited until careful inquiry has been made to its numbers and exact distribution." And yet Roosevelt obviously felt this injunction was not applicable to his son and him. It can only be assumed that the putatively scientific significance of the safari granted him absolution in his mind for the "game butchery" he seemed to be committing, and which he so strenuously denounced other hunters for indulging in–though when it came to hunting Bison in the Dakotas, he was reported to have said, before traveling Out West, that he wanted to shoot a Buffalo "while there were still buffalo to shoot."

Because Roosevelt revered the American buffalo since age twenty-five, in the way a hunter does the first true big-game animal he may hunt, he paradoxically went on hunting them, shades of the Northern white rhino, longer than absolutely commendable. Hearing in the fall of 1889, when free-roaming Bison in the United States outside Yellowstone were said, by census, to number eighty-five, that "a very few bison were still left around the head of Wisdom River," now called the Big Hole, he went there and found none. Later that year, hunting Moose somewhere in the wilderness west of Yellowstone, he found tracks of a band of six Buffalo, mostly cows and calves. His guide was a rheumatic elder man–which Roosevelt considered advantageous because the old man's arthritis hindered his carrying a rifle, which Roosevelt was confident he would have used to slaughter the entire herd, They tracked the animals into a glade where they waited for the bull to come out. When it did, Roosevelt held low behind the shoulder where he knew to kill a Bison, and fired. Without surprise or hesitation, all the Buffalo ran.

> Fifty yards beyond the border of the forest we found the stark black body stretched motionless. He was a splendid old bull, still in his full vigor, with large, sharp horns, and heavy mane and glossy coat; and I felt the most exulting pride as I handled and examined him; for I had procured a trophy such as can fall henceforth to few hunters indeed.

The most exulting pride? In some kind of hunting *droit du seigneur*? In reducing the lingering population to eighty-four?

The final male Northern white rhino, named Sudan by humans, died on March 19, 2018, at Ol Pejeta Conservancy in Kenya. It was forty-five-years old, its death due to senescence. Two females then survived.

...the Colonel wrote...
Roosevelt knew courage. He demonstrated genuine battlefield gallantry. He robustly extolled bravery as one of the cardinal virtues, informing his brand of muscular Dutch Reformed Christianity, and who knows if he did not secretly esteem it among the heavenly graces. But it colored his life with a hyper-martialism until nearly its end. While he lashed himself to it, it fed into his "exulting pride" that upheld the distortion that equates hunting dangerous wild beasts with warfare, which fails to comprehend that the courage of hunting dangerous game is not the courage of battle.

Ancient writers, for whom warfare was a more permanent fact of life than it ever was for Roosevelt, praised hunting not for what it taught in the way of killing, but what it built in the way of character. The Greek historian and military man, Xenophon, writing in his *Cynegeticus–On Hunting*–recommends hunting to young men because, more importantly than learning how to kill, "...the advantages that those who have been attracted by this pursuit will gain are many. For it makes the body healthy, improves the sight and hearing, and keeps men from growing old." It also benefits the warrior in "marching over rough roads under arms" without tiring; being "capable of sleeping on a hard bed and of guarding well the place assigned to them"; hunter-warriors can "make straight for the foe without a slip over any kind of ground, through habit"; if driven into retreat, "they will manage to save themselves without loss of honor and to save others"; and if "their post is in the van they will not desert it, because they can endure."

Nowhere does Xenophon say that he recommends hunting because it makes superior killers. There is no warfare with wild beasts among hunters, at least not ethical and moral ones. Hunting is not single combat with animals because that would be a perversion of the chase. Wild animals are not hunters's enemies to be conquered, enemy implying an innate equality of intelligence and objective and armament. The hunt cannot be a substitute for battle, as long as humans and animals remain separate species. The Spanish philosopher José Ortega y Gasset in his *Meditations on Hunting*, writes that hunting is not about the outwitting of wild game but the "imitation" of it, a form of homage, that is "indigenous to hunting." More than that, [s]trictly speaking, the essence of sportive hunting is not raising the animal to the level of man, but something much more spiritual than that: a conscious and almost religious humbling of man which limits his superiority and lowers him toward the animal." Roosevelt, I think, would have bridled at the notion of his descending to the stratum of the animal.

Roosevelt was not present for the deaths of his two oldest sons, the death by suicide of Kermit, and his eldest, Ted, of a heart attack in France, both during the Second World War. In the Great War before, though, on Bastille day, eighteen months following the death of Selous and within sight of the Armistice, Roosevelt's youngest son, Quentin, just twenty, a pursuit pilot with the United States Army Air Service, said to share his father's positive traits while unencumbered by most of his outsized illaudable ones, was killed in the air over France. For the brief remaining time of his life, the Colonel wandered down to the stables at Sagamore Hill to be among the horses his boy loved dearly, keening his pet name for him, "Quenty-quee," as perhaps he would not have, had Quentin fallen headlong in the chase of wild game, different deaths bearing different griefs. In terrible coincidence, six months before the death of Quentin, one of Selous's sons, a pilot as well, died over Belgium, his already-dead father spared this news.

Every form of courage Roosevelt knew and practiced could not mail him against this loss, even when there was courage enough within him to carry into his children, in whom he had done his utmost to instill it. Would he have finally preferred them to be cowards, or a coward himself, to persuade those he loved not to venture into desperate circumstances? The truth is that cowardice spares nothing, either, while offering a thousand deaths. You have to wonder, though, by the end, with the horses, with all that had injured him, if he remained able not to be scared, the way Bill Sewall had taught. Or if perhaps the other title, the one without soldierly vainglory, the one not Colonel, called for the larger courage. Father.

Roosevelt lived those full sixty years he placed a secret wager on. At his death, his third son, Archibald, who like the other three showed his own Rooseveltian courage in warfare, telegraphed his brothers and sisters, "The old lion is dead." It came while the Colonel slept. Life was what hurt him and should have made him scared. For all the pain he knew, though, or because of it, you can imagine that the Lion regretted not being awake to meet death head on, even on ground of its own choosing–as long as he could be there for it. That is a portion, though, that cannot be warranted for any of us. The best we can hope to achieve is not victory, but abidance.

Chapter Fourteen: Nyama

...to commit to terrestrial bipedalism...

Another brain spurt came about half a million years ago, when *Homo bodoensis* and *Homo neanderthalensis* represented the two species of humans, and cranial capacity in neanderthals reached as much as seventeen hundred milliliters. *Homo sapiens* males achieved a fifteen hundred-milliliter brain. But in as little as the last three thousand years, with the beggaring of nutrition in the shift from hunting and gathering to, well, gardening, the human brain in fact shrank to around fourteen hundred milliliters in males.

...an organ that at 2 percent of bodyweight requires 20 percent of our energy...

The expensive brain

The argument begins with the basic fact that the brain is a metabolically expensive organ. On the basis of *in vivo* determinations, the mass-specific metabolic rate of the brain is approximately

11.2W/kg (watts per kilogram). This is over 22 times the mass-specific metabolic rate of skeletal muscle (0.4 W/kg) (Aschoff *et al.*, 1971). A large brain would, therefore, be a considerable energetic investment. For example, an average human has a brain that is about 1 kg larger than would be expected for an average mammal of our body size (65 kg) and the metabolic cost of this brain would be just under five times that of the brain of the average mammal (humans = 14.6 watts, average mammal = 3.0 watts) (Aiello and Wheeler, 1995).

–Leslie C. Aiello, "Brains and guts in human evolution: The Expensive Tissue Hypothesis," *Brazilian Journal of Genetics*, March, 1997

I know, I know, the numbers look a little screwy; but what it says is that it costs us to have a brain as large as we have.

...easier to brazen it out with them than with Lion prides...

Modern Africans still engage in kleptoparasitism, taking from Lion kills. And they don't always patiently out-wait the hunters. Even a small phalanx of humans, armed only with spears or knobkerries, advancing with deliberate confidence can rout a large number of Lion from a carcass.

...bovine lard's singular arrangement of lipids...

As carnivory among hominins became persistent some two million years ago, it was not only terrestrial mammals we ate but aquatic animals such as fish, turtles, and even crocodiles, all possessing an abundance of lipids. Another element in our ancestors's diet then was honey collected from wild bees. Along with substantial amounts of concentrated energy, wild honey also provided protein in the form of the bee larvae in it, something we now take pains to filter out. The Olduwan tool kit–the type of flaked tools discovered at Olduvai Gorge in Tanzania by the Leakeys–was well suited to breaking-open hives. Hominins likely used hollowed-out gourds or emptied Ostrich-egg shells to transport honey back to their troop. Because of low moisture content, its bactericide level of acid, and enzymes from bees's stomachs, honey when stored in sealed ceramic jars keeps indefinitely–edible honey more than fifty five hundred years old has been found. Despite our delirious modern-day hysteria at the thought of feeding infants raw honey, because of the fear of botulism, Africans do, and no doubt did, spoon it blithely into the mouths of weaning babies.

...nerve- and tissue-growth processes...

Arachidonic acid, commonly–and inexactly–considered bad fat, is irreplaceable in the diet of an infant for brain development, and should be fed from birth. Hardly coincidentally, one of the richest sources for it is mother's breast milk.

...made to order for breaking bones...

Hyena and Lion, and others of the Carnivora taxon, have carnassial teeth for slicing into meat. Lacking them, we resorted to edged stone tools for breaking down carcasses.

...Simple rocks at first, could be lifted and dashed down...

This type of tool-making–the smashing of larger rocks on hard surfaces–is known as Lomekwian for the three and a third million-year-old Lomekwi 3 archeological site in West Turkana, Kenya, acknowledged now as the earliest record of human-made implements.

...the rock fracturing into smaller pieces...

The intentional process of making cutting and hammering tools from larger rocks is termed lithic reduction. Beginning from about seven hundred thousand years ago, many of the finest examples created by master flint knappers are regarded as art. One of the best is housed in the Metropolitan Museum of Art in New York. From the Acheulean, the two-pound, ten-inch biface, or hand ax, is conspicuously fashioned with faces and edges more symmetrical than would be of practical utility. Its main function may have been an aesthetic one, far earlier than the creation of petroglyphs.

...easier to chew and digest...

If we ate the same raw-food diet as that of the Chimp, adjusted for our greater body size, it is estimated we would spend five hours ever day chewing.

... setting grass fires let hominins modify landscapes...

Burning releases captured carbon into the atmosphere. But if the land is not broken by the plow and turned over to agriculture, the natural regrowth reabsorbs that carbon in a climate-neutral circuit.

...the blood-brain barrier...

This is the semipermeable cellular border that blocks the passage of various pathogens and large molecules in the blood into the cerebrospinal fluid, while actively transporting others, such as those of bovine fat, which the brain invites.

Chapter Fifteen: Happy

...*"The More Dangerous Game"*...

In a footnote to his essay on Hemingway in *The Wound and the Bow*, Edmund Wilson writes, "There would probably be a chapter to write on the relation between Hemingway and Kipling, and certain assumptions about society which they share. They have much the same split attitude toward women. Kipling anticipates Hemingway in his beliefs that 'he travels the fastest that travels alone' and that the female of the species is more deadly than the male..."

...September, 1936, issue of *Cosmopolitan*...

Noted Kentucky-born illustrator Dean Cornwell did an oil painting of the story for the magazine, titled *He Lay Face Down*. Margot Macomber looks rather like a slightly stunned, early version of Betty Crocker, as she kneels over her husband's dead body, which she never does in the story. There is a double express rifle, presumably Wilson's, though he shot a 505 Gibbs bolt action, held butt-down by the muzzles in the hand of a tracker who is indiscernibly black. Another rifle may be Margot's full-stocked Mannlicher, leaning against the large rock the tracker stands upon. Wilson seems some remove from his description in the story. Macomber's wound is suggested by a minimal swirl of paint strokes on the back of his head, as if his hair was merely mussed. The foliage under which the Buffalo lies, dead, is a distinctly fall maple-leaf red. The overall well-done painting's style is something like photorealism meets impressionism. In a magazine aimed at a female readership, Cornwell seemed to have paid particular attention to male buttocks and bare calves.

...a travesty of the hunter and man he had known...

Marginally less strident than the prevailing mumblecore opinion of feminists and progressives would be that of the conservative writer Barton Swaim's:

...an inveterate liar, prone to hedonism and violence, vicious beyond belief to wives and friends, and culpably stupid on political subjects.

Yet he was Hemingway, for all that.

...unhearing his shot in the roar...

Hemingway's onomatopoeia for this sound of the double rifle: "*ca-ra-wong!*" One does one's best not to think of the televised *Batman.*

...saw fragments like slate...

For those keeping score at home, Hemingway is using the technique here of repetition–"shot," "fragments," "horns"–that Frank O'Connor believed he learned from Joyce.

...his friend Charles Thompson's firing...

When John Dos Passos declined Hemingway's invitation to join him on his 1933-34 safari, knowing that Hemingway could not help but turn it into a grinding *mano a mano*, Hemingway asked another of his closest friends, Charles Thompson, to come with him.

Thompson, his family owners of the largest marine hardware store in Key West along with in time, as recounted in a newspaper article, a marina, a fleet of fishing boats, a fish-processing company, an icehouse, a cigarbox factory, a trucking company, a pineapple plantation, a guava-jelly factory, and a turtle-fishing operation that included a fleet of turtle boats, met Hemingway in 1928 when the then-young "writer," as Hemingway compulsively introduced himself, came into the store looking for information about fishing. Thompson happily took him out in his boat and introduced the writer to salt water.

Thompson became Karl in *Green Hills of Africa.* On the safari itself, Hemingway was consumed with envy over Thompson's casually consistent besting of him in the taking of trophies, especially when for Thompson the hunting was all about sport and enjoyment, not about scorekeeping. The writer took revenge on his friend by ridiculing him in the pages of the book, something that visibly upset Thompson even forty years later when he was interviewed about it; yet Thompson refused to say anything against the man he considered, even in death, to be a great friend, classifying the book as merely fiction.

...his Springfield rifle...

Hemingway grew up with shotguns at a time when the big game populations of northern Michigan, where he first hunted, were at historic lows; and he had little experience with rifles when he met an old friend, Milford Baker, an experienced big-game hunter with whom he drove ambulances in Italy in World War I, in Abercrombie & Fitch in New York in 1929 as Hemingway was making plans to hunt in the high country of the Yellowstone and eventually in Africa. Abercrombie advertised that it could customize one of the abundant surplus Springfields into a genuine sporting arm. The famed writer and authority on rifles, Colonel Townsend Whelen, personally selected the best new and unfinished–in the white–Springfield barreled actions for the rifles, and Abercrombie added a handmade walnut stock, blued the steel, and checkered the bolt handle. Baker, according to the book *Hemingway's Guns*, advised Hemingway to buy one of these rifles and had him join the National Rifle Association, then an organization devoted to marksmanship, so he would be eligible to order the barreled action through the Director of Civilian Marksmanship. Hemingway, as might be expected, paid extra to have his 30-06 built to best-rifle standards, adding Circassian walnut for the stock and a Water-buffalo horn fore-end tip. The rifle included a Zeiss Zeilklein 2¼× riflescope on a detachable mount, which Hemingway, upon receipt of the Springfield, almost at once detached and never used.

...killing over thirty Hyena...

What Hemingway wrote about Hyena implies more contempt than hatred, or perhaps it was another manifestation of escalating paranoia. His picture of killing them–and on his first safari in Africa, when the Hyena was classed as vermin and its take unrestricted, so no conflict with authorities could arise, he killed thirty by his own meticulous recording–is nearly unbearable. Granted, he is only telling us this to relay the wonderful pleasure his tracker M'Cola–a primitive, to be sure–took in seeing Hyena shot, and not the portion of it in which he, Hemingway, may have shared.

"Highly humorous," he wrote in *Green Hills of Africa*, "was the hyena...who, shot from the stern, skittered on into speed to tumble end over end. Mirth provoking was the hyena... hit in the chest, [who] went over on his back, his four feet and his full belly in the air. Nothing could be more jolly than the hyena...who raced his tail in three narrowing, scampering circles until he died."

To what end such scrupulous observation, even if it were a venting of his "satirical steam," this time at the expense of an African hireling–he did famously upbraid fellow writer Bob McAlmon, en route to their first bullfight in Spain, for turning away from the maggoty corpse of a dog in the Madrid rail yard; you had to look unblinkingly at reality to capture the "tru gen," to make it actual in your writing and not mere facsimile?

Satire or not, it "was funnier" though, "to see a hyena shot at a great distance, in the heat shimmer of the plain...to see him start that frantic circle, to see that electric speed that meant that he was racing the little nickeled death inside him. But the great joke of all, the thing M'Cola waved his hands across his face about...the pinnacle of hyenic humor, was...the classic hyena...snapping and tearing at himself until he pulled his own intestines out, and then stood there, jerking them out and eating them with relish"–Hemingway, even though using the masculine pronoun, repeated the false claim that the Hyena was hermaphroditic, based on the elongation of the female's clitoris, up to seven inches, employed in birth, urination, and copulation. During birth through the clitoris, a majority of cubs suffocate; but because a Hyena has only two nipples for nursing, there is a practical advantage to losing cubs, while females can die if the clitoris ruptures. Females run Hyena clans, being stronger and more aggressive than males, three times as much testosterone coursing through their bodies.

Was Hemingway's mockery in the name of illustrating the cruelty inherent in all men? If so, then he neglects to acknowledge that he is the agent of what his savage tracker finds so damn funny–if there were no shooting, there would be no laughing.

Like any agonizingly injured animal, the Hyena may react by biting at its wounds, and could pull out its own intestines. But as far as standing and eating them, what can be said? If you watch that happening, it means implicitly that you made an extremely bad shot–for which Hemingway repeatedly ridiculed Thompson-Karl in *Green Hills*–and do not have the modicum of compassion necessary to finish off even a hated animal, who is obviously *in extremis*, hunting for the source of its hurt in the only way it knows. But whatever his motives, Hemingway cannot help but find something lyric–"racing the little nickeled death," possibly *le petite mort*?–in "the sequence of motion and fact" he looked for, to create the actual emotion he felt.

...there may be no known examples of African buffalo in arenas...

While there seems to be no record of an African buffalo in the ring, that I could find, there is a story of Bison in the arena in Juárez, Mexico in January, 1907.

When Mexican officials visited Scotty Philips's private Bison herd in Fort Pierre, South Dakota, it was their opinion that no Bison would be a match in a fight with a *toro de lidia*.

Feeling his animals's honors at stake, Philips offered to ship down two Bison bulls, one a full-grown adult, eight-years old, the other a four-year-old, and settle the issue.

The train carrying the two Buffalo left Fort Pierre in a blizzard but made it to the border and Juárez in a few days. The arena was full for the fight, and the first Buffalo to be put in was the older. Named Pierre, it walked to the center of the ring and lay down on the sand in the sun. The fighting bull was let in, skidding to a halt at the sight of the alien beast. After several puzzled moments, the bull began its approach to the Bison, which rose lazily to its hooves. As the Bison just stood, the bull finally gathered itself into an outright charge and slammed its head into the standing Bison's. It was the bull that staggered back.

Regaining its senses, it charged again, and again crashed skulls with the Bison, once more appearing to suffer the worse for it. Thinking better of this tactic, the bull tried to charge at the Bison's flank to gore it; but the Bison, unlike a fighting bull that turns on its hind legs, was able to pivot swiftly on its front ones and met the bull head on. The bull repeated this attack a few more times with no greater success. By now the Bison was growing disgruntled; and when the bull attacked one more time, the Bison squared up to it and charged itself, the collision nearly knocking the bull unconscious. After that, all the bull wanted was to find the exit out of the ring. Three more bulls were turned into the arena that day, the Bison growing more testy with each. After these bulls were as flat-footedly defeated as the first, Pierre ambled back to the center of the ring and proceeded to wallow luxuriantly on its back in the soothing sand.

The following Sunday a traditional bullfight was staged; but the bulls on the card had all faced Pierre the week before and been ruined for the matador, capable only of pitiably circling the ring next to the barrera, searching for an escape, unwilling to advance into the center of the arena. The younger Bison, Pierre, Jr., was then sent in, to face the matador; but after a witnessing a few perfunctory passes with the cape, the governor of Chihuahua interceded to halt the contest, perhaps out of fear of the matador's being humiliated.

The pride of American Bison upheld, Pierre and Pierre, Jr., were ready to return to South Dakota in triumph. Mexican authorities, though, perhaps in sectarian retribution for the loss of face, wouldn't permit the Bison to clear the border. So Scotty Philips had them slaughtered in Juárez and the meat taken to a butcher in El Paso for sale. *Sic transit gloria mundi.*

...and one recibiendo, receiving...

Ernest Hemingway, *Death in the Afternoon*:

> According to historians Pedro Romero [*considered the father of modern tauromachy*], who was a matador in Spain at the time of the American revolution, killed five thousand six hundred bulls between the years of 1771 and 1779 and lived to die in his bed at the age of ninety-five...Historians speak highly of all dead bullfighters.

...to be true in the writing...

It is notable that Hemingway could find no better way of affording praise to his friend and fellow novelist, John Dos Passos, than to say of him that he was "brave as a damned buffalo."

...Dieu! que El son du...

Vigny wrote his verse in 1826. Hemingway, or his wife Pauline, may have been recalling lines Paul Verlaine wrote in his 1870 poem, La Bonne Chanson: La note d'or que fait entendre/Un cor dans le lointain des bois–*The golden note by which one hears/ The horn in the depths of the woods.* In either case, Verlaine read Vigny.

...in tow by the Stalinists, wrote Wilson...

In a 1935 letter to his Moscow translator, Ivan Kashkin, Hemingway stated his decidedly non-fellow traveler politics of the day:

> Everyone tries to frighten you now by saying or writing that if one does not become a communist or have a Marxian viewpoint one will have no friends and will be alone. They seem to think that to be alone is something dreadful or that to not have friends is to be feared. I would rather have one honest enemy than most of the friends that I have known. I cannot be a communist now because I believe in only one thing: liberty. First I would look after myself and do my work. Then I would care for my family. Then I would help my neighbor. But the state I care nothing for. All the state has ever meant to me is unjust taxation. I have never asked anything from it. Maybe you have a better state but I would have to see it to believe it. And I would not know then because I do not speak Russian. I believe in the absolute minimum of government.

From *Green Hills of Africa*: "If you serve time for society, democracy, and the other things quite young, and declining any further enlistment make yourself responsible only to yourself, you exchange the pleasant, comforting stench of comrades for something you can never feel in any other way than by yourself." The scars from his own young body were the receipt for his completed service.

In Hemingway's single four hundred twenty-two-word sentence about the Gulf Stream, also in *Green Hills*, he wrote about the way the empty condoms of our great loves float with no significance against the current. Entire oeuvres may be based on the empty condoms of great loves and adjudged of lasting critical seriousness. Yet writing about a subject such as angling, horses, dogs, or hunting, and others exiled to the Kolyma of trivial pastimes, risks pronouncements of fakery and superficiality when "it is as important and has always been as important as all the things that are in fashion"–Hemingway.

About the writing of *The Old Man and the Sea*, Anthony Burgess in *99 Novels* said, "Hemingway's long hours of learning the marlin-fisher's craft–hours which, according to his left-wing critics, he had wasted in an escapist reactionary pursuit–had paid off. Writers must know about things as well as words." The difference between the things of hunting and those of romantic passion or the rest of the acclaimed themes such as war, peace, race, sex–or stupidly, gender–politics, economics, family, and more, in terms of the gravity as a worthy subject, is not even nugatory. What matters is not the subject, but what it creates.

An added point, to resort once more to Ortega y Gasset and one of his most famed quotes:

> In our rather stupid time, hunting is belittled and misunderstood, many refusing to see it for the vital vacation from the human condition that it is, or to

acknowledge that the hunter does not hunt in order to kill; on the contrary, he kills in order to have hunted.

...the very thin portfolio of such...

At the moment, I can think of one novel that is set around the African buffalo. That is the late Robert F. Jones's–Bad Bob as we knew him–*The Diamond Bogo: An African Idyll.* Based on Jones's hunting experience, and set in a land that is clearly an African exclave of his Hassayampa country from his first book, the classic, and likely today cancelable, *Blood Sport.* A professional hunter, seeing the end of the game, takes on one last safari so he can find the legendary Buffalo with a diamond as big as the Ritz embedded in its boss. For the rest, the book needs to be read.

As few good African buffalo stories as there may be, there is one exceptional one about Bison, John Graves's "The Last Running." In 1923 in the story, an old Comanche, Starlight, and eight braves come to the Texas ranch of Tom Bird, a likely stand in for Charles Goodnight, and demand that he give them his prized Bison bull, that he keeps in a fenced pasture *in memoriam,* so they can kill it with arrows and lances in one last ritual hunt. Starlight and Bird fought in the old days, and now they match wills.

In the end, the story resides in Tom Bird's words to his young great-nephew, no more or less sentimental than the ending of "Macomber."

"'Damn you, boy,' he said. 'Damn you for not ever getting to know anything worth knowing. Damn me, too. We had a world, once.'"

...their feet in mosquito boots...

These were high, soft footwear you put on in the evening after coming in from hunting, for sitting around the fire and waking out to the 'loo at night. Some could be tightened around the tops. Their use in repelling mosquitos seems intuitive. What has only recently been learned, though, is that certain foot odors are extremely attractive to mosquitos, especially *Anopheles gambiae,* a notorious vector of malaria. The odor produced by *Staphylococcus* bacteria presents a particularly powerful pull on mosquitos and can linger in dirty socks. Regular foot washing and clean socks can help repel the insects, as do mosquito boots.

...he had seen or heard, or read...

Hemingway biographer Michael S. Reynolds cataloged two thousand three hundred and four books, newspapers, and periodicals that Hemingway either owned or borrowed between 1910 and 1940. Patterson's *The Man-Eaters of Tsavo* is not among them.

...it was that the Irish-, and perhaps illegitimately, born Patterson...

In *The Seven Lives of Colonel Patterson,* the biographer Denis Brian takes note of its seeming that the British Empire, whenever faced with a situation, turned to the Anglo-Irish, such as T. E. Lawrence, for a solution.

...until his death in Bel Air, California, in 1947...

Patterson's cremated remains, along with his wife's–she dying but weeks following him–were buried in Angelus-Rosedale Cemetery in Los Angeles. My four years in Jesuit preparatory school were passed across Venice Boulevard from his grave, my never knowing, then. After more than half a century, with the aid of Israeli Prime Minister Benjamin Netanyahu, Patterson's ashes were reinterred in the village of Avihayil, beside the bodies of many of the Jews he commanded and with whom he fought.

...One who disagreed was Winston Churchill...

On a fact-finding and hunting trek from Lake Victoria to Gondokoro in southern Anglo-Egyptian Sudan in 1907, when he was Undersecretary of State for the Colonies, Winston Churchill was wont to say at the end of each day, "Sofari, so goody!"

...a beauty product she never used...

Hemingway drew on his professional hunter Philip Percival and the coquin Bror Fredrik von Blixen-Finecke–husband of Karen Blixen–for the character of Wilson. The model for Margot Macomber was apparently far more specific.

Jane Kendall Mason, described as someone who in her life came close to being famous, was twenty-two when she met Hemingway on the Île de France when he was crossing to America with wife Pauline, who was seven-months pregnant with son Gregory. Jane lived on a large estate outside Havana with her first husband, Grant Mason, the "'nice jerk,'" who headed Pan-Am Airways in the Caribbean while being wealthy in his own right. For her beauty, Jane was indeed paid to endorse a beauty product, Pond's cold cream, her picture taken by the English photographer, artist, and costume and set designer, Cecil Beaton. She was also an adventurous sportswoman–equestrian, angler, hunter, as well as a drinker and hell-bound driver, and because she was unable to have children, a sought-after sexual partner. With his family parked in Key West, Hemingway was frequently in Havana to fish and to carry on an erratic four-year affair with Jane, often in his room 511 in the Hotel Ambos Mundos–Hemingway, in his evening *Papa doble*-daiquiri-fueled braggies, asserting that she scaled the side of the building and climbed through his room's window to lie abed with him.

Jane was too much for any one man and didn't give a damn. She left her two sons, adopted from England, with their governess and went to Africa to hunt with Blixen. She did think enough of her children to shoot a Zebra colt and to have the skin made into a mount for a rocking horse.

She was wild, difficult to live with, and unstable. There was at least one suicide attempt, thought not sounding to have been overly serious. After serial marriages by both, Arnold Gingrich, founding editor of *Esquire* and erstwhile Hemingway friend, became her final husband, following many years of their having been sporadic lovers.

It is difficult to know if Jane was as hard and cruel as Hemingway made her out to be as Margot Macomber. He thought she should be proud to have been immortalized in one of this best stories.

She said of him, as quoted in Denis Brian's *The True Gen*, "I liked Ernest, but didn't love him."

Hemingway may have been exorcising her hold on him through his writing after their final break up. Maybe he resented the fact that as a woman she could compete head-to-head with him in the skills he valued in himself as an outdoorsman–he could barely stand being rivaled by another man. It was, however, never Hemingway's obligation to be evenhanded.

Though she remained married to Gingrich till the end of his life, the marriage was never peaceful. Jane's ways and indulgences probably culminated in the stroke that at age fifty-five in 1964 left her, in the words of food writer and Gingrich's long-time mistress, M. F. K. Fisher, a "helpless paralytic and ex-alcoholic." She lived on for seventeen more years, never forgetting Hemingway, as he surely never forgot her.

...according to the columnists...

Hemingway's comings and goings were of no less interest to the press then as the fictional attention the Macombers attracted. This, from the April 4, 1934, *The New York Times*:

Hemingway Here, Avid For Lion Hunt

> Ernest Hemingway, the author, arrived home yesterday and told reporters that for the present he had forsaken the bull-fighting arenas of Spain for big-game hunting. Mr. Hemingway, accompanied by his wife, returned on the French liner Paris after a three-month safari in Kenya Colony [*his safari was primarily in Tanganyika*], East Africa.
>
> The author spoke enthusiastically of the trip and of several encounters with African lions. The animals can cover a hundred yards in three seconds [*more like four in their highest bursts of speed*], he said, adding that "they are upon you before there is any time to act."
>
> "The lion is a fine animal," Mr. Hemingway remarked. "He is not afraid or stupid. He does not want to fight, but sometimes man makes him, and then it is up to the man to shoot his way out of what he has got himself into."
>
> Mr. Hemingway said he had found the East African buffalo somewhat more considerate. The buffalo, he said, is vicious enough and charges repeatedly, but the hunter has more opportunity to bring down this type of game than he does when dealing with lions.
>
> The Hemingways had been abroad since last August. Mr. Hemingway said he hoped to return to Africa next Winter and later to write a novel with lion and buffalo hunting as the framework.
>
> "The bull-fight has become formalized," he said. "My interest is now in Africa, and all I am here for is to make enough money to return to East Africa."

He intends to return to his home at Key West, Fla., for a season of intensive writing.

...his ex-slave second wife Florence...

Baker hunted with the Maharaja Duhleep Singh in Central Europe and the Balkans when in 1859 they came to the Danube River port of Vidin in what is now Bulgaria. On a lark they visited the slave market where Baker saw a beautiful Transylvanian teenage girl, marked for the seraglio of an Ottoman pasha. Smitten, Baker joined in the bidding for her but lost; afterward, though, he bribed her guards so he and the slave girl, Florence, could escape together in a speeding carriage. They married, in time; and wherever Baker went, even when he searched for the source of the Nile, hunted grizzly in the Bighorn Mountains in Wyoming Territory, or engaged in skirmishes with slave traders, she was there, the natives of northern Sudan calling her Anyadwe, Daughter of the Moon, for her long blond hair.

...or more likely trek or climb or ski...

The story was made into the 1947 Gregory Peck movie, *The Macomber Affair*, but the same situation–a husband's showing himself "very publicly, to be a coward" to his wife–is portrayed in a modern setting in the very good Swedish film, *Force Majeure*, in which a husband and father abandons his wife and children at a ski resort when they all appear to be threatened by an avalanche. Hollywood, of course, remade it into a comic atrocity, *Downhill*, six years later. There is another film, from the Republic of Georgia, entitled *The Loneliest Planet*, this about a wealthy couple on a hike when the husband flees a dangerous encounter. Hollywood, apparently, has yet to find that one. Blessedly.

"...at the Mathaiga [sic] Club?..."

It is spelled Muthaiga–the name of the greenheart tree–for the exclusive Nairobi suburb where it is located. The colonial administrators had their Nairobi Club, so in 1914 the farmers and professional hunters, the Honorable Berkeley Cole central among them, formed a club of their own, where, according to an article on the club's centenary, a bell would summon a cocktail on a spotless tray and you could play mixed doubles. The drinking day started in the morning and progressed to jumping horses over tables, firing random shots into the ceiling, and enjoying the sight of a local socialite dancing naked in the men's-only bar at night.

...the little openings the solid bullets had made in his tawny hide...

Why Macomber was using solid bullets on a thin-skinned animal such as a Lion is baffling. It may be assumed that this is the load Hemingway used to kill his Lion, but he shouldn't have. One hundred eighty-grain, soft-nosed bullets would have been more effective in a 30-06. A solid is more likely to pass through a Lion's body, wounding it possibly fatally but not stopping it the way an expanding bullet would. The purpose of a solid is to give deep penetration on a very large, heavily muscled and boned animal such as the Buffalo. Prewar softs were not the most reliable–today, expanding hunting bullets may use bonded jackets, partitions, or perhaps best of all, monolithic copper to produce larger-diameter wound channels with lethal penetration–but they were a better choice for a Lion than solids. Wilson should have known that, and had Macomber load softs in his rifle instead, unless he thought that softs were too unreliable, or that solids would do less damage to the hide for the taxidermy, hardly a sound reason for not using proper ammunition. Or perhaps specifying solids was a way for Hemingway to make the wounding without killing more plausible.

...a lifetime of torments scorched from him...

It may be an allusion too far, but you think of Turgenev when you think of Hemingway, and here of Bazarov's father in *Fathers and Sons* applying the lunar caustic to his son's typhus-infected finger, too late to save him. The courage Wilson burned into Macomber was ultimately too late, too, his needing to have left his wife far earlier.

...double size cot...

Windfalls were not some invention of Hemingway's. His friend Bror Blixen had a double cot in his tent for the same reason Wilson did, which Hemingway knew.

Wilson complains to himself about Macomber, after sleeping with his wife, "What does he think I am, a bloody plaster saint?" Few professional hunters were. Bunny Allen, living into the twenty-first century, claimed Romany descent and grew up among poachers in the Thames Valley, which included Windsor Forest–his skill at snaring rabbits earned him his nickname–before joining his brothers on a farm in Africa, from which he took clients shooting. He worked with Blixen and Finch Hatton, and was reputed to capture Cheetah by being driven alongside and leaping out onto them. He may also have been the paradigm of the amorous professional hunter, though always discreet. After World War II he fell in with movie safaris–*King Solomon's Mines*, *The African Queen*, *Mogambo*–doubling for Clark Gable, who suffered delirium tremens on the shoot, and by many accounts as a stand-in for Frank Sinatra with his wife, Ava Gardner–Gardner's first, off-screen line in *Mogambo*, as she is bathing in an outdoor shower, is a bit of a mixed Shakespearian Easter egg: "Who's there? Bunny?" Living into this twenty-first century on the Kenyan island of Lamu, Allen remained a much-loved husband, father, and grandfather.

Today it may be that the professional part is in greater evidence than the hunter. P. H.s seem to conduct themselves more like concierges, with virtues rigorously intact all around, and something ineffable lost. Though it may also be that a larger vulgarity has infected the occupation.

Some years ago, though past the time when Allen was a hunter, a friend was after Buffalo near the Luangwa River. Zambia was still wild Africa, and the sight of another vehicle was an uncommon occurrence. When one appeared across the dambo wetlands, my friend's professional hunter roared the Land Cruiser toward it. When they pulled up, the driver of the other vehicle handed him a letter.

My friend's P. H.. tore open the envelope and read the message.

"The bloody bitch got the bloody abortion," he yelled in relief, tearing up the letter and letting the fragments flutter into the wind. He then returned my friend to the pursuit of Buffalo. At least when Karen Blixen cabled Finch Hatton that she was pregnant with a baby she meant to name Daniel, and Finch Hatton cabled back, "Suggest you cancel Daniel's visit," he probably had the good manners not to share the information with his safari clients.

Back when the temptations encountered by professional hunters were not confined to celebrity or the ignoble, J. A. Hunter, slayer of a thousand Rhino, recounted in his book *Hunter* a wry anecdote from when he led a French count and countess on safari–no, he should tell it:

> One evening after I had turned in, the flap of my tent opened and the countess came in wearing a lace Parisian nightgown that covered her but poorly and carrying a beer glass full of whisky. She sat down on the edge of my cot, offered me a drink, and then took one herself. "Hunter, my friend, I am lonely," she told me sadly. "Countess, where's your husband?" I asked her. She looked at me a long time. "Hunter, you Englishmen ask the strangest questions," she said and flounced out of my tent. For the next few days she was a bit cool toward me but when the safari was over, both she and the count kissed me as they said good-by. A very affectionate couple. I enjoyed meeting them.

...was an exceedingly strange man...

Frederic Manning, son of a New South Wales politician, was the proverbial sickly child. He traveled to England at sixteen with the scholarly poet, editor, translator, and literary critic–and onetime Catholic priest–Reverend Arthur Galton. Living with Galton, Manning read and tried to write. He produced some books of verse and one on religious topics, all indifferently received by the public. In London he met with the likes of Max Beerbohm and Ezra Pound. Meanwhile, an asthmatic since boyhood, he smoked and drank heavily. In his thirties at the outbreak of the Great War, he persisted in trying to enlist until he was finally accepted by the army. His dependency on tobacco and alcohol prevented him from becoming an officer, but as a lance corporal he saw action at the Somme and Ancre. Following the Armistice, Manning continued residing with Galton until the reverend's death. Manning was thought to be uncomfortable with intimacy and likely lived a celibate life. After Galton died, Manning began staying in a hotel not far from where T. E. Lawrence, a friend, served in the Royal Air Force under the name of John Hume Ross–Lawrence joining at the time in flagellation parties in Chelsea. As war novels became extremely popular in the late 1920s, Manning's publisher urged him to write about his experiences, and Manning anonymously produced *The Middle Parts of Fortune*. Manning died in a nursing home in 1935, aged fifty-two, three months before Lawrence was killed on his Brough Superior SS100 motorcycle.

...working out of a personal problem...

Hemingway read De Maupassant. If he didn't read the story "The Duel," he still echoed its question of courage–that potential title for Macomber, "The Fear of Courage." In De Maupassant's brief tale a Viscount impetuously challenges a stranger to a duel with pistols that will end only in one of the participants being "grievously wounded." As the day for the affair draws closer, the Viscount tells himself, "'I must prove that I am not afraid.'" That was of course the feeling that drove Macomber into the tall grass with Wilson after the wounded Lion, when all of him wanted not to go. It was also what made him ask Wilson, pleading with him, really, "'It doesn't have to go any further, does it?'"

If you have read the De Maupassant story, you know that the Viscount's greatest fear is that if "in the presence of the other men" attending the duel "he did not have that calm, noble bearing that he should have, he would be lost forever." So the ultimate fear isn't death or wounding but of displaying fear in front of others. Macomber is lucky to experience what Varlam Shalamov tells us, from the vantage of "prolonged starvation" in the Kolyma Gulag, is "the most lasting of human feelings," "resentful anger" toward Wilson for sleeping with his wife, and toward his wife for her adultery, the ideal combination for searing away fear. The Viscount can muster no such rage. And while Macomber's cowardice occurred deep in the African bush, the Viscount's will be public knowledge. The ultimate solution he latches onto is a loaded Gastinne-Rennette pistol, one of the pair he would have used in the duel. Discovering a "confused, inexplicable joy" in this answer to the threat of "dishonor, of the whisperings in his circle, of the laughs in the drawing-rooms, of the scorn of the ladies, of the allusions of the journals, of all the insults that cowards would throw at him," he, like, apparently, Audley James Blyth, opened his mouth and "brusquely thrust the barrel into his throat," becoming a man to die literally of fright.

Unluckily for the Viscount and Macomber 1.0, they were not Chewong tribesmen from Malaysia. This is the rare indigenous peoples whose ancestors and gods were said to display fear, timidity, and flight when they perceived danger. They are even proud of their cowardice, an oral tradition among their elders including tales of the times they ran away.

...validity enough for anyone...

Again, the bones of the story have led to at least four films. The problem, then, seems at least valid enough for that.

...no lonelier man in death except the suicide...

With time the difficulty of not seeing Hemingway's life as a deliberate premise grows more and more. Almost everything Hemingway did, from hunting, fishing, drinking, eating, being an aficionado of the corrida and boxing, loving, fatherhood, all of it, even writing, came from some premeditated intention, in the service of something else, perhaps his art. Arbitrary and cruel circumstances–those of Jack London, nursed by a former slave after his mother attempted suicide following his birth, going to sea as a teenager to escape the cannery, and to the Klondike later to stay out of the jute mill; of Knut Hamsun, sent off at nine by his family to live with and work for an uncle who starved and beat him, the title of his first important work, *Hunger*, saying everything; of Hans Fallada, run over by a horse cart and kicked in the head at sixteen, failing to die but killing his boyhood friend in a fumbled suicide pact, addiction, incarceration, institutionalization, Joseph Goebbels–informed others's writing, while Hemingway's can look suspiciously like the product of pantomime. A pose. Even to the production of his death, which he rehearsed countless times before audiences.

While saying he was much interested in suicide, Hemingway also qualified it as banal. He would not have written the scene of his own death when he lived at 74 rue du Cardinal

Lemoine, because he would have recognized it as travesty. If it contributed to a story at all, it would have been in the "seven-eights" part that was under the water. His death did not happen out of something but was resorted to in order to escape something–like the Viscount? He might have only written it later, when his gifts were vitiated, as the false ending to a work that does not continue on to satisfactory completion. It was as the way a bull could be destroyed if it were "over-caped." He meant to over-cape, not a bull, but the other thing he was afraid of, and had always been, because, like the bull a matador fears, it was "too big, too fast…too strong" to stave off any longer. He thought he could defeat it with a gesture, like El Gallo's *pase de la muerte*, the pass of death, which wasn't as much as what it seemed.

…Hemingway's heroes end in physical defeat

Not just Hemingway's, but from the beginning of world literature with the first of all heroes. The Polish science-fiction and futurist writer, Stanisław Lem, wrote, "Man's fate as a battle that leads inescapably to defeat–that is the final sense of *Gilgamesh*." Lem made that astute judgment in the review of the very nonexistent three hundred ninety-five-page book, with eight hundred forty seven pages of endnote commentary, *Gigamesh*, authored by the entirely fictitious Irish Patrick Hannahan.

…a matter far from settled in the story…

Hemingway's second wife, the former Pauline Pfeifer, carried a Mannlicher on safari with Ernest in the 1930s. According to a 1930 letter Hemingway wrote to Milford Baker–who, recall, advised him on his Springfield–quoted by Ellen Andrews Knodt in the Spring 2019 issue of *The Hemingway Review*, and as noted in a Facebook post by Silvio Calabi, co-author of *Hemingway's Guns*, Hemingway had the rifle's standard set trigger replaced by Griffin & Howe with a single stage. A set trigger could be pushed forward into a hair-trigger position, so that only a glancing touch would fire the rifle. A single stage required a constant pull. Hemingway thought that with the set trigger he would "get in trouble" sometime on game. He also worried that with it on the Mannlicher in Pauline's hands, he "would never be sure [she] might not shoot me with it by mistake." Or not by mistake.

Chapter Sixteen: Hona

…tonight would go on with whiskey…

I don't think I ever saw my father truly drunk–Mother was another matter. He was not an adept drinker, though he liked a gin martini, up, with a restaurant meal.

"I only like to drink martinis when I am alone or with someone," he'd say, wanting to sound waggish.

He was swooning drunk on his wedding night after his friends saw the joke in spiking his drinks at the reception. In the honeymoon suite, he dolphined amain in and out of drowsiness, as if he rode the bow wave of a ship, at one juncture thinking he caught sight of his bride kneeling at the foot of the bed, praying a decade of the rosary on her beads in deterrence.

He also got drunk at Roy's house a few days after the death of his father, though that seemed the expected thing, a conscious decision because it was what you were supposed to do when your father died.

...it lighted in an instant...

Shot Galileo, carried out in the Nevada Test Site two hundred miles from the Dove fields around Tulare was part of the Plumbbob Series of twenty-nine above-ground test explosions during 1957. It took place on September 2. An eleven-kiloton device on a five hundred-foot tower was detonated at oh-five-forty. The stated objectives of the Department of Defense for this blast were:

(1) To test performance of military personnel as affected by witnessing a nuclear detonation
(2) To perform AFSWP [Armed Forces Special Weapons Project] military effects experiments to measure the effects of a nuclear weapon with a known yield and characteristics on military equipment, material, structures, and ordnance
(3) To provide DOD personnel an opportunity to observe a nuclear detonation and to become familiar with its effects
(4) To evaluate military equipment and tactics.

Troops two-point-seven miles away from ground zero witnessed the explosion, then performed various exercises such as weapons disassembly and assembly, crawling under obstacles, and hurling dummy grenades, to test how the sight of mushroom clouds close at hand affected the performance of human beings.

...the courage necessary to stand for myself...

Depression and fear differ. Depressed people–and angry ones such as Macomber–may act bravely, even recklessly. Fear and anxiety exist, as an early warning system, to protect from harm. Our natural tendency to be anxious has been described as "a complex mixture of cognitive, affective, behavioral, and somatic components [with complicated] relations to other aspects of motivation such as arousal." We face it every moment of living, and would in fact be at an, to use an overworked word appropriately for once, existential disadvantage if we never experienced it.

The Chewong are reputed to have a saying, "To be angry is not human; but to be fearful is." Utter fearlessness is an evolutionary dead end, literally. Negotiating fear–overcoming it ultimately too much to ask–may be the permanent object of our existence. Even Buffalo can be scared. But they are also so wonderfully brave in their large pulsing souls.

...Ad te clamanus...

To you we cry, banished children of Eve.

HUNTING TH